Frontiers in
Asian Christian Theology

1162

D0887642

Frontiers in Asian Christian Theology

Emerging Trends

R. S. Sugirtharajah, Editor

ORBIS BOOKS

Maryknoll, New York 10545

DEC 2 1 1994

BT
30
.A8
F76
1994   ALUMNI MEMORIAL LIBRARY
ST. MARY'S COLLEGE
ORCHARD LAKE, MICH. 48324

The Catholic Foreign Mission Society of America (Maryknoll) recruits and trains people for overseas missionary service. Through Orbis Books, Maryknoll aims to foster the international dialogue that is essential to mission. The books published, however, reflect the opinions of their authors and are not meant to represent the official position of the society.

Copyright © 1994 by R. S. Sugirtharajah

Acknowledgment is gratefully extended for permission to reprint the following:

"Recovering Jesus for Outcasts in Japan: From a Theology of the Crown of Thorns" by Kuribayashi Teruo (*The Japan Christian Review*, 1992, 58); Overseas Ministries Study Center for "My Pilgrimage in Mission" by M. M. Thomas (*International Bulletin of Missionary Research* 13 [1], 1989); "Hindu-Christian Funeral" by Stanley J. Samartha (*National Christian Council Review* 108 [4], 1988); "Ethnic Conflict in Sri Lanka and the Responsibility of the Theologian" by Tissa Balasuriya, *Responding to Communalism: The Task of Religions and Theology,* ed. S. Arokiasamy (Gujarat, India: Gujarat Sahitya Prakash, 1991); "Some Perspectives on Homeland Theology in the Taiwanese Context" by Wang Hsien Chih (*CTC Bulletin* 6 [2 & 3], 1986); The United Society for the Propagation of the Gospel, London for "Who Is God for Us Today?" by Jyoti Sahi (*Thinking Mission* #2, April 1989); Asian Women's Resource Centre for Culture and Theology, Seoul, Korea for "Feminine Images of God in Korean Traditional Religion" by Choi Man Ja (*In God's Image,* June 1989) and "My Marriage Is Not a Sacrament" by Astrid Lobo Gajiwala (*In God's Image,* September 1990); "Mothers and Daughters, Writers and Fighters" by Kwok Pui Lan, reprinted from *Inheriting Our Mothers' Garden: Feminist Theology in Third World Perspective,* edited by Letty M. Russell, Kwok Pui-lan, Ada Maria Isasi-Diaz and Katie Geneve Cannon. Used by permission of Westminster/John Knox Press; "The Language of Human Rights: An Ethical Esperanto?" by Felix Wilfred (*Vidyajyoti Journal of Theological Reflection* 56 [4], 1992); Christian Study Centre on Chinese Religion & Culture, Hong Kong for "Dancing, Ch'i, and the Holy Spirit," by Peter K. H. Lee (*Ching Feng* 34 [3], 1991); Christian Institute for the Study of Religion and Society, Bangalore, India for "A Theological Interpretation of the Tribal Reality in India" by Nirmal Minz (*Religion and Society* 34 [4], 1987) and "Theological Perspectives on the Environmental Crisis" by Samuel Rayan (*Religion and Society* 37 [2], 1990); "Toward a Christian Dalit Theology" by Arvind P. Nirmal (*Asian Journal of Theology* 6 [2], 1992); "The Dragon, the Deluge, and Creation Theology" by Archie Lee Chi Chung (*Doing Theology with People's Symbols and Images,* ATESA Occasional Papers #8, ed. Yeow Choo Lak and John England (Singapore: ATESEA, 1989); "Theology of Reunification" by David Kwang-sun Suh (*Theology and Politics* Vol. I).

All rights reserved. No part of this publication may be reproduced or transmitted in any form or by any means, electronic or mechanical, including photocopying, recording, or any information storage or retrieval system, without prior permission in writing from the publishers.

Queries regarding rights and permissions should be addressed to:
Orbis Books, P. O. Box 308, Maryknoll, New York 10545–0308

Published by Orbis Books, Maryknoll, NY 10545
Manufactured in the United States of America

ORBIS/ISBN 0-88344-954-4

Contents

Section III
SPEAKING OUT OF OUR PERSONAL ENCOUNTERS
Examples of Asian Sociotheological Biographies

Section IV
SPEAKING FOR OURSELVES
Current Theological Concerns

Acknowledgments

Some of the great Asian texts and narratives remain authorless, but we owe their unknown authors a first expression of thanks for all they have bequeathed to humanity.

Though this Asian collection carries my name, I owe a special debt of gratitude to a number of people: Robert Ellsberg and Susan Perry of Orbis Books, who, over the years, have become more than publishers in supporting and encouraging me at every stage of this project; Daniel O'Connor, who, in different incarnations as venerable guru, affectionate critic and even at times willing collaborator because of his shared interest in the subject, provided stimulus and sustained my enthusiasm; Meline Nielsen, Louise Wilmot, Katrina Youster, Griselda Lartey, Gill Davies and Jane Lorimer — the Central Library staff at the Selly Oak Colleges — who as always went out of their way to secure the books and articles I needed; course participants in the Third World Theology class at Selly Oak Colleges, who enthused and agonized over the materials and ideas I shared with them; all the copyright holders of the articles for their kind permission to reproduce them; and finally, Sharada, my wife, who consistently reminds me that the Christian narrative is only one among many narratives in Asia.

R. S. SUGIRTHARAJAH

Introduction

R. S. SUGIRTHARAJAH

In an era in which the meaning of a narrative resides with the reader, and texts themselves offer preferred readings, let me begin with my own interpretation of the Parable of the Prodigal Son. If we were to read the parable, overvalorizing its narrativity and detaching it from its context, we could discern certain parallels between the life and times of the Prodigal Son and some of the Asian theologians.

Like the Prodigal, some of us received our portion of the scholarship and spent our theological youth in faraway cities like Rome, Heidelberg, Oxford, and Berkeley, where we learned exotic things such as demythologization and structuralism, thus intellectually binding ourselves to the citizens of the country. After riotous living in the academic fleshpots of the West and dabbling in fashionable theories, we felt impoverished and found our way to a pigsty. It was here, among battered women, exploited workers, and undernourished children, that our academic honor was brought to shame, and that our scholarly neutrality and credibility were challenged. What one of the characters of Japanese novelist Shusaku Endo said in a different context could be equally true of us as well: "Your Latin is good. But your faith is rotten. Your study abroad was in vain."[1] We learned that in switching temporarily to the Hebrew Scriptures for a mess of academic pottage, we had sold our own rich religious and cultural birthright. Our scholarly purity defiled, we decided to go home and become servants and apprentices of the people. The essays in this volume are the accounts of Asian theologians coming to themselves and their journey back to their home — Asia.

This volume is the fourth in a series of anthologies on Asian Christian discourse. It is almost a decade since the last one appeared in the West under the editorship of John England.[2] Interestingly, the preceding four years had seen a burst of publishing on Asian theological thinking.[3] The essays assembled in those volumes generally reflected the theological mood and the ecclesiastical needs of the late 1960s and 1970s. Since then, as they say in feminist circles, things have moved on. No two decades have the same questions, nor are new questions formulated without interacting with the earlier ones. The intention of this volume is to capture the ongoing conversation on some of the issues raised in the previous volumes and also to document the essence of the new emphases. Thus the essays assembled here continue to probe and clarify some of the thrusts and trends sketched in the earlier volumes; at the same time, they wrestle with fresh issues that have emerged more recently. This volume, in other words, is the logical and latest extension of the interpretative trends reflected in the earlier anthologies.

New Emphases

Let me begin with two fresh aspects of Asian theology.

The Rise of the Subalterns

One of the vibrant voices in the Asian scene in the 1980s has been the subaltern sector of Asian society — namely, women, Indian dalits (the new name chosen by the former untouchables), Japanese Burakumin people (the defiled indigenous group and the tribals). Their questioning of the church's concern and care for them is one of the major theological themes of the 1980s.

The last two decades have been a time of extraordinary energy and accomplishment in feminist theological thinking all over the world. There is no doubt that this had an enormous influence on Asian women. Building on, and at the same time taking issue with, their counterparts, Asian women have been able to work out their own specific discourse based on two interpenetrating realities — Asianness and womanness. In carving out their own theological niche, women were able to free themselves from the dominance of the Asian male liberation theology under whose shadow they had existed in the initial stages, and which had ironically failed to notice their presence. Interestingly, of nearly sixty essays in the earlier four volumes, only one touched on the plight of women. Though the present collection does not make claims of an adequate larger numerical representation of women's writings, the essays gathered here acknowledge the fact that women's issues are at the center of Asian theological thinking and no longer a peripheral matter.

Along with the emergence of Asian feminist thinking, the 1980s saw the birth of liberation movements among the Indian dalits and the Japanese Burakumim and different tribal peoples in Asia. They, too, collectively try to recover their often denigrated past heritage, and in doing so, seek to control their own theological discourse. These people see themselves as "twice discriminated" among Asian elites and high castes. Many of them feel, and rightly so, that the dominant Asian Christian theologies, liberation, ecumenical, or denominational, have made them once more invisible and have reproduced a theological agenda which was primarily hierarchical, elitist, and casteist. Discovering their self-worth and reclaiming their cultural heritage, dalits, Burakumin, and tribals have recently raised their voices against their own indigenous elites who not only tried to displace their discourse but also to determine the content of it.

Ways of Doing Theology: Extratextual Hermeneutics

The other significant shift in the 1980s was in the method of doing theology. There were two major influences: the impact of the liberation hermeneutic and the emergence of extratextual hermeneutics — the audacious and daring way Asia's literary and nonliterary resources were woven into theological discourse.

In the essays of the earlier volumes one could detect the reigning theologies of the West and the ecumenical thinking of the time. These theologies — secular, political, and revolutionary — were European in origin and content but had found their way into Asian theological circles. Dietrich Bonhoeffer, Johann Metz, Harvey Cox, and Arend Van Leeuwen were some of the cherished names. Similarly, the theological output of the ecumenical movement could be discerned in the Asian thinking of the time. Two important conferences at that time were the Second Vatican Council (1963–65) and the Church and Society Conference of the World Council of Churches in Geneva (1966). Though these ecumenical conferences assembled out of different ecclesiastical needs, some of their deliberations and pronouncements had a deep impact on Asian thinking. Issues such as how to respond to a world ridden with conflicts, how to rectify institutional violence (the cause of much injustice, misery, and degradation of the people), the redefinition of salvation as a contemporary historical process, and the acknowledgement of truth values in different religious traditions rightly found their way into Asian theological reflection.

But the 1980s also saw a fresh way of doing theology initiated with the formation of the Ecumenical Association of Third World Theologians (EATWOT). Until that time, theological activity meant dealing with ideas and concepts drawn from Christian Scriptures and church traditions. It meant expounding, elucidating, and explaining inherited concepts. Latin American liberation theology challenged this view and proposed another way of discovering the theological truth, which was, as Ezekiel had done (3:15), to start where people were and with their concrete experience. This new way could be defined as dialectical reflection on the current situation and on the biblical data from the perspective of the poor and the exploited. The Latin Americans who first mooted this notion argued that the content of Christian theology was liberation and that it was inseparably linked to the struggles of the victims. In explicating this in their turn, Asians have modified it to suit their context. Whereas Latin Americans begin with analysis of the social reality and move on to the biblical narrative for illumination, Asian theologians, on the other hand, with no disrespect to the merit of such an approach, have worked out a hermeneutic which takes into account Asia's religiocultural values and its multiple sacred textual traditions.

It is in the attempt to integrate faith and culture that Asian Christians are chalking out a new path. There is a move now to go beyond the earlier monotextual approach, which puts so much emphasis on the canonical Christian texts, and to use literary and nonliterary resources that are common to all the peoples of Asia. It may be a coincidence, but the emergence of greater literary interest in biblical texts, especially among American scholars, has occurred at a time when Asian interpreters' attention was drawn toward literary and nonliterary genres of different religious traditions. The extratextual hermeneutics that is slowly emerging as a distinctive Asian contribution to theological methodology seeks to transcend the textual, historical, and religious boundaries of Christian tradition and cultivate a deeper contact with the mysterious ways in which people of all religious persuasions have defined and appropriated humanity and divinity.

Such a rethinking reverses the earlier missionary approaches to the same texts and stories. These polemical attempts invariably resulted in according a privileged status to Christian texts and in affirming the superiority of the Christian story, thus distancing and creating skepticism among the very people such interpretations sought to understand and influence. The new endeavors, on the other hand, assume and demonstrate that diverse textual and nontextual expressions of divine-human encounters are more valuable and enriching than they were once perceived to be. Archie Lee Chi Chung's words encapsulate the thrust of the new enterprise:

> A cross-textual approach aims at going beyond comparative studies and inter-faith dialogue. It is a way to do theology which is meaningful to Asian Christians and theologians who have both the identity of being Asian as well as being Christian and who value both their cultural-religious text and the biblical text.[4]

Continuing Concerns

Moving beyond Contextualization

There have been various attempts to re-inscribe the gospel in Asian terms. They have gone through different phases such as acculturation, indigenization, and so on. When the essayists in the earlier volumes were at work, the idea of contextualization seemed to be the accepted norm for integrating the gospel and Asian culture. But over the years, some Asian theologians have felt that this concept, too, has its limitations. The earlier contextualizers assumed the following:

1. that the Christian gospel is immutable, and Asian culture, thought patterns, and religious traditions are convenient vehicles for it. Such an insertion of the gospel will gradually usher in the Kingdom of God, and Christian values will ultimately triumph over the other religious values of Asia. In other words, they assumed a Christendom framework and saw the Christian church as the beacon of hope amidst all the ills of Asia. The mood was triumphalistic. One of them proclaimed, "We have been set in the world, for the sake of the world."[5]

2. that the Christian gospel was an uncontaminated and neatly packed, wholesome product that had universal validity. They also accepted the Christian Scriptures and church dogmas without challenging the gender, racial, religious, and cultural biases inherent in them.

3. that the Christian manifestation is final and unique. They assumed God's absence from Asia's religious and cultural history and that this history had nothing theologically worthwhile to contribute.

But in a changed mood, which Raimundo Panikkar terms "Christianness,"[6] current theologians are questioning the legitimacy and relevance of such contextualizing efforts. They are well acquainted with new and more critical understandings of the Christian gospel and their own society. They see these earlier efforts as apologetic and polemical. They also find the overt Christocentrism in them a hindrance: such an uncompromising position cuts Asian Christians off from the wisdom of Asia.

Unlike the contextualizers, these theologians do not understand the gospel as a pure and unalloyed substance. They reckon that the gospel itself has gone through a series of enculturation processes: first, when it left its Palestinian village setting and moved into the hellenistic milieu; and later in the West, when it was recast in the light of colonial needs, before it started its journey toward Asia. As Sebastian Kappen says in one of his essays, "by uncritically transplanting dogma and tradition one cannot develop a liberative Asian theology."[7]

The basic thrust now is not the declaration of the gospel in an Asian style but discerning it afresh in the ongoing broken relationships between different communities and between human beings and the created order. The task is seen not as adapting the Christian gospel in Asian idioms, but as reconceptualizing the basic tenets of the Christian faith in the light of Asian realities. The new mood is not to assume the superiority of Christian revelation but to seek life-enhancing potentialities also in the divine manifestations of Asia.

Hence they are more audacious and robust in their use of cultural resources. There is a willingness to integrate, synthesize, and interconnect. They want to refashion and reformulate the gospel. The following two quotations, one by Roy Sano, an Asian-American theologian, and the other by the Korean feminist Chung Hyun Kyung, reflect and typify the new mood thus:

> Because of warnings against syncretism, I once asked myself: How can I be Christian and yet Buddhist? Through time, however, as I became aware of the extent to which Buddhism permeated my Japanese cultural heritage and I recognized how impossible it was to eliminate everything from that heritage, my question changed. I now ask: "How can I be Christian without being Buddhist?"[8]

> I discovered my bowel is a shamanistic bowel, my heart is a Buddhist heart and my head is a Christian head.[9]

In this revised view, the gospel and the Christian church are no longer seen as in charge, and society and culture no longer belong to them. These Asian theologians see that the Christian church in Asia needs a huge reappraisal of itself. The gospel is seen as one among many divine manifestations. This is not seen as a disaster but as an opportunity. It does not mean abandoning the arena but seeking to reinvent anew from a position of humility and vulnerability.

Greening of Theology

The other continuing concern has been the challenge posed by environmental issues and the concomitant political, economic, and social ramifications raised by them for Asian people. Reverence for the created order is not totally new to Asian Christian thinking. An early interest in the theology of creation was shown in the writings of P. Chenchiah, P. D. Devanandan and C. S. Song. The basis for such a concern was theological interest in religious plurality and cultural diversity. What is new is the affirmation of an inextricable connection between ecological issues and justice from the perspective of the poor. The earlier essayists were not unaware of nor unconcerned with these economic problems. They were articulating the Christian faith in the aftermath of independence. Nation building and economic development were the issues that were uppermost in their theological agenda at that time. The processes of urbanization and industrialization were seen as the fruits of the gospel. In the 1980s it gradually dawned on Asians that the enthusiasm with which the development programs were initiated to help alleviate malnutrition, underdevelopment, and illiteracy did not bear fruit. Rather, it helped to create a new form of colonialism, and moreover, it tended to help the powerful elites of Asia and their counterparts in the industrially advanced countries. Furthermore, the development that took place was achieved at the expense of the Asian poor and their environment. People's welfare and natural resources were sacrificed for the growth of the gross national product and the numerical magic of per capita income. The beneficiaries were the investors and not the local people for whose welfare these programs were supposedly initiated.

Asians today are questioning the system that perpetuates this inequality and seeking to affirm the intimate link between ecology and justice from the perspective of the underprivileged.

A Word about This Volume

It has not been easy to choose from a vast amount of literature. As editor, I have applied two simple ground rules in selecting the pieces: (1) whether the writings reflect the current cultural, historical, political and religious realities of Asia; and (2) whether they incorporate Asian symbols, stories, images, ethos, and thought patterns in their theological enterprise. In selecting the materials, I was looking for items that were in touch with everyday life and that integrated Asian feeling, creativity, and imagination. I am aware that the selections here are not an exhaustive inventory of all the available materials. They are only representative samples of current Asian perspectives and styles of doing theology.

This volume is assembled around four themes:

Section I, "Speaking among Ourselves: Emerging Subaltern Voices," captures the ongoing dialogue between Asia's dominant theologies and the continent's subalterns — women, Indian dalits, tribals, and the Japanese Burakumin people. The theology of subalterns, like all theologies of emancipation, springs from the experience of being hurt and wounded. Once hidden, neglected, sidelined, and subjugated, the subalterns have now emerged to tell their own story on their own terms, and in the process have discovered a new self-identity, self-worth, and self-validation. By reclaiming their personal, communal and group stories, the four essayists representing these constituencies — Kurubayashi Teruo, Arvind Nirmal, Nirmal Minz, and Chung Hyun Kyung — not only remove the distortion and mystification perpetuated by the reigning Asian theologies but also use them to reinstate their legitimate position and affirm their wish to be accomplices in reinvigorating Asian theology.

Section II, "Speaking out of Our Own Resources: Using the Asian Heritage as Illumination," provides examples of how Asian Christians are reclaiming folktales, fables, myths, and stories from their own heritage to enhance their theological reflection. It is through such stories that Asians come to grips with their humanity, environment, and ultimate reality. Ever since Macaulay asserted that "a single shelf of a good European library was worth the whole of native literature," these stories have been dismissed as pagan, vain, and useless, and regrettably have been excised from the Christian consciousness. Besides, they were held to be not a proper vehicle to elucidate lofty and serious matters such as theology. The examples reproduced here rectify such a notion. This section contains examples of extratextual hermeneutics. Peter K. H. Lee and Archie Lee Chi Chung use Chinese resources; Jyoti Sahi employs Indian tribal folktales; Choi Man Ja delves into the Korean shamanistic myths, and Samuel Rayan imaginatively mixes textual traditions of three faith communities: Jewish, Hindu, and Muslim. These essays bring home an important interpretative lesson: it is the stories of people rather than preconceived theological ideas or hermeneutical criteria that lead to deeper truths about humanity and God.

Section III, "Speaking out of Our Personal Encounters: Examples of Asian Sociotheological Biographies," contains theological reflections in story form based on personal experiences. The spell of the story has always exercised a special potency in Asia, and Asians have characteristically sought meanings for complex situations through the narrative format. Narrative theology allows for directly integrating experience with theology — a decisive prerequisite for any vibrant theology. Standing within the tradition of storytelling, four theologians relate the impact of their autobiographical experiences on their theology. Aloysius Pieris recalls how his encounter with Buddhist clergy and a poor university student enabled him to rethink his received theological wisdom; Kwok Pui Lan relates how digging into the personal histories of her foremothers prompted her to work out an inclusive theology for the Chinese context; M. M. Thomas shares his ecumenical odyssey and affectionately names those ecumenical luminaries who influenced his thinking; Astrid Lobo Gajiwala recounts her experience around her decision to marry a Hindu and the theological impediments posed by such a union, and goes on to describe the eventual marriage and the birth of her first child. Stanley J. Samartha concludes this section by inviting us to join him at the funeral of his Hindu friend and in his wrestling with the theological issues prompted by the occasion. Though academic theology may treat these recollections as personal, anecdotal, and subjective, the experiences recounted here enabled the essayists to renew their theological vision.

Finally, Section IV, "Speaking for Ourselves: Current Theological Concerns," documents some of the ongoing crucial issues addressed by Asian theology. Wang Hsien Chih, the Taiwanese theologian, highlights one of the lesser-known theological aspirations: a homeland theology for his people. Noh Jung Sun illustrates the next urgent task of Korean *minjung* theology: the unification with North Korea. Felix Wilfred redefines the concept of human rights from a third-world perspective. Samuel Rayan tackles the issue of ecology from an interreligious point of view, and Tissa Balasuriya defines the task of a theologian in a communally torn context.

It will be seen that this collection does not include the question of how Asians perceive Jesus or how they articulate spirituality or how they use Christian Scriptures. The reason for their omission here is that these have been adequately covered in recent anthologies.[10]

An explanation is needed about the sexism in the language. For most of us, English is not our first language, and the vocabulary we use is an inherited one. The most worrying concern for us is that the continual use of English alienates us from our own people and their vernacular mode of articulation. Some of us still continue to think in our mother tongue before we translate into English. Now we have been told that we have learned English wrongly and must relearn it. For those who have been displeased by sexist language, may I assure you that at least some of the languages in which most of us converse have been sensitive to this issue and do not observe this gender division.

My hope is that the essays in this volume illustrate the way Asian Christians are trying to articulate their faith in an ever-changing and ever-challenging continent.

They may not provide completely satisfactory answers to Asia's religious plurality or its poverty or its environmental depletion, but I believe they do suggest where we should begin to look for these in Asia itself. What A. K. Ramanujan, the Indian literary critic, said in another context may be equally true here as well: "... we may say that we are moving indoors, into the expressive culture of household to look for our keys. As it often happens, we may not find the keys we are looking for and may have to make new ones, but we will find all sorts of other things we never knew we had lost, or ever even had."[11]

Notes

1. Shusaku Endo, *Foreign Studies* (London: Peter Owen, 1989), p. 51.

2. John C. England, ed., *Living Theology in Asia* (Maryknoll, N.Y.: Orbis Books, 1981; and London: SCM Press, 1981).

3. Barbara and Leon Howell, *Southeast Asians Speak Out: Hope and Despair in Many Lands* (New York: Friendship Press, 1975); Gerald H. Anderson, ed., *Asian Voices in Christian Theology* (Maryknoll, N.Y.: Orbis Books, 1976); Douglas J. Elwood, ed., *What Asian Christians Are Thinking: A Theological Source Book* (Quezon City, Philippines: New Day Publishers, 1976) and *Asian Christian Theology: Emerging Themes* (Philadelphia: The Westminster Press, 1980). For a more recent volume, produced in Asia, see Dayanandan T. Francis and F. J. Balsundaram, eds., *Asian Expressions of Christian Commitment* (Madras: The Christian Literature Society, 1992).

4. Archie Lee Chi Chung, "Cross-Textual Hermeneutics in Asian Context," *PTCA Bulletin* 5 (1), 1992, p. 5.

5. Elwood, p. 44.

6. Raimundo Panikkar, "Christendom, Christianity, Christianness," *Jeevadhara: A Journal of Christian Interpretation* 21 (124), 1991, pp. 324–30.

7. Sebastian Kappen, "The Asian Search for a Liberative Theology: Theology and Transformative Praxis," in *Bread and Breadth: Essays in Honor of Samuel Rayan,* ed. T. K. John (Anand, Gujarat: Gujarat Sahitya Prakash, 1991), p. 109.

8. Roy Sano, "'Holy Moments at Canberra," *Christianity and Crisis* 51 (10/11), 1991, p. 228

9. *Christian Century* 109 (9), 1992, p. 271

10. For Asian christologies see *Asian Faces of Jesus,* R. S. Sugirtharajah, ed. (Maryknoll, N.Y.: Orbis Books, 1993 and London: SCM Press, 1993). For spirituality see *Asian Christian Spirituality: Reclaiming Traditions,* Virginia Fabella, Peter K. H. Lee, and David Kwang-sun Suh, eds. (Maryknoll, N.Y.: Orbis Books, 1992). For biblical interpretations see *Voices from the Margin: Interpreting the Bible in the Third World,* R. S. Sugirtharajah, ed. (Maryknoll, N.Y.: Orbis Books, 1991 and London: SPCK, 1991); *Readings in Indian Christian Theology Vol. I,* R. S. Sugirtharajah and Cecil Hargreaves, eds. (London: SPCK, 1993), especially the section on Indian biblical hermeneutics; see also the special issue on "Asian Hermeneutics" by R. S. Sugirtharajah, ed., in *Biblical Interpretation: A Journal of Contemporary Approaches* (forthcoming).

11. A. K. Ramanujan, ed., *Folktales from India: A Selection of Oral Tales from Twenty-Two Languages* (New York: Pantheon Books, 1992), p. viii.

SECTION I

SPEAKING AMONG OURSELVES

Emerging Subaltern Voices

Theology at 120°F in the shade seems, after all, different from theology at 70°F. Theology accompanied by tough chapatis and smoky tea seems different from theology with roast chicken and a glass of wine. Now, what is really different, *theos* or theologian? The theologian at 70°F in a good position presumes God to be happy and contented, well-fed and rested, without needs of any kind. The theologian at 120°F tries to imagine a God who is hungry and thirsty, who suffers and is sad, who sheds perspiration and knows despair.
— Klaus Klostermaier, *Hindu and Christian in Vrindaban*
(London: SCM Press, 1970), p. 40

Chapter 1

Recovering Jesus for Outcasts in Japan

KURIBAYASHI TERUO

In popular perception Japan is seen as a booming economy with a homogenous community. Both these presuppositions are challenged by a group of indigenous minority people whose existence is little known to the outside world. They are the Ainu, Okinawans, Korean residents and the Burakumin people, who are discriminated against on the basis of the concept of ceremonial pollution. The article reproduced here traces the history of the discrimination against the Burakumin, formerly known as Eta and Hinin, and offers a distinctive perception of liberation that moves beyond the one espoused by other liberation theologies.

Kuribayashi Teruo is Professor of Theology at Shikoku Gakuin University, Zentsuji, Japan. His doctoral dissertation focused on the outcasts of Asia and is titled: "A Theology of the Crown of Thorns: Towards the Liberation of Asian Outcasts" (Union Theological Seminary, 1985). He is actively involved in the Burakumin liberation movement and has written articles highlighting their plight.

Source: *The Japan Christian Review*, 1992, 58.

"We have learned to see the great events of world history from below, from the perspective of outcasts."
— Dietrich Bonhoeffer, *Letters and Papers from Prison*

"The Suiheisha Declaration is our Bible for the unliberated Burakumin."
— Imai Kazuichi, *The Crown of Thorns*

Suffering and Liberation

The basic theme of this article is the suffering and liberation of outcasts in Japan. This theme is the natural outgrowth of my belief that our theological task in contemporary Japan is to reflect critically on the liberating activity of God in the midst of oppression, taking as our focus the concrete sociohistorical context of Japan's three million outcasts, the Burakumin.[1] This paper, therefore, seeks to analyze the suffering and pain historically experienced by the Burakumin and to discuss their situation as it relates to the biblical theme of liberation. The sole purpose of such theological reflection is to articulate the meaning of God's redemptive work in the anguished communities of Japan, thus giving the Japanese outcasts to understand that their striving for freedom is not only consistent with their legitimate desires and expectations as human beings but also is itself the central theme of Christian faith.

I do not intend to imply by my specific focus on the suffering of the Burakumin that their victimization alone is worthy of meaning granted by Christian theology. In Japan other minorities are discriminated against in various ways — Korean residents, Ainu and Okinawan people, the physically and mentally handicapped, women, and so on. However, the condition of being a Burakumin best illustrates what oppression means in Japanese society today. Every conceivable brutality visited upon its least-valued members — humiliation, persecution, social marginalization — has been suffered by the Burakumin minority, and their communities are paradigmatic of victimization in specifically Japanese terms.

Although this article also deals extensively with a theme of liberation, I disclaim the mere extension of "liberation theology" that has become fashionable in the ecumenical world. "Liberation," as I am using the term, is actually a translation of a Japanese word, *kaiho,* that has been used for more than seventy years by the Burakumin themselves in the struggle for justice and freedom.[2] The Buraku Liberation League, for example, uses *kaiho* as opposed to a word such as *dowa* (integration) or *yuwa* (assimilation). Its function here reflects the Burakumin's self-understanding as oppressed people and their recognition that their marginalized state is the result of mechanisms of domination. This is a harsh revelation to assimilate — that one's marginalization is not a matter of being "insufficiently integrated" into society or "not yet fully equal" with common Japanese but of being systematically kept outside of society and dominated as inherently unequal.

It is true that during the Meiji period (1868–1912) the Japanese government tried to implement a policy of integration with respect to the Buraku communities, but the policy incorporated no long-range goal to eliminate discrimination against them. Indeed, the policy presupposed the continuation of oppression and served instead to create a safety valve to prevent radical opposition on the part of the Burakumin. The price paid for this process of alleged "integration" or "assimilation" was excessive: the growing alienation of large sectors of the outcast communities and the consequent repression of all forms of self-respect. The situation eventually culminated in the Burakumin's critical opposition to integration and in their opting for the language of liberation. Thus the language of liberation implies a need to go beyond the possibility of integration to self-determination. The first principle of the program adopted by the National Levelers' Association (Zenkoku Suiheisha), the first militant organization for Buraku liberation, established in 1922, was that the Burakumin "shall achieve their liberation through their own acts." The policy of self-help thus introduced a new way of consciousness and action among the Burakumin, and the language of liberation has retained a tremendous overall function of increasing self-awareness and pride among them.

Rooted as it is in the historical experience of the Japanese outcasts, our theological language of "suffering" and "liberation" cannot but assume a sociopolitical dimension, which must affect the content and the methodology of reflection on faith as a specific historical event. But this vocabulary can be easily deprived of its radical character. "Suffering" and "liberation" can be used in an exclusively spiritualistic sense to imply that Christian suffering is the endurance of pain and Christian liberation is the liberation from self and pride. This personal affirmation cannot be denied wholesale. Faith is not merely a psychological process. A human being is undeniably a social entity, and a reflection on faith in a context of societal repression necessarily goes beyond contemplation of individualistic terms. "Suffering" and "liberation" both acquire another dimension, becoming a condemnation of those who repress social and political contradiction as the locus of genuine Christian awareness and praxis.

The new social consciousness among the Burakumin is to be understood as an occasion for renewing the theological debate on the meaning of the liberating activity of God. Challenges to the theme of this debate are often raised by reducing the issue to an either/or proposition: "What is the good of changing the structure of the social system without first changing the human heart?" But psyche and structure are not opposed in the way this question implies. Changing a discriminatory social structure *is* one way of changing the human heart. The relationship between the human heart and its social milieu is reciprocal, one of mutual dependence. To believe that political change will somehow make for a new humanity is naïve and mechanistic, but so is the idea that a "personal" change guarantees the transformation of an oppressive social structure. This either/or proposition denies the radical dialectic unity of self and society. To change a social structure is to change the way in which the self perceives reality, to change the reference points required to maintain a discriminatory system of beliefs.

As stated at the beginning, the main purpose of this paper is to model the kind of theological reflection possible in the context of liberation for the Japanese outcasts. The main questions to which my discussion will constantly return include: What challenge do the Burakumin pose both to our theological reflection and to the church in Japan as a whole? How might our theological agenda be set within their concrete historical context? What fundamental contribution can theology offer to the ongoing reflection on and the attempt to overcome the discrimination against the outcasts in Japan? What new perceptions and directions can theology gain from their struggle for equality?

The Suiheisha's Adoption of the Crown of Thorns

On March 3, 1922, at the inaugural convention of the Suiheisha, the following declaration was read aloud to some two thousand representatives from almost all the Buraku communities in Japan:

> Burakumin throughout the country, unite! ...Brothers and sisters! Our ancestors sought after and practiced liberty and equality. But they became the victims of a base contemptible system developed by the ruling class. They became the martyrs of industry. As a reward for skinning animals, they were flayed alive.

As a recompense for tearing out the hearts of animals, their own warm, human hearts were ripped out. They were spat upon with the words of ridicule. Yet all through these cursed nightmares, their blood, still proud to be human, did not dry up. Yes! Now we have come to the age when men and women, pulsing with this blood, are trying to become divine. The time has come when the martyrs' Crown of Thorns will be blessed. The time has come when we can be proud of being Eta.[3] ...Let there be warmth in the hearts of people, and let there be light upon all humankind. From this, the Suiheisha is born.[4]

The official flag of the Suiheisha was unfurled for the first time. It was black, emblazoned only with a round crown of thorns dyed blood-red, intentionally symbolizing the passion of Jesus. The flagpole was fashioned in the shape of a bamboo spear, symbolizing the militancy of traditional Japanese peasant uprisings against injustice. Similarly, a year later, when the central office of the Suiheisha sent out a message urging the Burakumin to attend the second national convention, the text repeatedly emphasized the crown of thorns in a messianic manner as the symbol of the association's militancy:

The flag with a Crown of Thorns of the color of blood should be the symbol of our suffering and martyrdom. Come and gather in front of an altar and mourn for the tens of millions of our ancestors groaning underground. Once we were lowly people (senmin). Now, we are chosen people (senmin). Three million beloved brothers and sisters, for a "better day," let us unite.[5]

"Martyrdom" and "suffering" are Christian terms rendered by the Japanese outcasts as symbols to express their pain, their groaning, and their long history of oppression. "Chosen people" and "blessing" have been rendered in like manner to express their "eschatological" expectation and hope for liberation. Most of the Suiheisha founders, including Saikō Mankichi, the principal author of the declaration, were not Christian. It is significant, therefore, to note their utilization of Christian symbols, along with their use of Buddhist and Marxist terms, to recall and interpret their experience in the past and to express hope for the future.[6] In the declaration, Saikō denounces the dominant class of his country who have systematically oppressed the Burakumin on the basis of their "mean and filthy" occupations such as animal-slaughtering, butchering, and skinning. It is the rulers themselves, says Saikō, who have "ripped out" and "flayed alive" the human hearts of the Burakumin to make them scapegoats of a semifeudalistic society. He also challenges that oppression. Indeed, his voice is prophetic, echoing the similar cry of Micah, who fiercely denounced the rulers who did "flay men alive and tear the very flesh from their bones."

And I said:
Listen, you leaders of Jacob, rulers of Israel,
Should you not know what is right?
You hate good and love evil,
You flay men alive and tear the very flesh from their bones;

You devour the flesh of my people,
Strip off their skin, splinter their bones. (Micah 3:1–3)

The various biblical stories with their themes of suffering and liberation, such as the Exodus story and the parables of Jesus, provided rich symbolism for the Japanese outcasts to understand and to interpret the destiny of their people. Their instinct sharpened by the experience of oppression, they rightly found in the Bible images that could bear the weight of both their struggle and thirst for justice. The appeal for the second national convention in 1923 evoked the event of Exodus, comparing the enslaved Burakumin to the people of Israel led by Moses. It reads:

> March 3rd of 1922 shall be remembered as the glorious foundation day of the National Suiheisha. It was the day when our three million brothers and sisters under curse chose the path towards liberation. It reminds us of the people of Israel who used to be the despised in Egypt, tried to be free from oppression, led by day in a pillar of cloud and by night in a pillar of fire, and marched into the desert of Paran. Since then a year has passed, and now our day of the Second National Convention has come. Though the wilderness is endless and the promised land of Canaan is still far, our marching tone is even higher and more brave. History is a process of liberation. Three million brothers and sisters and six thousand unliberated Buraku, unite under the flag of the crown of thorns![7]

More than anything else, however, the Burakumin came to relate their experience to the biblical symbol of Jesus' passion. For these people, the crown of thorns is not a symbol of militancy in the sense of conquest or triumph over others in society, nor does it function to adorn in the manner of the Japanese imperial family's use of the "throne of chrysanthemums" crest. It is a symbol that has led the oppressed Buraku communities to experience fellowship with one another and to extend solidarity to other exploited and marginalized people. It is a symbol that calls all people under oppression into solidarity with one another.

It should be emphasized that it was the Burakumin themselves who first took Jesus' crown of thorns as the symbol of their suffering and liberation. Most of them were not churchgoers. They simply took the Bible and read in it their daily experience. Some Christians, however, have found in the Burakumin's interpretation of Jesus' crown a symbolic vehicle for their identity of faith, witnessing to the dimensions of divine activity working among the outcasts in Japan.[8] For them the crown of thorns has become a symbol of the solidarity of God with the marginalized, the oppressed, and the exploited. It has come to signify the person of Jesus, who makes the groaning of the despised his own cry for liberation. The symbol reveals that God is also suffering with them, while promising their freedom from that oppression. The crown of thorns has become a sign of the divine purpose that redeems history from the effects of human evil.

But is this process of symbolism and interpretation by the Burakumin and some Japanese Christians really legitimate in the light of Christian faith? Or is the symbol of the crown of thorns merely used as an image corresponding to a pseudo-messianic character of the Suiheisha? Do we really have here a new way to articulate the truths inherent in faith, or do we have a "false ideology," divorced from authentic Christianity? One way to approach these questions is to examine the original meaning of the crown of thorns, as it has been understood in the Bible and theological traditions.

The Crown of Thorns in the Bible and the Church

The first obvious meaning of the crown of thorns is in its implicit and explicit differences between the priestly and princely crowns of the Old Testament. The Hebrew kings and aristocrats were thought to be set apart by Yahweh in the wearing of royal crowns (*nezer*).[9] Josephus describes the priestly crown as a three-tiered diadem worn over the turban around the nape of the neck. Both crowns indicated "dedication and consecration" to Yahweh. They signified not only the noble rank and authority of the wearer but also the sacred religious nature of his office, given by God. They were called the holy crowns; they were engraved with the words "Holy to the Lord" and decorated with pure gold. Among the priestly class, only high priests could wear this crown, and they were few. It conferred authority to intercede for the nation of Israel and to offer sacrificial rituals to Yahweh in the Holy Temple of Jerusalem. In a word, a crown in the ancient world of Israel was a symbol of high rank and special achievement in society.

Jesus' crown of thorns is significantly different from those of the high priests and kings of Israel. It is a mere crown of thorns (*akanthinos stephanos*) that accords him neither glory nor respect in this world. According to the description of Jesus' crowning with thorns (Mark 15:17, Matt. 27:29, John 19:2, 5), Jesus was first scourged, then clothed with a mock royal cloak, crowned with thorns, beaten on the head with a rod, spat upon, mocked by soldiers, reclothed with his own garment, and finally led out to be crucified. The crown that was forced down on Jesus' head was nothing more than a braided circle of thorny stems, which the Roman soldiers used to deride Jesus after Pilate sentenced him to death. This crown was intended to mock and humiliate him as a criminal who had imagined himself to be the "King of the Jews." The crown of thorns signifies mockery, humiliation, and dishonor.

The apostle Paul, however, saw in Jesus' crown of thorns the exaltation that was the ultimate outcome of his humiliation. A symbol carries the freight of what was, what is, and what is to come, and the crown of thorns is not limited to its past meaning as a sign of mockery. At the very center of Paul's faith lies the assertion that a humiliated and despised man named Jesus was, and is, and will be the glorious Son of God, the messiah who delivers the world from sin. The most high and powerful God has been incarnated in the human figure of the lowest and most powerless. From the very beginning, this central paradox marked the difference between the new faith in Christ and the various religious streams current in the world of his time. Paul was aware of the fact that the proclamation of a suffering messiah was foolishness to enlightened Greeks and a scandal for orthodox Jews. But for Paul as well as for the people of the early church, Jesus' crown, together with the cross, was a symbol of victory. The New Testament states that the faithful would wear the crown of rejoicing (1 Thess. 2:19), of righteousness (1 Pet. 5:4), and life (James 1:12; Rev. 2:10). The crown given by Jesus Christ to the persecuted is "an unfading crown of glory" (1 Pet. 5:4). God crowned Jesus with thorns so that he would taste suffering and death for the world, but as God redeemed him from death, exalting him and turning his dishonor into honor, God will crown men and women in their sufferings "with glory and honor" (Heb. 2:7). In the faith of the early church, Jesus' crown of thorns became the symbol of the solidarity of God the Father with Jesus the Son through his passion and resurrection, inviting the rejected and despised of the world into the joyful fellowship of the Kingdom.

According to Lanternari, the Christian faith among the poor in medieval Europe preserved the character of a "religion of the suppressed,"[10] and the poor farmers and artisans knew their faith would bring them into spontaneous fellowship with a mystical Christ. The cross and the crown of thorns became the objects of popular faith among them, and during times of persecution, war, poverty, and starvation, a Christ crowned with thorns was often experienced as directly present. At the great Christian pageants during Lent and Holy Week, the wretched people would carry in their processions a statue of the crucified Jesus crowned with thorns. Jesus' passion was a major Christian pageant for the marginalized in general. Here we could contend that their daily experience rightly grasped the authentic element of the Christian faith in the Passion story; a profound insight into the meaning of the gospel for the poor and the marginalized underlies that emphasis.

The official church, however, did not recognize the crown of Jesus as a radical symbol of the authentic originality of the Christian faith. Reflection on the crown of thorns was generally devotional or contemplative, and by the end of the Medieval Era, church tradition had elaborated around it a "mystique of sorrow and suffering." That is to say, Jesus' crown was grasped in passive terms, understood to represent an inward experience for each individual and not for communal transformation. Its message of suffering and liberation was understood to imply endurance in this world and freedom in the next or at the end of time. The symbol had become dissociated from Jesus' historical cause for the poor and the oppressed and was utilized as a cult object — fragmented, as it were, from the whole, along with Jesus' "Five Wounds," "Precious Blood," and "Sacred Heart."

When the period of the Enlightenment began to affect the church, theologians and modern humanists came to despise and abhor the miserable image of the suffering Christ; it was understood as a contradiction of everything that modern and progressive spirituality represented. Instead of seeing the crown of thorns as a symbol of suffering and liberation, liberal theologians exchanged the dark cultic image of medieval faith for the bright crown atop the glorious figure of a triumphant Christ — more representative of the righteousness, beauty, and morality of the humanist ideal. In a time of progress and human advancement, the longing for fellowship with an abandoned and tormented Jesus and his unpleasant crown appeared to deny the evolutionary impetus toward the good, the true, and the beautiful. The crown of thorns of the suffering Christ has never been a valued symbol for a bourgeois faith in modern society.

It is the oppressed Burakumin themselves, and not the church theologians and biblical scholars in Japan, who have rightly recovered the radical meaning of Jesus' crown of thorns. Their revived focus on the crown of thorns is much more praxis-oriented in character than either modern or medieval European-counterparts. Among them Jesus' crown is no longer seen as an object of personal cult nor as an expression of misery or inescapable fate in one's individual life. It is not, as seen in many medieval paintings of the Passion, or *Anfechtung,* an expression of the inward wrestling of the tormented soul with self and sin. On the contrary, when interpreted in the eyes of the Japanese outcasts, Jesus' crown of thorns has become a symbol representing, in an oppressive world, the Kingdom of freedom and justice to come. It goes beyond the "golds and roses" draped around the crown by an interpretation formulated to fit the needs of civil religion. It has become a symbol that both points to the pain of the marginalized and reveals the hope of their final victory. Recovered through the eyes of the Burakumin, the symbol of the crown of thorns confirms Christian faith as the faith in the liberating work of God for the outcasts in the world.

A New Name for Jesus

How can we in the church recover the originality of Jesus' crown of thorns when the way we think about him has been so conditioned or, one might say, "distorted"? Pastors and theologians in Asia, orthodox and liberal alike, have presented images of Jesus that are mostly alien to the daily experience of the Asian people in general, and to that of the outcasts in particular.

One powerful voice protesting this alien image of Jesus is that of playwright Kim Chi Ha, a Korean Catholic, who was tortured and imprisoned during the 1970s for his human rights involvements in Korea. The setting of his play, *The Gold-Crowned Jesus,* is a ghetto in a small town.[11] A leper, a beggar, and a prostitute — the three main characters — are obviously the social victims of Korean society. They sit down together, with empty stomachs, and lament their misfortune. Nearby stands a statue of Jesus with a golden crown on his head. It was constructed by a company president who, in the play, prays the following prayer:

> Jesus, the gold crown on your head, it really suits you. It's perfect. You are truly the king of this world, when you wear that crown. You are the king of kings. You are handsome, you are really handsome in that crown. Dear Jesus, never forget that your gold crown was made from the cash contributed by yours truly last Christmas....Please, Jesus, help me make more money. And if you do that for me, Jesus, next Christmas I will cast your whole body in gold.[12]

One cold night, however, this statue suddenly cries out to the leper, one of the most despised in the Asian world, that he must liberate Jesus from captivity. The statue says that if he is to come and save those who are toiling, he must first regain his own freedom. Priests, bishops, business industrialists, not to mention powerful government officials, will not free him. The leper asks in awe, "What can be done to free you, Jesus, to make you live again so that you can come to us?" To this question, Jesus replies:

> It is your poverty, your wisdom, your generous spirit, and even more, your courageous resistance against injustice that makes all this possible....It is sufficient that I keep The Crown of Thorns. The crown of gold is merely the

insignia of those ignorant, greedy, and corrupt people who value only displays of external pomp and showy decorations.[13]

In the statements "I keep the crown of thorns" and "the crown of gold is the insignia of those greedy and corrupt people," Kim pits the crown of thorns against the crown of gold forced on Jesus' head by the rich and the powerful. And this is the hermeneutical principle by which we need to find Jesus anew in the church and to recover him for the Asian outcasts. Needless to say, the mission of the church is to proclaim Jesus' Good News to those who are suffering and tormented. But this is not the whole story. Paradoxically speaking, those who are suffering and oppressed are not only the objects of evangelization, but also the subjects of evangelizing the church from which they received the gospel. The true figure of Jesus could be revealed through their "poverty, wisdom, generous spirit, and courage." It is the church that needs to be evangelized by the suffering people if it is to retain its vigor and strength for the proclamation of the gospel of Jesus Christ.

Discussing the exact part of Kim's play, C. S. Song argues that it is not a shock to hear that Jesus first asks the outcast to release him from the cement statue.[14] Song asserts that the church in Asia has alienated Jesus from the poor for a long time by allying itself with the establishment. Those who control society dress Jesus in golden splendor, hoisting him high above the altar. They have taken him away from the hands of the marginalized, sealing his mouth with solemn liturgies and sophisticated sermons. "Kim vigorously protests this captivity of Jesus in the institutionalized church," says Song, "and Jesus' image has been identified with the titles and names of the powerful in the world." If Jesus is to have any meaning for the Asian peoples, he must take off the gold crown as Kim alludes to in the play. He must regain a simple crown of thorns and join the oppressed in their suffering and joy. If Jesus is a savior merely for the powerful, he has nothing to do with the wretched in Asia.

It is an obvious fact that churchgoers in Japan belong mostly to the middle-class intellectuals and that they understand Jesus Christ through their position in society. But the Burakumin outcasts understand him quite differently. They have understood him and the preaching of the Kingdom in terms of their sociohistorical experiences of suffering and dreams. They would interpret him from the underside of history and start to liberate Jesus from the captivity of those who boast of rank and honors. Confronted with the person of Jesus in the Bible, the Japanese outcasts have begun to associate him with images that would correspond to their living experience of his inexhaustible reality. For example, as early as the 1920s, a man named Mori Yuichi said that "Jesus crowned with thorns" is a "liberator for us, the Burakumin."[15] He related the New Testament story of Jesus to the story of fellow captives in Japan. He argued that Jesus had made the declaration of emancipation nearly two thousand years ago, long before the Emancipation Decree was issued by the Meiji government in 1871. What impressed him particularly was Jesus' opening words of his ministry in Luke 4:18–19:

> "The spirit of the Lord is upon me
> because he has anointed me;
> he has sent me to announce good news to the poor,

> to proclaim release for prisoners
> and recovery of sight for the blind;
> to let the broken victims go free,
> to proclaim the year of the Lord's favor."

Unless our Christology is analyzed in the light of the Japanese outcasts' anguish, hopes, and dreams, we cannot bring out what Jesus' good message means for the segregated villages, crowded ghettos, and daily battles for freedom fought in their communities. The most serious weakness shared by Japanese academic theologians and biblical scholars is that they grant the sociohistorical life of Jesus with the oppressed only a secondary role. Salvation is understood to occur at the ontological level rather than being genuinely historical and communal. Liberation is interpreted only in terms of the individual dimension. In order to avoid that co-optation of academic tradition, our investigation of Christology must study what Jesus Christ did in terms of the concerns of Asian outcasts. Our questions are: What name can we give to Jesus that expresses a liberative understanding of his message and person? Who is Jesus for those who suffer under the oppression of casteism? What title would emerge from their analysis of the figure of Jesus?

Jesus as the One Crowned with Thorns

Jesus as Co-Sufferer

Of all the possibilities, the "One Crowned with Thorns" could become the Christological title par excellence for the Burakumin. Jesus as the "One Crowned with Thorns" has two main characteristics. First of all, Jesus appears before them as a co-sufferer. Because the Japanese outcasts are suffering discrimination and suppression, the Christological importance must be found in this reality of suffering with the marginalized. If Jesus is not suffering as they are, then his life and death will have little significance for them. We must make clear that the Spirit of Jesus is suffering with them. Even now, the exact pains of the outcasts in Japan are felt as his own.

What was absurd to Greeks and offensive to Jews (1 Cor. 1:8) was the Christian faith in which a messiah suffers. A suffering messiah was a totally absurd notion for the highly cultured Greeks. A messiah, as conceived within the powerful city-state of Athens, would have been a sage-king full of power, wisdom, and glory who would preside over the world of generals, philosophers, and thinkers with leisure time in which to mediate and to argue; meanwhile, the rest of the slave population would have to toil and labor. Such a messiah would possess military skills and would be able to lead his armies into battlefield, conquer enemy territories, and enslave captives. His messiahship would be consolidated by his capacity to empower the nation. On that basis, the Greeks dismissed Jesus as the suffering messiah, absurd and useless.

For the Jews, a suffering messiah was also a highly offensive notion. Like the emperor of Japan before World War II, the messiah awaited by the priests and the Pharisees had to be free from every contamination of the world. That is what "sacred" and "holy" means — to be set apart from all people and things that are unclean and defiled. In the figure of Jesus, however, the concept of messiah took a radically different form. Moltmann observes: "As an outcast Jesus brought the gospel to outcasts through his death. Through his self-sacrifice he brought God to those who had been sacrificed. Through his death under curse he brought liberating grace to those who are cursed according to the law."[16] Jesus took the form of an outcast and thus the identify of the despised and the powerless. This identification reached its climax at the Passion, when Jesus was crowned with thorns and crucified. As Hebrews 13:13 reminds us, Jesus not only died once and for all but continues to bear upon himself the affliction and wounds of all the despised. He shall continue to be crowned with thorns until the day of the final redemption. He is still present among the forsaken, the wretched, and the marginalized. If all of this statement is christologically true, then it must also be true that Jesus stands today with the three million Burakumin in the midst of their sufferings. Wherever there are cries and groaning, there is the Spirit of Jesus; he is suffering together with the marginalized in Japan.

Shusaku Endo, a Japanese Catholic novelist, pictures Jesus as co-sufferer most vividly in the last part of his well-known book *In the Vicinity of the Dead Sea*. He describes a Jew named Kobarsky, who is about to be handed over for execution in the Nazi concentration camp:

> I looked at Kobarsky as he waddled along accompanied by a German guard on his left. For a moment — just a flash — I saw with my own eyes another man waddling along beside Kobarsky, a person who was dragging his feet just like the prisoner. The man on his right also wore the same prison garb and like Kobarsky had a stream of urine dripping to the ground behind him.[17]

From the context of the novel, "the man" accompanying Kobarsky on his death march is understood to be Jesus himself. This is Endo's image of Jesus as cosufferer. Though Endo himself employs the word "companion" (*dohansha*) rather than "co-sufferer" (*kyokusha*) for Jesus, it is clear that Endo is depicting the person of Jesus as present in the life of the people who toil and suffer. He argues that insofar as Jesus has assumed the identify of the hurt and the weak, he is with them.

A theology of Buraku liberation must affirm that Jesus continues to be identified with those who are discriminated against under suppression. It must be announced that he is present among the Burakumin farmers in the villages and low-paid workers in the cities. Jesus took the form of an outcast in his Incarnation, becoming totally identified with humanity in its most miserable form. To call him the "One Crowned with Thorns" is the ultimate symbolism of this identification.

But our understanding of the person of Jesus remains one-sided if we see this meaning only in his being a co-sufferer. A new life in Jesus means also the overcoming of suffering and bondage. Endo's one-sided emphasis on Jesus as a companion leads to a dead end wherein Jesus is conceived as merely meek and docile and cannot serve as a source of strength to break the cause of sufferings. One cannot proceed from Endo's standpoint to criticize the traditional images of Christ that do not foster liberation.[18] A Christ who suffers but does not liberate is a Christ embodying the "interiorized impotence of the oppressed" (Hugo Assmann). The image of a suffering Son of God might serve as a critique of the powerful and monarchical Christ, or of God as the Almighty King. But it little supports efforts to achieve political, social, and historical liberation for the Burakumin. This is why it is important for us to cultivate theologically as well the person of Jesus as liberator.

Jesus as Liberator

We have seen previously that the Burakumin themselves explored the image of Jesus as liberator of the oppressed. For our concerns, however, Kim Chi Ha's ballad, *Chang Il Tam,* which portrays Jesus as a man for Asian outcasts par excellence,[19] is also useful. It was confiscated by the late Park regime as proof of his "conspiracy to publish subversive materials." Chang Il Tam, the hero of the ballad, was born at the bottom of society as a son of the Paekchong (Korean outcasts similar to the Japanese Burakumin). Since childhood he had seen the misery of his people, and his experience of agony eventually led him to become "a preacher of liberation." He followed the way of Im Kok Chong, a legendary Korean thief, believing that the Paekchong and other poor people of Korea ought to regain what the rich and powerful had taken from them. He started robbing affluent aristocrats and giving money to the poor. He was arrested and thrown into prison, but even there he shouted to his fellow prisoners, "We must be liberated! Down with the degraded bourgeoisie!" He then escaped from the prison and, chased by the police, ran into a ghetto where some women were being forced to work as prostitutes. Chang called those women his mother and kissed their feet, declaring, "The soles of your feet are heaven," and "God's place is with the lowest of the low!"[20]

Later Chang climbed Mount Kyeryong and preached to beggars and prostitutes that a new Kingdom could be established on the land of the Eastern Sea. He advocated social change, political resistance, and the practice of "the communal ownership of property."[21] His major theme, "the transformation of the lowest into heaven," required radical praxis and the consciousness raising of the outcasts themselves. He asserted that the most despised is God's noble agent to bring justice and peace into the world. He openly claimed that it was the sacred duty of the outcasts to "purge the wild beast that lurks within human hearts," which alluded to a symbolic act of the Paekchong's traditional occupations of butchering and cleaning.

Then one day, Chang asked the people to gather around an altar in the wilderness and organized a march to "the evil palace," the capital city of Seoul. Led by him, the poor and the marginalized started their march to make the "eternal journey toward paradise where food is shared by all."

The story continues, but it is enough to know that Chang Il Tam is Kim's image of Jesus who offers the hope of freedom to the outcasts in Asia. The heaven to which the beggars and prostitutes are marching is a kingdom of this world where justice and peace prevail. It is not an other-worldly place after death, as is often preached by the church. Kim's approach to Christology is mediated through an analysis of the communal reality of sufferers. But, contrary to Endo's work, Kim attempts to detect the social mechanism that generates the agony of the people. He tries to elaborate a praxis that is liberative in a historical context. Chang Il Tam does not simply seek an inner-directed conception of compassion as the oriental sages often do to reach enlightenment by themselves. Like legendary sages, he climbed the mountain of Kyeryong, but he did not stay there forever. He came down to the reality of the people, strove to be truly with them, and proposed that they change the oppressive structure itself.

In our present historical situation in the various Buraku communities, a Christology devoid of a liberating praxis would signify acceptance of the existing discriminatory society and lend support to those who oppress. A Christology for the Burakumin must not only take the side of the outcasts and give them consolation but also compel one to emancipatory praxis by faith in Jesus as liberator.

We have followed the person of Jesus in the light of our concerns with the contemporary Buraku issue. We have found that Jesus was crowned with thorns as a result of his mission to the marginalized and the despised in the world. He was hostile to the religious ideologues of his day and was eventually condemned because of his relentless attack on an ideology that promoted oppression of the poor. He was resurrected from death to show that the final victory will be in the hands of the socially abandoned. He not only suffers with them but also gives hope for their liberation in history.

Towards a Church with the Crown of Thorns

Jesus was folly to the wise, a scandal to the devout, and a disturber of the law in the eyes of the mighty. That is why he was crowned with thorns and ridiculed. As Paul says, if anyone identifies with Jesus, this world is negated to him or her. When a person realizes that one has been on the side of discriminators against the powerless but wants to walk in the light of Jesus' freedom, that person has to give up his or her previous identity and gain a new identity in Jesus. That person has to obtain a new citizenship in the world of the despised to make a real conversion from the sin of discrimination. This is why struggling with the Burakumin is a necessary part of the church in Japan.

The church in Japan, however, has long failed to recognize its own inherent oppression against them.[22] Some may try to tone this down, or to offer various interpretations of it, but that does not change the fact. It is not widely known in the ecumenical church community that Japan is guilty of oppression and continues to discriminate against its own minority. Much attention has been paid to the "miracle" of Japan's economic prosperity, but certainly among the Japanese who did not benefit appreciably from that success are the Burakumin. A report of the World Council of Churches states:

> Perhaps the least-known case of the group oppression is that against the Buraku in Japan, which shows only too vividly that once an identifiable group has been marked out for oppression at some point of history, it is extremely hard to eliminate the stigma.[23]

Long gone is the time when the church in Japan could handle the question of Buraku oppression by simply stating that God created all men and women equal and that there exists no discrimination in the church. Today it is the church itself that is called to answer for oppression. It is being called into question by many who have experienced in their daily lives the terrible distance that separates the church from the issue of Buraku discrimination. It is even being called into question by non-Christians who are far away from the life of the Christian community but who are involved in the struggle for liberation and see the church as an obstructive force in the effort to eliminate Buraku oppression and construct a more just society.

The dominant churches in Japan have been mirroring the North American and European churches, uncritically borrowing their theologies, institutions, canon laws, spirituality, and even lifestyles. They have not found new forms appropriate to the world of the outcast communities in the process of liberation. The people who want to shape their life to the demands of those communities find it extremely difficult to accept ecclesial structures that do not take serious account of the causes underlying the present social reality of Japan.

Today a new type of ecclesiology has begun to be worked out among Burakumin Christians. The reflection of the church that identifies with Jesus' crown of thorns is being conducted from within the concrete experiences of suffering and hope in their communities. It is trying to proclaim solidarity with the pains of the Burakumin and to do a liberating praxis with them. If this mission is seriously promoted, a new church could eventually emerge that takes seriously the figure of Jesus Christ who was born as and died as an outcast and was resurrected for the despised.

The majority of churches in Japan have not given much attention to the problem of Buraku oppression, but I am convinced that the time will come for them to assume a more active role in the struggle for freedom.

Beyond the undeniable fact that Buraku oppression exposes millions of people to daily hostilities ranging from verbal intimidation to segregation in marriage, housing, and employment, ultimately the credibility of the gospel of Jesus Christ — and thus the future of the church in Japan — is at stake. The task of the church in Japan is somewhat comparable to that of the prophet Isaiah, who was struck by a vision of God to liberate his people, but he was also keenly aware of the blocks in himself that served to negate that vision. "Woe is me! I am lost; for I am a man of unclean lips" (Isa. 6:5). He understood the deep sense in which he was a part of the problem. But in spite of this difficulty in himself, in a moment of faith and decision, he responded courageously, saying "Here I am! Send me" (6:8).

In the pursuit of the vision of a liberated society in which there exists no oppression, the church in Japan must rise above the blocks within itself and respond to the call of God, as the prophet did, even though the church, too, has been a part of the problem. The responsibility of the church is to proclaim the vision of the Kingdom of God, transcending the narrow boundaries of caste and bringing justice to the world. The church in Japan is facing a great challenge. It has been chosen for great causes. It is being challenged on its ability to speak the truth of faith. Its trial has just begun, and before it are only two choices: either the church keeps the golden crown for the powerful and the respected, or it takes it off and recovers the crown of thorns that has been revealed in the eyes of the despised and the forsaken in Asia.

Notes

1. For reading the history of Buraku oppression in English, see George De Vos and Wagatsuma Hiroshi, *Japan's Invisible Race,* rev. ed. (Berkeley: The University of California Press, 1972); Minority Rights Group, ed., *Japan's Minorities: Burakumin, Koreans & Ainu* (London: Minority Rights Group, 1974); Roger Yoshino & Murakoshi

Sueo, *The Invisible Visible Minority: Japan's Burakumin* (Osaka: Buraku Liberation Publishers, 1977); Buraku Liberation Research Institute, *Long-suffering Brothers and Sisters, Unite!* (Osaka: Kaiho Shuppan, 1981); Suginohara Juichi, *The Status Discrimination in Japan* (Kobe: Hyogo Institute of Buraku Problems, 1982); Mikiso Hane, *Peasants, Rebels & Outcasts: The Underside of Modern Japan* (New York: Pantheon Books, 1982).

2. Inoue Kiyoshi, *Buraku no Rekishi to Kaiho Riron* (History of the Buraku and theories of liberation) (Osaka: Tabata Shoten, 1969), pp. 125–26.

3. "Eta" literally means "much filth." Outcast status and social codes of untouchability in Japan were set during the medieval period, reflecting a complex network of economic, political, and religious conditions. It was in the rigid stratification of society under the Tokugawa Shogunate, beginning in 1600 A.D., that the degraded outcast status of those practicing "defiled" jobs was formally established. The lowest status of the outcasts were called the Hinin, or "nonpeople," a heterogeneous group made up of beggars, prostitutes, entertainers, mediums, diviners, religious wanderers, executioners, tomb-watchers, and fugitives. Above the Hinin were the Eta, hereditary outcasts who were forced to perform occupations considered ritually polluting, including animal slaughter and disposal of the dead. Since outcasts who practiced jobs involving death and blood were seen to be subhuman by nature, Eta status was inherited through birth or was obtained through marriage or close associations. See Herbert Passin,"Untouchability in the Far East," *Monumenta Nipponica,* 12 (1956).

4. Buraku Mondai Kenkyusho, ed., *Suihei Undoshi no Kenkyu* (A study of the history of the Suihei movement) vol. 2 (Kyoto: Buraku Mondai Kenkyusho, 1971), p. 143.

5. Ibid., p. 173.

6. Inoue Kiyoshi, *Buraku Mondai no Kenkyu* (A study of Buraku problems) (Kyoto: Buraku Mondai Kenkyusho, 1959), pp. 107–8. Wagatsuma argues that the founders of the Suiheisha were probably influenced by Christian socialism and the social gospel in the 1920s when Japanese Christian liberals introduced Christian symbolism into social issues. See De Vos and Wagatsuma, *Japan's Invisible Race,* p. 43.

7. Buraku Mondai Kenkyusho, p. 173.

8. Seminars and study groups have been organized by pastors and theologians to reflect theologically on the issue of Buraku liberation from the early 1960s. See The Christian Conference for the Buraku Liberation, ed., *Buraku Kaiho Kirisutosha Kyogikai Sanjyu Nenshi* (The thirty years of the Christian conference for the Buraku liberation) (Osaka: The Christian Conference for the Buraku Liberation, 1992).

9. See *International Standard Bible Encyclopedia,* 3d ed., s.v. "crown"; *New Bible Dictionary,* 2d ed., s.v. "crown of thorns"; *Dictionary of Subjects and Symbols,* 2d ed., s.v. "crown" and others.

10. See Vittorio Lanternari, *The Religions of the Oppressed: A Study of Modern Messianic Cults* (New York: MacGibbon & Kee, 1963).

11. Kim Chi Ha, *The Gold-Crowned Jesus & Other Writings* (Maryknoll, N.Y.: Orbis Books, 1978), pp. 85ff.

12. Ibid., pp. 109–10.

13. Ibid., p. 124.

14. Song Choan Seng, *The Compassionate God* (Maryknoll, N.Y.: Orbis Books, 1982), p. 111.

15. Quoted by Fujino Yutaka in his article, "The Foundation of the National Suiheisha and Christianity," *Fukuin to Sekai* (The gospel and the world) (March, 1989).

16. Jürgen Moltmann, *The Church in the Power of the Spirit* (London: SCM Press, 1978), p. 87.

17. Shusaku Endo, *Shikai no Hotori* (In the vicinity of the Dead Sea) (Tokyo: Kodansha, 1978), p. 323.

18. Endo's Jesus as companion seems to function only in terms of a personal paradigm. Endo identifies himself with the tax-collectors and sinners as in Luke 15:7, 18:13, and Matthew 18:14. He seeks to follow Jesus who is the companion of sinners, but in reality Endo stands socially and politically on the side of the establishment by struggling only against his own "darkness of inner self." Only subjectively does he call himself a sinner. See criticism of Endo in Arai Sasagu, "Jesus, the Companion," *CTC Bulletin,* no. 3 (April, 1982), p. 29.

19. Kim, pp. 23–30.

20. Ibid., p. 28.

21. Here Kim is influenced not by Marxism but by the teaching of the Tonghak Movement. The Tonghak, or "Eastern Learning," founded by Ch'oe Che Un in 1859, is an eclectic (partly Christian) religious sect that attracted the poor peasants and workers. See Chi Myong Kan, "The Tonghak Peasants Revolution and Christianity," *Seisho to Kyokai* (The Bible and the church) no. 7 (1983), pp. 8–13. On the history of the Paekchong, see Rhim Soon Man, "The Paekchong: Untouchables of Korea," *Journal of Oriental Studies,* vol. XII, nos. 1 & 2 (1974).

22. Kudo Eiichi, *Kirisutokyo to Buraku Mondai* (Christianity and the Buraku problem) (Tokyo: Shinkyo Shuppansha, 1983), p. 5. According to Kudo, the evangelical mission toward the Buraku communities was started at the Hiromae Church in Aomori Prefecture in 1877 by Protestant missionaries. The Japan Episcopal Church (Sei Ko Kai) built a church in Tokyo in 1878. In 1888 the Burakumin in Okayama began organizing a Bible study group at Takeda. However, the leaders of the mainstream churches hardly realized the needs of the Burakumin for freedom, and eventually the churches in Japan retreated from almost all Buraku communities.

23. Barbara Rogers, *Pace: No Peace Without Justice* (Geneva: World Council of Churches, 1980), p. 29.

Chapter 2

Toward a Christian Dalit Theology

ARVIND P. NIRMAL

Indian Christian theology, in its eagerness to relieve itself from the stranglehold of Hellenistic, Latin, Germanic, and Anglo-American influences, reclaimed uncritically brahamanical philosophical insights to work out its own indigenous theology. Though it looked innovative at that time, especially the imaginative way in which Hindu religious categories were grafted onto the Christian theological scheme, it is now clear that it overlooked and surprisingly made no impact on the majority of Indian Christians who are dalits. This group of people have been variously known as *harijans* (Children of Hari [God] Mahatma Gandhi); *avarnas* (casteless); *panchamas* (fifth caste); *chandalas* (worst of the earth); Protestant Hindus (Ambedkar); depressed class (British colonial days); scheduled caste (Indian Constitution). This article is one of the initial attempts to look at the dominant Indian theologies and work out a theology of dalit liberation that would incorporate the pain, wounds, and hopes of the dalits.

Arvind P. Nirmal is the head of the Department of Dalit Theology at Gurukul Lutheran Theological College and Research Institute, Madras, India. He is one of the pioneers in articulating dalit theology and has written widely on the subject. His recent edited volumes are *Towards a Common Dalit Ideology* and *Reader in Dalit Theology,* both published by the Department of Dalit Theology, Gurukul Lutheran Theological College and Research Institute.

Source: *Asian Journal of Theology* 6 (2), 1992.

"When they divided the *Purusa,* into how many parts did they arrange him? What was his mouth? What were his arms? What are his thighs and feet called?

"The *brahmim* was his mouth, his two arms were made the *rajanya* (warrior), his two thighs *vaisya* (trader and agriculturist) from his feet the *sudra* (servile class) was born."

—*Rig Veda,* X, 90:12

27

"But a *sudra,* whether bought or unbought, he may compel to do servile work; for he was created by the self-existent *(svayambhu)* to be the slave of a brahmin.

"A *sudra,* though emancipated by his master, is not released from servitude; since that is innate in him, who can set him free from it?"

— *Manu Dharma Sastra,* VIII, 413–14

"I had the misfortune to be born with the stigma of 'untouchable.' But it is not my fault, but I will not die a Hindu, for this is within my power."

— Dr. B. Rambedkar

"There came a woman of Samaria to draw water. Jesus said to her, 'Give me a drink.' ... The Samaritan woman said to him, 'How is it that you a Jew, ask a drink of me, a woman of Samaria?' For Jews have no dealings with Samaritans."

— John 4:7, 9–10

"There is neither Jew nor Greek, there is neither slave nor free, there is neither male nor female; for you are all one in Christ Jesus."

— Galatians 3:28

Jesus answered, "It was not that this man sinned, or his parents, but that the works of God might be made manifest in him."

— John 9:3

Introduction

This is an historic moment for Indian Christian theology. At this moment Indian Christian theology has ceased to be an enterprise of the elite, on behalf of the elite, and has allowed itself to be an enterprise of peoples. These peoples are the dalits: one, the broken, the torn, the rent, the burst, the split; two, the opened, the expanded; three, the bisected; four, the driven asunder, the dispelled, the scattered; five, the downtrodden, the crushed, the destroyed; and six, the manifested, the displayed.

If we want to grasp the full significance of this historic movement, we must look back at the tradition of Indian Christian theology. In the seventies, I had made the following observation in one of my articles:

Broadly speaking Indian Christian Theology in the past has tried to work out its theological systems in terms of either Advaita Vedanta or Vaishisahtha Advaita. Most of the contribution of Indian Christian theology in the past came from caste converts to Christianity. The result has been that Indian Christian theology has perpetuated within itself what I prefer to call the *Brahminic* tradition. This tradition has further perpetuated an institutional interiority-oriented approach to the theological task in India. One wonders whether this kind of Indian Christian theology will ever have a mass appeal.

This brief observation can be spelled out a little more fully. To speak in terms of the traditional Indian categories, Indian Christian theology, following the Brahminic tradition, has trodden the *jnana marga,* the *bhakti marga,* and the *karma marga.* In Brahrnabandhab Upadhyay, we have a brilliant theologian who attempted a synthesis of Sankara's Advaita Vedanta and Christian theology. In Bishop A. J. Appasamy, we had a *bhakti margi* theologian who tried to synthesize Ramanuja's Vishishtha Advaita with Christian theology. In M. M. Thomas we have a theologian who has contributed to theological anthropology at the international level and laid the foundations for a more active theological involvement in India — the *karma marga.* In Chenchiah we find an attempt to synthesize Christian theology with Sri Aurobindo's "Integral Yoga."

If we look at India's involvement in the ecumenical movement, we recapture the following story. The International Missionary Conference held at Edinburgh in 1910 set an official seal on the "Fulfillment Theory" expounded by J. N. Faruhar. The second International Missionary Conference held in Jerusalem in 1928 encouraged the efforts of the supporters of the fulfillment theory but warned against the danger of "syncretism." It also said that different world religions should cooperate with one another against the common enemy of "secularism." Between the Jerusalem conference and the Madras meeting of the same body in 1938, Barth's neo-orthodoxy became the dominant theology of at least continental Europe. Hendrik Kraemer, the Dutch theologian, applied the Barthian insights to the "problem" of non-Christian faiths. He worked out what might be called the "gospel-judging religion" model. Kraemer argued that there was a basic difference between the gospel or revelation on the one hand and religion on the other. All religions were human attempts at salvation, and as such they had to be judged by the gospel. Christianity, on the other hand, was not a religion, but a gospel — the gospel of Jesus Christ. It was revelation from above. The gospel was not addressed to a Hindu or Muslim or Buddhist but to a sinful and fallen human being. Kraemer's thesis was published under the title, *The Christian Message in Non-Christian World,* on the eve of the Third International Missionary Conference in 1938.

Thus, from the early days of India's ecumenical involvement, it had concerned itself with the "problem" of other faiths. Out of this ecumenical involvement emerged the concern for dialogues with other faiths, and this concern continues to be taken seriously. But this concern again has contributed to Indian Christian theology's obsession with the Brahminic tradition. As a matter of fact, in connection with the International Missionary Conference at Tambaram, several research studies in the economic social environment of the Indian church were conducted by various Christian colleges. They gave a very sober picture of the economic condition of rural Christians. It also became clear that depressed-class converts continued to complain of indifference and neglect. All this, however, did not make any change to Indian Christian theology's obsession with the Brahminic tradition. It had no time or inclination to reflect theologically on the dalit converts who formed the majority of the Indian church.

The situation did not change till the seventies. It was in the seventies that Indian theologians began to take the questions of socio-economic justice more seriously. The Indian theological scene thus changed considerably and there emerged what is known as "third-world theology." The advocates of the third-world theology were held together by their allegiance to "liberation theology." It was yet another imported theology. Its chief attraction was the liberation motif, which seemed entirely relevant in the Indian situation where the majority of the Indian people face the problem of poverty. But somehow I felt that liberation motifs in India were of a different nature, the Indian situation being different, and we had to search for liberation motifs that were authentically Indian. Latin American liberation theology, in its early stages at least, used Marxist analysis of socio-economic realities — the haves and the have-nots. The socio-economic realities in India, however, are of a different nature, and the traditional doctrinaire Marxist analysis and these realities are inadequate in India. It neglects the caste factor, which adds to the complexity of Indian socio-economic realities. A journalist-scholar like V. T. Rajashekar Shetty tells us *How Marx Failed in Hindu India.*

The Indian advocates of the third-world theology also ignored the incidents or violence against dalits in the seventies. The seventies saw several caste wars. Belchi in Bihar in 1977, the urban area of the North and the South (Agra and Villupuram), both in May 1978, and Kanjhawala near the heart of the country's capital are a few of the places that witnessed organized violence against the dalits by caste-Hindus in the seventies. This real-life context was overlooked by our Indian third-world theologians, and they continued to engage in the Latin American liberation rhetoric. The sixties and the seventies were also the decades when the dalit *sahitya* (literature) movement and the dalit Panther movement were making headway in Maharashtra. Somehow our theologians did not see in these dalit movements and struggles a potential for theological reflection.

To sum up, then, whether it is the traditional Indian Christian theology or the more recent third-world theology, our theologians failed to see in the struggles of Indian dalits for liberation a subject matter appropriate for doing theology in India. What is amazing is the fact that Indian theologians ignored the reality of the Indian church. While estimates vary, between 50 and 80 percent of all the Christians in India today are of scheduled-caste origin. This is the most important commonality cutting across the various diversities of the Indian church that would have provided an authentic liberation motif for Indian Christian theology. If our theologians failed to see this in the past, there is all the more reason for our waking up to this reality today and for applying ourselves seriously to the task of doing dalit theology.

My friend, Professor John Webster, in his article, "From Indian Church to Indian Theology: An Attempt at Theological Construction," has seen three stages in the history of the Depressed Class Movement in India. The three stages are somewhat overlapping chronologically, but they all have their own distinctive characteristics. The first stage is dated from the 1860s or 1870s through the 1930s. The chief characteristic of this first phase is the phenomenon of mass conversion, especially to Christianity. The second stage of this movement begins around 1900 and goes up to 1955. The chief characteristic of the second stage is the caste Hindu efforts to improve the condition of the depressed classes. Initially, voluntary organizations such as the Depressed Classes Mission (1906) and the all India Shuddhi Sabha (1909) were involved in these efforts, and later Mahatma Gandhi and the Harijan Sevak Sangh (1932) expanded the work. After 1937 the government agencies were used to pass laws and to finance and administer programs for the welfare of the depressed classes. The third and the last stage is dated from the 1920s to the present day. The stage is characterized by self-assertion on the part of the depressed classes themselves. Webster's study is important because it underlines the point I have made earlier: the fact that so much was happening on the dalit front, but Indian Christian theology failed to take note of it.

It is the contention of this article that the struggle of Indian dalits is a story that provides us with a liberation motif that is authentically Indian. This story needs to be analyzed and interpreted theologically. The struggle is far from over. All the documentation on the situation of the dalits is clear indication of the fact that the liberation story of Indian dalits is incomplete as yet. Theirs (or rather ours) is an ongoing struggle. This liberation struggle needs to be undergirded theologically.

Having looked at the background of and the need for a Christian dalit theology or dalits theologies, we should now attempt to answer the question: What is dalit theology? It is rather difficult to answer this question in simple and straightforward language. For one thing, dalit theology is still in the process of emergence. We are still trying to construct a dalit theology or theologies. This is why I have entitled this essay "Toward a Christian Dalit Theology." What I am trying to do in this paper is to indicate the possible shape or form that Indian Christian dalit theology may take. The task that I have set before myself is to anticipate the possible shape of dalit theology in terms of our understanding of the Holy Trinity.

What Is Dalit Theology?

This question, according to Webster, may be answered in at least three different ways: The first answer may be that it is a theology *about* the dalits or theological reflection upon the Christian responsibility to the depressed classes. Second, the answer may be that it is a theology *for* the depressed classes, or the theology of the message addressed to the depressed classes and to which they seem to be responding. Third, the answer may be that it is a theology *from* the depressed classes, that is, the theology which they themselves would like to expound.

This article will expound the third answer, as I happen to be a dalit Christian myself. There is a parallel for my stand in dalit literature of Maharashtra. In 1970, Bagul published his long story entitled "Sood" (Revenge) with the foreword by the late M. N. Wankhade, the former principal of Milind Maha Vidhyalaya. Wankhade defined dalit literature as "Sahitya produced by dalits about dalits giving expression to their anger against those who have made them dalits." Wankhade's definition of dalit literature was followed by a stormy discussion in the traditional circles of literary criticism. Along with Wankhade, I would say that a Christian dalit theology will be produced by dalits. It will be based on their own dalit experiences, their own sufferings, their own aspirations, and their own hopes. It will narrate the story of their pathos and their protest against the socio-economic injustices they have been subjected to throughout history. It will anticipate that liberation is meaningful to them. It will represent a radical discontinuity with classical Indian Christian theology of the Brahminic tradition. This Brahminic tradition in the classical Indian Christian theology needs to be challenged by the emerging dalit theology. This also means that a Christian dalit theology will be a countertheology. I submit that all people's theologies are essentially countertheologies. In order that they should remain countertheologies, it is necessary that they are also exclusive in character.

This will be a methodological exclusivism. This exclusivism is necessary because the tendency of all dominant traditions — cultural or theological — is to accommodate, include, assimilate, and finally conquer others. Countertheologies or people's theologies therefore need to be on guard and need to shut off the influences of the dominant theological tradition.

In such a theological venture, the primacy of the term "dalit" will have to be conceded as against the primacy of the term "Christian" in the dominant theological tradition. This again will be a question of methodological primacy. What this means is that the non-dalit world will ask us, "What is Christian about dalit theology?" Our reply will have to be: "It is the dalitness which is 'Christian' about dalit theology." That is what I mean by the primacy of the "dalit." The "Christian" for this theology is exclusively the "dalit." What this exclusivism implies is the affirmation that the Triune God — the Father, the Son and Holy Spirit — is on the side of the dalits and not of the non-dalits who are the oppressors. It is the common dalit experience of Christian dalits, along with the other dalits, that will shape a Christian dalit theology.

Historical Dalit Consciousness

The historical dalit consciousness is the primary datum of a Christian dalit theology. The question of dalit consciousness is really the question of dalit identity, the question of our roots. If we leave aside the so-called Apostles' Creed and the so-called Nicene Creed and examine some of the biblical creeds and confessions, we will see the question of identity is an integral part of any faith-affirmation. Take, for instance, the Deuteronomic Creed found in Deuteronomy 26:5–9:

> "And you shall make response before the Lord Your God, 'A wandering Aramean was my father; and he went down into Egypt and sojourned there few in number; and there he became a nation, great, mighty, and populous. And the Egyptians treated us harshly and afflicted us, and laid upon us harsh bondage. Then we cried to the Lord the God of our fathers, and the Lord heard our voice, and saw our affliction, our toil and our oppression; and the Lord brought us out of Egypt with a mighty hand and an out-stretched arm, with great terror, with signs and wonders; and he brought us into this place and gave us this land, a land flowing with milk and honey.' "

I would like to expound this passage in full because it has tremendous implications for a dalit theology. For the Latin American liberation theologians, it is the Exodus experience which is important. It opens with the calling to memory the roots of the people who experienced the Exodus liberation. A creed, a confession, a faith-affirmation, therefore, must first exercise in laying bare the roots of the believing community: "A wandering Aramean was my father" recalls the nomadic consciousness. To confess that "once we were no people" is also an integral part of a confession before we come to claim "now we are God's people." It is only when we recognize our roots, our identity, that we become truly confessional. A truly confessional theology, therefore, has to do with the question of roots, identity, and consciousness.

Second, we notice that this wandering Aramean is also described as "few in number." The Aramean ancestor, therefore, stands for the entire community. The question of identity and roots is inseparably bound with the sense of belonging to a community. In our search for a dalit theology, it is well worth remembering that what we are looking for is community identity, community roots, and community consciousness. The vision of a dalit theology, therefore, ought to be a unitive vision — or rather, a "communitive" vision.

Third comes the recalling of their affliction, the harsh treatment meted out by the Egyptians and their bondage. Then comes their cry to the Lord; Christian dalit theology, therefore, is a story of the affirmations, the bondage, the harsh treatment, the toil and the tears of the dalits. A genuinely dalit theology will be characterized by pathos, by suffering.

Fourth, the Exodus liberation is symbolized by "a mighty hand," "an outstretched arm," and by "terror." "Signs" and "wonders" are low in the order. Liberation does not come only through "signs" and "wonders." A certain measure of "terror" is necessary to achieve it. In terms of dalit theology, this would mean that the dalits cannot afford to have a fatalistic attitude to life. They must protest and agitate to change their lot. The late Dr. B. R. Ambedkar's mantra for the dalits was "unite, educate, and agitate."

Finally, we should also notice that the "land flowing with milk and honey" comes last. It is an outcome of the liberation already achieved. Liberation is its own reward. The "land flowing with milk and honey" is not the chief goal of the Exodus. Rather it is the release from the captivity and slavery and the liberation from the Egyptian bondage that is the chief goal of the Exodus. The implication for a dalit theology is that the liberation struggle we are involved in is primarily a struggle for our human dignity and for the right to live as free people created in the image of God.

This historic Deuteronomic Creed has paradigmatic value for our dalit theological construct.

The historical dalit consciousness in India depicts even greater and deeper pathos than is found in the Deuteronomic Creed. My dalit ancestors did not enjoy the nomadic freedom of the wandering Aramean. As outcastes, they were also cast out of their villages. The dalit bashs (localities) were always and are always on the outskirts of the Indian village. When my dalit ancestor walked the dusty roads of his village, the *Sa Varnas* tied a branch of a tree around his waist so that he would not leave any unclean footprints and pollute the roads. The *Sa Varnas* also tied an earthen pot around my dalit ancestor's neck to serve as a spittle. If my dalit ancestor tried to learn Sanskrit or some other sophisticated language, the oppressors gagged him permanently by pouring molten lead down his throat. My dalit mother and sisters were forbidden to wear any blouses, and the *Sa Varnas* feasted their eyes on their bare bosoms. The *Sa Varnas* denied my dalit ancestor any access to public wells and reservoirs. They denied him the entry to their temples and places of worship. That, my friends, was my ancestor — one among many in Maharashtra. My dalit consciousness therefore has an unparalleled depth of pathos and misery, and it is this historical dalit consciousness, this dalit identity, that should inform my attempt at a Christian dalit theology.

Our paradigmatic creed tells us that "signs" and "wonders" are not enough for the liberation we are seeking. We need a "mighty hand" and an "outstretched arm" and a certain measure of "terror" — in short, we need an activist struggle for liberation, a movement informed by its action towards its theological reflection. Our pathos should give birth to our protest — a very loud protest. Our protest should be so loud that the walls of Brahminism should come tumbling down. A Christian dalit theology will be a theology full of pathos, but not a passive theology.

The Gentile-consciousness of the New Testament can confess that "once we were no people but now we are God's people." The dalit consciousness in India cannot say even that much. We were not only "no people" but we were also "no humans." For the *Sa Varnas,* humans were divided into four castes: the Brahmins, the Kshatriyas, the Vaishyas, and the Shudras. But we were the outcasts, the *Avarnas,* no-humans, below even the shudras in the social ladder. We were the *panchamas,* the *chandals,* and the *Mlenchhas.* This "no-humanness" also should become a part of our theological affirmation or confession.

The dalit consciousness should realize that the ultimate goal of its liberation movement cannot be the "land flowing with milk and honey." For a Christian dalit theology, it cannot be simply the gaining of the rights, the reservations, and the privileges. The goal is the realization of our full humanness or, conversely, our full divinity, the ideal of the *Imago Dei,* the image of God in us. To use another biblical metaphor, our goal is the "glorious liberty of the children of God."

Our Exodus Experience

The ideal of the *Imago Dei* in us leads us to the question of God. What kind of God are we talking about? What kind of divinity does dalit theology envision?

But before that question is answered, I must make one final comment about the Deuteronomic Creed under study. The creed speaks not only about the roots and the historical nomadic consciousness of the people of Israel but also about their changed status and their thanksgiving. The nomadic experience is brought to memory, but so is the Exodus experience. "Few in number" are now a "nation," great, mighty, and "populous." "No people" are now "God's people." But Christian dalits in India also affirm their own exodus experience. What I mean is that as we should be aware of our historical consciousness, our roots, and our identity, we should also be aware of our present Christian consciousness. We are not just dalits. We are Christian dalits. Something has happened to us. Our status has changed. Our exodus from Hinduism — which was imposed upon us — to Christianity, or rather to Jesus Christ, is a valuable experience — a liberating experience. The non-dalits of this country have teased us as "rich Christians" or "bulgar Christians." But we know that this is not true. Both the 1935 Constitution under the British and the Constitution of the Indian Republic deprived us of our economic rights, political rights, privileges, and reservations. We have been discriminated against in the past, and we continue to be discriminated against in the present. Notwithstanding all this, we have followed Jesus Christ. Our exodus to him enabled us to recognize our dalitness, the dalitness of Jesus of Nazareth, and also the dalitness of his Father and our Father — our God; in our exodus to Jesus Christ, we have had a liberating experience. Although we have not reached our ultimate goal, we are confident that the Jesus of Palestine or the more immediate Jesus of India is in the midst of the liberation struggle of the dalits of India. A Christian dalit theology, therefore, should also be doxological in character. Our struggle is not over as yet, but we ought to be thankful that it is undergirded by our own exodus experience and our own exodus hope.

The Question of God

Now I return to the question of God. I have already said that our exodus experience has enabled us to recognize the dalitness of Jesus and his Father. It is in this recognition that the mystery of our exodus lies. This recognition means that we have rejected non-dalit deities. A non-dalit deity cannot be the God of dalits. This is why our other dalit friends have rejected Rama (the deity whom million of Hindus worship and pray to). The story goes that Rama killed Shambuka — dalit — because Shambuka had undertaken *tapascharya,* a life of prayer and asceticism. The dominant religious tradition denied to the dalits the right to pray. Rama, therefore, simply killed Shambuka and performed *dharma* (a religious act). This is why dalits have rejected Rama. For dalits, Rama is a killer-God — killer and murderer of dalits.

But the God whom Jesus Christ revealed and about whom the prophets of the Old Testament spoke is a dalit God. He is a servant-God — a God who serves. Service to others has always been the privilege of dalit communities in India. The passages from *Manu Dharma Sastra* say that the shudra was created by the self-existent (Svayambhu) to do servile work and that servitude is innate in him. Service is the *sva-dharma* of the shudra. Let us remember that fact that in dalits we have peoples who are *avarnas* — those below the shudras. Their servitude is even more pathetic than that of the shudras. Against this background the amazing claim of a Christian dalit theology will be that the God of dalits, the self-existent, the Svayambhu, does not create others to do servile work but does servile work himself. Servitude is innate in the God of dalits. Servitude is the *sva-dharma* of our God; and since we, the dalits, are this God's people, service has been our lot and our privilege.

Unfortunately, this word "service," *ministry* or *diakonia,* has lost its cutting edge. A shop tells you, "service is our motto." Is it? Isn't profit the real motto? A dentist plucks your tooth out and sends you a bill saying, "for the professional services rendered." A member of the state cabinet or of the central cabinet calls himself or herself a "minister" — a servant — whereas what he or she really enjoys is power (*satta*) and not *seva* (service). The word has become an "in" thing. Originally, the word *diakonia* was associated with waiting at the dining table. The "servant," therefore, means a waiter. Our housemaid, or the sweeper who cleans commodes and latrines, is, truly speaking, our servant. Do we realize that? Let us be prepared for a further shock. Are we prepared to say that my housemaid, my sweeper, my *bhangi,* is my God? It is precisely in this sense that our God is a servant-God. He is a waiter, a *dhobi,* a *bhangi.* Traditionally, all such services have been the lot of dalits. This means we have participated in this servant-God's ministries. To speak of a Servant-God, therefore, is to recognize and identify him as a truly dalit deity. The Gospel writers identified Jesus with the Servant of God of Isaiah 53. In his service, he was utterly faithful to God. But what kind of language is used to describe his servant?

He has no form or comeliness that we should look at him,
and no beauty that we should desire him.
He was despised and rejected by men,
a man of sorrows, and acquainted with grief,
and as one from whom men hide their faces.
He was despised, and we esteemed him not.
Surely he has become our griefs
and carried our sorrows;
Yet we esteemed him stricken,
smitten and afflicted.

He was oppressed, and he was afflicted,
yet he opened not his mouth;
like a lamb that is led to the slaughter,
and like a sheep that before its shearers is dumb,

So he opened not his mouth.
By oppression and judgment he was taken away
and as for his generation, who considered
that he was cut off out of the land of the living,
stricken for the transgression of my people?

That is the language used to describe the servant-language, full of pathos. That is the language used for God — the God of dalits. But that is also the language which mirrors our own pathos as dalits. The language that mirrors the God of dalits are dalits themselves. Incredible, isn't it? Isaiah also thought so. Therefore, he asks a question right at the beginning of this passage, the Servant Song: "Who has believed what we have heard? And to whom has the arm of the Lord been revealed?" We Christian dalits in India can answer that question. We should, with full confidence, tell Isaiah, "We have believed what you have heard. And to us has the arm of the Lord been revealed. That is why, Isaiah, we are Christian dalits and not just dalits."

Dalit Christology

But what does it mean to say that we are Christian dalits and not just dalits? This statement has christological implications that must be faced boldly. It means, first of all, that we proclaim and affirm that Jesus Christ, whose followers we are, was himself a dalit — despite his being a Jew. It further means that both his humanity and divinity are to be understood in terms of his dalitness. His dalitness is the key to the mystery of his divine-human unity. Let us note some of the features of his dalitness. Let us forget for a moment the wonderful story of his birth colored by the angelic choir, the bright star, and the wise men. Let us have a close look at his genealogy as given in the Gospel according to Matthew (1:1–17). We seldom read this genealogy carefully. Among Jesus' ancestors are few names that should startle and shock us. The first name is that of Tamar, the daughter-in-law of Judah. She outwitted her father-in-law by sleeping with him and conceiving by him (Genesis 38:1–30). Second, there is Rahab — the harlot who helped the Israelite spies (Joshua

2:1–21). Third, there is King Solomon. We should not forget that Solomon was an illegitimate child of David. These small details of Jesus' ancestry should not be forgotten, as they are suggestive of his dalit condition. He is also referred to as a "carpenter's son." That sounds like looking down on his father's profession.

The title that Jesus preferred to use for himself was "the Son of Man." The title is used in three different ways, according to the New Testament scholars. First, it simply means "man" in an ordinary way. For instance, in one place when a scribe wanted to follow him, Jesus said, "Foxes have holes, and birds of the air have nests; but the Son of Man has nowhere to lay his head" (Matt. 8:20). The second group of the Son of Man sayings is indicative of Jesus' present suffering and imminent death. The third group of the Son of Man sayings is called the Eschatological Son of Man sayings. There is some debate about the order of the second and third groups. The second of the Son of Man sayings is significant for developing a dalit Christology. These sayings speak of the Son of Man as encountering rejection, mockery, contempt, suffering, and finally, death. Let us look at a few of these sayings:

And he began to teach them that the Son of Man must suffer many things, and be rejected by the elders and the chief priests and the scribes, and be killed, and after three days rise again. (Mark 8:31)

And he said to them, "Elijah does come first to restore all things; and now it is written of the Son of Man, that he should suffer many things and be treated with contempt." (Mark 9:12)

For the Son of Man also came not to be served but to serve and to give life as a ransom for many. (Mark 10:45)

These sayings indicate that Jesus as the Son of Man had to encounter rejection, mockery, contempt, suffering, and death — all these from the dominant religious tradition and the established religion. He underwent these dalit experiences as the prototype of all dalits. The last saying quoted above also connects the theme of service with the Son of Man.

Another noteworthy feature of Jesus' life is his total identification with the dalits of his day. Again and again Jesus is accused of stealing and drinking with publicans, tax collectors, and "sinners" of his day (Mark 2:15–16).

In his study entitled, "Jesus' Attitude to Caste — A Bible Study" (*Madras Diocesan News and Notes,* January 1982), M. Azariah has drawn our attention to Jesus' approach and attitude towards Samaritans, the dalits of his day, and has demonstrated that Jesus loved and cared for the dalits.

The Nazareth Manifesto in the Gospel according to Luke has often been commented on recently, especially during the Emergency of the seventies. Some of our church leaders even compared it with the twenty-point program of the Indira Congress. What is generally overlooked is its significance for a Christian dalit theology. When Jesus quotes the passage from Isaiah and declares, "Today this scripture has been fulfilled in your hearing," we read that "all spoke well of him and wondered at the gracious words which proceeded out of his mouth." But then Jesus goes on to tell his audience for whom his liberation is meant. His two illustrations indicate that the liberation he is talking about is meant for the dalits and not for non-dalits. In his first illustration he speaks about Zarephath the widow in Sidon, to whom Elijah was sent. And he also makes the point that there were many widows in Israel, but Elijah went to none of them. Similarly, it was only Namaan the Syrian, the leper whom Elisha cleansed. Of course, there were many lepers, in Israel, but they were not cleansed. The "dalits" were set over against "Israel." The gospel that Jesus brought was the gospel for "dalits" and not for non-dalits — not for Israel. The whole situation changes at Jesus' explosive words and we read, "When they heard this, all in the synagogue were filled with wrath. And they rose up and put him out of the city, and led him to the brow of the hill on which their city was built, that they might throw him down headlong" (Luke 4:16–29). The Nazareth Manifesto then is really a manifesto for dalits.

Another episode from Jesus' ministry, full of significance for a Christian dalit theology, is that of the cleansing of the temple. The account is as follows:

> And they came to Jerusalem. And he entered the temple and began to drive out those who sold and those who bought in the temple, and he overturned the tables of the money changers and the seats of those who sold pigeons; and he would not allow any one to carry anything through the temple. And he taught, and said to them, "Is it not written, My House shall be called a House of Prayer for all the nations?" But you have made it a den of robbers. And the chief priests heard it and sought a way to destroy him; for they feared him, because all the multitude was astonished at his teachings. And when the evening came they went out of the city. (Mark 11:15–19)

This incident is interpreted in various ways by New Testament scholars. The evangelists other than Mark tell us that Jesus was angry on this occasion. On the other hand they omit the words "for all the nations" in their account and leave the quotation from Isaiah incomplete. It has been suggested that the evangelists see in this passage a fulfillment of Malachi 3:1, Zechariah 14:21, and Hosea 9:15. All these passages refer to God's final intervention in history. Jesus' action then would seem to be that of the messianic king on his final visit to his father's house and people and embodying God's ultimate judgment upon the life and religion of Israel. The second suggestion is that Jesus' cleansing of the temple was in line with the prophetic antithesis between prayer and sacrifice and, like the prophets before him, upheld the first and condemned the second. The third suggestion is that Jesus' anger was directed against the greed and dishonesty of the dealers and the way they were fleecing the poor. But we must note that Mark omits any reference to Jesus' anger. The fourth and final suggestion comes from Lightfoot, who maintains that the incident must be understood in terms of its implications for the Gentiles. All the buying and selling and money exchanging took place in the part of the temple that was reserved for Gentile worship. It was the Gentile court. The Gentiles has no access to the inner precincts where the Jewish worship was conducted. The bazaar that was in the Gentile court thus effectively prevented them from conducting their worship in a peaceful and quiet manner. Jesus the messianic king thus restores to the Gentiles their religious rights. Lightfoot's interpretation makes sense to the Indian dalits, who had to struggle for the right to temple entry, and we know about temple entry legislation in the various states of India. Indian dalits know what it means to be denied the entry to temple and to be denied the right to pray and worship. Ambedkar and his followers had to agitate for the entry to the Kala Rama temple in Nasik. We know about many such temple entry agitations. In his act of restoration of the Gentile right to worship, we see a prefiguration of the vindication of the Indian dalit struggle for their prayer and worship rights.

There are many other examples of Jesus' sympathy for the dalits of his day. But his dalitness is best symbolized by the cross. On the cross, he was the broken, the crushed, the split, the torn, the driven-asunder man — the dalit in the fullest possible meaning of that term. "My God, my God, why hast thou forsaken me?" he cries aloud from the cross. The Son of God feels that he is God-forsaken. That feeling of being God-forsaken is at the heart of our dalit experiences and dalit consciousness in India. It is the dalitness of the divinity and humanity that the cross of Jesus symbolizes.

The Holy Spirit

My treatment of a dalit pneumatology will be necessarily brief and sketchy, as I did not have enough time to work it out. In our understanding of the beneficial activity of the Holy Spirit, we will have to make use of the metaphors and images of the Holy Spirit. Read, for example, the story of the valley of the dry bones in Ezekiel 37. "Can these bones live?" is the most important question. I am aware of the fact that bones in Ezekiel represent Israel. But Israel here is under dalit conditions. The bones are dead, dry, and lifeless. The Holy Spirit revives these dry bones, gives them life, unifies them, and makes an army out of then. For us dalits, then, the Spirit is the life-giver, unifier, and empowerer for the liberation struggle of the Indian dalits. In our dalit experiences, the Spirit is our comforter who "groans" along with us in our sufferings.

In the story of Cornelius, Peter says, "How God anointed Jesus of Nazareth with the Holy Spirit and with power; how he went about doing good and healing all that were oppressed..." (Acts 10:38). The Holy Spirit, the Spirit of Jesus, heals all that are oppressed. While Peter was preaching, the Holy Spirit descended on the Gentiles. The baptism was to come later. The Holy Spirit did not wait for the baptism of the Gentiles — the dalits — to descend upon them. The Holy Spirit is the Spirit on the side of the dalits.

This is a very brief statement of the triune nature of a Christian dalit theology.

In John 9:3 we read, "It was not that this man sinned, or his parents, but that the works of God might be made manifest in him." This is also true of ourselves as dalits. We have suffered in the past, and we continue to suffer in the present. This is not because of our own sins or the sins of our ancestors. We need not and should not subscribe to any doctrine of *karma samsara*. Our suffering and dalitness have their place in the economy of salvation foreordained by God. It is in and through us that God will manifest and display his glorious salvation. The sixth group of meanings associated with the term "dalit" is "manifested" or "displayed." It is through us that God will manifest and display his salvation. It is precisely in and through the weaker, the down-trodden, the crushed, the oppressed and the marginalized that God's saving glory is manifested or displayed. This is because brokenness belongs to the very being of God. God's divinity and humanity are both characterized by his dalitness. God is one with the broken. God suffers when his people suffer. He weeps when his people weep. He laughs when his people laugh. He dies in his people's death, and he rises again in his people's resurrection.

This is one possible version of a people's theology — shall I perhaps say "No people's theology"? But there again, it is always the "no-people," the "dalits," who are the real people — God's very own people.

Chapter 3

A Theological Interpretation
of the Tribal Reality in India

NIRMAL MINZ

Next to Africa, India has the largest tribal population. Like the dalits and women, the tribals in India have been for a long time largely unrepresented and unrecognized by the mainstream theologies of India, including the indigenous liberation variety. Their corporate myths, rituals, and religious practices have been despised, sidelined, and unacknowledged by the mainline Indian theology. The following piece is an attempt to work out a tribal theology, beginning with their present existential reality and at the same time reinventing their future, linking it with the biblical paradigm of the covenant of God with the people.

Nirmal Minz is Bishop of the Gossner Evangelical Lutheran Church, Ranchi. He has been long active in the struggle for the full recognition of the tribals. He has also written extensively espousing their cause.

Source: *Religion and Society* 34 (4), 1987.

Need for a Theological Interpretation

Anthropological Studies and Discussions

There are more than seventy million tribal people in India. Tribal communities are found in small and big groups in almost all the states. They are divided into four major sectors as they are geographically located: (1) the north-eastern tribes of Mongoloid origin; (2) the north central tribes of West Bengal, Bihar, Orissa, and Eastern Madhya Pradesh; (3) the tribals of Western India: Gujarat, Rajputana, Western M.P., and Maharashtra; and (4) the tribals of Karnataka, Tamilnadu, Kerala, and Andhra Pradesh. In the central tribal belt, a major concentration of the Kharia,

Munda, Ho, Santhal, Oraon (Kurukh), and other minor tribes is found in Chotanag-pur and its adjacent areas. The Agneya (Austric) and Dravidian language families are found among them. Our discussion on tribal reality in India will be illustrated from this area.

Missiological Interpretation on Tribals

These studies are done mainly with a political, missiological, and social science bias. Our purpose is to attempt a Christian theological interpretation of tribal re-ality in Chotanagpur and its adjacent areas in the central tribal belt of India. The German, Belgian, English, Norwegian, and Danish missionary societies worked in this region. The missionary attitude to and understanding of tribals is seen in their preaching and writings. They were conditioned by the nineteenth century missionary concern in Europe for the "heathens" of Africa and Asia. The British government described them as the aborigine people of India who had no culture and there-fore were backward people. The missionaries found them to be one of the most exploited, suppressed, and oppressed people in India. They had no social stand-ing in the Indian social structure of caste hierarchy. To begin with, their religion was disregarded, as they have no written scriptures and organized religious bodies like others. In this sense the tribal people of Chotanagpur became a great object of mission. In saying this one must not minimize the fact that the white Aryan mission-aries had an extremely difficult task in becoming friends and brothers of the Oraons, Mundas, Kharias, Hos, and Santhal, sometimes at the displeasure of their powerful Aryan brethren. Missionaries like Dr. A. Nottrott, Fr. J. F. Hoffman, and Rev. P. O. Bodding are noted for what they did in regard to tribal lands in Chotanagpur and Santhal parganas in Bihar.

Indigenous Theological Discussions

Theological discussions are going on in this region. The Roman Catholic Theological Centre at Ranchi is attempting an indigenous theology, adopting the principle of inculturation. We do not want to enter into debate with this school of thought here. We have noted their efforts and at some future time discussion with them will be undertaken. Our frame of reference and our efforts to theologi-cally interpret tribal reality in this region has a different methodology and subject matter.

Tribal Reality

A tribe is a homogeneous community occupying a contiguous geographical area, with a language of its own. Therefore a fairly well defined homeland is an in-tegral part of definition of a tribe. Some forces are trying to distort the idea of identity and tribal reality in the central tribal belt. These forces are calling tribals *"Banbasis"* (forest dwellers) and their homeland is described as *ban kshetra* (forest areas). Such distortions of tribal reality have far-reaching consequences of a po-litical and social nature. Tribal reality includes four major ingredients: the people, their homeland, power, and God (gods). The interactions, interrelations, confrontations, conflicts among these realities, in the context of the central tribal belt — and a possible resolution of the problem — will be the substance of our discussion within a biblical framework. We are making this approach a conscious option for our future undertakings. This may be questioned, but this seems to be a fruitful way of interpreting tribal reality around us.

Biblical Paradigm for Contextual Interpretation of Tribal Reality

We have mentioned that tribal reality has its four basic ingredients — the people, the land, power, and God. Why not people only?

We all know that a people without land is just like a bird without a nest or like "boat people" floating on an immense ocean. Conversely, a land without people is like a desert or a colonized land. And a people without participation in a political decision-making body is like a cow or a prostitute. It is because we bear the image of God that we can affirm and reaffirm our human dignity, from which we are commissioned to be God's stewards to rule over the land. The power to rule in accord with the *Imago Dei* brings the problems of people and land into dipolar confrontation in the history of human development.

The existence and identity of tribal people cannot be imagined without land and the spirit around. Indigenous people have declared in their 1974 Consultation in Auckland, New Zealand, that "land is life" for them. No land, no people.

The biblical paradigm of covenant of God with people provides a principle of contextual reinterpretation of tribal reality in the central tribal belt of India. For our purpose we will group them into separate categories.

The Noachic Covenant (Genesis 9:8–19)

Verses 9–10 make the covenant clear: "I now establish my covenant with you and your descendants after you, and with every living creature that was with you — the birds, the livestock, and all the wild animals, all those that came out of the Ark with you — every living creature on earth." This is a universal covenant with people and nature as a whole, including the earth. Such a universal covenant is well within the tribal vision of the human being-nature-spirit continuum. The tribal understands that land and forest or nature as such are all God-given. No human being has earned them or made them. The close relationship of tribals with all living creatures in these lands and forests is inalienable. Therefore no individual ownership was possible in tribal land tenure. The entire community was the custodian of land, forest, and all living creatures within the geographical territory and community inhabited. If any other human community came in contact with the original one, it shared the land, forest, and the entire natural wealth. No question of grabbing this piece or that, by one or the other person or the group of persons, if they were real human beings as the tribals themselves were. Tribal humanity rested in harmonious or balanced relationship of human being-nature-spirit. It is, therefore, the primacy of spirit (God) over human beings and nature which sets things in proper harmony and balance. Any disruption of this balance meant the dehumanization of human beings, and the unhealthy pollution of the environment.

The Abrahamic Covenant (Genesis 12:1–4)

"Leave your country, your people, and your father's household and go to the land I will show you.... I will make you into a great nation and I will bless you.... I will bless those who bless you." The story of Abraham can be taken as an archetype for all peoples on earth. It is a story of a process by which a tribe, a people, learns to relate itself with others. The covenant has three ingredients — a land, a great nation, and a blessing and mutual blessing. It has the implication of formation of a nation. The patriarchal archetype of Abraham may not be easily detectable in tribal history. But the migration from Indus Valley to the present homeland is a real one. Each tribe can trace back to the historical archetypal figure who could link them with the past before they occupied the present land. As over against the Abrahamic story, mutual blessings among the tribals have been realized to a much greater degree than mutual killings. The spirit of adaptation and adjustment for mutual living held the tribals in their present homeland for thousands of years before they were disturbed by the Aryan invaders even in the present homeland of Chotanagpur and neighboring areas.

In the Abrahamic covenant, primacy of people over land becomes clear but for the tribals of the central tribal belt such a distinction between people and land did not emerge. The basic universal covenant of God with Noah continued. People and land remain an integral part of the life of tribals till the initiation of Nagbansi kings over all the tribals by the creation of a myth by Brahmanic magic on the Chotanagpur scene, as late as 64 A.D.

The Mosaic Covenant (Exodus 19:1–24)

Deliverance from Egypt and the journey towards the Promised Land is the key to the making of the people of Israel. God actively participates in delivering his people from Pharaoh in Egypt. Therefore, the making of a people and the revelation of God are two sides of the same coin. "I will take you as my own people, and I will be your God. Then you will know that I am the Lord your God who brought you out from under the yoke of the Egyptians" (Ex. 6:7). Yahweh makes a definite covenant with Moses. "You yourselves have seen what I did to Egypt and how I carried you on eagle's wings and brought you to myself. Now if you obey me fully and keep my covenant, then out of all nations you will be my treasured possession. Although the whole earth is mine, you will be for me a kingdom of priests, a holy nation" (Ex. 19:4–6).

The Mosaic covenant has two basic bearings regarding the tribal people of Chotanagpur. Pharaoh for them is not in Egypt, a foreign land, but in the homeland of the tribals themselves. It is a very peculiar situation that the tribal people are under the yoke of different kinds of pharaohs in their own homeland.

The Nagbansi Kings

With the beginning of Nagbansi kings here, direct social, economic, and political contacts were made with the plains people. Nagbansi kingship became the source and channel of Sanskrit culture coming into this region, making a religious and social impact. They married the daughters of the kings of Orissa and of the northern plains. With the marriage relationship, Brahmins came over in good number, at different stages. The Nagbansi king had to maintain law and order, as he was the supreme ruler. He brought the Rajputs and gave them the zamindaris of different sections of tribal land and population. The network of zamindari, and later jagirdari, strengthened the position of the king against the tribal chiefs. Along came the traders and Mahajans in this area under the protection of the raja and the zamindars. The zamindars acted as agents of the police. Also a strong Pharic structure was built up, and social, economic, and political exploitation of the tribals began in that early period, about two thousand years ago.

Tribal life has always been accommodative and adaptive to change. Strangers and newcomers have always been welcomed by the tribals. They would have liked coexistence with others in their own homeland if the others had no home. Instead of coexistence and fellow feeling, the outsiders began to dominate and exploit and oppress the peace-loving, democratic, and egalitarian tribals. Stratification of society in Chotanagpur began with the initiation of Nagbansi kings — a Sanskrit tradition deeply incorporated in the life of the people of Chotanagpur.

The Muslim Invasion

The coming of Muslims into Chotanagpur introduced property holding systems completely different from the existing one. Raja Durjansal brought pomp and glory to his court and an alien culture which displaced the folk culture and participation by all in dance and music. The singing and dancing of individuals with the whole crowd watching was encouraged by the Nagbansi rajas, the zamindars, and jagirdars all over the land of the tribal people. Along with the political, economic, and social bondage, cultural erosion began to take place in tribal life.

British Rule

The British invaded the land of the Adivasis. They did three major things: (1) They introduced individual ownership of land. (2) They made alliances with the rajas and zamindars to control and keep the Advasis under their thumb. They entrusted the police force to their control. (3) They introduced the English system of education. They began to destroy the collective ownership of land, the village democracy, and discipline of the people out of an ethical imperative. And finally English education degraded tribal educational values and systems, dealing a death blow to the cultural values of the tribal people.

What happened to the people, land, power, and God (gods) in this process? First of all, the tribals were made subservient to the dominant Aryan (Sanskrit) culture. Their cultural and human values were pushed to the background, and corrupt human relationships gained currency in their ordinary life. Honesty, truthfulness, equality, dignity of labor, collective ownership of land, and democratic principles were completely done away with. A stratified, caste-ridden Indian social system began to build itself up, leading to social alienation, degradation of the tribals in the eyes of the latecomers, and a low self-image. This affected the tribals deeply.

The Majhias Land

The best lands in each village were declared or recorded as Majhias belonging to the ruling administrative machinery, the zamindars, or their representatives at various places. The principle of individual ownership of land, right to do whatever one liked to do with one's landed property, initiated the idea that land was a commodity to be bought or sold. God-given land now became personal property. The same process affected forests also as they were taken under government control. Social control of forest and land was snatched away and, therefore, an imbalance between human being-nature-spirit took place. This started the dehumanization process of the tribal people in Chotanagpur.

The Mosaic covenant is a process of making a people out of a non-people, whereas the process in Chotanagpur is forcing the people (tribals) to become non-people. Slowly and surely tribals — the subjects in their own land — were made the objects with no participation in the decision-making process to shape their own destiny in their own homeland. The Israelites had only forty years of desert experience and a few generations of bondage under pharaohs in a foreign land. But the tribals have been under the yoke of different kinds of pharaohs for at least two thousand years.

Attempt at Second Exodus

Exodus from the homeland of the Adivasis has taken place in the past. This exodus again is a peculiar one. It is leaving the "promised land" or one's own homeland and going in search of a second-rate shelter. The raja and zamindar oppressions and suppressions sometimes forced some people to go out of Chotanagpur. Leaving their home, they went as laborers to the tea gardens of Assam and North Bengal or under the British government to work in the Sundarbans and in Andaman and Nicobar Island, on plantations of cane, sugarcane and indigo. They went to Mauritius and even to the West Indies. Going away from the homeland proved to be of economic advantage for a few, but as a people they completely lost their identity. They are not recognized as tribals in Assam. In all other places they are almost bonded laborers of a capitalistic system.

One of the major theological questions in this context is to discern the God who is directing the destiny of the tribal people under such a life of bondage to the pharaohs of different kinds. How long will the pharaohs turn a deaf ear to the voice of this God in and through the *Vedna* (suffering) of the people? When will the pharaohs let these people go and rediscover their homeland and become again the people worthy of their name in Mother India?

The Davidic Covenant (2 Samuel 7:1–17)

The Davidic covenant was made after 450 years of occupation of the Promised Land beyond Jordan, the land full of milk and honey. After the Israelites settled down in the Promised Land of Canaan, they asked God for a king. "They said to Samuel: You are old and your sons don't walk in your ways, now appoint a king to lead us such as all the other nations have.... Listen to all that people are saying to you; it is not you they have rejected, but they have rejected me as their king. As they have done from the day I brought them up out of Egypt. . . . Now listen to them but warn them solemnly and let them know what the king who will reign over them will do" (1 Sam. 8:5–9).

Demand for a king and granting one under compulsion is a stage in the history of Israel that can be compared to the introduction of the king over the tribals by the Brahmanic craft of myth-creation. Yahweh politics is now being taken over by kingly politics in which defense and offense, invasion and subjugation, become the order of the day.

Messianic kingly politics meant a trial of strength among them. In his own home Absalom revolted against his father and wanted to be given power even before the time was ripe. After King Solomon, the country was divided into North and South. An internal conflict arose and fightings and killings became the order of the political scene in the Promised Land. One of the most important theological issues emerges here for our contextual reinterpretation of tribal reality in Chotanagpur. The Israelites occupied the land with military and physical power, killing the Adivasi tribes as mentioned above. And they did it in obedience to the command of Yahweh (Deut. 20:16–18). The people of Lord — the colonialists — are supported by a God who is unmindful of the poor Canaanites, Hittites, Amorites, Jebusites, and others. This pattern of the occupation of land of the indigenous people by the so-called people of God has continued till the present time. North America was occupied and made into what it is today at the expense of the Native Americans. New Zealand is occupied by the English overrunning the Maori Adivasis there and so also in Australia and all Latin American countries. This raises a serious question whether might is right or right is right in the world, particularly today in the context of Chotanagpur tribals.

The Chotanagpur tribals have put up fights against the oppressors and suppressors and exploiters in the past. The Sata Ho Santhal rebellion of 1851, Sardar larai, Birsa movements, and Tana Bhagat movement come under the political messianism in which confrontation of Satta Sakti (government power), Artha Sakti (economic power) and Jati Sakti (caste power) played their roles against the tribals. All the rebellions and revolts of the tribals against the colonial power supported by local rajas and zamindars proved fatal for the tribals. The military and state power clamped down on peoples' uprisings to reassert their identity and regain their homeland in which they wanted to be the subjects. Is the history of indigenous people going to be repeated here in Chotanagpur and the Adivasis wiped away, making room for the latecomers, be they the Nagbansis, the Muslims, the British, or finally, the peoples of the plains of Bharatmata? What kind of God is this who takes the side of the strong and leaves the weak and helpless alone? The Adivasis will fight against such a God (or gods) who encourage and promote injustice, corruption, and oppression of people by people. The tribals are looking to a God (or gods) who will take the side of the poor and neglected, exploited and oppressed Adivasis and show them a vision of their homeland, a land flowing with milk and honey in Chotanagpur itself. Yahweh is not such a God for the tribals of Chotanagpur.

God's New Covenant in Jesus: The Paradigm of Jesus — Servant Politics (Mark 10:45, John 10:10)

Except for the Noachic covenant, the Abrahamic, Mosaic, and Davidic covenant paradigms have not enlightened or opened possibilities of solution to the tribal problem — the liberation and the regaining of the homeland of Chotanagpur. The universal covenant with Noah should be reinterpreted for us in the light of the second chapter of Isaiah and the life, teaching, and works of Jesus Christ. Deutero-Isaiah saw the problems of people like the tribals here and raises a fundamental issue of human relationships in our world. It asserts that the creator God must be the redeemer of not only Israel but of all people in this world. The creator God is also the redeemer of Israel in history, who shows love for all human beings by calling Jacob (Israel) to witness as servant to all nations. Israel cannot be a messiah any more because the messiah politics of Assyria, Babylonia, and Persia were a mere repetition of ugly power politics that was destined to pass away. However, the servant politics that transcended the old ethnocentrism of Israel will heal the ugliness of power by vicarious suffering as it witnesses to God's creative power and redemptive love for all people (Isa. 55:3–5). God's covenant in Jesus Christ is not for any one selected nation or peoples, but it is a covenant for the good of the whole world.

The Potential for New World Order through Servant Politics

Jesus loved the poor, the unwanted, the crowd over against the organized religious and political powers of his day. His life, teaching, and work directly challenged the religious hierarchy and social and political colonial powers. The crowd wanted him also to enter into the political messianism and come into direct confrontation with the powers of that day. But Jesus refused to yield to the will of the people in the ethnocentric sense. Jesus challenged the meaning of power as it was currently understood and used. In his mind the power to dominate should be transformed radically into the power to serve with the self-offering of his own life as a paradigm (Mark 10:45).

The holy triumphalism of Israel over the natives in Canaan ought to be eradicated and replaced by a new universal brotherhood and sisterhood in Jesus Christ (Col. 3:10–11). The prophetic vision of Creator-Redeemer-God who loves all nations and peoples and takes the form of a suffering servant to recreate all things must be recapitulated and reclaimed as an operative principle in human relationships, not only between person and person but between peoples and nations on this planet. The kingdom of tribal people, "Lok," has to be established as a stage towards the Kingdom of God in this world. The struggle for human dignity inherent in the *Imago Dei* must continue in the homeland of the tribal people in the central tribal belt of Chotanagpur. Human liberation rather than purely a political emancipation must catch our imagination at the depth of our being. This would mean achieving universal human freedom by overthrowing the existing basis of oppression and exploitation all over the world, particularly in Chotanagpur. Nationalistic interest distorts this vision of human liberty in any situation, but this has been much more so in Chotanagpur than in any other place in our world.

Demographic Picture of Chotanagpur Now

We have not concretized the problems and issues in our discussions above. It is time now to come to the grass-roots level and try to reinterpret the tribal context in the light of the Jesus-servant paradigm. Here is a God in Jesus Christ for all people including the tribals in this region, and therefore something new can emerge for the good of the tribal people, their homeland, and God.

Before independence in 1947, the tribal population in Chotanagpur was over 52 percent of the total inhabitants here. Today, after forty years, the percentage of tribal population in their own homeland has gone down. The reasons for this demographic change are obvious. The systematic, indirect colonization of tribal land by nontribals has gone on for the last two thousand years. The influx of outside population increased under the British government's protective policy with regard to the kings and zamindars, traders and officials from the plains of our motherland. Now this influx has billowed and the floodgates have been thrown open under the guise of national interest. Heavy industries, central and state government offices, the University of Ranchi and its colleges, the formation of new districts, divisions, and so on, have opened a regular channel of movement into the tribal homeland in massive numbers. There is no one to question this movement of people invading Chotanagpur for milk and honey, alas, at the expense of the tribals of this region.

Social Analysis of Chotanagpur Population

Gone is the day when one could think of a homeland for tribals only. Two thousand years of history, and the history of forty years after independence, forces any serious scholar or theologian to reconsider the previous stand. One must face the social fact: There are two major groups of people in the land of the Adivasis. First, the Adivasi and the backward communities with them have lived here together in harmony from time immemorial. The Kharias, Mundas, Santals, Hos, Oraons, Kurmis, Kunihars, Lohars, Ghancis, Turis, Chick Baraik, and Ahirs, the Mehtars and others make the major block of *Lok* (people) who claim to be the "sons of this soil." Taking the tribals and the backward communities and the dalits in this region, they can form an overwhelming majority of people with the same social, economic, political, and religious handicap in relation to the latecomers. Second, the Sadans, the former rajas, zamindars, Brahmins, business community — the Mahajans and the Marwaris have lived here for more than a hundred years. They are not the "sons of the soil" in the same sense as the tribals claim to be, but they have related themselves with the homeland of the Adivasis for more than five generations. They are not tribals, but they are Chotanagpuris. The point at issue here is not that they belong to Chotanagpur. But where is the cut-off point for us to determine the segment of population here called Chotanagpuris? There are two suggestions for consideration. First a family, whoever they may be, who has lived for a hundred years or more in Chotanagpur is a Chotanagpuri. Second, a person, family, or a community that has come before 1947 and made their home, staying permanently, should be considered Chotanagpuris for our purposes. Let us remind ourselves that we do not ignore the shifting and changing population who work in government offices and industries. We take them as a floating population that has no stake in the homeland of the tribals.

Among the first group of people — the "sons of the soil" — the problem of intertribal, and tribal-non-tribal relationship needs to be analyzed, understood, and interpreted. As in the land of Canaan, the two kingdoms struggled for their supremacy over each other, so rivalry for being number one on the ladder has crept in. The contact with Aryan sociocultural values has injected this poison into the minds of some people. Tribal identity in the composite sense of the term, with its spirit of accommodation, has to be revived and lived in this land. The strangers have come; we have given them shelter under our roof or under the tree of our homeland. All the backward community people are part and parcel of our identity as a people. Then we also are conscious of the fact that the *sadans* of various kinds and types, including the descendents of rajas, zamindars, and jagirdars, have become our inalienable neighbors. They are our neighbors though they ill-treated us, exploited and oppressed us in the past — and still continue to do so in certain pockets of Chotanagpur. The Muslim population in this region is by and large a group of converts from the Adivasis and there are some blood relations between the tribals and the Jolha (backward Muslims) in this region.

Power Politics in This Context

The homeland of the Adivasis has been very conveniently placed between two superpowers — the central government and the four state governments, particularly in the State of Bihar. The Adivasis alone, and even together with the other Chotanagpuris as discussed above, are being crushed to pieces. And this is being done in a most polished manner. The people here, both the Adivasis and Chotanagpuris, are deprived of participation in the decision-making process in the real sense of the term. Homeland is a God-given gift for the tribals and a human right. This is slowly but surely being snatched away from the people. Adivasis and Chotanagpuris are made objects of welfare for the central and state governments, and this has been accepted by the tribals. In this process further erosion of tribal and Chotanagpuri identity is going on. Any people's movement in Chotanagpur becomes either separatist/antinational or missionary and foreign instigated. The superpowers play this game in order to keep the Adivasis and Chotanagpuris under perpetual bondage. They still operate under the principle of the Davidic covenant in which power politics of nationalists and ethnocentrism continues. The political messianism has already been tried several times, beginning from the early Santhal Rebellion till the present Jharkhand movement of different kinds, none of which have been able to deliver the goods to us. The vision of Isaiah and the servant politics of God's covenant in Jesus Christ have not been tried. Let us at least entertain this idea and see how it shapes future programs and action to regain the identity of the tribals by recovering their homeland in Chotanagpur and neighboring areas.

Introduction of Servant Politics through God's Covenant in Jesus

God's covenant in Jesus is a universal covenant for the people in this world. Such a paradigm seems to be acceptable and applicable to tribal reality in India and in Chotanagpur. It is one of the most important historical facts in this region that the tribals had no friends in the real sense of the term. The oppression, exploitation, and suppression they experienced for about two thousand years have given them a bitter experience of the inhuman relationship of human beings in Mother India. So tribals were friendless people for many centuries. But the Christian missionaries — of German, English and Belgian origin — proved to be their sympathizers and real friends. These Christian missionaries came as the servants of God with full commitment to serve the people with great personal sacrifices. One cannot imagine the difficulties and hardships they faced in becoming the friends of tribals. It was at the displeasure of the rajas and zamindars that they served the downtrodden. The British government supported this cause indirectly, as it was against the interests of their allies in keeping law and order in this region. The word of Fr. J. Hoffman and Dr. A. Nottrott for the protection of Adivasi land and Rev. P. O. Bodding's help in framing the Chotanagpur and Santhal Pargana Tenancy Acts speak for themselves. Tribal languages and grammar were given written form by the missionaries. It gave the tribals self-respect, identity, and a new consciousness about themselves.

With devoted service rendered to the tribals, a substantial Christian community has come into being in Chotanagpur and its neighboring areas. In fact, it is one of the heavily Christian areas in North India. The Lutheran, the CNI (former SPG) and the Roman Catholic denominational churches are well established with their congregations, schools, hospitals, and colleges. It could be expected that this new element connected with the servant politics of Jesus should have played its major role in the liberation of the people and the gaining of a homeland of their own. We have already mentioned political messianism, where power politics confront each other, was tried in the past but has failed so far. The two superpowers mentioned above have successfully maneuvered the course of history to the best of their vested interests and have worked against the aspirations of the people.

The demographic picture shows that a homeland for the tribals is a basic issue. The tribal adaptability and accommodative capacity must extend its horizon to include the latecomer Chotanagpuris, according to the agreed cut-off point. Here the servant politics of Jesus is essential to bring a cohesion among the Chotanagpuris — both tribals and non-tribals. And then both together should offer themselves and the land for the service of Mother India as a people with their homeland Chotanagpur and adjacent areas. Not confrontation but reconciliation with justice and service to each other here, and service to the nation as a whole, should be the prime motive of being a people in their own homeland of Chotanagpur.

The role of the Christian church as the body of Jesus Christ in this context must be explored anew. Here is a chance to reconcile all factors and forces and to help achieve the goal of Chotanagpuris to be the subject of destiny and regain their homeland in the future.

Chapter 4

"Han-pu-ri"

Doing Theology from Korean Women's Perspective

CHUNG HYUN KYUNG

Asian women in the early stages of their theological enquiry were either largely enthused by the efforts of their Euro-American counterparts or were under the influence of their Asian male colleagues for inspiration and impetus. Increasingly they have come to realize that such a status cannot bring emancipation for them and that they need to be more aware of their distinctive voices as both Asian and women. To achieve this, they are seriously turning to Asia's cultural symbols and their own lived experience of helplessness and humiliation. The essay below is an example of such an attempt to construct a truly Asian women's theology using Korean shamanistic tradition.

Chung Hyun Kyung is Professor of Theology at Ewha Women's University, Seoul, and came to prominence with her electrifying presentation at the Canberra meeting of the World Council of Churches. Along with her teaching, she is active in women's groups. She is the author of *Struggle To Be the Sun Again: Introducing Asian Women's Theology* (Maryknoll, N.Y.: Orbis Books, 1990).

Source: *We Dare To Dream: Doing Theology as Asian Women,* Virginia Fabella and Sun Ai Lee Park, eds., Asian Women's Resource Centre for Culture and Theology, Hong Kong, 1989 and Maryknoll, N.Y.: Orbis Books, 1990.

I

Last April in New York I had the chance to see an exhibition of recent woodcut prints from the Korean people's movement. When I entered the exhibition room I was overwhelmed by the power of the work. I cried. I cried because I could see the opening of a new horizon in these prints, something I had been longing for in my theological work for a long time: discovering, naming, claiming, and creating our own reality. I could not see any apologetic attitude in these prints. They simply said what they felt, with confidence. They trusted their experience.

A Korean art critic who had brought the prints talked about the cultural movement of young artists in Korea. Most were well trained, he said, in the Western fine-arts style. However, they had overcome the cultural captivity of Western art and had created their own styles, which could express the content of people's everyday lives and their struggle for liberation. The artists' personal styles mirrored the style of our national heritage. This same concern was demonstrated several years ago in Korea in a landmark exhibition of paintings entitled "Vomiting" where, for example, a painting done in the Western high-art style was covered with Korean cartoons. From the time of this exhibition, the most vital of Korean artists have sought to evolve an art that could give a life-giving power to the Korean people. One artist whose works were included in this exhibition emphasized the key to this change in people's art: it was the artists' belief in their own aesthetic feelings as opposed to a need for approval from their teachers or Western standards.

I call these artists and myself second-generation liberationists. Our teachers, who were the first-generation liberationists, mainly reacted against the colonial heritage. They did not realize that they were involved in a subconscious attempt to prove themselves to their former colonizers. They said they knew their enemies and could think as well as or better than their colonizers. Our teachers clearly knew what they did not like, but they did not know where they should go in their own works. We members of the second generation owe a lot to our teachers because they gave us the colonizers' tools and the space to create. We second-generation liberationists are not unaware of the neocolonial power surrounding us, but we also know our own power. We know what we like and we construct our own life-giving works. We believe in our experiences and are not intimidated by outside authorities any more.

Doing theology from a third-world woman's perspective must be understood in this context. My teachers' generation felt compelled to prove their theological abilities to (in descending order) white male theologians, white feminist theologians, and finally Korean male theologians, in order to justify the validity of Korean women's theology. But in my generation we start our theology from owning our own feelings and experiences. We know that the most dangerous thing for an oppressed people is to become benumbed through internalizing alien criteria and ignoring our own gut feelings. If we do not permit ourselves to fully experience who we are, we will not have the power to fight back and create our own space. We have to touch something truly real among and around us in order to meet God. Just as young Korean artists from the people's movement find their aesthetics in ordinary people's everyday lives, so we emerging women theologians find God's revelations in our ordinary everyday experiences. As the artists use Korean styles to express their artistic aspirations, so too we theologians try to use our national and cultural traditions to express the God-experiences of our people.

I do not try to articulate Korean women's God-experience from biblical or orthodox theological perspectives in a traditional sense. Instead I like to name Korean women's experience within our cultural context of suffering and life-giving using our traditional symbols and metaphors in an organic way. Then I try to make connections between Korean women's experiences and the Christian tradition. In this article I will approach Korean women's God-experiences through our overwhelming sense of the presence of haunting ghosts in our land.

II

I was raised in a ghost land. My childhood memories are filled with various kinds of haunting ghosts. Ghosts are everywhere. There are kitchen ghosts, toilet ghosts, house ghosts, river ghosts, and mountain ghosts. As a young girl, it was difficult for me to live with so many ghosts. I knew ghosts would hurt me if I did not behave. I heard awful stories about ghosts from many people. They said most ghosts carried swords in order to kill people whom they hated. These ghosts were the spirits who could not rest because what had happened to them in their earthly lives was too cruel and unjust to forget or forgive. They were therefore wandering around seeking the chance to inflict revenge or to tell the truth.

Even though I could not see them, I always felt the ghosts' presence. I was afraid of them. I was especially afraid of baby and children ghosts. I should be careful not to make them jealous of me. Too many cookies, too many toys, or too many beautiful clothes might make baby and children ghosts angry at me. I had to share with other children. Otherwise baby or children ghosts would not tolerate me because they had never had the privilege to enjoy those things in their short earthly lives.

I never went outside by myself after sunset. Whenever I wanted to go to the bathroom, which was located outside the house in Korea, I went there with an adult. I kept the bathroom door open while I was doing my business because I was afraid of bathroom ghosts. People said bathroom ghosts had bleeding hands which pulled people into the dung hole. I also never slept by myself. I always slept with adults until I was thirteen.

There were some fun moments in the ghost land. One of them was watching the ancestor worship. The ancestor worship was a really big family event. Many relatives gathered together, prepared meals, and had big feasts. We opened all of the windows and doors to let our ancestors into the house. Ancestors were friendly ghosts. Most of them had families to take care of their tombs and to remember them. They were not wandering ghosts. They rested in paradise and visited us annually on the ancestor worship day.

Ancestor worship day was like homecoming day for all of us. At midnight we lit candles and burned incense and worshiped them. All the men in the household bowed down to the ancestors' spirits. My mother, aunts, and I watched the worship from outside the room when my father, uncles, and brother bowed down. I was very envious of my brother. As a little girl I could not understand why I was not allowed to bow down to my grandfather's and grandmother's spirits. I loved them too! One ancestor worship day — I think I was five or six years old — I cried and screamed, asking my father to let me join the ancestor worship. I kept crying, lying on the ancestor worship room floor. Finally my father let me join him.

In Korea women prepared the feasts but were not allowed to participate in the worship itself. I felt sorry for my mother. However, she was in charge of feeding all of the visitors, including the wandering ghosts. She always left generous amounts of food in front of the main gate of our house for wandering ghosts. She said to me she should not forget to leave food for the wandering ghosts, as they did not have relatives to take care of them. Mother told me they were constantly hungry. My favorite part of the ancestor worship was the feast. We shared food after finishing the ancestor worship and shared our life stories with one another until dawn. Another fun activity in the ghost land was watching in my neighborhood the shamanistic rituals we call *"kut."* Since my mother was a Christian, she did not want me to see *kut.* Therefore I had to go there without my mother's knowledge. There was always music, dancing, and excitement in *kut.* I felt my body was moving, following the drum beat. The shaman wore beautiful, colorful dresses and sang and danced until she reached a state of ecstasy. She then called to the ghosts and talked to them. Other times the shaman consoled the ghosts, played with them, or negotiated with them. There were many people who watched the shaman and responded to her.

During my junior and senior high school days, I gave up my interest in ghosts. The Korean public education system, which was influenced by the pragmatism of John Dewey, brainwashed me into believing that all ghosts stories were superstitious fantasies. It was an age of enlightenment and independence. I could sleep alone and go to the bathroom courageously by myself!

The ghost world returned to me when I went to college and studied Korean history with others in the student movement. It was a revelation for me. I realized Korean history was full of wars, invasions, and the cruel exploitation of my people by foreign powers and domestic power elites. So many people have died unjustly throughout our history. Where have all these people gone? Where are they now: heaven or hell? According to Korean beliefs, these people's spirits could not rest in eternal peace. All of these people had to become restless wandering ghosts!

Since my college days, wandering ghosts have not been objects of fear for me. I started to believe that these ghosts were the voices in the wilderness which could unveil and proclaim all of the injustices in our history. I must listen to their voices because they must clearly contain God's voice as it has resonated throughout our history.

In Korea we call these wandering ghosts *han*-ridden ghosts. *Han* is a very peculiar feeling. According to the late *minjung*[1] theologian, Suh Nam-Dong, *han* is "the suppressed, amassed and condensed experience of oppression caused by mischief or misfortune so that it forms a kind of 'lump' in one's spirit."[2] This is the typical, prevailing feeling of the Korean people. Another Korean *minjung* theologian, Hyun Young-Hak, described our deep, shared feeling of *han* very vividly: "*Han* is a sense of unresolved resentment against injustice suffered, a sense of helplessness because of the overwhelming odds against, a feeling of total abandonment ('Why hast thou forsaken me?'), a feeling of acute pain of sorrow in one's guts and bowels making the whole body writhe and wiggle, and an obstinate urge to take 'revenge' and to right the wrong all these constitute."[3]

This feeling of *han* comes from the sinful interconnections of classism, racism, sexism, colonialism, neocolonialism, and cultural imperialism that Korean people experience every day. I want to think of *han* as the Korean people's "root experiences" or "collective consciousness." I think any meaningful Korean theology must start from the understanding and articulation of *han*. Korean *minjung* theology arose out of this consciousness in the 1970s.[4]

The direct translation of *minjung* is "people." But *minjung* is not a neutral term. *Minjung* means a specific people. According to a Korean *minjung* theologian, Suh Kwang-Sun, *minjung* are "the oppressed, exploited, dominated, discriminated against, alienated and suppressed politically, economically, socially, culturally, and intellectually, like women, ethnic groups, the poor, workers and farmers, including intellectuals themselves."[5] Therefore the term *minjung* is a bigger and broader concept than the "proletariat." *Minjung* theologians try to articulate theology out of the concrete historical experience of the Korean *minjung*.

Korean women's theology shares many things with Korean *minjung* theology. However, it clarifies the content of oppression further. Just as Mercy Amba Oduyoye named the third-world women's status as "irruption within the irruption,"[6] we Korean women could name our status as *"minjung* within the *minjung*."[7] Korean women have taken within their whole being the poisons of injustice and suffering in our history and have survived. The Korean woman was at the bottom of the oppressive system but has not always been a passive victim. She is also an agent of liberation. She has given birth to a new life and hope for our country.

III

What are the specific aspects of Korean women's *han?* In order to articulate Korean women's theology out of Korean women's root experience, *han,* we have to know the concrete context of Korean women's *han.* Korean women have been suffering with Korean men under colonialism, neocolonialism, and military dictatorship throughout our painful history. The oppression of women, however, has taken specific forms in addition to all of the experiences of suffering that women share with men. I want to call this aspect of women's suffering "gender specificity." Women suffer just because they are women. The people with power of domination have exploited women in particular ways using the female gender ideology. I would like to unveil the Korean women's *han* in the perspective of the gender specificity of women's suffering. While I am uncovering the mutilated "her-story" in Korean history, I will also try to discover the signs of active resistance within women's culture. Sometimes Korean women were destroyed as "passive victims" due to lack of power bases and support systems. Other times Korean women were "active agents" of liberation and wholeness for both men and women in our society. Following are some prototypes of women's suffering or active resistance in Korean history.

Women's Han under Religiocultural Gender Ideology

In ancient Korea, Korean women enjoyed more or less equal status with men. We can find the traces of matriarchal society in Korean history. However, since the time Korean society was organized into rigid social and religious systems, female gender has been the target of oppression and exploitation. Especially after the Yi dynasty, which established Confucian ethics, women's oppression has deepened. (Confucianism was based on the adult male leadership in the family and others' obedience in the name of harmony.) The elite group of the Yi dynasty developed the ideology of female chastity and obedience.

Once women's sexuality and chastity belonged to her family, women had to live under severe sexual censorship because, under the Confucian social order, losing her virginity hurt the social advancement of male members of her family. For example, they prevented widows from remarriage. Widows' remarriage, it was thought, made the blood of the family unclean. Women are responsible for the purity of their family's blood. When a widow got married, she was punished along with her parents, new husband, and children by blocked social advancement of the whole family. Even a ten-year-old girl who was engaged through her parents' arrangement had to keep to her widowhood in the in-laws' house if her future husband died before marriage.[8] The young, never-married widow's life was constantly guarded by both families. In some cases a young widow's room was locked and she was prohibited from coming out — in order to maintain her chastity. The young girl's sexual desire was the object of her family's fear. In the worst cases, the young widow was encouraged to commit suicide or she was secretly killed to keep the family reputation intact. Even now we see the presence of this oppressive culture when living singly as unmarried women is discouraged or when widows are encouraged to maintain their celibacy. Korean women have endured all such social, cultural, and religious control over their lives. But they have also actively fought against double standards in our cultural and religious life by creating and sharing songs, poems, and stories among women.[9]

Women's Han under Colonialism

Under Japanese colonization many Korean women's bodily integrity was violated by Japanese colonial and military power. During World War II, Japan recruited poor, rural Korean women for their labor forces. These women were forced to be official prostitutes for Japanese soldiers. About one hundred thousand Korean women were used by Japanese soldiers in the various battle fronts. According to one Korean woman who survived the war, she and others had to receive Japanese men all through the day and night.[10] Even though their private parts were swollen and they cried from pain, the women were forced to continue to receive the soldiers.[11] Many Korean women died of venereal diseases. Other Korean women were either abandoned in foreign lands or were killed by the soldiers when the Japanese retreated from their battle lines. When Japanese soldiers reported the death toll to their superiors, they simply reported these women's deaths as "a few lost war supplies."[12] Some Korean women survived this hell. Many of them could not return to Korea, however, because they were ashamed of themselves and "virtuous" Korean morality would not accept these "dirty" women back. Many of them died in alien lands. The Japanese government deliberately destroyed the reports on these Korean women. Their pain could thus be erased permanently from history. I am sure these women have become wandering *han*-ridden ghosts.

Women's Han under Neocolonialism

The struggle of women workers at the Tongil Textile Company shows the sinful interconnection between neocolonialism, military government, and sexism. Tongil

Textile Company was an export-oriented company. As in many other textile factories, the majority of workers were women. Behind the rapidly increasing GNP of Korea in the 1970s were many women who worked under miserable conditions in the textile companies. These companies provided the main materials for Korean export. At Tongil Textile Company about 80 percent of the workers were women. Male workers originally led the union. Women workers' consciousness was raised by their participation in the labor movement, and they finally elected a woman as their union leader.

Some of the male workers who belonged to the union would not tolerate a woman as head of the union, so they received money from the company and tried to destroy the woman-led union with the help of the police. Women workers were disillusioned by this betrayal by their male comrades and resisted. When this resistance became stronger, some of the male workers and policemen threw feces and urine at the women. Some women workers were force-fed feces and had their breasts smeared with feces. All this did not destroy their struggle. Rather, it made the woman-led union stronger. When police tried to arrest them by force, women workers took off their clothes and protested naked. This symbolic action made a qualitative leap in the Korean women workers' movement. Rev. Cho Wha Soon, who staunchly supported the women workers, confessed that this event raised her and other women's consciousness as women.[13] Before the event, women workers did not pay much attention to the women's movement because they considered it a middle-class movement. But after the betrayal by their male comrades, they began to realize their need for liberation from sexism. When the women workers of Tongil Textile Company took off their clothes, they also took off male domination over their lives.

Women's Han under Military Dictatorship

Kwon In-Sook, a twenty-three-year-old labor activist who was expelled from her university for her involvement in the student movement, was arrested in June 1986 as a subversive. Police detective Moon Kwi-dong (thirty-three years old) began examining her on alleged connections with other people in the movement. When she refused to reveal the names, the police detective took off her clothes, beat her, and sexually tortured her.[14]

Ms. Kwon was deeply humiliated. She confessed that she wanted to kill herself due to extreme shame and pain. Her liberationist consciousness would not allow her to commit suicide. She decided to let the whole world know what she experienced. She wrote out a request to arrest the torturer; her request was discarded by the chief of security. Upon hearing of the incident, women prisoners who were in the same prison as Ms. Kwon went on a hunger strike in order to support her. The next day the male prisoners did the same. This was the first time in Korean history that a woman made a public issue of sexual violation. Many Korean women have been sexually tortured in various circumstances by the officers of the dictatorial government, but they did not dare to speak out for fear of endangering their families' reputation and out of fear of revenge by the government. Ms. Kwon broke the culture of silence on violations of women's sexual and personal integrity prevalent in Korea under the military government.

Children's Han under Poverty

Women's *han* is not just limited to adults. Children accumulate *han* in their hearts, too. Children are deprived of their childhood in the poor sections of Korean society. Let us listen to the poem written by a twelve-year-old Korean girl in a slum:

My mother's name is worry,
In summer, my mother worries about water,
In winter, she worries about coal briquets
And all the year long, she worries about rice.

In daytime, my mother worries about living,
At night, she worries for children
And all day long, she worries and worries.

Then, my mother's name is worry,
My father's name is drunken frenzy,
And mine is tear and sigh.[15]

When poverty is the order, the people who suffer most from poverty are women and children. A Korean woman organizer, Kang Myung-soon, lives in a slum area and has talked about children's *han* in her community. Once some five- or six-year-old children in her community went to a wealthy church and were taunted as dirty beggars by some affluent children whose families belonged to the church. These children asked Kang Myung-soon to return with them to attack the wealthy church. The children carried stones in their hands.[16] When these poor children grow up and their individual *han* join to become a collective *han*, what kind of future can Korean society expect?

IV

How can we then solve and untangle the accumulated *han* of Korean women? In Korea we call the release of *han* "*han-pu-ri.*" I think *han-pu-ri* must be the purpose of doing women's theology in Korea.

Originally the term *han-pu-ri* came from Korean shamanistic tradition. Korean shamans have played the role of the priest or priestess of *han-pu-ri* in his or her communities. Shamanistic *kut* (ritual) gave the opportunity for the voiceless ghosts to speak out their stories of *han*. The community then must solve the *han* of the ghost collectively either by eliminating the source of oppression for the ghosts or by comforting or negotiating with the ghosts. Therefore *han-pu-ri* has been an opportunity for collective repentance, group therapy, and collective healing for the ghosts and their communities in Korean society.

The most fascinating things about Korean *han-pu-ri* for me are the following three factors:

1. The majority (65–70 percent) of shamans who play the role of the priest or priestess of *han-pu-ri* in Korean society are women.

2. The majority of people who participate in the *han-pu-ri kut* in Korean society are women.

3. The majority of characters in ghost stories are women.

These factors provide an important clue for the "hermeneutics of suspicion." But why are women the majority in the above situations? When I look at the three factors with the "epistemological privilege" of third-world women, the answer is clear. Korean women have been the embodiment of the worst *han* in our history. They usually did not have the public channels to express their *han*. This developed a sense of impassibility among Korean women. Many of them died without releasing the sense of impassibility in their lives. That is why there are so many women ghosts in our traditional stories. Women who endured the helpless impassibility could understand one another through their shared life experience as women. *Han-pu-ri* became one of the few spaces where poor Korean women played their spiritual role without being dominated by male-centered religious authorities. *Han*-ridden women got together and tried to release their accumulated *han* through *han-pu-ri kut*.

There are three important steps in *han-pu-ri*. The first step is *speaking and hearing*. The shaman gives the *han*-ridden persons or ghosts the chance to break their silence. The shaman enables the persons or ghosts to let their *han* out publicly. The shaman makes the community hear the *han*-ridden stories. The second step is *naming*. The shaman enables the *han*-ridden persons or ghosts (or their communities) to name the source of their oppression. The third step is *changing* the unjust situation by action so that *han*-ridden persons or ghosts can have peace.

The Korean Association of Women Theologians (KAWT) developed a theological methodology by which they can assuage Korean women's pain. KAWT follows steps that are similar to the shamanist *han-pu-ri* when they articulate Korean women's theology.[17] According to the report of their second consultation for the establishment of feminist theology in Asia,[18] women theologians took the following steps. They started their theologizing from listening to the *han*-ridden women's stories. They invited women from the bottom stratum of Korean society, such as farmers, factory workers, and slum-dwellers, and listened to their life stories. After this step, the women theologians did social analysis with the help of social scientists and other women who knew the structural aspects of the problem. They then moved to the theological reflections with the questions raised by the former two steps. The next step was to check with the original storytellers and communities whether the articulated theology made sense to them and empowered them. The final step was action. KAWT participated in various demonstrations and organized protests in order to solve Korean women's *han*.

I can find four main theological sources in the Korean women's emerging theologies. The most important source for Korean women's theology is the Korean women's lived experience. However, this experience is not the universal, abstract, and standardized human experience as alluded to by some traditional European male theologians. The specific historical experience of Korean women is manifested in their experience as victims and agents of liberation, and through the experience of *han* and *han-pu-ri*. Korean women's experience is the starting point and ending point of Korean women's hermeneutical circle. The second source is critical consciousness. Critical consciousness is different from a neutral, detached, objective reason. Critical consciousness is an engaged subjective reason that takes sides. Critical consciousness is the thinking power that can uncover the ideology of domination. The third source is tradition. Korean women use all of the traditions we have in order to fully articulate Korean women's theology.

We use our own religious traditions, such as Shamanism, Buddhism, Confucianism, and Christianity, and political ideologies. However we do not use all the traditions uncritically. We distinguish from a specifically women's perspective the liberative traditions from the oppressive traditions. We women learn from our experiences that male-defined liberation did not always include women's liberation. We use liberative traditions to empower women and our critical analysis of the oppressive traditions to name the source of oppression. The fourth source is Scripture. We use the Old and New Testaments along with other scriptures from our traditional religions. We selectively choose liberating messages from the texts. Scriptural texts are our references for women. We learn by the texts, but we go beyond the texts to meet the community behind the text.

When we Korean women do theology with the above methodology and resources, we come up with the question of the norm for our theology. What makes our theology good theology? I will say the norm of Korean women's theology is the power of liberation (*han-pui-ri*) and life-giving. If a theology untangles the Korean women's *han* and liberates us from bondage, it is a good theology. If a theology keeps us accumulating our *han* and staying in our *han*-ridden women's places, it is a bad theology no matter how important church unity, the authority of the Bible, and church traditions are. If a theology has a life-giving power to Korean women and empowers us to grow in our full humanhood, that is a good theology. If a theology makes us die inside and wither away in our everyday bodily and spiritual life, it is a bad theology.

Can this Korean women's theology be a Christian theology with these two norms: liberation (*han-pu-ri*) and life-giving power? Surely it can because we Korean women believe in good news (gospel), not bad news. For us, the gospel of Jesus means liberation (*han-pu-ri*) and life-giving power. In that sense, we are Christians. Where there is genuine experience of liberation (*han-pu-ri*) and life-giving power, we meet our God, Christ, and the power of the Spirit. That is good news. We Korean Christian women define our Christian identity according to our lived inherited experience, which stretches five thousand years back, even beyond the birth of Jesus.

Notes

1. *Minjung* is a Korean word meaning "people," specifically, "oppressed people." Korean theologians did not translate *minjung* theology as people's theology in order to emphasize the particularity of Korean people's historical, cultural experience.

2. "Towards a Theology of *Han*," *Minjung Theology* (Singapore: Christian Conference of Asia, 1981), p. 65.

3. "Minjung, the Suffering Servant and Hope," a lecture given at James Memorial Chapel, Union Theological Seminary, New York, 13 April 1982, p. 7.

4. Suh Kwang-sun's article, "A Biological Sketch of an Asian Theological Con-

sultation," in *Minjung Theology,* pp. 15–37, shows the origin and the development of *minjung* theology in the Korean context.

5. From Suh Kwang-sun's class lecture given at the School of Theology at Claremont, August 1983.

6. "Reflections from a Third World Woman's Perspective: Women's Experience and Liberation Theologies," in *Irruption of the Third World* (Maryknoll, N.Y.: Orbis, 1983), p. 247.

7. Letty Russell used the similar term "Minjung of the Minjung" in order to name the Korean women's status. See her forthcoming article, "Minjung Theology in Women's Perspective," to appear in a book of critical reflections on the development of *minjung* theology in Korea (Lee Jung-young, ed.).

8. For the resource for women's life under Confucianism, see Lee Ock-kyung, "A Study on Formational Condition and Settlement Mechanism of Jeong Juel (Faithfulness to Husband by Wife) Ideology of Yi Dynasty," an M.A. thesis, from Ewha Women's University, Korea, 1985.

9. For concrete examples, see Lee Oo-jung, "Korean Traditional Culture and Feminist Theology," *The Task of Korean Feminist Theology* (Seoul: Korean Association of Women Theologians, 1983), pp. 63–78.

10. *Prostitution: Study on Women,* no. 2 (Seoul: Korean EYC, 1984), p. 13.

11. Ibid.

12. Ibid., p. 14.

13. Personal interview with Rev. Cho Wha-soon, New York, May 1986.

14. This fact sheet is based on a report of the Korean National Council of Churches Human Rights Association printed in local edition of *Dong-A il bo,* New York, 17 July 1986.

15. Taken from the cover page of *My Mother's Name Is Worry: A Preliminary Report of the Study on Poor Women in Korea* (Seoul: Christian Institute for the Study of Justice and Development, 1983).

16. Kang Myung-soon, "The Story of Poor People," in *Korean Culture and Christian Ethics* (Seoul: Moon Hak Kwa Chi sung sa, 1986), p. 381.

17. This is not the official position of the Korean Association of Women Theologians but my personal interpretation of KAWT's theological methodology.

18. Korean Association of Women Theologians, *Second Consultation for the Establishment of Feminist Theology in Asia* (Seoul: KAWT, 1983).

SECTION II

SPEAKING OUT OF OUR OWN RESOURCES

Using the Asian Heritage as Illumination

One dark night an old woman was searching intently for something in the street. A passerby asked her, "Have you lost something?" She answered, "Yes, I have lost my keys. I've been looking for them all evening." "Where did you lose them?" "I don't know. Maybe inside the house." "Then why are you looking for them here?" "Because it is darker in there. I don't have oil in my lamps. I can see much better here under the street lights."

— An Indian folk tale

Chapter 5

Dancing, *Ch'i,* and the Holy Spirit

PETER K. H. LEE

One of the emerging trends in Asian theology is extratextual hermeneutics — an approach that tries to use indigenous literary and nonliterary resources for theological enquiry. Articles in this section demonstrate how this is undertaken by Asian theologians. Here is an example inspired by a dance performance staged by a local company. The Hong Kong theologian moves beyond dancing and tries to interweave Chinese philosophical motifs with Christian concepts for mutual enrichment.

Peter K. H. Lee is Director of the Study Centre on Chinese Religion and Culture, Kowloon, Hong Kong. He has published numerous articles on Asian theology and hermeneutics. His specialty lies in the profound way he has juxtaposed biblical narratives and Chinese myths and developed hermeneutical insights for a multireligious context.

Source: *Ching Feng* 34 (3), 1991.

Some time ago at an Asian theological seminar I read a paper with the title, "Can Theologians Dance on the Top of a Pin?" The title is a take-off on a question raised by Scholastics of the Middle Ages: "How many angels can dance on the top of a pin?" I wrote that paper to encourage younger Asian theologians-in-the-making to make theology lively, as dancing is lively, by suggesting that creative theological thinking can come from even a small place like Hong Kong, which is the size of a pin's head on the map.

This article is a further exploration of the possibilities for doing theology which, like a wonderful dance performance, would leave a vivid and lasting impression on one's consciousness. I again use Hong Kong as a locus of theological exploration. I shall move into the level of theological thinking by way of the dancing scene in Hong Kong. But I find *ch'i* (meaning breath or air), as a Chinese philosophical category, a helpful frame of reference for rethinking the Spirit in the Christian sense.

Dancing on the Hong Kong Scene

Hong Kong is not noted for its development of dancing as an art form. But notwithstanding its critics' denigration of Hong Kong as a "cultural desert," in the last decade it has sponsored annual arts festivals and Asian arts festivals that feature outstanding musicians and performing groups from many parts of the world. In the dancing field, the world's top ballet companies, including Sadler's Wells Ballet, the Royal Danish Ballet, and the Bolshoi Ballet Company, have graced the stages of performing theaters in Hong Kong. Practically all of the countries in Asia have sent dancing groups to perform during the Asian arts festivals and on other occasions. This year there is a Chinese Minority Groups Dance Festival, featuring some eight dancing troupes from China. So Hong Kong is a place where one has the opportunity to see dance performances of many kinds — from Europe and North America, from Asia and China's various regions.

But has Hong Kong itself produced anything notable in the art of dancing? The answer, alas, is that Hong Kong has nothing specially its own in this field. One has to look very hard to find anything worthy about dancing on the Hong Kong scene. There is, as yet, no world-class dance emerging from the indigenous Hong Kong culture.

Lion Dance and Dragon Dance

Let me begin with a type of "dance" that has deep roots in the folk culture of the Hong Kong Chinese people, though it is not of a high art form. I refer to the lion dance and the dragon dance. They are centuries-old Chinese customs. They have survived to this day in Hong Kong's Chinese community. The two are not identical, but one or the other often appears at a New Year (lunar calendar) celebration or some other special occasion.

The lion dance uses a "lion" (papier-mâché head on a large wooden frame and a body made of a long piece of cloth). Two persons are needed to perform the dance, one at the head and one at the tail. The one carrying the head up and down must be a strong man, moving the head with his arms and turning it in various directions while doing fancy footwork. The one at the tail holds the cloth that is the "body" and takes agile footsteps. The lion dances to the beat of a drum or a gong. It can do tricks, such as teasing the firecrackers and jumping or climbing up a tree to pick a bundle of green vegetables hanging from a high place. Sometimes two lions dance, one male and one female. It is like a *pas des deux,* but of course it is not refined dancing as in ballet.

What does the lion dance signify? It is supposed to assure good fortune for the community. The lion, being a strong animal, is a symbol of power — power to defeat or dispel evil forces and power to bring good fortune. The "vitality" of the lion is acknowledged right at the start of the dance by the "dotting of the lion's eyes" with ink. This is done by an important personage.

The dragon dance is more elaborate because the dragon is more highly decorated and much longer. The dragon dance requires more people to hold up the head, the body, and the tail. If it is performed at a New Year's function, the function must be a big event. The dragon dance may also be a part of a celebration program on other occasions. Whatever the occasion is, it must be important.

The lion dance and the dragon dance are usually performed out-of-doors, in a public square or park. A large crowd gathers to watch the dance as a part of a community celebration.

Ch'an Dance

From the lion dance and the dragon dance, which are extroverted, noisy, and fast-moving, I turn to a *ch'an* (*zen*) dance performance, which is introverted, quiet, and slow-moving. *Ch'an* in Chinese (or *zen* in Japanese) is the word for "meditation." The *Ch'an* Buddhist sect, emphasizing meditation, takes its name from the word.

Actually, there is no type of dancing called "*ch'an* dance" as such; it was by coincidence that I saw a performance advertised as "*ch'an* dance." It was a performance choreographed by a Korean woman residing in Hong Kong, Madam Lee, who is convinced that meditation according to the *Ch'an* sect is a good tonic for the busy and restless life of a modern city like Hong Kong (and Seoul). A dancer and choreographer trained in modern dancing, Madam Lee developed her *ch'an* dance by working with a small group of dancers. Hers is a small company performing only occasionally. Out of curiosity I went to see one of its performances.

I have not kept a program of that dance performance, and I cannot recall the details. But I did have an over-all impression of what the dance endeavored to communicate. To put it in another way, the dance has transmitted to me a sense of *ch'an* or *zen*. The performance that evening was on the whole slow-moving; too much so, I am afraid, for fast-paced Hong Kong. Perhaps the slow movement was meant to be a contrast to the frenzied Hong Kong tempo. If so, the contrast could have been more effective by moving from a fast tempo at the start to a slower-paced performance.

At any rate, sitting in the audience, I was gradually drawn into a sense of wholeness — breaking up the usual box-like image of the stage, breaking down the barrier between the audience as onlookers and the performers as faraway "objects," and breaking through into an inner consciousness. The consciousness was inner wholistic space, which was not just a void but was illuminated by insights.

The *ch'an* dance may have been slow-paced, yet it was movement. One number reminded me of *t'ai-chi-chüan* movements. Those who are adept at *t'ai-chi-chüan* can practice meditation (*ch'an*) in motion. By the same token, the *ch'an* dance is a form of meditation in motion or slow movement. How? As I understand it, in this kind of *ch'an*, one meditates with bodily movement, which, in this case, is suppleness in strength. The "mind" itself is "mind-less" (emptied of any fixated ideas) but moves along with action, which is flowing and rhythmic. Accordingly, consciousness of the mind flows rhythmically, with the *tao* disclosing itself along the way. I may have read more into the *ch'an* dance than what was warranted, but for a few fleeting moments a sense of *ch'an* meditation was mediated to me.

The *ch'an* dance is by no means in the mainstream of the Hong Kong dancing scene. In fact, very few people know how to appreciate it. The performance that I saw was not particularly impressive. Yet I have noted it here for a special reason. *Ch'an* meditation does seem to have something to offer in a crowded and frantic place like Hong Kong. If a form of dancing can capture *ch'an* spirituality, credit is due to it.

A City Contemporary Dance Company Production

The City Contemporary Dance Company, formed in 1979, is Hong Kong's first professional contemporary dance company. Its choreographer-dancers, having received training in ballet and modern dance of the Western tradition, now go back to classical Chinese literary and artistic resources for inspiration and then make productions that speak to the contemporary age. The company's productions are gaining recognition among the younger generations in Hong Kong, and the troupes have traveled to neighboring Asian cities and elsewhere to perform.

I refer here to a production entitled "South Wind." The entire program is based on selections from the ancient classic, *Shih Ching* (the Book of Poems). As is often the case with the company's productions, this one seeks to reinterpret, by the dance, the classical texts in contemporary idiom. The *Shih Ching,* dating back to pre-Ch'in periods (twelfth to sixteen centuries B.C.), contains 305 poems (reportedly selected by Confucius out of several thousand). The poems are grouped under the sections, *"Feng"* (Wind), *"Ya"* (Grace), and *"Hsiung"* (Ode). "Wind" includes ethos, lifestyle, prevailing customs, *Zeitgeist* (the spirit of the times), and (by a play on the sound *feng*) satire (*feng-ch'i*). So poems under the section "Wind" grew out of the life and times of the people from various regions of ancient China. The poems are expressive and spontaneous, sometimes exuberant and sometimes sorrowful, and at times with a touch of satire or humor. Under the section "Grace" are collected poems written by the gentry for court ceremonies and feasts. "Ode" is the collection of songs that were sung during royal ceremonies. We can see that the *Shih Ching* is a remarkable book. Confucius, whether or not he was the actual editor, reportedly valued it highly. *Shih Ching* is one of the "Five Classics."

The "South Wind" dance production has adopted sixteen numbers from the "Wind" section, one each from "Grace" and "Ode." The sixteen "Wind" numbers range widely in theme and style. They include harvest in the plantation, a man longing for a woman, the sadness of an abandoned woman, a wedding, twilight, the panic of a woman running away with her lover, the mother-child relationship. The original poems are all short and focused, and the dances also speak to a single theme pointedly.

Let me refer to three numbers to illustrate how the choreographers and dancers seek to translate ancient texts into contemporary idiom. "Wind from the South" has plants growing under the gentle breeze to signify the growing up of children under their mother's care, but the mother becomes tired (suggested by the wilting of tree leaves), and the children regret their failure to return their filial care to her (as shown by the unruliness of the young plants). This kind of poignancy in the mother-child relationship is not uncommon in modern urban Hong Kong, where motherly love, given to the point of self-sacrifice, is as valid as anywhere else, and where traditional filial piety is still found, though at times neglected. Poignancy comes when the children realize their failure to live up to their expected duty.

"Moon Rising" depicts a man yearning for his dream-lover, to no avail. The dream-girl is compared to the shining moon, and the man looking at it has his heart torn by emotions. The dancing against the background of a moon effectively portrays the conflict of emotions.

Many a poem in the *Shih Ching* gives dancing a special place. One of the poems, "Heavenly Dance," celebrates the art of dancing:

> Oh heavenly and heavenly,
> Let's all dance and dance,
> During high noon,
> At the front of the stage
>
> With my robust body,
> I dance and dance in a public court.
> I am strong as a tiger;
> The reins are in my grasp like ribbons.

The dancers in this number dance with clean and vivacious steps, making their own rhythms with bright clapping sounds (by slapping their belts?). It gives the feeling that dancing is pure joy and wholesome fun.

Only one number is selected from the "Grace" section. It is the "Song of the Gentry." The dance is a decorative, extravagant, and fast-flowing piece of work. The backdrop and sidedrops (made up of vertical panels of cloth in a gradation of light colors from cream to yellow to gold to green) and the costumes (silvery gray silk with faint, simple designs for both sexes) suggest a modern setting which has good taste, such as one would find amongst the younger affluent professionals in a place like Hong Kong. The dance movements are lively all right and rather expressive, too — but lively over what and expressive of what? That is not clear. The program notes say that the choreographer tries to show "the emptiness of bourgeoisie festivities on a bounded stage." That dance made me think of a "yuppies" party — smart people enjoying the pleasures of a consumer society but devoid of meaning in their conversations and lives. Watching this number, l did enjoy it and found it engaging, but I could not see the point — perhaps the point of the dance is that there is not much meaning to the kind of boxed-in existence (suggested by the bounded stage set by the cloth backdrops and sidedrops) of the modern "gentry."

The "Ode" number staged is entitled "National Anthem." By that is not meant a song for the whole nation but a religious hymn expressing a people's aspirations. In this presentation the dance movements are based on traditional Chinese court gestures such as walking, stopping, kneeling, kow-towing, and so on, but contemporary dance steps are combined, quite successfully. The costumes, background design, and music are contemporary. The overall effect is a sense of majesty without being stilted. Where can this kind of scene be found? A modern society with Chinese cultural ingredients and advanced technology, perhaps, and yet, interestingly, piety and respectfulness are found there, too. It can only be in the future, "an ending of an era," as the program notes say. The futuristic (or eschatological?) note is accented by the roaring sound of jet engines and the flashing of revolving red police lights, but I failed to grasp all the meaning.

Overall, even if the dancing artistry was not first-rate, the production showed creativity. Creativity is evidenced in transcribing inspirations obtained in ancient

literary texts into the contemporary scene by the medium of dancing. The choreographers and dancers, as well as the composers and stage designers, together
succeeded in capturing something of the spirit of the age. To the extent that they
heightened the sensibility of the audience, they were effective artists. With the latest production of the City Contemporary Dance Company, modern dance in Hong
Kong has come-of-age — not fully mature, but an adolescent ready to enter the
world of grown-ups.

From Dancing to *Ch'i*

The City Contemporary Dance Company production of "South Wind" involves
a process of transcribing from one art form, poetry, into another, dance. The
transcribers, in this case the choreographer and the dancers, can read the poems
intelligently and then use another medium at which they are adept, the dance, to
interpret what they read. In turn we now undertake a process of transcription from
the dance to words, words conveying theological ideas. Actually it is not direct transcription or word-for-word translation but rather free adaptation into a theological
idiom.

Recapitulations

Let me first recapitulate what has impressed me in the dance performances
mentioned.

1. All the performances generate energy. The lion and the dragon are symbols
of vitality — vitality not only in the people but also in their culture. Whereas the
lion symbolizes prowess in general, the dragon has been the age-old symbol of
majestic or imperial power. In the Hong Kong context, energy is channeled especially through commercial enterprises. (Hence Hong Kong is known as one of the
"four little dragons" of Asia, along with Taiwan, Singapore, and South Korea, where
either the Chinese race is in the majority or the influence of Confucian culture is
pronounced.) On festive occasions, like the New Year and the commemoration of
a special event, the lion dance or the dragon dance is on hand to celebrate economic success or to ensure prosperity. The dance numbers in the "South Wind"
production, too, all exhibit energy and agility.

2. Dancing can have a dimension of spirituality. Spirituality induces an attitude
relating one to a realm beyond. It has a sense of the ultimate to which the subject
is responsive or open. It is an attitude, a spirit, a dynamic state of being, but if
it is worthy spirituality, it has a "beyond" as reference. The *ch'an* dance emitted
such a spirituality. The "Ode" number in the City Contemporary Dance Company production had implied spirituality in the attitude of reverence and gesture
of offering.

3. Rich emotions are transmitted by dancing. The contemporary dance numbers,
especially under "Wind," danced to a wide spectrum of human emotions: thanksgiving at harvest time and lament over the shortness of life, pining for the beloved
and fear at a time of eloping, the sense of futility over chasing after the unsatiable,
and the exuberance of dance. One of the great values of the *Shih Ching* is that

human emotions are expressed undisguisedly, and the dances patterned after the poems try to give free rein to the emotional expressions too.

4. The dance exemplifies grace. Dancing is freedom of bodily movement following a pattern that is pleasing to watch. The contemporary dance performers apparently had training in ballet, which accounted for their graceful steps; their modern dance movements were free but not untutored. The *ch'an* dance that I saw was subdued gracefulness. The lion dance and dragon dance are not a high form of art, yet their movements are agile.

Ch'i

As I recapitulated how the dances have impressed me, I asked myself if there was some force or power that ran through all. The Chinese philosophical concept of *ch'i* then suggested itself. The simplest English equivalent of *ch'i* is "breath" or "air," but in the course of philosophical development it acquires the connotations of "spirit," "energy," "essence." *Ch'i* is an important category in Chinese philosophy. Indeed *ch'i* has a rich history from antiquity to the present.[1] *Ch'i* is subject to materialistic, idealistic, naturalistic, and metaphysical interpretations. But it is worthy of note that as a philosophical or metaphysical (these two terms in Chinese are sometimes indistinguishable) category, *ch'i* has a unifying character — it runs through the myriad manifestations of things and it is related to other fundamental principles or concepts like *tao* (way), *li* (reason or principle), *yin-yang, pen-t'i* (ontology). Of course it would be out of place here to present the variety of views of *ch'i* in Chinese thought.

Fortunately, in the thought of an important philosopher, Tai Chen (1723–1777), we can find a doctrine of *ch'i* that helps us to gather the threads into a meaningful whole in the light of our interest in the spirit of dancing. Tai Chen lived at the beginning of the Ch'ing dynasty. Toward the end of Ming, a number of thinkers took special interest in *ch'i* as a philosophical category. The Sung and Ming neo-Confucianists had already built imposing philosophical systems that were almost watertight. The demise of Ming as a dynasty under the threat of the Manchus, a foreign race, was a cause for reflection. It seemed as though *ch'i* was like air released from a vast vessel, yet it was an essential substance, so to speak. So *ch'i* served as a means for philosophers to rethink many thoughts. Moreover, *ch'i* has affinity to spirituality, which, being more immediate to the heart/mind than concepts, is more satisfying to a distressed soul. However, in the thoughts of the philosophers, *ch'i* is not just something ethereal, unrelated to the central concerns of thinking persons, and must be understood wholistically.

Wang Fu-chi (1619–1692) made a grand synthesis of the various schools of thought on *ch'i*. *Ch'i* was elevated to an unprecedentedly high metaphysical position. Yen Yüan (1635–1704) and Li Kung (1659–1733) had a more pragmatic bent, insisting on *chi's* presence in the practical world while giving *ch'i* a metaphysical basis. Fang Yi-chih (1611–1671) combined *ch'i* (air) and *huo* (fire) ontologically and there, with a touch of *ch'an* (zen), brought *chi-huo* into unity with *hsin* (heart/mind).

Ta Chen followed this tradition of rethinking on *ch'i*. His thinking on the subject, too, forms a coherent whole, in that there are a number of points that correlate with what I have noted about dancing. First, *ch'i* is both metaphysical and physical. *Ch'i* in the metaphysical sense and *ch'i* in the physical sense are of one piece, though in different forms. Metaphysically *ch'i* is the ground of existence and production of all things. *Ch'i* is the physical content of *tao,* and *tao* is in *ch'i.* In the physical sense *ch'i* includes *yin* and *yang* and the "five elements" in all their combinations. In a word, *ch'i* is the unifying ground for all that exists.

Second, *ch'i* is productive motion or process. In the five elements (water, fire, wood, gold, earth), *yin* and *yang* interact to produce the multitude of things, with *ch'i* as the dynamic power behind all. *Ch'i* is alive, incessant. It is self-sufficient and self-directing. Outside *ch'i,* nothing else exists, and *ch'i* by itself provides the dynamics of productive motion. "Productivity" includes productivity of life — vegetable, animal, and human life certainly, and "life" or "liveliness" in everything else too. That is not made clear, but Tai Chen had a sense of cosmic aliveness, as expressed by the words *sheng-sheng,* literally meaning "production and production." Reproduction, transformation, creativity are all implied. *Sheng-sheng* follows a meaningful pattern and a natural order.

Third, *ch'i* certainly manifests itself in the human person in an especially notable way. What distinguishes human beings from things is that *ch'i* is clear and distinct. *Ch'i* in humans includes not only *hsüeh ch'i* ("full-blooded" spirit) but *hsin-chih* (understanding in the heart/mind), *ren-hsing* (the nature of being human). Desires, emotions, and morality all have their legitimate places in human nature. Tai Chen criticized the traditional neo-Confucianists for deprecating human desires and emotions. He thought that desires and emotions cannot be treated in isolation from mortality. Morality is certainly important. In this he adhered to the Confucianists' emphasis on *ren* (kindness), *yi* (righteousness), *li* (propriety), *chih* (wisdom), and *hsin* (trust). But desires and emotions should be taken into account in moral behavior. *Ch'i* works in the whole personality and makes the human personality all the more alive and rich. Tai Chen was one of the last systematic thinkers of China using *ch'i* as a central theme prior to the modern age, when Western thinking invaded China.

Ch'i and Holy Spirit

Whether or not it was by coincidence, a number of thinkers at the close of the Ch'ing dynasty again took up the subject of *ch'i* and found in Tai Chen's thought some important clues. These thinkers include Kang Yu-wei, Yen Fu, Tan Tze-t'ung, Chang T'ai-yen, and Sun Yat-sen, who were all exposed to Western thought in one way or another. Passing up these figures, I, in my exploratory rethinking on the Holy Spirit by way of my enamor with dancing on the Hong Kong scene, came upon a useful framework in Tai Chen's thinking on *ch'i.*

The Spirit as Energy

Taking the cue from dancing, I wish to underline that the Holy Spirit (or Spirit for short) is energy. Traditionally, Christian theologians, when dealing with the subject of the Holy Spirit, are preoccupied with the problem of relating the Spirit to God and to Christ. If one works within a strict trinitarian framework of God as three Persons, arguments have been waged as to how the Spirit can be a Person, and whether the Spirit proceeds from the Father or the Son or both. It would not be the central concern of this paper to go over the intricacies of these arguments. What is of interest now is the point that the Spirit is energy or dynamic power. Western theology is not short on arguing that the Spirit is power, as wind (the meaning of the Hebrew word for spirit, *ruach,* or the Greek *pneuma*) is an agent of power. Power to do what? To accomplish what God wills, as the Book of Acts so well testifies. That is fine. Although it is nothing new, the point is emphasized nevertheless that, in theologizing, we must not lose sight of the Holy Spirit as an enabling or energizing power.[2]

Dancing is energetic motion, and my fascination with it prompts me to think of the Holy Spirit as a dancing spirit. Now, in thinking of the Spirit being likened to a dancing spirit, I conceive of it as acting in human life in a real way. To go back to the lion dance and the dragon dance, they symbolize energy in a people. In down-to-earth terms, the energy is in the people's world-affirming attitude, in their way to do business and in the community's prosperity. Similarly, can the Holy Spirit be an energizing power in the ethos of the people in down-to-earth terms? It is not just in making money but in the people's outlook in life — according to God's will. When and where do we see this happen?

I recognized a higher spiritual power at work in the Chinese students' animated mass demonstration at Tiananmen Square for political reform in May 1989. Tremendous energy was generated. The exuberance was symbolized at one point by the students singing and dancing. I witnessed the same spirit working in three Sunday marches on the streets of Hong Kong, each time numbering one million people, and an evening of singing and dancing in the open air by television performers to raise millions of dollars, all in support of the reform rallies in Beijing. I saw spirit-moved rallies in the theaters and stadiums in Hong Kong early in August this year, with hundreds and thousands of people in attendance, to raise money — several billion Hong Kong dollars in all — for relief work on behalf of flood victims in the eastern region of China.

No doubt mixed motivations were involved in these mass activities. Christians and the churches as such did very little on those occasions. It would be a gross over-simplification to call these activities the sheer work of the Holy Spirit. Yet it is possible to identify elements that were in tune with the Spirit of Christ. Where there is genuine concern for freedom and justice, where there is compassion for others in trouble, there Jesus Christ is present, and his followers have the right to identify certain signs as bearing the marks of the Holy Spirit. That the Spirit works outside the church does not matter; the parameter of the Spirit is larger than the church. What matters is that it comes from a transcendent source, God, and that elements in it are identifiable by what is known to be Christ's life and teachings.

The mass movements which I have just mentioned were extraordinary events, but can we see that the Spirit operates in ordinary life as well? Let me refer again to the dragon dance and lion dance, which are symbolic rituals with deep roots in Chinese culture. Tai Chen is helpful here when he suggests that *ch'i* is not floating air but is embodied in culture and other human conditions. I shall start with the dragon dance, linking it up with the nickname, "four little dragons." The "four little dragons of Asia" are all under the impact of Confucian culture. Though geographically small, they are known for their economic achievement in recent years, hence the nickname, "little dragons." These countries are not without woes, brought on by unruly economic endeavors. Still, using the dragon as a cultural symbol, it is fierce and aggressive. Elsewhere I said that the four little dragons (traditionally male figures) have too much *yang,* to the deprivation of *yin.* I thought that they needed a better balance between the *yang* and the *yin,* and I fancied that the dragons need the company of their phoenixes. (In Chinese culture, the phoenix is female, symbolizing feminine royalty.) I even invoked the fable (of Middle Eastern origin) of the phoenix rising from the ashes as a resplendent creature. In a similar vein, the four little dragons need a rebirth of culture to become "gentler and kinder societies." I do not know how to engraft these thoughts in Chinese culture. If I were a choreographer, I would devise a dragon-and-phoenix dance for the students to perform on special occasions. This is to heighten the awareness of the need for a rebirth of culture.

I believe it is possible to bring out the gentle and compassionate side of the people by using the cultural symbols. Recently the Third Olympics for the Disabled (called "Abilimpics") was held in Hong Kong. Hong Kong as the host was generous in providing hospitality. A dragon dance was performed at the closing ceremony. The dragon, specially made for the occasion, was one thousand feet long, a record for the *Guinness Book of World Records.* It was not fierce-looking at all, and the long body twirled and twirled gracefully. The dragon was supported by several hundred able-bodied together with disabled "dancers." That was a significant act meant to symbolize mutual support and cooperation. The dance added gaiety to a happy party. If the dragon dance — and the lion dance too — can be used more not only for celebration of economic success but for a joyous occasion for the whole community where benevolence, cooperation, and peace prevail, then the cultural symbols perform a beneficial function.

One more word about the lion dance. In some instances, both a lion and a lioness are in the dance. I am one who goes for the right balance of *yin* and *yang* in a culture. By the way, Tai Chen and other Chinese thinkers are helpful in speaking of the *yin-yang* interaction in *ch'i.* We need not take *yin-yang* literally; I take it in a symbolic sense, to signify the balance of cultural forces. *Ch'i* is relevant here as dynamic power. If I were a choreographer, I would design a dance featuring the male and female lions — and lion cubs, too — to bring out the humanized elements in the midst of celebration of life.

Where does the Holy Spirit come in? The Christians need not at every turn announce the Christian name, but they can rejoice when they see elements that they recognize according to their faith tradition. Empowered by the Christian Spirit, let them participate in the building up of the community along with the rest, enriching or purifying the spirit of the whole, but ever ready to learn from others and cooperate with them. The Christians really need not be anxious to make the Christian claim; if they follow the lead of the Holy Spirit at the right time, people will know the Christian meaning.

Spiritual Discipline

I would next like to consider the Holy Spirit in relation to spiritual discipline. The *ch'an* dance performance that I saw disposed me toward this interest. That performance demonstrated to me that dancing, with its external movements, has an inner consciousness. When dance is deliberately linked up with meditation (which is what the word *ch'an* means), it becomes a spiritual exercise. Real spiritual exercise is not a wooden activity; it is a disciplined activity. But if it is truly spiritual, it is an activity in which the Spirit becomes alive. How the Holy Spirit comes in, we shall consider later. Presently I shall say more about an activity like dancing adaptable to spiritual exercise.

I have never performed as a dancer, and so I do not have firsthand experience of dancing. Now, that *ch'an* dance performance I attended had in one number some movements taken over from *t'ai-chi-chüan.* I have taken lessons in *t'ai-chi-chüan,* but I have never become an expert at it. *T'ai-chi-chüan* is not only a physical exercise but can be a spiritual exercise, too. In simplest terms, in doing *t'ai-chi-chüan,* one's consciousness flows, following supple bodily movements, through a series of "acts." Moving through the acts, the mind "empties" itself, but as the movements are supple, so becomes the mind. Meditation by *t'ai-chi-chüan* is a relaxing and freeing experience. Relaxing is a beneficial tonic for people living in a busy city like Hong Kong. And freeing for what? Of that I am not sure. I need to consult with those who know better.

I know a Catholic priest who seeks to integrate *t'ai-chi-chüan* into Christian meditation. I really want to learn from him as to how the Spirit fits in here. I also know a retired minister who "dances" with the sword (*wu chien*) every morning. Now over eighty years old, he is in robust health. He probably does not think of "dancing with the sword" as a spiritual exercise, but at any rate I would like to talk with him about the subject.

I would now like to describe briefly my experiment with swimming, as a spiritual exercise. I swim in the morning. Certainly it is a good physical exercise. Just now I am experimenting with it for spiritual significance. I swim laps in the pool. In swimming the breast stroke, I have a sense of the depth of water in the pool through the corners of the eyes, while my mind usually thinks of nothing. Yet sometimes ideas come to my mind; I do not consciously seek answers, but thoughts enter my mind. Not long ago I was asked to compose the lyrics for a hymn on the subject of the Holy Spirit. Some words sprang to my mind during swimming. Several days later I completed the lyrics (in Chinese), four verses in all. I am not going to show all the words here except the first line in each verse:

> The Spirit is like fresh wind...
> The Spirit is like spring water...
> The Spirit is like burning flame...
> The Spirit is like bright light...

For the last two weeks I have been swimming to these lines, one line for each lap (back and forth), repeating the same words in my mind as I stroke. I repeat the lines again for more laps. As I swim, ramifications of the rest of the words I wrote, if not the very words, arise in mind. The meaning of the ideas becomes clearer or verified later on during the day. I also use other hymns for my "swimming meditation," like "Holy Spirit, truth divine...love divine...power divine...peace divine..." I am still new at this experiment. But several things have become clear. One, my swimming meditation is an enjoyable experience. Every morning I now cannot wait until I swim. Two, I know what it is to have a sense of inner space as I have never known before. Three, unexpected inspirations come at some time during the day (or night) if not while swimming. I hope to report more on my experiment at a later time. By uttering certain words, is it merely autosuggestion? I do not think so, for the meaning of the words is verified or expanded. If that is autosuggestion, so is any hymn singing, so is the "Jesus prayer," or any prayer, for that matter.

The Spiritual Life in Active Service

Going beyond spiritual exercises, I would now like to speak of the spiritual life in active service. Actually, the principle at work in a spiritual exercise also applies to a life of service. In spiritual exercise, the individuated consciousness is lifted to a higher level of dedication, and the Spirit on high in turn animates the mind — and body — as nothing else can. A life of active service, dedicated to a higher cause, is motivated and empowered thereby, in fact, "to do far more abundantly than all that we ask or think" (Ephesians 4:20).

Dag Hammarskjöld, the Swedish diplomat who was Secretary General of the United Nations from 1953 to 1961, combined a contemplative temperament with a life of action in the interest of world peace. He recorded in his diary (Whitsunday, 1961): "But at some moment I did answer yes to someone — or Something — and from that hour I was certain that existence is meaningful and that, therefore, my life, in self-surrender had a goal."[3]

Outwardly an austere man, Hammarskjöld was a tireless worker, utterly devoted to what he did. The following lines are a characterization of his way of life:

> With all the powers of your body
> concentrated in the hand on the tiller,
> All the powers of your mind concentrated
> on the goal beyond the horizon,
> You laugh as the salt spray catches
> your face in the second of rest.
> Before a new wave —
> Sharing the happy freedom of the
> moment with those who share your responsibility.
> So in the self-forgetfulness of
> concentrated attention — the door
> opens for you into a pure living intimacy,
> A shared, timeless happiness,
> Conveyed by a smile,
> A wave of the hand.[4]

A man of action though he was, Hammarskjöld had a sense of the lyrical quality of life enveloped in the Spirit: "Thou takest the pen — and the lines dance. Thou takest the flute — and the notes shimmer. Thou takest the brush — and the colors sing. So all things have meaning and beauty in that space beyond time where Thou art. How, then, can I hold back anything from Thee?"[5]

Can we see spiritual-minded people in active service in a place like Hong Kong? There is a hospital that has a section to serve terminal cancer patients. The nurses there are most unusual. They serve with dedication, patience, skill, and buoyancy of spirit. The head nurse said that they have to have a sense of commitment; otherwise, they would not work in the hospital. They are dedicated to the belief that even terminal cancer patients are entitled to spend their last days on earth with the least pain possible, in peace and trust, and spiritually in readiness for self-surrender. Certainly the dedication is of a thoroughly spiritual nature. Then doing unpleasant chores and seeing patients in suffering becomes bearable.

I know some Hong Kong individuals who are convinced that the protection of human rights and greater progress in democratization are of the highest priority for the sake of the future of Hong Kong. They are not arguing or thinking in the abstract but have a keen sense of the dignity of the human person with all his or her endowments from God. They also have a lively awareness of how much more meaningful life in the community can be if the people can have more participation in the governing process. These people know that they are fighting an uphill battle, but they brace themselves for the fight, and they learn quickly to play the game of politics adroitly — according to fair rules. They are at times discouraged, but recently they are encouraged by the response of the people — and the unexpected changes in world events in favor of the cause of freedom and democracy. Some of them believe that a higher power is at work mysteriously in the affairs of the world.

Tai Chen's theme of *tao* being in the processing of *ch'i* for ceaseless productivity has implications here. He said, "The *tao* for humans is applicable in day-to-day human relations and personally exemplifiable."[6] In heaven and earth, *ch'i* flows ever creatively: that is *tao* in human affairs. Whatever is creative cannot but have *ch'i* flowing through: that is *tao*. Tai went on to expound the Confucian virtues of *en* (benevolence), *yi* (righteousness), *li* (propriety), *chih* (wisdom) in terms of the *ch'i* flowing through heaven and earth and in human affairs, all in productivity and creativity. In other words, the person who follows the *tao* is receptive to *ch'i* and shows all the classical virtues as Confucius and Mencius taught. Conceivably this is realizable even today.

Tai Chen's conception of *ch'i* (like that of most Chinese philosophers) is not commensurate with the classical Christian understanding that the Holy Spirit belongs to God, who is at a distance from the world or transcendent to it. This difference is apparent where the Christian believer prays, albeit with the Spirit present, to God who is "the other." Human beings and God are not unitive even if communication of one with the other is granted. In one sense God is one "who is not far away and in whom we live and have our being" (Acts 17:7), yet in another sense God is beyond all our concepts of spatial dimensions (as Christ's love surpasses all length, width, height, and depth, [Ephesians 3:19]), and this "beyondness" or distance makes a difference in one's relationship to God.

The poems in *Shih Ching* (Book of Poetry) do have a conception for "The Lord on High" (Shangti, the Chinese name that is adopted by Protestant Christians for God). The "Ode" number (adapted from *Shih Ching*) in the City Contemporary Dance Company production has the dancers showing reverence, petition, and praise to a supreme being.

The Spirit and Human Emotions

Last, I would like to come to the idea that the Spirit allows human sentiments to give full expression. One of the great merits of the poems in the *Shih Ching* is that rich human emotions of a wide range are allowed to unfold themselves. The dance production "South Wind" adopts sixteen poems and portrays human emotions in a variety of scenarios. Human emotions in the poems and dances are not raw emotions but sublimated into fine sentiments.

Tai Chen was one of the rare philosophers who accorded a place for the expression of human sentiments. He criticized the scholastics of the Sung and Ming periods for "killing humanity by rationalism" and bureaucratic officials for "killing humanity by legalism." He said that human desires and passions, like eating and drinking, the love between a man and a woman, are "givens" of life. These need to be ordered and balanced, however. Hence *li* (principle) is important. He said, "What may be in accord with *li* is that sentiments have not lost their blindness and sensitivity. There can be no situations of expressing sensibilities satisfactorily without satisfying the requirement of *li*."[7] Also, "In heaven and among persons, emotions subsist, and where emotions are neither excessive nor suppressed, there *li* prevails."[8] "Following *li* (principle) and *yi* (righteousness) is pleasing to the heart, just as tastiness pleases the palate, music pleases the ears, and color pleases the eyes: all that is called *hsing* (being true to the nature of things)."[9] *Li* is in *ch'i,* which is in command of things, and when *ch'i* works properly, everything is true to its nature. Tai Chen recognized Mencius' admonition to moderate desires so as to nurture the heart, but he at the same time appreciated Mencius' approval of a joyful life and willingness to share joy with people. Tai Chen's criticism of the inhumanity of Confucian scholasticism by suppressing human sentiments reminds one of Jesus' condemnation of jaded people, like the Pharisees and legalists, for having lost their capacity for joy and sorrow. He compared these people to children sitting in the market place and calling to one another,

> We piped to you and you did not dance;
> We wailed, and you did not weep.

To those whose hearts and minds are in Christ, Paul wrote, "Whatever is true, whatever is honorable, whatever is just, whatever is lovely, whatever is gracious, if there is anything worthy of praise, think about these things" (Phil. 4:8). Tai Chen would have liked this saying. On many occasions he taught, "Let sentiments [interact] to purify sentiments" and "When 'full-blooded' *ch'i* knows the heart then one realizes one's being." But he would not have understood why and how somebody else, like Christ, would be needed besides *ch'i* and *li* and *tao*.

Christ is the embodiment of God's grace. "From his fullness have we all received, grace upon grace" (John 1:17). In Bali I once saw an amateur Christian dance group (in Bali everyone loves to dance, and professionals and amateur dancers alike dance for the love of dancing) that brought out the graciousness of forgiving love in the scene of the father accepting the Prodigal Son and in another scene of Jesus' telling the woman caught in adultery, "Go, and sin no more!" The graceful dancing portrayals of these scenes have indelibly etched in my mind that God's Spirit is supremely gracious.

Concluding Words

Let me now conclude with words from Ecclesiastes (3:1–4):

> For everything there is a season,
> and a time for every matter under heaven:
> a time to be born, and a time to die;
> a time to plant, and a time to pluck up what is planted:
> a time to kill, and a time to heal;
> a time to break down, and a time to build up;
> a time to weep, and a time to laugh;
> a time to mourn, and a time to dance...

The Book of Ecclesiastes has a sense of the rhythmic movement of events in heaven and earth. Breathing is rhythmic, the beating of the heart is rhythmic, the waves and tides of the sea are rhythmic, the moon waxes and wanes rhythmically,... and of course, music and dance thrive on rhythm. Why should we be surprised to know that *ch'i* (breath, air, *ruach, pneuma*) is rhythmic in having *yin* and *yang* interact in all things? I cannot pretend to have given a new theory of the Holy Spirit. But at least this I know: there is a time or a season when the Holy Spirit is a dancing spirit.

Notes

1. Zhang Liwen, ed., *Ch'i* (Beijing: Chinese People's University Publishing Association, 1990).

2. Krister Stendahl recently wrote a small book entitled *Energy for Life* (Geneva: W.C.C. Publications, 1990). The subject of the book is the Holy Spirit.

3. Dag Hammarskjöld, *Markings,* trans. L. Sjoberg and W. H. Auden (New York: Alfred A. Knopf, 1959), p. 205.

4. Ibid., p. 96.

5. Ibid., p. 118.

6. Tai's essay on "Tao."

7. Tai's essay on "Li."

8. Ibid.

9. Tai's essay on "Hsing."

Chapter 6

Feminine Images of God
in Korean Traditional Religion

CHOI MAN JA

When Asian women began to work out their own contextual theology, the traditional religious perceptions of women became one of the major subjects for
research and reflection. Such an investigation enabled them to expand the received biblical image of God, which reiterated their inequality, and to reclaim
creatively from their own religiocultural resources concepts of a goddess, which
stress the strong and positive aspect of women in spite of being neutralized by
patriarchal culture. The article reproduced below is an attempt to reclaim the
metaphors for God/Goddess from the Korean shamanistic tradition.

Choi Man Ja is a Korean feminist thinker and has been long active in the Korean
women's movement.

Source: *In God's Image,* June, 1989.

The Negative Influence of the Masculine Image of God
in the Korean Church

Most Korean Christians believe that God is the Father who is head of the world
and families. This conviction goes very deep into the hearts, minds, and beliefs of
my people. This masculine image of God is very authoritarian and imperialistic, and
it has justified and guaranteed male dominance over women and the subordinate status of the female. Furthermore, this image of God related to the Father God is very
deeply woven into worship and prayer for both men and women. Many Christians
habitually say Father God more than five or six times within only one sentence
when they pray. Of course, God is not male, but Korean Christians experience God
as masculine. In other words, we imagine God anthropomorphically as male.
    Once formed, the image organizes and interprets our experience so that what we

actually experience as well as its meaning and significance is largely the function of our imagination. Thus, Korean Christians cannot escape this patriarchal and hierarchical structure which was formed from beliefs in a Father God. Concretely, this masculine image of God is usually related to church Constitutions which often prohibit the ordination of woman.

The Presbyterian Church of Korea is the largest denomination in Korea, with a membership of one million, two-thirds of whom are women. Yet, it has excluded women from the ministry and decision-making processes. The petition for the ordination of women was rejected by the male-dominated governing body based on a biblical interpretation in which the imagery for God is so patriarchal and imperialistic that it seems to justify male dominance over women.

I feel it is very urgent to expand the imagery for God into one that conveys the most significant metaphors for the Christian faith. Much Korean feminist theology, therefore, is involved with reclaiming goddess images in traditional culture, or reclaiming the feminine images of the biblical God, or both.

Female symbols for God are essential for maintaining the fullness of the image of God and promotion of equality. Goddess images are also helpful. In order to overcome inequality in the Korean church, as a first step, Korean feminist theology is searching out the feminine images of God in the Korean culture. The Korean Association of Women Theologians plans to develop the concept of goddess for Korean feminist theology by studying the concept of goddess in Korean culture as revealed in Korean folk literature.

Korean Shamanism

Shamanism originated in northeast Asia or in Siberia. Shamanistic religion did not arise out of Buddhism or any other religion. It originated among Mongolic nations and consists not only of superstitions and shamanic ceremonies but also of a certain primitive way of observing the outer world, nature, and the inner world, the soul.

Shamanism is one of the most significant and representative religions of the Korean people. Through shamanism we can find the pulse of the Korean people's mind. Shamanism is the oldest folk religion of the religious life of the Korean people. It is said to be the original religion of Korean folk music, dance, and play. All of these are closely related to shamanistic religious practices.

The characteristics of Korean shamanism are cultural phenomena transmittable by ordinary people. It is a part of people's lives and the lives of religious people particularly. It can be regarded as a natural religious phenomenon originating from the people's lives for driving away calamities and inviting blessings by the spiritual power through the shaman priest — *mudang*. Shamanistic faith or custom is the most pervasive form of religious culture in Korea. The shaman ritual, the *kut*, gives expression to the very soul and essence of the Korean people and their culture. Scholars of Korean shamanism carefully avoid the term "religion" in defining the *mudang* phenomenon. In Korea, they call it "custom of *mudang*," not *kyo* or religious teaching, but *sok* or custom. And *musok*, or the custom of *mudang*, may be defined as "a form of people's faith in traditional religious phenomenon centered around the *mudang*." When scholars call this religious phenomenon "custom of *mu-*

dang," they contrast it with religion, which has teachings and doctrine. They want to call it "people's faith" or "folk beliefs."

The Korean shamanism base was formed in the lives of ordinary people before foreign religions came to this land. Shamanism is the pervasive religious custom and culture of the Korean *minjung* (the common people). Shamanism has no hierarchy, no church, no building, and no doctrine. Korean shamanism has no known founder, no prophet, no leading priests. Spiritual exorcism, direct communication with holy spirits, and healing through *mudang* are typical phenomena. Korea is one of the representative countries in Asia in this respect. In spite of the fact that foreign religions have come into the land, they have not been able to permeate into the Korean people, since they are very different from the Korean people's lives and consciousness. Therefore, despite its lack of teachings or doctrines, Korean shamanism still deserves to be called a religion. The original meaning of the term religion, "a contractual obligation with a divine being," is fulfilled in the "custom of *mudang*." Consequently, we find the understanding of God formed in the lives of the Korean people through Korean shamanism. Accordingly, we can analyze the feminine images of God through the Korean people's perception of God.

Outlook on the Concept of God in Korean Shamanism

Korean shamanism has no concept of monotheism; rather, it is polytheistic. It is mostly dependent on animism, which originated in *anima*. Animism is a belief that holds that all kinds of animals, plants, and natural things have *anima*, spirits. When people set up "spirits" for all kinds of things, they give very detailed names to the things that are closest to their daily lives, experience, and knowledge. For example, they have detailed gods (spirits) for aspects of the home, such as the spirit of the kitchen, the tutelary spirit, the gate spirit, the harvest god, three gods governing children's birth, and so on. On the other hand, people did not set up "spirits" that are neither close to nor useful for their daily lives. Spirits center on the house and family.

This family-centered animism also includes worship of ancestors, those who have died and been deified and worshiped by the people. Shamanism pursued practical blessing in this world by the help of spirits. So shamanism perceives spirits as a means of blessing, not as the object of life. According to Im Chul Je, shamanism has five kinds of spirits:

1. Spirits of all things: mountain, sea (dragon), local, tutelary, harvest, and so forth.
2. Spirits of deified human beings:
   a. Ancestors.
   b. Ordinary children who, as they grow up, experience extreme difficulty, which they overcome, and then become special deities by indication of the Majesty. Many myths have stories of these deified spirits.
3. Spirits of the dead,
4. Spirits originating from foreign religions.
5. Ghosts.

Kim Tae Kon divides shamanistic spirits into two kinds of gods. In general these are natural gods and human gods. Examples of natural gods are heaven, earth, mountain, water, fire, wind, rock, animal. Human gods are a king, a queen, a general, an ancestor of Mu, and so on. Spirits of shamanism each have a special function, and each spirit has a great power related to its special function. But the spirits use their power not through a reasonable revelation but through giving punishments to human beings. So human beings have to serve them by offerings to prevent their anger.

Spirits have power to control life and death, rise and fall, blessings and calamities, and the health and disease of human beings. Shamanism does not have any vision of salvation for the future. On the contrary, it is concerned with this world's problems and reality. Spirits of shamanism use their power to solve the problems of human beings' basic needs.

Feminine Images of Gods in Korean Shamanism

General View of Shamanist Gods

Korean shamanism has thirty female gods among 273 gods. In general, Korean shamanism has a male-god centered conception. According to his *Mu Sok* study, Kim Tae Kon says the highest god is Chun-sin (heavenly god), which is considered a male god. There are four classes among the gods in shamanism — upper, middle, low, and lowest. Yun Sung Bum insists that male gods were stronger and higher than female gods in their power and role. Female gods played the role as the assistants of male gods. Then he suggests that Korean culture had districts of origin, northern and southern. The northern district had been formed from a nomadic patriarchal culture, whereas the southern part was formed from a matriarchal culture. So we can get the idea from him that, although he insists on the superiority of male gods, he implies that there were strong female gods in the southern culture that belonged to a more ancient time than the northern culture. Therefore, we see that the images of female gods might have been transferred from the southern part to the northern culture, and gradually changed to patriarchal images of god by the cultural development in the North.

Im Chul Je claims that shamanism originally considered god as female. So the Mountain Spirit, Sea (Dragon) Spirit, Wind Spirit, and Sam-sin (god of giving birth), are all goddesses in shamanism. Generally, in ancient times, people thought of the sun as a goddess in many countries. Thus, the primitive image of God was probably of a female god.

After the introduction of foreign religions such as Buddhism, Taoism, and Confucianism to Korea, the sex of Korean shaman gods became confused and many became of indistinct sex. Some gods changed their sex to a hermaphroditic spirit. For example, the tutelary spirit and home visitor spirit have images close to female but are of both sexes.

Now, let me search for the feminine images of shaman spirits according to their characteristics and the myths that were expressed in Mu Ga's song of shaman when she organized the ritual. Mu Ga explains the origin of the spirits.

Feminine Images of the House Spirits

In Korean shamanism, house spirits are very close to the people and served by women. People believe that their houses are filled with all kinds of spirits. For example, they believe that the kitchen has a kitchen spirit (Jowang Sin), the gate has a gate spirit (Su Mun Jang), the housing site has its spirit (Tu Ju De Gam), and there is a guardian spirit of the home (Sung Ju De Gam). These house spirits are served mainly by women. Women also serve the spirits outside the home, such as the sun spirit, star spirits, moon spirit, dragon (sea) spirit, and spirit of richness. We could say that, in general, women serve the natural gods.

On the contrary, men have been interested in the worship of their ancestors. Men try to keep their family line and to dominate family members. But the faith of women is close to their daily lives — very practical, useful, concerned with blessing and calamity in reality. Women believe that the house spirits give them food, help them give birth, give them a safe life, clothes, a house, and bring health to their family. They want stability and peace in their family life. Even the house spirits are a mixture of male and female god, but the character of their function is explicitly related to feminine images (childbirth, feeding, supplying food, taking care, curing).

Let me introduce the myth of Sam Sin Hal Ma Ni (*Hal Ma Ni* means grand-mother), the most representative female god among the house spirits — the female god of giving birth. In the beginning, before any human being lived on earth, Dang Gum Ae Ki, the virgin god, lived in heaven. She married the monk god, and they had three sons. Thus she became the god of giving birth. She began life on earth being the life-giver for human beings. Thus people believed that babies were born through her orders. This belief has continued till the present. Women desiring to become pregnant serve Sam Sin with rites in their bedrooms. After a child is born, other rites are followed to win Sam Sin's protection for keeping the child healthy and safe until it is seven years old. On the third and seventh days after birth, the mother's underwear is placed on the table. After the child is seven, another house spirit, Chil Sung Sin (Seven Stars God), is responsible for the welfare of the child and can decide whether or not to give it long life. Sam Sin has strong powers to give birth, and she works very freely and autonomously without the interference of other gods, even of Chun Sin, the god of heaven. Women serve the house spirits, whose concerns are those of the women for the well-being of the home and family.

Myth of the First Ancestor God of Korean Shamanism

According to Mu Ga, the first ancestor of Korean shamanism is Ba Ri De Gi. She is both divine and human. The Baridegi myth gives us the most representative goddess image. It presents not only a feminine image but also an image of one who transcended sex as a savior. Here is the story of Baridegi.

Once upon a time, a king named Ogu married Byong-On. They had many children, but they were only daughters, seven in all. The seventh daughter was abandoned because the baby was not expected to be a girl. Her name was Baridegi, which means a deserted or abandoned child. Left alone in the back court of the palace, she was fed and protected by birds in the daytime and beasts in the night-time. When the king found out his daughter was alive and well, he devised another way to get rid of her. She was to be offered as a sacrifice to the Dragon King in the western sea. She was placed in a jade chest and cast into the sea. However, the jade chest floated. Then a gold turtle appeared and carried the chest with the baby in it to a mountain. An old couple passing that way were attracted to the glowing jade chest. Surprised to discover a baby inside, they considered her a gift from heaven and took her home to raise as their own.

Meanwhile, her parents, Ogu the Great and his wife Byong-On, were dying in bed. Despite the best doctors and medicine, they did not improve. Finally, they consulted a fortune-teller who told them, "Since the disease of the king is the punishment of heaven for abandoning his daughter, the chosen one, he cannot be healed with any medicine made in his country. Only spring water from the west can cure him." So Ogu the Great called his six daughters and asked them to bring this spring water for him. They all refused to do this. So he ordered his servants to search for the Baridegi princess. After bidding her stepparents farewell, she was brought to the palace. When she learned that her parents were dying, she was sad and wept. Even though they had abandoned her as an infant, she agreed to travel to the west for the spring water that would cure them.

The west was far from King Ogu's country. The journey was so tough and difficult that anyone setting out on it must accept with resignation that there might be no return. Whenever the Baridegi princess asked directions, some work was required of her. So she made her way by washing clothes and helping with the construction of a bridge and the building of a tower in exchange for directions. After she had walked a long way, she came upon Buddha and Amitabha playing Badug. They warned her that she was only halfway there with another three thousand lee over difficult roads to go. Nevertheless, the Baridegi princess told them she would continue in order to get the spring water that would save her parents. They gladly gave her directions and gifts, three bunches of flowers and a gold stick.

Now she had left the world of humans. She had to go through long miles of hell, as many as eighty-four thousand hells. There were a burning mountain and a sword mountain, an ice-filled hell and a snake-filled hell, a water-filled hell and a darkened hell. With her mind concentrated only on helping her parents, the Baridegi princess endured all these. Next she passed through a place where she heard the desperate moans and shouts of people. Then she came to a big river three thousand lee wide. With the aid of the gold stick, she crossed the river riding on a rainbow. On the other side, she was met by a fearful-looking giant who demanded to know why she was there. He was tall as the sky, with eyes like lanterns; his feet were three squares and three inches. When she explained of her search for the spring water to heal her parents, he required tribute money of her. Since she had no money, he asked her to do something for him. He ordered her to cut trees for three years to clear a path for a road, to keep the fire going for three years for her clothing, and to carry drinking water for three years. So the Baridegi princess worked for the giant for nine years. But the fearful giant still demanded more of her. He told her that if she married him and bore seven sons, he would then accept her will. There was nothing else she could do but marry him and bear him seven sons.

After all this, the Baridegi princess could finally take the spring water and return to her parents. While she was searching for three colored peach flowers, the giant decided to go with her. As they returned they saw a boat on the water with no anchor and no light. On it were the bodies of dead women — those who did not have children when alive and those who died during childbirth. These women were still wandering around after death. The Baridegi princess prayed for them and blessed them.

Finally she reached the human world. When she arrived home, her parents were about to be buried. She stopped the funeral march and let her parents drink the spring water she had brought. They were revived. The Baridegi princess and the giant were formally married before her parents and lived happily thereafter. After the death of the Baridegi princess, she became a goddess. Her story has been handed down from generation to generation.

In this myth, we can observe the patriarchal social consciousness which is favorable to sons rather than daughters. We also see that a woman was able to save her parents and society in spite of the inhuman treatment she had received under the patriarchal system. The disease of the patriarchal parents was overcome by the generous effort of an oppressed woman.

I would like to focus on two main points of the story. First, the way in which the Baridegi princess integrates the human and divine, life and death. She integrates the principles of this world and the other world. Through her suffering, she overcame the disease and death of human nature. Eventually she became the founder goddess of the shaman religion. Second, we note that she had the power to heal people. Healing is a major function of the shaman. A shaman spends most of *kut* (the rite of shamanism) in healing people. The power of healing shows the divine power that transcends the power of human nature. Healing is perhaps the most earnest and common request of most human beings.

In conclusion, we see that the image of Baridegi is of a female savior. Her divine power transcends human nature yet is at the same time in the midst of the difficulties experienced by human beings. She is great, but she never used any destructive power or military force to save her parents and their society. She sacrificed herself for others. The Baridegi myth is similar to the new humanity of Jesus who gave himself for all human beings.

The God of Cereals — The Female God of Earth
from Se Kyung Bon Pu Ri Mu Ga of Che-ju Island

Se Kyung means god of earth, god of cereal, and Bon Pu Ri means the song about the origin of god that discloses or interprets the meaning of that god. The heroine of Se Kyung Bon Pu Ri is Ja-chung-bi, who is also a divine-human. Ja-chung-bi became the mother goddess of earth with power to control the fertility of five grains and of cattle. Ja-chung-bi was the daughter of Kim-jin-kuk and Jo-jin-kuk. She wanted to be the wife of Mun-do-ryung, the son of the God of Heaven. However, his parents refused to allow her to become his wife. She eagerly appealed to them. Finally, the Heaven Gods required that Ja-chung-bi take a hard test. They asked her to stand on the blade of a sword surrounded by flaming fire. Ja-chung-bi endured all of the suffering given by the Heaven God and eventually she became the wife of Mun-do-ryung. However, knaves killed Mun-do-ryung and captured Ja-chung-bi. She was able to exclude them and bring her husband back to life with the flower of rebirth from the western world. At last, Ja-chung-bi received the seeds of five grains from the Heaven God. She was given the power to control the fertility of grains and cattle and the power over wind and thunder. She became the goddess who loves people.

This myth has the same divine-human pattern as the Baridegi myth. Ja-chung-bi is related to the earth, to nature, to that power which gives fertility to earth and cattle. These are considered the power of women's production. The story does not focus on women's productive power. Rather it focuses on Ja-chung-bi's wise, active, and strong divine-human image. She received divine power through her struggling and suffering. So her image is not feminine in the common sense, but as a superior feminine image, as divine.

Image of the Great Mother

In Korea there are many legends and myths of the Great Mother who is described as a cosmic-human. From Che-ju Island come a great number of myths of feminine deities. One myth of Che-ju Island is about Sun-bum-de-hal-mang. *Hal-mang* is grandmother in the dialect of Che-ju. The myth describes her as a giant: She was as tall as the length from Halla Mountain to Pental Island located before Che-ju City. She is the mother of the cosmos who made mountains, rocks, springs, islands, and built bridges. It is generally thought that Sun-bum, the Great Mother, is the original goddess from whom Sam-sin-hal-mang, Se-kyung-hal-mang (Ja-chung-be), and Jowang-hal-mang (the spirit of the kitchen) were derived.

As mentioned above, these goddesses have important roles in giving birth, the feeding and caretaking of children, in motherhood generally. As the faith in the Great Mother was passed down from generation to generation, the image of the Great Mother was changed by the different cultures. A number of myths about the foundation of the country involve the Great Mother. In many of them there was no father, just the mother and her son. The child was conceived by a divine being, born of the Great Mother, and then became the founder of the nation. The myths depict the mother as wise, strong, and active. The image of this Great Mother also absorbed Korean folktales of girl heroines. These folktales have the same pattern as the divine-human myths. Following are two examples of folk tales of female heroines.

The Story of Ji-ne-jang-tu. There was a shrine of big centipede Ji-ne in the town of Chung-Ju city in Choon Chung Province. Inhabitants of this village had as one of their rites the sacrificial offering of a girl to the big Ji-ne. This sacrifice was to ensure the people of the village peaceful days.

In that village lived a girl named Soon-i with her blind father. Once Soon-i found a big toad called Duggubi in her kitchen. She cared for Duggubi in her heart. Soon-i and her father were too poor to live. Soon-i decided to give herself as the sacrificial offering for Ji-ne so that her father would have enough wealth to live. Soon-i was bound with rope and left in the shrine. The big Ji-ne came to take her. Suddenly Duggubi appeared and attacked Ji-ne. They fought furiously until both were killed. Soon-i was able to return to live happily with her father. Ji-ne never again appeared in the village for a girl sacrifice.

The Story of Sim-chung. Once upon a time there was a girl whose name was Sim-chung. Sim-chung's mother was dead, and she lived with and cared for her blind father. She worked as a day laborer to support her father. One day she heard that her father could regain his sight if they would offer three hundred bags of rice to the temple.

At that time, some sailors were visiting the village to buy a girl to be an offering for the Dragon (Sea God). Whenever these sailors passed In Dang Su, in the middle part of the sea, the Dragon God showed great anger toward them. They believed the Dragon God would remain angry until they made an offering of a girl. Sim-chung decided to give herself for the Dragon God's offering if the sailors would pay the three hundred bags of rice so her father could regain his sight. This was arranged and the rice was given to the temple. The sailors took Sim-chung and threw her into the sea. However, the Dragon God saved her and invited her to the sea palace. The Dragon God prepared a very large mudflower, put her on it, and floated her across the sea. When the flower came to land, it was found by a king. He met and married Sim-chung. Sim-chung wanted to meet her father, so the King prepared a great party and invited all the blind people in the country. At the moment when Sim-chung met her father, he opened his eyes and was able to see.

These two stories have several things in common: the blind fathers cared for by daughters, no sons or mothers present. The situations are very similar. The blindness of the father presents his powerlessness. He is totally dependent on his daughter. The lack of power of the father is caused by the absence of the wife. There is no patriarchal authority of the father in these stories. In contrast, the daughters have brave, strong images that give new life to their fathers. The mothers were hidden in these stories, but we could imagine that the mothers were divine beings such as the mascot Duggubi and the Dragon God. Even today the image of the Great Mother is revealed in women's strong and active works.

Conclusion

Shamanism can be regarded as a natural religious phenomenon originating in the lives of the people and their needs for driving away calamities and inviting blessings.

The Korean shamanistic faith was formed within the lives of ordinary people before foreign religions came to Korea. Other religions have not been able to supplant it in the lives and consciousness of the Korean people. Thus Korean shamanism is the main religion of the people. The main content of this shamanistic faith is to repulse calamity and invite blessings. Koreans myths and folktales have a very strong image of women, and goddesses are close to the daily lives of the people. However, because Korean society was strengthened by the patriarchal structure, God was not identified as female. The original images of God in Korean culture have been forgotten.

To summarize:

1. The original image of the goddess is strong, active, and wise, yet the highest gods are not expressed as female. The patriarchal culture has changed the original image of the goddess.

2. The feminine image of God came from the role of motherhood. The role of the house spirit is especially close to the mother's role. But spirits can only use their power to control.

3. Female divine-humans present the image of a savior.

4. Female gods have strong power and used it very autonomously.

5. Female spirits are very close to women's lives.

This paper has several limitations. First, only images from Korean shamanism are presented. I did not relate them to a feminist theological perspective. Second, because Korean shamanism is so closely related to women's lives and deaths, the historical and sociological dimensions should be included. But that would be a very vast undertaking. This is just the beginning of searching for a feminine image of God in Korea. Much can be gained by further developing the feminine images of God found in Korean culture. Then feminist theology will be able to stand steadily on our own culture.

The Bible must be investigated to find God's maternal activities. Many biblical images picture God as the one who cares, feeds, protects, heals, guides, disciplines, comforts, washes and clothes her human children (Isa. 46:3, 4; Ezek. 36:25; Hos. 11:3, 4; Num. 11:12, 13, 16). God is even pictured as a midwife (Isa. 66:9). There are a lot of similarities between the function of Korean shamanism's spirits and the biblical God's maternal images. This study and comparison needs to be continued.

Chapter 7

Who Is God for Us Today?

JYOTI SAHI

The article below is an example of how nonliterary sources, especially the myths of marginalized communities, can be used to evolve an ecologically sensitive Christian spirituality. What is remarkable about this essay is that it goes beyond the traditional judgmental missionary hermeneutics and employs primal myths and legends of the tribal peoples of India, which came out of their sociopolitical experience, as a resource for theological enquiry.

Jyoti Sahi lives in Silvepura, a village near Bangalore, India, where he and a community of artists are engaged in the development of Indian Christian art forms. His book, *Stepping Stones: Reflections on the Theology of Indian Christian Culture,* recounts his theological journey as an artist working for the Indian church.

Source: *Thinking Mission* #2, April, 1989, a quarterly published by the United Society for the Propagation of the Gospel (London).

Over the last two years we have been making a study of creation-based spirituality to be found among various oppressed tribal groups in India. We have increasingly focused on the myths and legends of these marginalized cultures because it is often here that we can find a counterculture that has a prophetic thrust, questioning the existing oppressive structures of the world. These stories of suffering people come from their experience and therefore speak to our own times, when institutionalized violence has reached an even greater sophistication of cruelty.

Generally speaking, when people talk about Indian culture, they mean the "great tradition." It seems to be a general characteristic of philosophical and transcendental worldviews found in cultures all over the world that these are often body or earth denying, based on a spirituality that was known in the West as a *via negativa.* In order to arrive at what is universal the temporal is denied as basically illusory. Some suggest that this abstract worldview may be responsible for our present ecological crisis. It has encouraged in many spiritually minded people a basically negative attitude to the sensory world. In this context spirituality implies something that transcends the physical and sensory. This can easily lead to an exploitation of nature for the sake of human advancement.

Those who are now concerned that the human community must realize its dependence upon and responsibility toward the rest of creation have come to question certain aberrations found in a kind of spirituality understood by a dominant and ultimately exploitative class. Thus we cannot escape the fact that many mystics subscribed to an attitude not only to nature but also to fellow human beings that believes in the superiority of a few realized souls over the masses.

There is, however, another approach to spirituality that stresses the living spirit present in all human beings and the whole of natural creation. This approach affirms the close interconnectedness between mind and body, the sensual and the highest aspirations of the soul. The one is not just opposed to the other but rather fulfilled by the other. There is a need for the *via positiva,* a spirituality that sees the beauty in the physical world around us and believes that this is not just an illusion but a real experience of the Divine Creator.

Such an approach to spirituality characterizes the deepest insights of tribal and folk religions that see life in terms of a cosmic worldview. Such cosmic faith systems are to be distinguished from the transcendental faiths, which believe that God is totally outside the created cosmos and can be reached only by going beyond creatures. Unfortunately, too often those who believe in a transcendental God have looked down on the adherents of cosmic faiths, calling them animists, pantheists, idolaters.

It is only now that we are beginning to realize that those who have found God in creation have in fact been sensitive to the spiritual significance of the earth. The great metacosmic faiths, which have tended to assume the leading position in our modern world, have created the impression that nature is something lowly, if not harmful, for spiritual progress. This attitude towards nature has often had a disastrous effect on society's sense of responsibility for the environment, leading to the destruction of nature in the name of both spirituality and science.

In fact it could be demonstrated that the concept of scientific progress, so important in our modern secular world, is closely aligned to a notion of spiritual progress in that both are essentially concerned with the mind and make claims to a universal understanding of nature. Both the scientist and the spiritual human being seem to assume a position outside nature from which they are able to judge nature and use its resources for purely human ends.

What tribal and folk cultures stress is a more participatory and humble approach to reality, one that emphasizes that the human mind is itself an aspect of a much greater mind operative in the whole of nature. Humility, by the way, comes from the earth (*humus*) and is characterized by a kind of earthy common sense. Taking this humble, earth-affirming viewpoint as the basis for our own spirituality as creative artists, we have been looking at a number of models found in the folk cultures of India. These models are communicated through stories, themselves the work of the creative imagination. Underlying these stories we can find a spirituality.

It is important to look at these stories not just as fanciful ideas about humanity and creation but as ways of understanding our relationship to society and nature as a whole. The stories are not only descriptive; they are prescriptive. They tell us what it is to be truly human. They are also particularly important because they have taken shape among groups who have suffered in the past and have tried to understand their alienation in the light of a wider vision of creation.

As artists, we have also found that these stories tell us something about the creative process. It is in this context that I would like to set out four models that we have found particularly meaningful in our search for a theology that is firmly grounded in creation.

The Creation Model

There are many myths concerning the way in which people were created out of the earth to participate in the natural rhythms of nature and to celebrate the joy of all with song and dance. A creation myth is fundamental to the spirituality of many tribes, such as the Uraon tribe of Chota Nagpur. These tribes tell how the first human beings were made by God out of clay. The myth narrates how earth first came out of a primal earthworm, and it was from this clay that Dharmes fashioned the first man and woman, leaving his freshly created figures in the sun to dry. The heavenly horse, called Hamsraj Pankraj (a flying horse), came down to earth and stamped on the clay figures, destroying the first human models. This flying horse seems to have a rather negative function in the myths of this tribe. In this myth the flying horse represents the negative forces of the cosmos.

Dharmes had to make the human couple again, but this time he took the precaution of also making two fierce dogs to guard the clay figures as they lay drying in the sun. These dogs chased away the flying horse when it came down to earth. Dogs have an important role to play not only in relation to the creation of human beings but also as companions of God. The dogs also seem to be associated with the underworld through a very ancient level of Indian myth in which the dog is related to knowledge and faithfulness. The dog is thus symbolic of a protective power in nature. This animal seems to project something animal in the human person. There is a close tie between the human community and the animal world.

The Deluge Model

Many ancient myths are concerned with the end of the world. The Santali tribe of east India has a central myth which describes the rain of fire or the way in which the human race was destroyed by God on account of its sinfulness. Here again we have the pattern of an initial creation gone wrong because of the way in which human beings polluted the whole environment. The Creator had to purify creation by pouring down a rain of fire followed by a flood of waters. Only one couple called Bilcha Burhi escaped the seven days and seven nights of deluge by hiding at the base of a mountain. Later the couple were protected by the wife of the Creator, who was called Sita. She hid the little human creatures in the knot of hair at the back of her head. She also taught them to plough, and they became the first cultivators of the earth. The furrow is also known as Sita.

Here we find a very ancient idea of the human being as created to till the earth and make it fruitful. But there is also the fear that humanity will destroy the earth by polluting it.

The Work Model

This legend, which is central to the religious system of the Munda tribe, an ancient Kolarian tribe, tells of the coming of the Iron Age. We hear the story of how the Creator, who is called Haram, gave to all the tribes various works to do. Only one tribe got left out — the Asura tribe. This tribe therefore came to the Lord Haram and asked him what they could do. Haram allotted them the task of smelting iron. The Asuras subsequently worked so hard at their smelting that the whole of nature became destroyed by their fires and the smoke from their furnaces — so much so that all the animals went to God to complain that nature was being ruined. Then Haram sent three pairs of birds to warn the Asuras that they should not smelt iron day and night but only in accordance with the rhythms of day and night.

But the Asuras had now become very proud and claimed that they were equal to the Creator, as they knew the secret of transforming fire, and there was nothing that could stop them from burning their furnaces both day and night. Because they would not listen to the birds, Haram decided himself to come to the Asuras in the form of a leprous child. He came to the iron smelters to ask them for employment as a servant in their smithy, but he was refused work on account of his leprous condition.

They sent him to an old woman, of lower caste, who was childless and who worked in the forest making charcoal. This old lady agreed to give the child employment on condition that he look after her parboiled rice and make sure that the birds did not eat it when it was out in the sun drying. The leprous child began to show miraculous powers, so that whereas the iron smelters found that they were getting less iron from the earth, the old woman found that her store of rice was increasing mysteriously.

The Asuras, suspecting that the child was a magician, asked him what had to be done to make right the balance, so that they might once again get plenty of iron from the earth. He suggested that a sacrifice should be made, but the usual sacrifices proved ineffective. Then Haram said that there would have to be a human sacrifice. At that point the leprous child offered himself, saying that since he had no parents and was covered in sores, his life was not worth living. He then explained to the Asuras how they must close him up in their furnace and keep the fires going for three days and three nights before opening the furnace again.

The Asuras followed his instructions, and when finally they opened the furnace, Haram stepped out of the fire no longer a leprous child, but like the rising sun, covered in golden ornaments. The Asuras were very impressed and cried: "So far we have only managed to get iron from the earth, but now it seems that you have found the way of getting gold. Teach us your secret."

Then Haram said: "You have seen the way in which I was transformed by entering the furnace." So then the Asuras were all eager to enter the furnace themselves and asked their wives to close them up while keeping the fires burning for three days and three nights. At first the wives noticed that there was a great commotion going on inside the kiln and asked Haram what was happening, but he suggested that the Asuras must be fighting over the gold.

When the furnace was finally opened, the women found only the burned bones of their menfolk. They lamented their loss and accused Haram of cheating them, but he said: "I sent to you the three birds, and you would not listen. Then I even came myself to work in your furnace, and you despised me as a polluted child. This is the result of your pride." Haram then ascended back into the heavens while the women tried to cling to him. However, they fell back to the earth, one falling by a stream, the other on a hilltop, another in the forest, and one other in a field. Haram made a covenant with human beings that they must respect the rhythms of nature and not destroy creation with their work.

The myth clearly indicates how human work has to cooperate with nature and not destroy it. Those who use their creativity to destroy nature will themselves be destroyed by their own greed.

The Spiritual Knowledge Model

The story is told in North Kerala of the cultural hero Pottan, who belongs to the Pullaya community. This community, which is believed to have been a tribal group originally, has become absorbed into the prevailing Hindu society, as an out-caste group. In fact outcastes are divided into three types. There are those who are supposed to remain six meters (twenty feet) from the high caste, those who must keep twelve meters (forty feet) away, and the lowest of the low, who must remain eighteen meters (sixty feet) away. The Pullayas belong to this lowest category.

The story narrates how the great Shankaracharya of Kaladi, the most celebrated Brahmin sage and mystic of Kerala, was on his way to attaining the highest spiritual knowledge of Advaita. He was passing along a narrow path and came to a place that had a tank on one side of the road and a thorny wilderness on the other side. On this stretch of road, Shankaracharya met with the untouchable Pullaya called Pottan, who was half naked, carrying a burden on his head. In his arms and on his shoulders he carried his eight children, who are supposed to represent the eight directions of space. "Move out of my way!" cried the Brahmin. But the Pullaya hero stood his ground. "How can I move?" he asked. "On one side of this road is the tank, and on the other side is the thorny wilderness. I am carrying a heavy burden, and in my arms and on my shoulders are my eight children. It is not possible for me to step off the road."

The Brahmin Shankaracharya was adamant, however. He could not risk pollution on this journey. The lowest outcaste had no right to block the way of the highest sage of all time. But Pottan continued to argue. "As you feel hunger, I, too, feel the pangs of hunger. When your body is cut, red blood flows and, in the same way, blood flows from my body when I am injured. In what way then, O Brahmin, are you different from me, an outcaste Pullaya?"

The legend has been interpreted in two ways. There is the high-caste way of understanding the myth as just one of the final revelations of God to show the Shankaracharya the ultimate reality beyond all name and form. Here the Lord Shiva merely appeared in the form of an outcaste Pullaya to test the spiritual insight of the Brahmin sage. But for the Pullayas, the legend has a different significance. It is a prophetic indictment of the caste system itself, which has marginalized their whole community and led them to great experiences of suffering. Shiva is their God, and he is here challenging the spirituality of the Brahmins of whose wisdom Shankaracharya was the epitome.

These various models give us some idea of how tribal and folk cultures in India have tried to relate the human community to the rest of creation. The human being cannot live in isolation, for the destiny of the human person is interconnected with the future of the whole planet. At the present time we are urgently in need of a new spirituality that is ecologically sensitive. Can the four models outlined here give us some insights into ways in which we can approach our environment more responsibly?

Justice and peace are not separate issues, quite distinct from ecological concerns, but are all interrelated. Without a common sense of responsibility for the environment and the relationship of mind to matter, the human community cannot be just and at peace.

The pattern we have observed of mind dominating the physical leads not only to the enslavement of nature but finally to the oppression of the poor, who are thought of as incapable of higher forms of spirituality. Spirituality has to be something which springs up from below. Otherwise, it will be for only the elite few, whereas every human being is called to discover herself or himself as a deeply spiritual being.

One of our main concerns is to interpret myths in the light of present-day experience and conflicts. The myth, if it is to continue to be a living force in a community, must mediate between the present reality and the ultimate world, which gives significance to all experience. A myth becomes dead and irrelevant when this connection with the immediate issues confronting a community is lost. We wish to recover the insights of what might be called a mythic vision, as a resource for present-day theologizing in the Indian context. It is from this perspective that we began to study the myths and local cultures of various marginalized communities.

In the four models outlined here, the first two belong to the primal, cosmic type, concerned with the processes of creation and destruction. It is within this all-embracing worldview that the specific experiences of tribal and oppressed communities have been localized.

The second two models belong more properly to the category of legends, in that they border on the historic experiences of particular communities — in the first case the experience of a tribal community in the early Iron Age and, in the second case, the painful sense of alienation imposed on a primitive community by a dominant caste structure developed in classical Hinduism.

Reflecting on these primal myths and legends, is it possible for us to evolve an understanding of Christ that will address itself to this worldview? The tendency so far has been to associate Christian theologizing with a metacosmic worldview, which has sought to go beyond the cosmos to a transcendental God. Here, in these myths and legends, we find an effort to understand God as a creator, participating in the rhythmic processes of creation. There is clearly a concept of divine intervention in creation at a point where creation is endangered, especially by human pride and concupiscence. God becomes a human person, willing to be sacrificed, in order to re-establish a world order in which the human community is covenanted into a more responsible role as co-creators, but not oppressors of other creatures. There is a clear perception that the oppression of other creatures and the enslavement of human communities is interrelated. Tribal society is not only participatory in its relationship to nature but is also profoundly egalitarian. That is to say, it questions the domination of the whole community by a privileged few. True spirituality is to be found where equal respect is shown between fellow creatures and, hence, the unity of all creation is ultimately preserved.

This unity is symbolized by the Divine Person at once fulfilling all creatures in a heightened Personhood and also exemplifying the essential self-realization in each creature. The primal concept, then, of the king is not just a hierarchically superior person but rather one who manifests the essential nobility of each creature within its order of being. In the kingdom of nature, every creature is entitled to a kingly status. The Pullaya Pottan reveals himself, in all his nakedness, as a king of the universe. The image of the king is very closely associated with the role of a creator — the king manifests on the level of the creature the indwelling presence and dignity of the creator. To say that every creature is an aristocrat, and capable of being realized as a king, is to comprehend the essential dignity communicated to every creature by the indwelling immanence of God as creator.

Sacrifice, like the image of the king, is also a creative act. It is important to note that in all the myths or legends we have outlined as typical of the primal worldview, the Lord is a suffering person whose involvement in creation is an act of self-sacrifice. Those who are mystified as to how a suffering Lord can be squared with a Lord of the dance have not properly understood how the act of creation itself demands this kind of polarity: the joyous celebration of life as a blessing, on the one hand; and, on the other hand, the struggle with death and the in-built forces of entropy in nature in the creative effort to transcend the grave.

Perhaps this is the inner logic behind the repeated motif of the "two creations." One creation goes wrong and ends in death and destruction. This is followed by re-creation. Here, through the medium of story, the essential mystery of the creative act is represented, for creation is always an act of re-creation, carrying within itself the mystery of its own dissolution and death. What the rational, discursive mind finds incomprehensible is communicated through the intuitive knowledge of the symbol. What appear to be logical opposites — death and life, chaos and order, entropy and evolution — are discovered at another level as identical.

The mandala is not simply an orderly patterning of the universe; it is rather the unfolding of an evolving complexity of structure. It is at once simple and involved, comprehensible and mysterious. It cannot be finally grasped by the calculating mind because, in the very act of imagining the cosmic balance, it transcends all natural symmetries. It prefigures a random convergence of all energies, which science is only just beginning to find the language to describe, but which myths have always narrated, from the very dawn of the oral tradition. It is in the light of this rediscovered wisdom that we want to reinterpret the myths, not just as vestiges of outgrown superstitions but as the harbingers of a more profound understanding of the world in which we live.

Chapter 8

The Dragon, the Deluge, and Creation Theology

ARCHIE LEE CHI CHUNG

Folktales common to Asian peoples were dismissed under the influence of missionary teaching as pagan and not a suitable resource for a lofty subject like Christian theology. As a result, they were banished from the collective memory of Christians. These stories were shaped by the life experience of ordinary Asian people. After long years of neglect, there is now an enthusiastic move not only to reclaim these stories but also to use them as a resource to reinvent the future. The example reproduced here not only points out the pitfalls of using these traditional symbols but also the possibilities they offer.

Archie Lee Chi Chung is on the staff of the Department of Religion, Chinese University of Hong Kong, Hong Kong. He is also Associate Dean of Program for Theology and Cultures in Asia. His current research interest is in crosstextual hermeneutics in an Asian context.

Source: *Doing Theology with People's Symbols and Images,* ATESEA Occasional Papers #8, ed. Yeow Choo Lak and John England (Singapore: ATESEA, 1989).

We read in the *Shih Chi* (Records of the Historian), written in the first century B.C. by Ssu-ma Ch'ien, a story about Confucius going to Chou to be instructed in the rites by Lao-tzu. After the visit Confucius said to his disciples:

> I know a bird can fly, a fish can swim, and an animal can run. For that which runs a net can be made; for that which swims a line can be made; for that which flies a corded arrow can be made. But the dragon's ascent into heaven on the wind and the clouds is something which is beyond my knowledge. Today I have seen Lao-tzu who is perhaps like a dragon.[1]

What did Confucius mean when he compared Lao-tzu to a dragon? What was common to both of them? As for the other creatures, Confucius could find ways to catch them, but it was beyond his knowledge how to catch a dragon. Perhaps Confucius found the teaching of Lao-tzu too difficult to comprehend. For him both the way the dragon ascended into heaven on the wind and the clouds and the thought of Lao-tzu are too mysterious and difficult to understand. In the mind of Confucius, the dragon was a powerful symbol.

Among Chinese communities the symbol of the dragon has become very popular. In Chinese art and paintings, stories and songs, films and television documentary series, the image of the dragon is often used and the Chinese character for "dragon" (*lung*) is found in their titles. The popular song "The Descendants of the Dragon" and the fact that 1988 is the "year of the dragon" in the Chinese lunar calendar have helped tremendously in reviving and cultivating the symbol that has become deep-rooted in the mind of the Chinese. The song has the following words:

> A dragon there was in the ancient East. China was her name. A people there
> was in the ancient East, descendants of the dragon they were. Under the feet
> of the huge dragon I have grown up, to be a descendant of the dragon.

In recent years, owing to the open-door policy of China and her commitment to modernization, the national sentiment and sense of racial identity of many people of Chinese descent have been aroused. We can see the Chinese being stimulated and motivated to treasure their ancient but rich civilization. The huge dragon of the East, lying dormant but now waking up and getting ready for creative action, is an image of China on its road to modernization.

Hong Kong will revert to China under the "one country, two systems" ideology, to be a "Special Administrative Region" (SAR) of China as of July 1, 1997. The present concern of the people in Hong Kong is whether the promotion of nationalism and Chinese sovereignty by the cultural symbol of the dragon, which undoubtedly has a strong grasp on the spirit of the Chinese people, is appropriate to achieve the goal of modernization in China and so to maintain the stability and prosperity of Hong Kong.

The purpose of this essay is to examine the symbol of the dragon, to evaluate its strengths and limitations. It will be shown that the symbol, powerful though it be, has its limitations, because it is an imperial emblem and therefore static and outdated. It can easily become a stumbling block or a cultural burden to the people in their striving for modernization and political reform, as well as in their aspiring to fit into a modern, secular socio-economic and political world.

We have seen that Confucius found the dragon to be an incomprehensible and inscrutable creature. Conceived thus, the dragon cannot be a meaningful symbol for communication. It does not generate any motivation for meaningful participation and creative action in building a community and developing a country. Furthermore, we shall suggest a people's symbol for the Chinese heritage to take the place of the symbol of the dragon: The Chinese story of the hero combating the flood waters could provide the basis of a relevant and meaningful symbol for the Chinese people of Hong Kong.

In reassessing the theological symbol of the dragon, we discover that in the Bible the dragon is a symbol of the sea/water monster or chaos creature that constantly threatens God's created order. According to the Ancient Near Eastern myth of creation, the creator-god fought against the dragon during the creation and has been fighting it ever since in order to maintain the cosmic and social order. The Bible adopts this myth to describe Yahweh's creativity. The study of the dragon symbol in this article will therefore naturally lead us to the battle between God and the sea monster. Similarly, the study of the story of Yu the Great, the hero who controlled the great flood water, is significant in doing Chinese theology in relation to people's symbols and images.

The Chinese Dragon Myth

The Chinese dragon is a legendary and fabulous creature of serpentine shape. Like its counterpart, the *naga* in Indian culture, it is a rain-bringing, beneficent deity with affinity to water.[2] It is regarded as a spirit of the waters or a water-god who, being associated with clouds and rain, blesses the parched earth with water. The author of the *Book of Chou Rites* (Chou Li), when speaking about painting and embroidering, comments that "water is represented by means of the dragon,"[3] and the commentator Chao P'uh of the Song Dynasty explains the line as follows: "The dragon is a divine being that dwells in the water. If one represents water without the dragon, there is nothing to show the divinity of the phenomenon."[4]

Since the need for water is primary among agricultural peoples for irrigation, the ancient Chinese people worshiped this water deity, who is believed to mount up to heaven and cause the rain to fall. There are records of the ritual performed by the people for praying to the dragon for rain.[5]

The dragon can become visible or invisible and has the ability to assume many different forms. Hsu Shen, in his classical work on the origin and meaning of Chinese words, has this to say about the dragon: "Senior among the scaled creatures, capable of occultation, capable of illumination, capable of slimness — capable of hugeness, capable of contraction — capable of extension. It climbs to the sky at spring's equinox. It plunges in the gulf at fall's equinox."[6]

This mutability of form, so characteristic of the dragon, makes it mysterious and inscrutable.[7] But this feature of variability and transforming power may provide an appropriate symbol of self-understanding for the Chinese people in Hong Kong. Historically they have demonstrated their strength of adaptability and their flexibility in industrial and commercial development. Hong Kong society has undergone rapid socio-economic changes and technological development. Yet it remains to be seen whether the challenge of the future and political changes of 1997 will be met by the people, who are supported by their considerable ability to adapt to new situations and cope with hardship.

Looking at any drawing of the dragon, one is often struck by the composite nature of this fabulous creature. It is well known that the dragon has nine components:

The horns of a deer
The head of a camel
The eyes of a devil
The body of a fish
The neck of a snake
The scales of a carp

The claws of an eagle
The palms of a tiger
The ears of a cow.[8]

Such a composite creature does not have a pleasant appearance, nor does it show any individual character. In addition the dragon does not give any impression of willingness to establish personal relationship with human beings. As a creature of the imagination, it conveys a kind of cold and distant feeling. It is a horrible creature, probably of sea-serpent[9] origin. One wonders whether it is really liked by people. In this respect a story can be cited to illustrate one attitude toward the dragon:

> Lord Ye was well known for his fondness of dragons. Dragons were painted on the walls and carved on the pillars of his house. In a word, he had dragons everywhere. Once, when a real dragon in heaven heard how much Lord Ye loved its kind, it flew down to his house. It struck its head through the southern window and coiled its tail around to the northern window. When Lord Ye saw this dragon, he shivered from head to toe and quickly hid himself away.[10]

From this incident, we can see that what Lord Ye appreciated was fake dragons painted on walls and carved on pillars, and not real dragons at all.

Another limitation of the symbol is that it represents the imperial authority, the unlimited and ever-expanding power of the emperor, who demanded absolute obedience and total submission from the people. Since the emperor was regarded as the lion of heaven and believed to be the incarnation of the dragon,[11] the people were expected to rely on his good will and were totally at his mercy. Even though it has been decades since the Chinese monarchy was overthrown in 1911, the dragon as an imperial symbol still remains alive today.

The symbol reminds people of the glorious past and a static society with fixed and assigned roles. It helps to nurture a complacent, conservative, and self-centered people with a parochial and arrogant attitude towards the outside world, combined with a mentality of servitude towards political leaders and patriarchal figures.[12] If the aim of Chinese society is to achieve modernization in its political structure, economic system, and cultural heritage, the Chinese people must overcome these limitations and be emancipated to take the future in their hands, to create a bright future through creative participation.

The Dragon-Serpent in the Bible

> In that day God shall bring his holy and great and strong sword upon the dragon, even the serpent that flees, upon the dragon, the crooked serpent he shall destroy the dragon (Isa. 27:1).

This passage is taken from the apocalyptic section (chapters 24–27) of Isaiah. The translation is based on the Septuagint (LXX), the earliest Greek version of the Old Testament. How did the first Chinese Christians react to such a passage? The God introduced by the missionaries was a slayer of the dragon, which, in the mind of the Chinese, was a beneficent being worshiped by many ordinary people and the emblem of their emperor.

There were devout missionaries who were either ignorant of the Chinese culture or who were simply of the conviction that the Chinese dragon symbol and myth were evil. They set upon themselves the "holy" task of destroying everything associated with dragons. I had a shattering experience of this denial of culture in Christian teaching put into action. At the time when my family, who were living in mainland China, became Christian, I still remember that the pastor and the "army" of Christians of the church marched to our house to demand that all art and literature and household items including furniture, bedding, bowls, and chopsticks that bore the dragon image be surrendered and then destroyed — that, is burned completely in front of the house. What a drama! These "Christian soldiers" won a triumphant battle in destroying the symbol of the dragon that once represented blessing and good omen in the culture of the new converts but which was regarded as evil and superstitious in the Western Christian teaching of that time.

To understand how the dragon symbol became the center of this battle, we must go back to the passage cited at the beginning of this section. In the Septuagint, the Greek word for "dragon" is used to translate a number of Hebrew words. In that passage the first two appearances of dragon have "Leviathan" as their Hebrew origin. The King James Version, Revised Standard Version, and New English Bible do not translate but transliterate the Hebrew word, probably because the passage itself has qualifying phrases to introduce Leviathan: "piercing serpent" (KJV; RSV has "fleeing serpent"; NEB has "twisting serpent") and "crooked serpent" (KJV; RSV has "twisting serpent"; NEB has "writhing serpent"). Moreover, in the Septuagint, "dragon" also translates the word *naha* ("serpent") in two other passages (Job 26:13; Amos 9:3).[13]

In Isaiah 27:1 the third dragon is *tannin* in Hebrew. RSV uses *serpent* (Exod. 7:9, 10, 12; Deut. 32:33; Ps. 91:13; 104:7, "dragon" in KJV), "sea monster" (Job 7:12, "whale" in KJV, Ps. 148:7, "dragon" in KJV) and "dragon" (Ps. 74:13) to render the word "dragon" found in the Septuagint.

On the whole, the word "dragon" is less often used in modern translations than in older versions, still less often in KJV than in the LXX, and less again in the RSV than in KJV. NEB usually replaces the "dragon" of the RSV with "sea monster" (Ps. 74:13) and "monster" (Isa. 27:1; Ezek. 29:3), except in Isaiah 51:9, where "dragon" is retained, and in Jeremiah 51:34, where strangely NEB replaces RSV's "monster" with "dragon."

Most of the modern Chinese versions have already eliminated all the words for "dragon" from the Old Testament. The commonly used Union Chinese Version, unfortunately, uses "alligator" for "Leviathan" and "big fish" or "serpent" for *tannin*,[14] and only *Lu's Translation* and *Today's Chinese Version* (1978) correctly render these beasts in the ancient Near East and the Bible as "sea monster," except in Isaiah 27:1 and Jeremiah 51:34. But all the above modern versions, both in English and Chinese, still consistently translate the dragon in the Book of Revelation as "dragon." Only *Today's Chinese Version* attempts to qualify the dragon by the perverse "dragon" (Rev. 12:3, 4, 7, 9, 13, 16, 17; 13:2, 4, 11; 16:13, 20:2).

To sum up, the "dragon-serpent" in the Bible has nothing to do with the Chinese *lung*. The former is the great sea monster in the mythology of the Ancient Near

East, which is a symbol of chaos and evil. It is presented as the opponent of the creator-god in the context of creation theology.

Creation: God's Battle against the Sea Monster

The "dragon-serpent" or "sea monster" in the Bible is mentioned primarily in connection with the creativity of God. It is personified as the chaos monster, which opposes the creator-god as his enemy.[15] It bears such different names as Rahab, Leviathan, Tehom, Tannin, Yam, or Nahar.

The Ancient Near East expresses the concept of creation in myth, which in Babylonia takes the form of Marduk's battle against Tiamat ("the deep") and in Canaan of Baal's battle with, and victory over, the chaos monster, Yam ("the sea") and Nahar ("the river"). Similar understanding of creation can be detected in the Bible. Psalm 74 embodies such a myth of creation:

> But thou, O God, thou king of old,
>   thou mighty conqueror all the world over,
> by thy power thou didst cleave the sea-monster (*yam*) in two
>   and break the sea-serpent's (*tannin*) heads above the waters;
>   thou didst crush Leviathan's many heads
>   and throw him to the sharks for food. . . .
>
> The day is thine, and the night is thine also,
> thou didst ordain the light of moon and sun;
>   thou hast fixed all the regions of the earth;
> summer and winter, thou didst create them both.
> (Ps. 74:12–14, 16–17, NEB)

The myth of God's battles with the sea monster, the sea serpent, and Leviathan represents " 'creation' in the sense of sustaining the created world against the threats of the chaos power."[16] Creation is then seen not so much in the cosmological sense as the founding of the physical world, but more significantly in the sociopolitical sense as the formation and maintenance of the human world. It expresses a process from "a state of social disorganization because of undertrained forces to structure and security in Yahweh's land" and an interest in "the emergence of a particular society, organized with patron gods and worship systems, divinely appointed king (or some other kind of leader), and kinship systems." The primeval forces of disorder and chaos, which were the opponents of the creator-god, could at any time find embodiment in history, in political oppression or economic exploitation. They threaten God's creation, and therefore it is God's task to check, eliminate, and destroy them so as to maintain the sociopolitical order.[17]

It is no wonder in the Old Testament that the description of Yahweh's victory over the chaos monster is immediately followed by Yahweh's saving deeds in history. Historical events are expressed in terms of mythological language, and creation myths are historicized. In Psalm 74, the crushing of the heads of the sea-serpent and Leviathan (vv. 13–14) is preceded and followed by an allusion to the division of the sea (v. 13) and the river (v. 15). The crossing of the Reed Sea is explicitly alluded to in Psalm 77:19–20:

> Thy path was through the sea, thy way through mighty waters...
>> Thou didst guide thy people like a flock of sheep,
>>> under the hand of Moses and Aaron. (NEB)

Deutero-Isaiah provides the best example of using the creation battle theme in the context of the concrete historical situation. The mythic-primeval is integrated with the historical-existential:

> Awake, awake, put on strength,
>> O arm of the LORD;
> awake, as in days of old,
>> the generations of long ago.
> Was it not thou that didst cut Rahab in pieces,
>> that didst pierce the dragon (*tannin*)?
> Was it not thou that didst dry up the sea (*yam*),
>> the waters of the great deep (*tehon*);
> that didst make the depths of the sea (*yam*) a way
>> for the redeemed to pass over?
> And the ransomed of the LORD shall return
>> and come to Zion with singing;
> everlasting joy shall be upon their heads;
>> they shall obtain joy and gladness,
>> and sorrow and sighing shall flee away. (Isa. 51:9–11, RSV)

In the Ancient Near East, the creator-god, Marduk or Baal, after achieving his creation battle over the chaos monster, is acclaimed king. Such an understanding is also expressed in the "enthronement psalms" (Ps. 47, 93, 95–99), and it forms the climax of the Song at the Sea (Exod. 15:18): "The Lord shall reign forever and ever."

As king, the creator-god Yahweh establishes his throne on the foundation of justice and righteousness (Ps. 89:14). He enters into a covenant with his people, whom he calls into being by his saving deeds, and chooses the earthly king as his son (Ps. 2:7) and his first-born (Ps. 89:26–27). The role of kingship is then properly understood in terms of maintaining the order of righteousness and justice (Ps. 72:1–4). The duty of his covenant people is to uphold that order by doing justice and practicing righteousness. In this respect, it is clear that the theology of creation in the Old Testament is actually "a theology of ordering,"[18] and it is exactly such a theology that is relevant to the people of Hong Kong in their strife for a brighter future and their quest for participation in molding that future.

Theology of Chaos Management (Ordering) and the Chinese Flood Story

In this section I want to propose that a theology of creation originating from the Old Testament can be formulated and then constructed with Chinese symbols.

It has been shown on the one hand that the creation myth in the Old Testament presupposes the existence of the dragon serpent or the sea monster, which is a personified chaos monster; and, on the other hand, the Chinese do not perceive chaos or evil in the dragon symbol at all.

With this as the point of departure, we shall explore what Chinese people regard as most fearsome and terrifying. What immediately comes to mind is *hongshui-mengshou,* "fierce floods and savage beasts," which can be traced back to Mencius:

> The world has existed for a long time, now in peace, now in disorder. In the time of Yao, the water reversed its natural course, flooding the central regions, and the reptiles made their homes there, depriving the people of a settled life. In low-lying regions, people lived in nests; in high regions, they lived in caves. The book of history says, "The Deluge was a warning to us."
>
> By the Deluge was meant the Flood. Yu was entrusted with the task of controlling it. He led the flood water into the seas by cutting channels for it in the ground, and drove the reptiles into grassy marshes. The water, flowing through the channels, formed the Yangtse, the Huai, the Yellow River, and the Han. Obstacles receded, and the birds and beasts harmful to humans were annihilated. Only then were the people able to level the ground and live on it.[19]

The flood is one of the earliest and the most popular of all the mythological themes in ancient China. The story itself is not homogeneous; traces of it appear in the Chou literature of *Shih Ching* (*The Book of Songs*) and *Shu Ching* (*The Book of History*) and extensively in later writings.[20] The hero who conquered the great flood waters was Yu the Great, believed to be the founder and so the first emperor of the Hsia dynasty (2783–1751 B.C.).

There are tales that attribute the success of Yu's saving of China from the great terrible deluge, which had ravaged it for nine or ten years, to Yu's intensive labor and hard work. The story has it that he even passed the door of his house several times without sparing the time to visit his family.[21] Yu was assisted by a winged dragon that used its tail to mark on the ground places where channels could be dug to drain the disastrous flood waters. T'ien Wen of the *Songs of the South* (Chu Tzu) presents the tradition in the form of a series of questions:

> How did he fill the flood waters up where they were most deep?
> How did he set bounds to the nine lands of the earth?
> What did the winged dragon trace on the ground?
> Where did the seas and rivers flow?
> What did Kun labor on, and what did Yu accomplish?[22]

What did Yu accomplish? Hsun Tze praises Yu's contribution in terms of his freeing the people from the evil of Kung-kung, the horned, serpent-like water monster.[23] In *Shan Hai Ching* there is recorded a version of Yu slaying the minister of Kung-kung, Xiang-liu, the nine-headed, human-face and snake-body monster.[24]

These fragmentary pieces of legends show that Yu had to fight against the serpent-like water deity or monster. In his draining the great flood water to the sea, Yu also expelled wild animals, harmful snakes, and dragons from the land so as to prepare the ground for cultivation.[25]

Yu's task was twofold: conquering the flood waters and expelling wild beasts. The outcome of his success was an ordered society and a settled agricultural life for the people. As in the Ancient Near East, Yu was also awarded kingship to rule the land. What Yu achieves is creation in the biblical sense of reducing chaos to order, as well as founding and managing the sociopolitical and economic order of the Hsia dynasty.

Ku Chieh-kang and T'ung Shu-yeh have convincingly argued that Yu was a divine being under the commission of the Lord on High to conquer the flood waters.[26] Historical events were later "created" and piled up on him, making him the sage-king after the great Yao and Shun. Yu was praised together with T'ang, Wen, and Wu as the sons of heaven who were obedient to the will of heaven. All of them were enriched and awarded with the heritage of the empire.[27] Derk Bodde concludes from his studies that "the intense historical-mindedness of the Chinese" and "their tendency to reject supernatural explanations for the universe — caused them to 'humanize' or 'euhemerize' much of what had originally been myth into what came to be accepted as authentic history."[28]

The flood story of Yu, having "the greatest hold on the Chinese consciousness,"[29] can contribute to the formulation of a Chinese theology of creation in terms of ordering and managing the human world. Many ancient philosophers and teachers have made reference to it in their writings. A few selected short quotations from the major works will illustrate its significant role in the mind of the Chinese.

The Book of Songs[30]

Yes, [all about] that southern hill was made manageable by Yu.

The Fung-water flowed on to the east [of the city], through the meritorious labor of Yu.

Very grand is the mountain of Leang, which was made cultivable by Yu.

When the waters of the deluge spread vast abroad, Yu arranged and divided the regions of the land, and assigned to the exterior great states their boundaries.

The Book of History[31]

Yu reduced to order the waters and the land, and presided over the naming of hills and rivers.

To him Heaven gave the Great Plan with its nine divisions and the unvarying principles of its method were set forth in their due order.

The Analects of Confucius[32]

> Yu and Chi, who devoted themselves to agriculture, came into possession of all that is under Heaven.

Tso Chuen[33]

> Wide and long Yu travelled about, when the nine regions he laid out, and through them led the nine-fold route. The people then safe homes possessed.

> "How admirable," said the viscount of Lew, "was the merit of Yu! His intelligent virtue reached far. But for Yu, we should have been fishes. That you and I manage the business of the princes in our caps and robes is all owing to Yu."

Chuang Tzu[34]

> In ancient time, when Yu dammed the flood waters and opened up the courses of the Yangtze and the Yellow River so that they flowed through the lands of the four barbarians and the nine provinces, joining with the three hundred famous rivers, their three thousand tributaries, and the little streams too numerous to count — he worked to establish the ten thousand states.

As quoted above and also in many more allusions to Yu, his combating the chaos and establishing order is a powerful symbol for the Chinese people in their participation in creating the future. The symbol of the dragon reminds us of our cultural heritage, whose decendents we are. The symbol of Yu motivates us to do what we ought to do. It also invites us to identify with Yu, as remarked by someone at the time of Hsun Tze: "The man in the street can become a Yu. How about this?" To this Hsun Tze gave a positive answer that every human being in the street can become a potential Yu.[35]

Notes

1. Ssu-ma Ch'ien, *Shih Chi* (Peking: Chung Hua Shu Chiu, 1959) vol. 7, p. 2140. The translation is taken from D. C. Lau, "Introduction," *Tao Te Ching* (Hong Kong: The Chinese University Press, 1982), p. x. Chuang Tzu recorded a similar story of Confucius' meeting with Lao Tzu; see Herbert A. Giles, *Chuang Tzu: Taoist Philosopher and Chinese Mystic* (London: George Allen & Unwin Ltd., 1926), pp. 148–49.

2. On the *naga* in Buddhism see the entry on *lung, Encyclopedia of Buddhism* (1984), pp. 1362–64. M. W. de Visser has shown that the Indian serpent-shaped *naga* exerted its influence on the Chinese dragon through the introduction of Buddhism to China, *The Dragon in China and Japan* (Freundlich genehmigter Neudruck der Ausgabe von 1913, reprinted 1969), pp. 21–25. E. T. C. Wermer says that the evil dragons found in a number of stories are those introduced by the Buddhists. The harmful dragons are associated with mountains. See his *Myth and Legends in China* (London: George G. Harrap and Co. Ltd., 1922), pp. 208–35.

3. Cheng Hsuan, *Chou Li, Cheng Shi Chu,* Section Tung Kwan, chap. 12.

4. The saying from Chou Li and the commentary from Chao P'uh are translated by M. W. de Visser and quoted from his book, p. 41.

5. Henry Doré, S.J., *Researches into Chinese Superstitions* (Shanghai: T'usewei Printing Press, 1918; Taipei: Ch'engwen Publishing Co., 1966), vol. IV–V, pp. 685–90. Marcel Granet, *The Religion of the Chinese People* (Oxford: Basil Blackwell, 1975), pp. 55–56. Jorge Luis Borges says, "Popular imagination links the dragon to clouds, to the rainfall needed by farmers, and to great rivers." *The Book of Imaginary Beings* (Penguin Books, 1974), p. 43.

6. Tuan Yu-ts'ai, *Shou Wen Chieh Tzu Chu* (Hong Kong: I Wen Publishing Co., 1966), chap. 11, pt. 2, p. 588. The English translation is taken from E. H. Schafer, *The Divine Woman* (Berkeley: University of California Press, 1973), p. 15. The word "equinox" in this translation is a substitute for the word "division" in Schafer's translation.

7. The dragon can be good and evil and can also be of all sizes and colors. See further, Laurence Binyon, "A Study of Chinese Symbolism," *Symbolism of Chinese Imperial Ritual Robes* (London: The China Institute, 1939), p. 16.

8. Lists with slight variations can be found in Henry Doré, p. 53 (the eyes of a rabbit as an alternative to the devil's eyes); Jorge Luis Borges, p. 53 (belly of a clam instead of the body of a fish); Paul Newman, *The Hill of the Dragon* (Bath: Kingsmead Press, 1979), p. 99.

9. On the origin of the dragon, there are various opinions. Many believe that it was a huge alligator or sea-snake. Yuan De-sing asserts that the dragon originates from the decorated snake for cultic purposes. "The Dragon in Art Designs from the Pre-Historic and Shang-Chou Periods," *The Dragon of the Imperial Palace* (Taipei: National Museum Publication, 1978), pp. 27–52.

10. Taken from *One Hundred Allegorical Tales from Traditional China,* trans. Jan & Yvonne Walls (Hong Kong: Joint Publishing Co., 1985), p. 49. I replaced Lord Ye for "Lord She" in the translated text.

11. C. K. Yang, *Religion in Chinese Society* (Berkeley: University of California Press, 1961), pp. 128–29. See also Laurence Binyon, p. 15.

12. There are a few short articles in Hong Kong Chinese monthly magazines around the time of Chinese Lunar New Year 1983: Qi Xin, "Be Not the Dragon's Heir," *The Ninety's,* 1983, monthly, 228: 14–16; Dai Qing, "Legal System, Not Modern Totemism — Interview with Mr. Yan Ziaqi," *Mingbao,* 1988, monthly, 268: 12–14.

13. The word "dragon" is also used to translate *tannin* ("serpent") in Exod. 7:9, 10, 12; Deut. 32:33; Ps. 91:13, 148:7; Jer. 51:34; and K pir ("young lion") in Job 4:10; 38:39; and even "he-goats" (Jer. 50:8) and "asps" (Jer. 20:16).

14. The Catholic Chinese Version still renders *tannin* by the "dragon" (Jer. 51:34), "the poisonous dragon" (Ps. 74:13, 91:13), "the flying dragon" (Job 26:13), "the flood water dragon" (Isa. 27:1; Amos 9:3), and "the monstrous dragon."

15. Benedikt Otzen, "The Concept of Myth," *Myth in the Old Testament,* ed. B. Otzen, Hans Gottlieb, and Knud Jeppersen (London: SCM Press, 1980), p. 67.

16. Hans Gottlieb, "Myth in the Psalms," *Myth in the Old Testament,* p. 68.

17. Richard J. Clifford, S.J., "The Hebrew Scriptures and the Theology of Creation," *Theological Studies* 46, 1985, p. 510.

18. Hans Heinrich Schmid, "Creation, Righteousness and Salvation: Creation Theology as the Broad Horizon of Biblical Theology," *Creation in the Old Testament,* ed. B. W. Anderson (Philadelphia: Fortress Press, 1984), p. 104.

19. D. C. Lau, trans., *Mencius* (Middlesex: Penguin Books, 1970), p. 113.

20. For a brief account of the outline of the story, see Derk Bodde, "Myths of Ancient China," *Mythologies of the Ancient World,* ed. S. N. Kramer (Garden City: Doubleday & Co., 1961), pp. 398–403.

21. On praising the hard work of Yu, see *The Complete Works of Han Fei Tzu,* trans. W. K. Liao (London: Arthur Probsthain, 1959), chap. 49, pp. 275–76; and Confucius, *The Analects,* trans. D. C. Lau (Hong Kong: The Chinese University Press, 1983), p. 75. See also Fung Yu-lan, *A History of Chinese Philosophy,* vol. 1 (Princeton: Princeton University Press, 1952), p. 239.

22. "T'ien Wen (The Heavenly Questions)," Ch'u Tz'u, *The Songs of the South* (Oxford: Clarendon Press, 1959), p. 48. Kun from whose belly Yu was born was punished and executed by the Lord in heaven for his theft of the "swelling mold" — "a magical kind of soil which had the property of ever swelling in size." He used the soil to build dams to hold back the flood waters. Derk Bodde, p. 399.

23. Liang Ch'i-hsiung, *A Brief Commentary on Hsun-Tzu* (Hong Kong: Chung Hwa Publishing Co., 1974), pp. 201, 348.

24. Yuan K'o, *Commentary on Shan Hai Ching* (Shanghai: Classic Press, 1980), p. 233. Kung-kung was euhemerized in Chou texts as a human "rebel" but in late Han writings described as a horned monster with serpent's body; see Derk Bodde, p. 387. In another late writing, *Taiping Guanchi,* Yu is reported to have captured another water monster. Yuan K'o, *Commentary on Selected Ancient Myths* (Peking: People's Literature Publishing, 1979), pp. 306–9.

25. Derk Bodde, p. 400.

26. Ku Chieh-kang and T'ung Shu-yeh, "The Legend of Kun and Yu," *Critiques of Ancient History,* vol. 7, part 11 (Shanghai: Classic Press, 1982), pp. 142–72.

27. Burton Watson, trans., *Mo Tzu, Basic Writings* (New York: Columbia University Press, 1963), pp. 78–83. Fung Y'u-lan, vol. 1, no. 96–97.

28. Derk Bodde, p. 403.

29. Ibid., p. 404.

30. James Legge, trans., *The Chinese Classics: The She King* (London: Oxford University Press, 1939), pp. 373 (Part II Book VI 6), 462 (Part III Book II 10), 546 (Part III Book III 7), 638–39 (Part IV Book III 4).

31. Clae Waltham, *Shu Ching, Book of History* (A modernized edition of the translations of James Legge) (Chicago: Henry Regnery Co., 1971), p. 231 ("The Marquis of Lu on Punishment") and p. 126 ("The Great Plan").

32. Arthur Waley, trans., *The Analects of Confucius* (London: George Allen and Unwin, 1938), p. 181 (Book XIV 6). By his effort to drain the land, Yu made the land suitable for agriculture. Chu or Hou Chi is the ancestor of the Chou people and the patron deity of agriculture.

33. James Legge, trans., *The Chinese Classics: The Ch'un Ts'en with the Tso Chuen* (London: Oxford University Press, 1939), pp. 424, 571.

34. Burton Watson, trans., *The Complete Works of Chuang Tzu* (New York: Columbia University Press, 1968), p. 366 (chap. 33, the world).

35. Homer H. Dubs, trans., *The Works of Hsuntze* (Taipei: Ch'eng-wen Publishing Co., 1966), p. 312 (chap. 23, "The Nature of Man is Evil"). See also Fung Yu-lan, vol. 1, p. 287.

Chapter 9

Wrestling in the Night

SAMUEL RAYAN

The rabbis of old used to say that the best commentary on any verse is another verse. The article reproduced here goes beyond this hermeneutical axiom and juxtaposes in an imaginative way three textual traditions, two ancient and one modern, but more significantly it brings together three different faith adherents — a Jew, a Hindu, and a Muslim. What is remarkable about this essay is that, in spite of the time span and different religious orientations, Job, Arjuna, and Gítánjali testify that sorrow and pain are universal. All three in their different ways wrestle with death, life, and God, and through sorrow and pain, grow in faith and love.

Samuel Rayan, a Jesuit, has established himself as a well-known theologian and much loved poet and often sought-after spiritual guide. He has written prolifically both in English and in his mother tongue, Malayalam. His writings reveal a harmonious combination of praxis and reflection, of contemplation and action.

Source: *The Future of Liberation Theology: Essays in Honor of Gustavo Gutiérrez*, Marc H. Ellis and Otto Maduro, eds. (Maryknoll, N.Y.: Orbis Books, 1989).

Reading Gustavo Gutiérrez's fine work *On Job*,[1] I became aware that several of its leading themes and emphases were, time and again, meeting, mingling, and parting in my mind with kindred concerns and accents of two other cherished works: the Bhagavadgítá (Gítá)[2] and the *Poems of Gítánjali* (*Poems*).[3] The Gítá is a sacred text, a poem, a dialogue, like the book of Job, and ancient, too; it is Job's near contemporary, being probably younger than Job by a century or two. The *Poems*, however, are quite recent and are not particularly sacred or religious though deeply human and spiritual. The author of the *Poems* was a schoolgirl who died of cancer soon after her sixteenth birthday; the authors of the other two poetic colloquies were, we may surmise, women or men of mature years, skilled in all the sophistication of philosophical theories and theological debates. The cultural and religious differences among the three works are deep. All the more remarkable is the overlapping of so many of their stresses, the coincidence of the spirit they breathe, and the convergence of their ultimate thrust.

Word of God

All three works represent our pursuit of God and God's pursuit of us through the tangled web of our painful, conflict-ridden, historical existence. Not only pursuit but struggle and wrestling of the human and the divine: wrestling in the night; wrestling with nameless, unnameable mystery, which in the end leaves us "dislocated," renamed, blessed, and equipped to face the world and build a future (see Genesis 32). All three works open on a scene of perplexity and pain with which it is hard to come to terms. Job is full of lament and rebellion; Arjuna of the Gítá raises questions and breaks down in anguish; Gítánjali too has some sharp whys, though she clothes her protests and laments in gentle trust. In all three works the sufferer finally stands face-to-face with God and finds peace or meaning or the strength to act and to endure not in intellectual and reasoned answers to questions posed by the critical mind but in direct spiritual experience that we can only describe as mystical. In each case the encounter is mediated by nothing but the clarity of intense innocent suffering or of dawning conversion. In each case, the new experience tends to subvert traditional positions in theology and piety.

In the Book of Job God speaks from the heart of the storm; God speaks only in response to Job's demands — and that, at the close of a lengthy debate among friends. In the Gítá, God (Krishna) takes the initiative and sustains the dialogue from start to finish. The use of dialogue to express and convey a spiritual experience is itself highly significant. Dialogue is not only a literary form but responds to the inner structure of spiritual experience, which at its higher reaches is interpersonal exchange, the weaving of a relationship in partnership between God and human beings. In the *Poems* it is only the young poet who sings her sad songs, but many a line is prayer directed to God or to loved ones; and it is not hard to discern behind the songs, within the songs, the answering, the prompting, the enabling voice of God.

Common to all three is a sense of the overwhelming gratuitousness of God's love and the call to respond, or actual response, in selfless concern for God, for God's project for the world, for God's people, for God's earth and ours. In each case disinterested faith and love are shown as correlates of God's gracious love made manifest in creation and, mysteriously, in history — even in the history of painful reeducation and testing by fire. There is in every case a distinct journey from despondency to joyful living or dying; from preoccupation with the ego to other-centeredness; from *dharma* (righteousness) as traditional way of life to *dharma* as innovative collaboration with God's love-designs and best wishes for our world; and from narrow individual or group interest to concern for the welfare of the world as a whole and of every created reality.

We cannot but take the three testimonies together. The voice of the great sufferers and questioners of ancient Israel has become our inheritance within the movement stemming from a unique Israelite, Jesus of Nazareth. The testimony also of the seekers, seers, and fighters of old who originated and molded India's culture and spirituality holds and nourishes some of the deepest roots of our life. And the witness of our simple and strong sisters and brothers like Gítánjali releases into the strife and confusion of our history a clarity and hope and faith from which we are able to live. The three words belong together and become God's word addressed to us and our community here and now, judging and gracing us, and challenging us to be creative and free for one another.

Job

Believing for Nothing

Gustavo Gutiérrez starts his reflections from the wager on which, from a literary standpoint, the Book of Job rests. The wager concerns the reality, even the possibility, of disinterested faith in God and love for God. The position of the satan is that religion is mercenary. Persons believe because believing pays and not because they view God as worthy *in se* of love and following. In human eyes God's worth lies in the wealth and welfare God can and does bestow. God is "buying" devotees and so gaining a foothold in human history. Should the flow of wealth and well-being cease, God would be discarded and religion would wither away. Such is the satan's estimate of human beings and of God.

God's estimate of human beings is different. Even God can be proud of human beings. They have in them enough of nobility and greatness to be able to "believe for nothing," to love disinterestedly, to live sacrificially, to be faithful to God and neighbor even in the midst of dispossession, ruin, and pain. Of this, Job is illustration and proof. God made the bet with the satan, and in Job human beings won it for God. There is a proud revelation of the human in that "the satan has lost his wager...for Job continues to cling to the Lord in his suffering even when he comes close to despair."[4] Gutiérrez concurs with the revolutionary conclusion of the author of Job that there is something shallow, debasing, demonic about a utilitarian religion in which faith and behavior hinge on expectation of reward. In self-seeking religion, all the relationships are vitiated; there is in it the construction of an idol instead of an encounter with God.[5] It leads to "contempt for human beings and a distorted understanding of God."[6] This point, debated in the subsequent dialogue in Job, will be treated at length with great subtlety in the Bhagavadgítá.

Job's painful journey, traced through the dialogues, lands him and us on a host of problems and many discoveries. Suffering of the innocent raises the problem of justice, which is basically a problem of God and of faith in God. Instead of rejecting God as torturer of the innocent, Job challenges the foundations of the prevailing theology of retribution. Eventually he comes to see that "if justice is to be understood in its full meaning and scope, it must be set in the context of God's overall plan for history."[7] This is a perspective to which careful attention and elaboration are accorded in the Gítá. When Job found that his experience at once of innocence and of suffering contradicted the doctrine of retribution, "he had the courage to face up to this contradiction and to proclaim it for all to hear." He rejected both the traditionally and officially upheld moral order and the God who was alleged to be its ground and guarantor.[8] His cry and quest is for a new image of God and a new language. Our cry and quest today is no different.

Shifts

In the process, a number of mental and spiritual shifts occur.

1. Job moves "from an ethic centered on personal rewards" to "another focused on the needs (and, we may add, the further possibilities) of one's neighbor."[9]

2. Along with that goes widening of concern and an expansion of the spirit when attention shifts from personal pain to the wretched condition of the vast masses of the oppressed of the land.

3. As a result, the conviction deepens that "real belief in God entails solidarity with the poor so as to ease their undeserved suffering by establishing 'uprightness and judgment.'" To go out of oneself, laying aside one's own problems and pain, in order to liberate and lift up other sufferers is "to find a way to God" and to a new language about God.[10] Gustavo makes the significant point that "vision of God . . . and defense of the poor . . . are combined in the experience of Job as a man of justice. They are two aspects of a single gift from the Lord and a single road that leads to the Lord."[11]

4. Once the truth is grasped that the suffering of the poor is not caused by God but by the wicked, the rich, and the exploiter, the whole argument takes a new turn. God is no longer the accused; God is seen as the challenger of the wicked rich, as the friend of the poor, and as an imperative of justice for the oppressed.

5. With that Job is able to transcend "a penal view of history" and finds himself enfolded in a world of grace. There unfolds a surpriseful awareness that the meaning of justice overflows its legal and prophetic definitions. Justice is far richer and more profound than retribution. Justice must be seen as situated within the framework of God's gratuitous love. May we hold, then, that it is love and not justice that has the final say?[12] We must be careful not to suggest a dichotomy and distance between love and justice. Justice remains crucial because it is love's basic form and prime imperative. In a situation of oppression, God cannot be revealed except as a call for and practice of justice and a clear option for the oppressed.

6. Perception of this unbreakable link between justice and love is a step toward recognition of the utter freedom of God, who cannot be shackled by anything, not even by our ethics and theologies of justice,[13] but can be encountered only within the practice of justice and loving relationships. That means concern for justice will unfold into contemplation of God's gratuitous love and abounding tenderness, which provide justice with its true horizons, reference points, and depths of meaning. The justice of God is God's love that gives and forgives endlessly. Among such gifts are opportunities and challenges, at times painful and mysterious, to grow to the Everest possibilities of the human heart — opportunities of the kind offered to Job and to Jesus.

7. One aspect of this growth is the insight that there is more to creation and God's ways than to serve human utility; not everything is for direct human use and control. Much in creation is God's freedom, God's joy, God's *leela* or play, as we would say in India. Nature is not all consumer goods or merchandise. Much of it

is art, and its meaning is contemplation through which nature becomes we and us become it.[14]

8. There is, then, the experience of growth from lament and bitter questioning to an attitude of wonder, worship, silence, and surrender. In the end, is Job renouncing his "lamentations and dejected outlook" rather than repenting of his rash questioning, as Gutiérrez suggests?[15] Why does his encounter with God not culminate in an ecstatic song of joy and praise as Arjuna's encounter does in the Bhagavadgítá?

9. That song is perhaps implied in Job's passage from a faith based on hearsay, dogmatic traditions, and external authorities to a faith based on direct engagement with the mystery of the Divine. The passage from ideas of God and pieties, gathered from conventions and fashioned in times of well-being, to others, springing from new spaces in the soul carved out by suffering, is big surely with songs of joy yet unsung.

Method

As we listen to Job and his friends, "it becomes clear that we are in the presence of two types of theological reasoning." Job's friends "take certain principles as their starting point and try to apply them to Job's case." Their method is a priori, doctrinal, abstract. Job, on the other hand, starts from the concrete reality of his experience, which he finds subversive of abstract principles. Gutiérrez emphasizes:

> Job's words are a criticism of every theology that lacks human compassion and contact with reality; the one-directional movement from theological principles to life really goes nowhere. A quest for understanding that is based on human and religious experience gives a glimpse of other ways of speaking (and keeping silent) about God.[16]

Within the experience-based approach itself, two phases may be distinguished. They mark Job's theological journey. The first phase raises questions, seeks to criticize and to unravel, to speak and to formulate. It then deepens into the second phase, which is one of contemplation, adoration, and silence. At this stage we live gently with questions to which no answers are available; the questions are no longer experienced as painful, nagging, or imperious because they have become reset within a larger horizon of mystery, which is best approached in worship and wonder and expressed in the language of doxology rather than that of dogma. The questions have become cherished symbols of our creaturely finiteness, the frontiers where we are unceasingly loved into being. We are happy that the God we adore is greater than our heart, our theology, and our church. We are glad we can sit in silence and joy over the unspeakable pressure of the real upon our heart. Apophatic theology is welcomed back. Our ancestors, the seers and *Rishis,* faced with the real beyond name and form, kept repeating *Neti Neti (na iti, na iti),* "Not thus, Not thus," but always other and greater, and greater still.

Job wrestled with himself and with unmerited suffering. He wrestled with his own theological convictions and their God as these were being undermined by his personal experience and the history of the oppressed masses. He wrestled with the God of his faith until, beyond the conventional conceptions of justice, he came to see the truth of the wonder of God's freedom and capacity for love — a love that is not shallow or sentimental but strong enough to put God's friends and God's children through tests like those that Job and Jesus underwent in order to foster what is most human and noble in them, what is unconditionally faithful and selfless. For God what matters is not painlessness but the making great of those God loves: fuller, richer, deeper being for women and men and things.

The Bhagavadgítá

The Thirst

This is a different kind of poem, a different drama. There is no explicit wager here as in Job. Nevertheless the central concern is identical. Is the human being, suffering from massive deprivation, humiliation, and despondency, capable of listening to God and working with God for the defeat of *adharma* (injustice) and the establishment of *dharma* (justice), not to gain anything for oneself but for the good of the world and the welfare of all creatures? The Gítá affirms the possibility and the necessity, and thus rejoins Job.

Being a dialogue between Krishna and Arjuna, the Gítá would correspond structurally to the last section of Job, where God addresses the sufferer after the latter had raised a point and taken a stand. In the course of the dialogue, themes are discussed that exhibit close affinity to themes in Job: God's graciousness, the gratuitousness of God's love, the position of that love as the ultimate source of reality; concern for human persons and respect for their limited freedom; being partial to the poor and taking sides with the victims; revelation in nature and the call to contemplation; the framing of nature within the horizons of history; challenge to conventional theologies and practices; encountering God in the midst of history's conflicts; and a deepening awareness of the divine as unspeakable mystery. The Gítá opens, as does Job, with a scene of crisis and pain. The turning point comes with a vision of the Divine, issuing into ecstasy and surrender. But the decisive factor that commits Arjuna to the historical tasks named by the Lord is the revelation of and encounter with the Lord's unconditional love.

The Setting

The Bhagavadgítá, a poem that proposes to probe deeply into "the verities of a life of integrity,"[17] stands in the *Bhíshma-parvan* (Bhíshma canto) of the massive Indian epic, *Mahabharata*. Though critics are divided in their view of the relationship between the epic story and the doctrinal elaborations of the Gítá, the reading of the Gítá is greatly helped by memory of its literary setting. The poem is a long dialogue between Arjuna, a warrior, and Krishna, his charioteer, the manifestation of the supreme person, in the battlefield of Kurukshetra. Arjuna is one of the five Pándava princes, of whom the eldest, Yudhishthira, was noted for his passion for justice and fair play. War broke out between the Pándavas and their hundred half-brothers, the Kauravas, the eldest of whom, Duryodhana, was an evil man. Yudhishthira became king, established suzerainty over all neighboring kingdoms, and celebrated the occasion with an extravagant show of wealth and power. Envy, fanned by this success, and hatred, provoked by the behavior of the Pándava prince Bhíma, a blustering giant and bully, led Duryodhana to plot the destruction of the Pándavas by fraud and arson. The scheme failed. Duryodhana then invited Yudhishthira to a fraudulent dice contest. The Pándava king lost, forfeiting all that he had. The blind father of the hundred brothers had the penalties canceled and got a new capital built for the Pándavas. Yudhishthira let himself be coaxed into a second dice contest in which he staked and lost everything again, including his freedom, his brothers, and their common wife, Draupadi. Draupadi was publicly insulted and humiliated by the Kaurava side. By the terms of the contest, the Pándavas had to live in exile in the forest for twelve years and incognito for an additional year.

Duryodhana's attempts to kill them or incriminate them having miscarried, and the thirteen years having elapsed, the Pándavas come back demanding the return of their authority and kingdom. Entrenched in power, Duryodhana refuses. All efforts at conciliation and a peaceful settlement foundered; all the efforts of Krishna and others to mediate were thwarted by the Kaurava chief. To avoid war and spare the people, the Pándavas offered to forgo their royal rights and be satisfied with five villages. Even this was denied. War was what Duryodhana wanted, and war was the one last resort left to the Pándavas to secure a minimum of justice and to curb fraud, crowned and enthroned in insolence. Both sides approached Krishna for help. This Yadava king would join one side as a noncombatant ally while his army would support the other side. The Kauravas chose Krishna's troops, and the Pándavas were happy to have Krishna with them as Arjuna's charioteer.

Arjuna's Grief

At zero hour, as the battle was about to begin, Arjuna, redoubtable archer who had never known defeat, suddenly broke down at the prospect of having to kill so many of his revered and beloved brothers, elders, teachers, and friends. He was overcome with compassion and sadness; his limbs quailed; his body shook, his mouth went dry, his skin burned all over; he felt unsteady, his mind began to reel, and the great bow slipped from his hand. His spirit overpowered by sorrow, he sank down on the seat of the chariot. Tears filled his troubled eyes. Stricken with weakness and bewildered about his duty, Arjuna resolved not to fight and became silent (G 1:28–30, 47; 2:1–11). It was as if the great archer had been struck down by invisible arms before the battle began — struck down like Job, whose determination to seek and find a way of speaking correctly about God led him, says Gutiérrez, "through a battlefield in which... the shots came at him from every side."[18]

Was this the shock of a crisis of conscience? Or the anguish of being caught in "the *dharmic* dilemma of a war, which was both just and pernicious?"[19] Or was it a failure of nerve and "a momentary collapse of morale?" Was the claim to a sudden flood of compassion a species of rationalization? Was Arjuna dismayed in reality by the fate that confronted him as he stood facing his own masters like Drona and Bhíshma, in the art of war? Was he retreating from the arena of history because the action he had to perform was painful?[20] It was at any rate "a swing into inaction, a virtual death of the spirit."[21] It was the dark night of the soul.[22] Arjuna is not, as Job was, struck down with malignant ulcers. He is afflicted with something far deeper, far more excruciating: doubt and despondency; the bitter memory of injuries heaped gratis on him and his brothers; the searing memory of Draupadi's humiliation. The Kurukshetra scene is the arrival point of a long history of fraud, frustration, and suffering, and of pride trampled underfoot. It was for Arjuna a galling moment and a crucifying dilemma. The question of innocent suffering is not raised; but it could be. Not that the Pándavas are faultless, but that this particular conjunction of events and the enormity of the situation are the result of evil Kaurava machinations.

Three other questions are raised and discussed. They concern (1) the traditional theology of withdrawal and inaction versus the new call to committed historical involvement; (2) the secret or open desire-driven, self-centered activity versus the ideal of self-denying, other-centered commitment; and (3) the realization of the interrelatedness of human beings and the universe of realities, together with their rootedness in God, who comprehends and permeates everything, holding them together and accompanying their evolutionary and conflictual journey toward completion.

Retreat versus Involvement

Krishna finds Arjuna's way of resolving the crisis simplistic and unacceptable. He would urge action: "Cast off thy petty faintheartedness and arise." Do not falter, but resolve on battle for that is every Kshatriya's duty (G 2:3, 31, 33, 37). If action is seen as tightening of ties to the unreality of "phenomenal," ephemeral existence, know that abstention from work will not make you free from action; there is no actionless existence. Do thou then thy allotted work (G 3:3, 4, 5, 8). There are reasons for this injunction: work is your contribution to the turning of the wheel of the world. Not to make a contribution, though benefiting from the world process, is to be evil, like the wicked who cook food for themselves alone; "verily they eat sin" (G 3:13, 16). Act in order to set an example to one another: What would happen if everyone abstained from work? God is ever engaged in work lest the world fall in ruin (G 3:30–34; 4:15). The world is of worth to God; it is no illusion; it is God's project. So precious is it to God that God labors unceasingly for its progress and accepts responsibility for being a model to human beings.[23]

We may not choose to drift passively down the streams of historical processes. We must choose action to affirm ourselves and accept responsibility for ourselves, for each other, for the earth. The war in which Arjuna is engaged is, we are told, a just war. What is one to do with those who care nothing for justice and, like the Kauravas, violate all *dharma* with impunity? Paul Mundschenk observes:

> There is a clear implication here that it is incumbent upon us to stand up and resist others when their actions are clear expressions of insolence or injustice.... With violence or without, we are to live by *dharma,* righteousness, which includes standing up to every measure of evil that comes our way. Not to do so becomes our own violation of dharma, and undermines our own inner journey, our sense of reconciliation.[24]

To withdraw is to leave the world as it is in its injustice, fraud, and conceit, and to decline responsibility for its redemption and transformation.

An old theology or ideology of flight from the world is rejected. It is in action that the self affirms, remakes, and realizes itself and the world. Are we not defined by what we have done, and still more by what we can yet do? Does not even physical science tell us that "action rather than matter is basic?"[25] In an earlier scene in the epic, during a debate with her husbands, Draupadi had passionately affirmed that life was action and no man of integrity and justice could abdicate action.[26] Conventional theology and spirituality bade Arjuna turn back from action on grounds that Krishna would subsequently show to be inauthentic and questionable because they fail to take into account the whole realm of reality, the complexity of historical situations, and above all, the world of God's grace and love, which must be the ultimate reference point in all matters whatever.

Mundschenk invites us to reflect that Arjuna represents us, "the variegated, protean community called humankind." We, too, start out confused. Arjuna's predicament, like ours, "arises from an elemental characteristic of human action in the world.... Human action must frequently be carried out within the context of moral uncertainty." Mundschenk adds that the uncertainty is "more poignantly felt in the context of modern capitalist society where competition is the fuel which feeds the social machinery."[27]

Nishkámakarma: Disinterested Action

Action is unavoidable; it is life. But action could spring from self-centered desire and greed or from a detached heart bent on doing what is right and what would benefit the whole community and the entire world. The denunciation of selfishness and greed, which is a major theme of the Gítá (1:38, 45; 2:5, 8, 60, 62, 70; 3:37, and so forth), receives the most poignant expression as the battle draws to a close with the Kauravas slain and Bhíshma, the patriarch of the clan, laid low. At that point one of the victorious Pándavas declare that selfishness is death, the desire to possess is death. Bhíshma concurs: selfishness is the basic factor that destroys the inner integrity of a people. The survivors realize that the real war has only begun: the war to be waged by the soul within the soul against greed.[28] Krishna advises Yudhishthira to recognize the enemy within and to prepare for the new war. The mind of the epic is that the total carnage in which the war ends is the bitter fruit of unmitigated greed, treachery, and egotism — of the Kauravas, obviously, but also of the Pándavas. The epic probes their hidden greed and pride. They had obtained certainty through conquest; they had indulged in empire-building activity. This and the subsequent exhibition of pomp and power lie at the root of the catastrophe.

It is made clear that Yudhishthira accepts the challenge to the dice contest in the hope of acquiring Duryodhana's land and wealth. He persisted in the game despite heavy losses and the evidence of cheating because of the "competitive frenzy of the excited gambler." The Pándavas practiced trickery and unfair means to kill Drona, Karna, and Duryodhana. Even the great Bhíshma was led by self-interest to equivocal and noncommitted answers when Draupadi raised the question of Yudhishthira's right to stake her in the contest after he had forfeited his own freedom. It was the clash of unbridled greed on both sides that led to the tragedy of total death.[29] Krishna Chaitanya states the message pointedly when he notes that "the world cannot survive if every man is predatory."[30] The alienation and disruption we experience today at the core of our personal and societal life stand in direct line with and direct proportion to the loyalty with which we have followed Adam Smith's capitalist doctrine of self-interest — that ultimate ground on which greed has been organized on world scale.

The Gítá, therefore, is pointing another way: a way of life instead of one of death, a way of being and acting in partnership with God for the re-creation and completion of the world. What saves our humanity is neither flight from the world nor immersion in it but discerning commitment. What matters is neither inaction nor action but "disinterested action," other-centered work, sacrificial living (G 3:3–10). "The world is in the bonds of action, unless the action is consecration" (G 3:9, J. Mascaro's version). For Arjuna renunciation *of* action was the only solution, but for Krishna the real solution consists in renunciation *in* action.[31] Gítá teaches not the abandonment of work but the conversion of all works into *nishkámakarma,* desireless action.[32] We have a right to action, not to its ultimate outcome; let not fruits of action, reward, and gain be our motive. The one who hugs desires attains no peace; the path to peace is action free of desires and longings, without any sense of I and mine (G 2:47, 55, 56, 70, 71; 3:19; 4:20, 21; 5:2, 10; 6:24; 18:6, 9, 10, 23, 26, 49, 54). It is the Yogin who goes beyond the fruits of meritorious deeds assigned to the study of the Vedas, austerities, and almsgiving who attains the supreme and final status (G 8:28). The best sacrifice, penance, or gift is that which proceeds from a sense of duty and faith, without the expectation of reward or return (G 17:11, 17–25).

Significantly, the last prayer Arjuna makes in the Gítá is for the knowledge of the true nature of renunciation and surrender (G 18:1). More significantly, Arjuna is told in the end to leave all duty and religion behind and care only for Krishna and the welfare of the world (G 18:66; see 54–66). Commercial religion and mercenary ethics, which hinge on hope of retribution and reward, are as firmly transcended here as in the Book of Job.

Going beyond this negative teaching on renunciation, the Gítá demands that work is oriented toward the noblest, most altruistic goals. The goal is *lokasamgraha,* the maintenance of world order, the unity of the cosmos, and the interconnectedness of society. The goal is to become *sarvabhutahite ratah,* taking intense delight in the good and well-being of all creatures (G 3:20, 25; 5:25; 12:4).[33] In disinterested action there is passionate interest, but it is other-centered, centered on God's purposes for the world, centered on God. As we have seen, work must be done as a sacrifice. The world arose from God's sacrifice. Sacrifice is the source of other-centered existence and life as community. And ultimately life is consecration to God (G 3:7–10; 9:27–34; 12:20; 18:54–65).

The conclusion is that renunciation of fruit and reward, and the surpassing of mercenary religion, is but the negative side of something profoundly positive: a way of attaching ourselves to God and God's program for the world. Going to the Lord and being with the Lord in the company of all creatures is the final fruit of life. Paradoxically, then, nonattachment is shown as yielding the highest reward, the inner fruit of other-centered action. The fruit of love is love and life. The fruition of disinterested devotion and service is "deepened being."[34]

Centering in God

Getting involved in history and striving for the unity and welfare of creation in its entirety, Arjuna is to seek and find God in all realities. As he makes progress, his transformation deepens. He is helped by Krishna to center himself and the cosmos on Krishna's person. Already in 2:61, a pointed reference to Krishna instructs Arjuna to "remain firm in Yoga, intent on me." From then on Krishna is presented both as the Absolute and as the Incarnate in history. He is the origin and the end, the ultimate resting place of the universe. The world holds together in him. He dwells in the heart of every creature. Those who know his birth and work "will come home" and will know no separation. Therefore, "resign all works to Me; take refuge in Me; see all existence in Me; see Me in everything and everything in Me" (G 3:30–32; 4:8–10, 35; 7:1–7, 13–20; 6:30–31, 47). Krishna's wonder, beauty, and saving power are presented in many colors and accents (8:4–7, 13–15; 9:4–7, 16, 19, 22, 26; 10:4–8), until the call sounds to total surrender:

> Give Me thy mind, give Me thy heart,
> Give Me thy offering and thy adoration;
> And thus with thy soul in harmony,
>   and making Me thy supreme goal,
>   thou shalt in truth come to Me.
> [9:34 = 18:65, Mascaro's version]

> He who works for Me, who loves Me,
> whose End Supreme I am,
>   free from all things, and with love for all creation
>   he in truth comes to Me [11:55].

The whole of chapter 12 is devoted to urging us to focus on Krishna, to fix our minds on him with worshipful faith, to lay all our actions on him, to set our thoughts on him, to make his service the supreme aim of life, and to perform actions solely for his sake. Those who do so "come to Me; in Me shall they live hereafter; they are dear to Me; and exceedingly dear are those who, with faith and love, hear and heed this life-giving word of Mine" (chap. 12; see also 13:2, 10, 18, 28; 18:54–58, 63–70).

The first outcome of this focusing on Krishna is a confession of faith on the part of Arjuna: Krishna is proclaimed the Supreme Brahman and all his words are accepted as true (10:12–18). Arjuna has been brought to the point where he now wants to meditate — center himself — on Krishna. How may he do it? He is instructed to think of whatever is the very best, the highest, the most excellent in any sphere or line of being or activity, and to see it as a symbol suggestive of something of the unutterable mystery that is Krishna:

> I am the Self seated in the heart of all things...
> Of the lights, I am the radiant sun...
> Of the senses, I am mind and of beings I am consciousness...
> Of weapons, I am the thunderbolt...

Of creations, I am the beginning...
Of Feminine beings, I am Fame and Prosperity, Speech,
Memory, Intelligence, Constancy, and patient Forgiveness...
I am the Beauty of all things beautiful...
I am the Goodness of all who are good...
I am the silence of all hidden mysteries...
And of the knowers of wisdom, I am the Wisdom [10:19–40].

In sum, then,

Know that whatever is beautiful and good,
whatever has glory and power,
is only a portion of my own radiance....
Know that with one single fraction of my Being,
I pervade and support the universe [10:41–42].

A revelation of the mystery in a riot of symbols; and a direct experience of the mystery given in a discourse (chaps. 9 and 10). We are far from the din and horror of the battlefield, and Arjuna is waking from his trauma. "My bewilderment is gone from me, says he, because I have been granted the grace of a Word concerning the Self, the Supreme Mystery" (11:1).

However, he does not yet commit himself to action on behalf of justice. That final conversion takes place only at the very end, when Arjuna will stand ready to do Krishna's word (18:70). It comes as the result of a further revelation, a deeper experience, given not in symbolic discourse but in direct vision, though that, too, is and cannot but be made up of symbols. From spiritual trauma and paralysis there is no exit via reasoning and argument. It is not his friends' theology nor his own outraged logic that transforms Job from a lamenting and debating sufferer into a contemplative capable of placing pain meaningfully within a world enveloped in God's gratuitous love. Job's conversion occurs within a transit from hearsay to vision. The same pattern is realized in the *Gítá*. It is as the *Kena Upanishad* says: "He is known in the ecstasy of an awakening" (Kena II.4).

That ecstasy is the content of chapter 11. The discourse-revelations already given bring Arjuna to prayer for vision (11:3–4). The vision is granted together with a new eye, an eye of faith and love, with which to perceive the vision (G 11:8). At the sight of Krishna's cosmic form, resplendent with the light of a thousand suns, with many mouths, eyes, ornaments, and weapons, with face turned everywhere, carrying all creation in his body, wonderful and terrible, Arjuna is overcome with astonishment, terror, and rapture. He is transported with devotion, praise, and prayer:

I bow before thee, I prostrate in adoration,
    and I beg thy grace, O gracious Lord!
As a father to his son, as a friend to his friend,
    as a lover to his beloved,
Thou, O Lord, should bear with me [11:44].

The chapter closes with renewed accent on unconditional love as the only authentic relationship between God and human beings. It is not by Vedic studies or austerities or almsgiving but by unswerving devotion alone can Krishna be truly seen and entered into (G 11:52–54).

Both Job and Arjuna had profound spiritual experiences that came to them in the hour of darkness and changed them. To Job God spoke of the mystery of creation; to Arjuna God gave a vision of the Divine in its cosmic dimensions. To the one, God spoke from the heart of the storm; the other was spoken to while a tempest of doubt and dismay was lashing his soul. Job was rendered speechless by a volley of questions from the Lord of the storm; Arjuna is enriched with words of joyous praise. Both are reestablished in freedom, enabled to walk in love and to work for the liberation of the victims of greed and of self-regarding religion, which uses God for private gain. Both Job and the Gítá bear witness to the truth of God's liberating presence in the midst of life's struggles and history's vicissitudes: a presence that does not tranquilize us but challenges and urges us to act against *adharma* and create a new world that could reflect and respond to the world of grace, which is God's best wishes for us.

Paul Mundschenk, struck by chapter 11 and the cosmic vision, muses that what Arjuna learns, or does not, and indeed cannot, learn, is more telling than what he sees.

> Is it not the case that Krishna is another name for Ultimate Mystery? The Gítá then amazingly explores the psychology of the sensitive, caring human being at a loss as to what to do in a world whose ultimate origin and meaning remain the mystery of mysteries. As then, now Arjuna is dazzled but he never really gets a straight answer.

Neither does Job, who also is dazzled into silence. But there is more than dazzle. There is insight. The heart has had a fresh touch and taste of the Divine. And the heart has its experiences of which the head may know little (as Paschal reminds us).

Mundschenk is right when he points out that

> a free and candid response to the immense cosmic mystery can only be an expression of deep elemental gratitude and appreciation — the sense of thankful goodwill that brings praise, benediction. One feels blessed. One overflows with the same goodness and thanksgiving at the very fact of being itself and one's own being in the world.[35]

Historically expressed, gratitude and appreciation would spell collaboration with the mystery to uproot *adharma*, to enhance life, and to shape a world of freedom and love within the range of the possible, which keeps expanding.

Of such "deep elemental gratitude and appreciation," the *Poems of Gítánjali* is a telling instance.

Poems

Gítánjali

She was born in Meerut on June 12, 1961. She died of cancer, in Bombay on August 11, 1977. For months she lived a lingering death, her frail body racked by pain, in her home or at the hospital, between which she journeyed every few days as her body broke down or recovered from time to time. A "blurb" on the jacket of the *Poems* says:

> Gítánjali's line of life ascends to the agonies of early disease, then rises to wrestle with her fate. In the ultimate suffering her faith is confirmed: nothing is without purpose. She dies into the earth to be miraculously reborn in the message of her poetry.

Gítánjali loved to write, paint, and watch the sea outside her window. Her suffering and loneliness found expression in her poems. Every piece she wrote was carefully hidden away "in little corners of her room; behind books and sofa seats or toys in the almirah; inside books, and cushion covers, or the pockets of old discarded skirts."[36] They were found by her mother and published through the miraculous collaboration of many persons whom they had touched and moved to tears.

Voices of suffering, the poems are nevertheless free of despair and self-pity and the horror of death. They are songs of beauty and innocence, full of wisdom and "the quiet dignity of one who had learned to live with hurt." They are witnesses to a beautiful child's simplicity, love of life, ear for the music of words, and implicit faith in God.[37] In the *Poems* we do not have first a scene of suffering, dilemmas, and traumatic experiences as in Job or the Gítá, followed then by long discussions, and culminating finally in fresh spiritual insights that enable one to face life with courage on a new level of awareness beyond agonizing questions. This structural pattern, common to Job and the Gítá, is realized in the *Poems* in almost every piece. Each poem depicts the entire journey from death to life; each voices the perplexity and the courage; each reflects the pain and the faith. Nearly every poem is the whole story in miniature: each encompasses the crucifixion as well as the resurrection.

There is no word from God. God never speaks to Gítánjali as God does finally to Job and throughout to Arjuna. And yet who could doubt that what the child writes is a response to some word she has heard? No more penetrating and purifying word could there be than her pain, her suffering, her sense of the nearness of death. In the depths of pain, in the depths of her shattered soul, the girl has heard and felt. Therefore, there are times when she requests us, "Please, be silent, let me hear the whisper of God."[38] There is no awe-inspiring vision here of cosmic mystery as there is in the Gítá; no passage as in Job from hearsay to sight. Yet who can miss the inner vision from which Gítánjali's simple words take on their poignancy and their power?

Pain

Gítánjali's is an experience comparable to Job's — perhaps more tragic and hurting than his. A child is being handed over to death, and she knows it. Everything is being taken from her: the life she loves, her beloved mother and father, her friends, her pets, her dreams, her childhood. She is on the cross all the time we see her. Job was there for a while, and Arjuna for a short spell. But this child is to remain nailed till the end. And yet she would not be extinguished. She would live; she has learned to love. Gítánjali knows how to turn her complete undoing into a song with wings of praise and thanks — to turn her little life into a thing of beauty forever, enshrined in a faith that suffering only deepens and illumines.

She prays in the night for mercy upon her wounded heart. She tries not to weep, but it is not easy to hide her grief or bring her aching heart to rest. Her heart, stung with the bitter truth of death's closeness, bleeds. It is a heart at the center of which waves of sorrow follow upon sorrow's waves. Gítánjali sees herself as a harp in the hand of God: now God caresses it tenderly, now God strikes it sharply, so her heartstrings quiver with pain — heartstrings already worn out and torn with the "stress and strain" of conflicting emotions overpowering. She had been a girl full of life, and fun-loving, who could laugh and cry at the same time. Now life for her has shrunk to medicine time and dreary nights. All that's left now is a handful of memories, bittersweet. "How beautiful life was!" The memory makes her "feel overwhelmed for all that she has lost." She sees herself as a wounded bird, paralyzed and helpless; her heart sinks when the sun goes down; her spirit is in turmoil, and a dark, sinister feeling creeps up her soul and "bruised and crushed lies my trust, faith, and soul."[39]

Death waits to claim her. She is not afraid; she will welcome death "with open arms." Gítánjali knows that death does not come on her own but on orders from the Lord. The girl's concern is that she has no costly gifts with which to receive the guest. All she has is some tears and "my wasted form." Of that form the young girl is tragically, pathetically conscious. She has nothing in all the world to claim as her own but "any distorted form." She recalls or imagines a visit to her school during an interval of recovery, and is stunned by the shocked, silent stare of friends at her shrunken form. For surely "Gítánjali is not unaware of her beauty shorn." Death was a great and welcome guest, yet at the thought of it a shudder passed through the child, and she swayed.[40]

There were times when she felt utterly miserable, past tears, "in the very gates of hell." Times when she saw her world crash at her feet. Times when she wished her heart could freeze and cease to be sensitive to hurt, when she felt her store of endurance had run out, when she feared her faith might fail and she might go mad. Before that should happen, please God, take me away. Even nature seemed to her to seek for ways of adding to her suffering. An angry night wind tore off the top of the beautiful tree she loved to watch from her window, "the only soothing sight" for her "fast-dimming eyes." That, too, was taken away.[41]

Questioning and Trusting

Is Gítánjali, then, on the dunghill with Job? The child would probably reject the metaphor. "Illness, too, is a gift of God, and Gítánjali accepts it with grace."

"Nothing is unimportant, not even death."[42] That does not prevent Gítánjali from raising questions, Joblike. "What have I done to deserve this?" she asks God. "What have I done to deserve this?" she asks happiness, which once loved to be where she was. Where have the happy days gone, O lord, and why? She tells God face-to-face that God has betrayed her trust and refused her all she yearned for. She speaks as Jeremiah spoke, and cries as Jesus cried on the cross. The child has many questions, which nobody cares to answer. "Perhaps there are no answers." The answer perhaps is silence. But "the sound of silence is overbearing her feeble heart" and "gnawing at her day and night." It is "deafening." The questions and the silences "bounce back and hit her hard." But when she thinks of God's kindness in the years gone by, she feels ashamed of herself for having asked, "Why, God, why?"[43]

Trust is Gítánjali's basic and abiding stance. It is what she deliberately cultivates. Trust and faith and gratitude, with a joyful conviction of being loved by God and fellow humans—not trust that health would be restored or life spared but the act of trust, of giving herself into God's keeping even as she saw her life ebbing fast and death standing by to claim her. In the cold and stormy night, a lamp burns steadily in her heart, guiding her through the dark to her destination. Gítánjali has given God all her trust and faith. She trusts God despite the clamor of sorrows, despite God's betrayal of her trust:

> I trust Thee.
> Yet,
> Though you have
> Betrayed my trust
> And refused me,
> All I yearn for....
> But dear God...
> Isn't it amazing
> For I trust you
> Still?

To Job God spoke from the heart of the storm; to us Gítánjali speaks from the heart of the storm that has gathered around her and is going "to gather her like dust." The child is afraid, "but yet I trust in God." "God alone knows what is best." As her desire to live burns bright, and yet her hope wavers and her dreams slip away, she decides, "with a trust most rare," to follow the beacon God has sent and let God steer her life's boat to where God wishes. When the awareness first dawned on her that only a short while was left for her on this earth, it hurt; but soon she mastered the moment and "placed myself and my trust in the palm of His hand."[44]

Your Will Is Best

Gítánjali's faith is not propped up by hope of reward, nor by fear of punishment. She is both afraid of death and not afraid of it: "I have not sinned or wronged any living soul." She prays for mercy, health, and life, and yet she has "long stopped begging for mercy." Her prayer to her dear God is for strength to accept his will and for faith to know that "your will is best." "Oh please, help me to trust you not from fear but because of love and faith." There is nothing this child seeks "save the truth." And in you, God, "lies the truth, and therefore, I seek you."[45]

She seeks God everywhere and in all things: in the rising sun, in eventide, in her pain, in her mother and father and their tenderness. She seeks God at all times: when she dreams and drifts, when God takes her pain away and rare moments of laughter come. She will seek God most when the hour of death descends. At that hour, "dear God, be by my side, hold my hand, take me where you want."[46] Gítánjali knows that God cares, "Oh, God does care." "People can let you down, God will not." She could, therefore, say in the tradition of Job that, when "sorrow, grief, and pain are near" and we lose "someone most dear," it is time "to reach out for God's hand." For God alone knows what is right. "Trust God and leave all else aside."[47] With death's shadow already falling on her and grief gripping her soul, she still has the clarity and the courage to say with Job and with Jesus: "If that's how you wish, thy will be done." Her prayer for her loved ones is that when the time of parting comes, they should just be near, hold her hand, and "with utter trust give in to God" and let her die with dignity.[48] Nights may be dark for her soul, too, but when day breaks "my heart sings glory to you, Oh God," for the gift of another day. Praise to God, for why should Gítánjali be sad "if flowers can die, which are so young and lovely to behold?"[49] We have in the poems many such resonances of the concluding part of Job and of the nature-contemplation in the Gítá.

The Welfare of All

What is most remarkable about Gítánjali is her ability to forget herself and become genuinely concerned with others, the courage and clarity of a wholly selfless spirituality. Herself dying daily, dying inch by inch, wrenched by pain, with death at her door, Gítánjali is not preoccupied with herself but anxious for others. There is evidence of a sustained struggle against the onslaught of self-pity. Even as her "tears flow silent, fast and free" she makes the brave promise "never to indulge in self-pity again." She prays for help "not to rail in self-pity," not to be swept away in its torrents.[50]

When her own heart breaks and her tears make "a permanent track" down her cheeks "like a shortcut through the lawn," her thoughts go to those who were caring for her, keeping watch, and trying to cheer her with songs. She does everything possible to lessen their suffering: she would act brave, control her tears, suppress her cry. She asks God to break her heart, break it, if necessary, but please be just, and do it "in such a way that no one should get hurt." Her own pain she can bear; what she cannot bear is the pain in the eyes of those who love her. In the stillness of the night she pleads with God: "Wipe out the scars in the hearts of those who loved me."[51]

Naturally, the child's first concern is for her parents: those "two loving souls who held her close to their heart" on "the night of the storm," when their eyes held no promise and avoided meeting their child's. She recalls the agony and tenderness of her father, the source of her faith and strength.[52] Her mother is special; very special, dear, and divine. To that brave woman her heart goes out. Her mother is the one Gítánjali most mentions next perhaps only to God. Her greatest pain is that her mother suffers in silence. May she not think unkindly of God, may she be there "when I meet my end," may she be thankful that her baby is at rest at last.[53] The girl makes adoring mention of her granny, affectionately names her brother, and remembers her friends with joy. May none of them suffer but take her departure in peace.[54]

Gítánjali's heart reaches out far beyond the circle of her relatives and friends. She seeks strength from God not only for herself and her loved ones to be able to bear the anguish day by day, but the grace to be merciful to all who hurt her or need her, the grace to spread whatever happiness she can. Her days are numbered, but she has so many tasks to fulfill. Her days are numbered, and she has so many dreams to bring to blossom: "to feed the down and the poor, and wipe their tears with my hands to see them happy."

As she turns to God, Gítánjali realizes that she is not the only afflicted person in this wide world. Therefore, before asking for mercy for herself and for the gift of a little sleep in the night, she would pray for all those "who like her are ill and cannot sleep for pain" and for all "who are poor and friendless, sad and lonely."[55]

Her sympathy extends to animals and all of nature. Once again she is at one with the Gítá in the ideal of joy, in the welfare of all beings. Micky and Judy, her pet dogs, are puzzled why their frolicsome friend is now so quiet. "They look upon me so dolefully, and it breaks my heart; these dumb friends are better than many human beings" who have no heart, who say they love but never serve. Oscar, the lame crow, was a friend for whom Gítánjali used to wait with a breakfast of crumbs. A bird song lingers in her thoughts and — was it a sad song or a song of joy? — teaches her not to stop singing "just because I am unwell." From her hospital bed of pain, Gítánjali's thoughts fly back home to Moti, the stray dog she had befriended and cared for. She misses him. She thinks of him each time she sees a loaf of bread. She asks others to see to it that Moti is fed. Is Moti shivering with lack of love, or has someone given him a rug? She remembers the paw he extended to her as she sat in the car to be driven to the hospital. "I care for you in a very special way, which you would never know, anyway." Her heart whispers a prayer for Moti: "May you find a friend to take care of you."[56] Bruce Allsopp finds "Moti My Friend" the most touching of Gítánjali's poems. It is "a crystalline expression of the anguish of a being prevented by illness from serving a fellow being who has become dependent."[57]

This girl's soul vibrates with all nature. Every evening with a sinking heart she watches the sun set, not knowing if she will see the glory of the rising sun again. The moon shining in a little puddle reflects the lamp of faith that burns in the temple of her heart, guiding her to her destination. The prospect of a visit home suddenly bathes the world in sunshine, and in the dazzling brilliance of her joy the rising sun looks dim. Gítánjali grieves over a tree broken and flowers scattered by a night wind. She contemplates the flowers standing by her bed and realizes that these young and lovely things too will die and be discarded "just as I will be." Why should I be sad in such company? "Praise to you, O God." Much of the nature with which her heart chimes is reflected in a presentation of a valley and dew-kissed grass and chirping birds, and treetops, cows, sheep, horses, and stray dogs as well as stagnant pools, clear springs, and sunrise greeting the world with warmth, till it sets, and lets the stars shine; the sun sets, "leaving behind the radiance of love."[58]

And in the silent, painful nights that follow, the moon strangely bathes the girl's aching heart and brings gushing endless childhood memories.[59]

Such is Gítánjali: wrestling with pain, with death and life, and with God. And she grows through it all in faith and love, surpassing herself and meeting the mystery — of life, of her own heart, and of her God, in the purity and transparency of childhood, in the intense fire of suffering. Gítánjali is another wager won. All clever, cerebral criticism of religion and all pretentious and verbose theologies have been silenced and bidden to simple faith and a song of praise. Gítánjali is the song of the Third World. With this young and broken mystic symbol, God has challenged us. Does not God too feel challenged and pressed to repentance? How could God have the heart to test so frail a flower so utterly and cruelly? To confound which modern satan and intractable cynicism did God make this bet? "Why, we ask with Pritish Nandy, should such unbearable agony come upon those who have never hurt anyone? Is sorrow our ultimate destiny in this imperfect universe?" I do not know, we answer with Pritish Nandy; "all I know is this: these poems have hurt me by an awareness. The miracle of pain that opens up worlds we never knew existed."[60]

Now that Gítánjali lives and has won the wager for God, God can be proud of her, as God is proud of Job, and Krishna of Arjuna. We are proud of her, too. Though the memory of her brings the tide rising in our eyes, we can see her as a revelation of what God can achieve, of what we can become, of what we are — a disclosure of human nobility and human possibility, the pure love and pure suffering of which the heart is capable; the wonder and the beauty of what God is able to create and nurture on this earth, beyond commodity culture, cold calculations, and the arrogance of power. We are called on to thrill with joy and thank God with Jesus for revealing these things to little ones.

Gítánjali means there is hope for humankind. She means we can "believe for nothing." Her meaning is that God is great, and is bent on making us great too. The meaning of this gentlest, frailest, fading, never-fading flower of a girl is that it is good to be a human being and live on this earth, even if the earth is soaked in our own tears. It is good to share life with persons and animals and trees and earth and sky. The message of her life is that it is good to believe and to adore. Gítánjali means God is here. It is good to love God for nothing. God is so worthy, so precious.

That is what Job and Arjuna and Gítánjali are telling us.

Notes

1. Gustavo Gutiérrez, *On Job* (Maryknoll, N.Y.: Orbis Books, 1987). Original title: *Hablar de Dios desde el sufrimiento del inocente* (Lima: C.E.P., 1986).
2. See S. Radhakrishnan, *The Bhagavadgítá* (London: George Allen and Unwin, 1948/1967); J. Mascaro, *The Bhagavad Gítá* (Harmondsworth: Penguin, 1962); R. C. Zaehner, *The Bhagavad Gítá* (Oxford University Press, 1969). The title means "the Lord's song."
3. Published by Oriel Press, London, 1982, with an introduction by Pritish Nandy. "Gítánjali" means a song-offering (from the title of a collection of Tagore songs).
4. *On Job,* p. 11.
5. Ibid., pp. 4–5.

6. Ibid., p. 30.

7. Ibid., pp. 30, 57, 67.

8. Ibid., pp. 82, 84.

9. Ibid., p. 31.

10. Ibid., p. 48, 88.

11. Ibid., p. 96.

12. Ibid., pp. 88–89.

13. Ibid., pp. 70–72, 77–79.

14. Ibid., p. 69.

15. Ibid., pp. 86–87.

16. Ibid., pp. 30, 27–29.

17. K. Chaitanya, *The Mahabharata. A Literary Study* (New Delhi: Clarion Books, 1985), pp. 206–7.

18. *On Job,* p. 93.

19. J. A. B. Van Buitenan, *The Bhagavadgítá in the Mahabharata* (Chicago: University of Chicago Press, 1981), p. 5.

20. Chaitanya, *Mahabharata,* pp. 279–352.

21. R. A. Malagi, "Dying into Life: The Prologue Scenes in the Bhagavadgítá and La Divina Comedia," in *New Essays in the Bhagavadgítá,* comp. Arvind Sharma (New Delhi: Books and Books, 1987), p. 191.

22. Chaitanya, *Mahabharata,* p. 249 (see Gítá 2:7 [Mascaro]).

23. Ibid., pp. 252–53.

24. P. Mundschenk, "The Psychology of the Bhagavadgítá," in *New Essays* (n. 21), p. 23.

25. Chaitanya, *Mahabharata,* p. 255, where reference is made to S. Petrement's *Simone Weil* (1976), to Arthur M. Young's *The Reflexive Universe* (1976), and to B. L. Atreya's *The Philosophy of Yogavasishtha* (1936).

26. *Mahabharata, vana-parvan* (forest canto), chap. 32.

27. Mundschenk, "Psychology," p. 17.

28. *Mahabharata, shanti-parvan* (peace canto) chap. 13, 16, 58.

29. Ibid., *vana-parvan* (forest canto), chap. 34. See Chaitanya, *Mahabharata,* pp. 190–95.

30. Chaitanya, *Mahabharata,* p. 275.

31. S. Gopalan, "The Concept of Duty in the Bhagavadgítá: An Analysis," in *New Essays* (n. 21), p. 8.

32. Radhakrishnan, *Bhagavadgítá,* p. 352, ad 18:2.

33. Ibid., p. 139.

34. Chaitanya, *Mahabharata,* p. 200.

35. Mundschenk, "Psychology," p. 22.

36. Nandy, "Introduction" to *Poems of Gítánjali,* pp. xv, xvii.

37. Ibid., pp. xv, xvi, xviii; Bruce Allsopp, "Foreword," p. xii.

38. *Poems,* p. 89.

39. Ibid., pp. 6, 7, 11, 19, 26, 38, 39, 44, 70, 84, 145, 146.

40. Ibid., pp. 9, 26, 27, 59.

41. Ibid., pp. 48, 54, 60, 150.

42. Ibid., pp. 27, 154.

43. Ibid., pp. 6, 40, 58, 56, 67; Jeremiah 20:7–13; Mark 15:34.

44. Ibid., pp. 39, 41, 56, 58, 82, 97, 98, 127.

45. Ibid., pp. 5, 6, 11, 20, 54, 68.

46. Ibid., pp. 3, 12–13.
47. Ibid., pp. 45, 50, 89, 147.
48. Ibid., pp. 20, 56, 84, 122.
49. Ibid., pp. 38, 64.
50. Ibid., pp. 11, 52, 54.
51. Ibid., pp. 137, 147.
52. Ibid., pp. 4–5, 28–29, 42–43, 63–64, 83, 130–31.
53. Ibid., pp. 32, 35, 42, 53, 77, 91, 104, 122, 125–26, 138.
54. Ibid., pp. 65–66, 32–33, 113–14, 120, 153.
55. Ibid., pp. 61, 81, 103, 110.
56. Ibid., pp. 14, 22–23, 28, 100, 115–16.
57. Allsopp, "Preface" to *Poems,* p. xii.
58. *Poems,* pp. 123, 124.
59. Ibid., pp. 2, 41, 57, 63–64, 79.
60. Ibid., pp. xvi, xvii.

Chapter 10

Lady Meng

A Liberative Play Using Common Folklore

R. S. SUGIRTHARAJAH, EDITOR

People articulate their faith in different media. They spin stories, recite poems, coin proverbs, enact dramas, and chant rhymed social-protest verses, thus reappropriating theology as the work of the whole people of God. The example reproduced here carries on that tradition and calls into question ground rules set by academic theology. It uses a common Chinese folktale that was popularized by the Taiwanese theologian, C. S. Song, in his booklet *The Tears of Lady Meng: A Parable of People's Political Theology* (Maryknoll, N.Y.: Orbis Books, 1982; Geneva: World Council of Churches, 1981), but moves beyond the narrative to the dramatic mode to express the historical experience of resistance and struggle.

This play was written by a group of course participants in the third-world theologies class at Selly Oak Colleges, Birmingham, England. It is often dramatized as part of their class work and followed by discussion of issues raised by the play.

The Tears of Lady Meng

EMPEROR: Chancellor, this must be stopped. Now! I will not tolerate any peasant soldier who allows the Huns from the Mongolian Steppes to break through our defenses in the North. These men must be disciplined. Our defenses will be impenetrable. There must not be one single gap in any border town or village that will allow the smallest slimy creature from outside this glorious land of ours to enter into it and disturb our peace. I despise these Mongolian Huns. Get them out of my country! Kill the collaborators, every man, woman, and child in every village along the border where these swine of the earth have taken cover. I *will* be secure only when every possible chink in our border has been closed.

NARRATOR: And so the imperial army patrolled the northern-most border in an attempt to stop the Huns from invading. This was an almost impossible task because the border stretched for over fifteen hundred miles, from Shanhai-kuan on the coast in the east to Kansu Province in the northwest.

CHANCELLOR: Oh, Most Worshipful Majesty, Emperor of all China, Son of Heaven, most magnificent and generous ruler of all, I have the reports you requested from the northern-most frontier of our glorious country. Tien-Ksien, most noble High Consol of Kao tai-hs in the extreme west, has reported that the soldiers of the Imperial Army only just held out against an invading force from the Huns and that 126 men, women, and children in the border village of Shan tan-hs were executed after fifteen of the enemy were found hiding in a barn. And from...

NARRATOR: From Kao tai-hs in the west to Shanhaikwai in the east, the chancellor read out report after report, each giving a graphic account about the imperial army fighting desperately to prevent the Huns from invading. After each report the emperor became more and more angry.

EMPEROR: Something *must* be done, Chancellor, and *now!* You cannot satisfy me with reports of mass executions of prisoners and peasants caught up in the border towns. The imperial army and the people must become an impenetrable wall against the enemy.

CHANCELLOR: A wall, you most wise and wonderful majesty?

EMPEROR: Yes a wall! The people shall become...no, better, they shall build a wall along the whole of the northern frontier. It shall be the greatest defense the world has seen. Call my finest architects and builders together and tell them I want a wall. It shall be thirty feet thick and sixty feet high and...

NARRATOR: And so the finest architects and builders met, drew up plans, quarried the finest stone, and set to work to build what would be the world's greatest monument to national defense. (*Wall-building — after each section is built, the previous section collapses.*)

NARRATOR: ...but all was not well.

EMPEROR: Chancellor! Give me reports on the Great Wall's progress. How long will it be before we are safe? Well? Why are you slow in speaking? Is the process not good? Speak, man, I am loosing my patience!

CHANCELLOR: Oh! Your Most Worshipful Majesty, I'm afraid the news is not, err...good. The builders are having problems.

EMPEROR: Not good? Not good? Work has been going on for six months now. Why have I not been told this before? What is the problem?

CHANCELLOR: The problem appears to be, Your Most Understanding Majesty, that no sooner has each piece of the wall been built than the previous section falls down, and so the wall, I'm afraid, your majesty, has made no progress.

EMPEROR: How can this be so, Chancellor? I employed the greatest architects and builders in the world. They have failed me?

CHANCELLOR: Your Most Worshipful and Wise Majesty, you are absolutely correct, their plans and techniques cannot be faulted.

EMPEROR: As I thought, Chancellor. Then the fault must lie with the materials used. But this cannot be so, since I ordered them to use the finest granite stone bound together with the finest mortar.

CHANCELLOR: Indeed, Your Most Gracious Majesty, this was done.

EMPEROR: Then why did it collapse, Chancellor, why? Are you telling me that it was sabotage by the workers, because if it was I will have the head of every worker, guard, general, and yours, too, Chancellor — yours, too!

CHANCELLOR: No, Your Most Kind, Generous, Most Worshipful Majesty, it was not sabotage. How could conscripted laborers under the strict oversight of the imperial army, outmaneuver your orders?

EMPEROR: Then why, Chancellor, why does the wall, the essential defense of this nation, make no progress? Why? Why?

CHANCELLOR: I'm afraid I am not able to answer this question, Your Most Worshipful Majesty, Son of Heaven. Perhaps I might take the liberty, if Your Most Worshipful Majesty will forgive me, to suggest that I consult with your wise counselor.

EMPEROR: Good, Chancellor, but not good enough. *I* will consult with my wise counselor. Bring him to me immediately.

NARRATOR: And so the most wise and trusted counselor was summoned to give an answer to the problem of the wall. He was fully aware of the problems, both of the wall and of the emperor wanting to defend his nation, his cause, and his religion, right and left. In the midst of great agitation the wise counselor entered.

COUNSELOR: Your Most Gracious, Worshipful Majesty, Ruler of all China, Son of Heaven, I have thought long and hard about the problem of the wall. Your Majesty, a wall like this, which is over ten thousand miles long, can be built only if you immure a human being in every mile of the wall. Each mile will then have its own guardian.

NARRATOR: What a counsel! Ten thousand lives for building a wall! This is insanity! This is inhumanity!

EMPEROR:	This is marvelous, wise Counselor, a true flash of revelation from heaven. My subjects are nothing but grass and weeds. It is right that they should be put to such a purpose so they may serve this magnificent nation. It shall be done.
NARRATOR:	And so plans were made to take ten thousand men from villages and towns along the border. From Kao tai-hs to Shaihaikwai, from the northwest to the east, all to be interred in between the stones at every mile along the wall to guard it from the spirits and evil influences that were causing it to collapse. The lives of ten thousand men as human sacrifices meant nothing to the wicked and unjust Emperor Ch'in Shi Huang-ti, for he regarded all the peasants as just grass and weeds to be trampled on. Even those who were above the peasants were worried for their lives since the emperor's cruel tyranny was unpredictable and they feared that the wall may require more noble guardians. Just before the emperor was able to command that these men were to be taken, a commotion was heard outside.
EMPEROR:	Chancellor, what is this disturbance? Quick, I have a decision to make!
CHANCELLOR:	Your Most Worshipful Majesty, there is a man outside who says he must speak to you on an urgent matter.
EMPEROR:	Can this not wait?
CHANCELLOR:	He says, Your Most Worshipful Majesty, that he knows "ten thousand" who would be easier to take and offer as a sacrifice to the wall.
EMPEROR:	Then why have you prevented this man from coming forward? Was he not consulted before you drew up your report?
CHANCELLOR:	I ask your forgiveness, Your Most Worshipful Majesty, but I did not know of his existence until this moment.
EMPEROR:	Chancellor, you are a foolish man. Bring this counsel to me! Man, do you bring me a good counsel?
MAN:	Your most worshipful majesty, ruler of all China, Son of Heaven, you are indeed a very wise man. You are right to suggest that ten thousand men should be sacrificed to act as guardians of the wall. Errr...
EMPEROR:	If you have come to tell me that, you are wasting my time. Tell me more or I will have your head.
MAN:	Thank you, Your Most Gracious Majesty. I have considered long and hard about the problems of rounding up ten thousand men and believe that this may encourage trouble on such a large scale that the whole plan may collapse as the wall has been doing. Therefore, may I suggest, Your Most Understanding Majesty, that it would be sufficient to sacrifice one man only.

EMPEROR: One man only! Are you mad? How can one man guard a wall as long as this when it is clear that ten thousand are needed?

MAN: If I may indulge a little further, Your Most Worshipful and Patient Majesty, ten thousand is indeed the key to keeping this wall standing. The one man to whom I refer is a man by the name of "Wan," since "Wan" means "Ten Thousand." Through him every valley shall be filled and every mountain and hill shall be brought low.

EMPEROR: This is indeed a revelation from heaven! If, as you say, this one man is all I need to bring peace to my country, then it will cause less trouble for the imperial army to deal with and will provide me with ten thousand laborers to build the wall. You are a wise and good man. I will trust in what you say and, if this works, then you will be appointed as my new wise counselor. But if it fails, I will have your head, and the heads of your family, and those of every member of your village! But for now, Guards! Find this man called Wan and immure his bones into the wall so that at last I might have peace!

NARRATOR: And so the soldiers were dispatched. The man who they were looking for lived in the town of So-Ping fu many miles from the imperial palace, where they eventually found him celebrating his marriage to Lady Meng at a large wedding feast, unaware of the emperor's interest in him.

GUEST: Today is a very important and very happy day for all the people of So-Ping fu, but especially for our friend Wan and for his beautiful bride, Lady Meng. On behalf of all the people who are gathered here to share this meal with you, may I wish countless blessings for today and for the rest of your life together, and may your life together be long and fruitful, with many children.

WAN: You are very kind, my friend. This is indeed the happiest day of my life, and I look forward to many years together with my beautiful wife, Lady Meng.

LADY MENG: It is the happiest day of my life also. We shall never be parted...(*Guards enter.*)

GUEST: What are you doing? You cannot come in here like this! This is a wedding feast, a day of celebration! How dare you do this?

WAN: What do you want? What is the purpose of this intrusion? (*The guards seize Wan.*) Take your hands off me! I have done nothing wrong. Where are you taking me? Let me go!

LADY MENG: Wan! Let him go! Wan! (*The guards take Wan away.*) (*Turning to the guest*) Why have they taken my husband, Wan? Why? I don't understand. What has he done? Where are they taking him?

GUEST: I don't know, Lady Meng, I don't know. But if you follow him, the imperial guards will take you also, I am sure, and they will lock you both up as far away from each other as possible, and you may never see each other again. As it is, they may just be taking him in for questioning, and he could be released in the morning.

NARRATOR: But this was not the case, for the emperor had decreed that Wan was to be the sole guardian of the wall. After many months of waiting, news about her husband's fate reached Lady Meng. Immediately she knew what she had to do. Her husband had been taken away from her and buried in the Great Wall. (*Wall is built with Wan imprisoned in it.*) The wall had been completed, but her duty towards her murdered husband was not completed. She knew that she had to bring back his bones and bury them where he belonged, in his ancestral home. It was a long and dangerous journey she had to make from her home to the wall. (*Lady Meng enters.*) Finally she reached the wall — the wall that took her husband's life, broke up her family, and deprived her of her joy and hope that the union of husband and wife alone could give. But at once she realized that she was confronted with a humanly impossible task.

LADY MENG: Why do you stare at me with cold hatred? Why do you show no emotions? You are a brutal and hateful monster that has a passion for power and enjoys seeing human misery. Why do you hold my husband prisoner?

NARRATOR: She was so exhausted from the journey over mountains and through rivers, and in pain from the wall's contempt, that she could do nothing else but sit and weep. She must have wept her heart out because during the night her tears affected the wall so much that it collapsed revealing her husband's bones. (*Wall collapses.*) The fact that the wall had collapsed was immediately reported to the Emperor Ch'in Shih Huang-ti in his imperial palace.

EMPEROR: Chancellor! Chancellor! Why is there so much commotion going on?

CHANCELLOR: Your Most Wonderful, Worshipful Majesty, Emperor of all China, Son of Heaven, I am afraid that I have just received rather disturbing news about the Great Wall...

EMPEROR: Go on.

CHANCELLOR: Well, Your Majesty, it appears that the Great Wall has, err, once again, err, collapsed.

EMPEROR: Collapsed? Collapsed? How did this happen? Wasn't the wall strong enough to hold off the invading Huns now that this man called Wan was immured as a sacrifice?

CHANCELLOR: The reason this has happened is, Your Majesty, very difficult to believe or understand, but it is the only explanation we have. It appears that the man Wan, who was immured in the wall as a guardian, was taken by the imperial army from his wedding feast. His bride, Meng Chiang, known as Lady Meng, vowed that she would find her husband's bones and return them to his ancestral home. When she reached the Great Wall, she could do nothing but weep, and it seems that her tears were so powerful that the effect on the wall was to make it collapse.

EMPEROR: This Lady Meng seems to be an incredible woman. I would like to meet her. Have her brought to me.

NARRATOR: So Lady Meng was taken by soldiers and brought before the emperor, and there she stood in all her beauty waiting for him to speak. Having done what she had done, Lady Meng expected to be put to death, but the emperor looked down at her in a strange, unnerving way.

EMPEROR: (*after a long pause*) Lady Meng, I have heard much about you, and it disturbed me greatly. However, when you came into my court, I was immediately struck by your beauty. You must be the most beautiful creature I have ever laid eyes on.

LADY MENG: Your Most Worshipful Majesty, Emperor of all China, Son of Heaven, I thank you for these kind words.

EMPEROR: Is it true what they say about you?

LADY MENG: You have said so, Your Majesty.

EMPEROR: Your unearthly beauty moves me so much, I will forgive you, and I want to make you my empress.

LADY MENG: Your Most Worshipful Majesty, you are so kind. I will agree, although if you will permit me to ask, I would be grateful if, before we are married, you would do three things.

EMPEROR: Whatever you wish, My Empress.

LADY MENG: First of all, Your Most Worshipful Majesty, I would like you to hold a festival lasting forty-nine days in honor of my husband; secondly, I would be grateful if Your Majesty would be present at my husband's burial, along with all your officials; and finally, Your Majesty, could you build a terrace forty-nine feet high on the bank of the river, where I could make a sacrifice to my husband?

EMPEROR: If this is all you want me to do, then it shall be done immediately. Chancellor!

CHANCELLOR: Yes, Your Most Worshipful Majesty?

EMPEROR: See to it that the wishes of Lady Meng, my future empress, are granted this instant.

CHANCELLOR: Yes, Your Majesty.

NARRATOR: When everything had been completed, Lady Meng climbed onto the terrace and looked down on the emperor and his officials forty-nine feet below and began to curse him in a loud voice.

LADY MENG: (*Curses emperor in Chinese.*)

NARRATOR: Hearing Lady Meng saying, "You are wicked and brutal! You do not care about the people in the towns and villages. You use them as a mat on which to wipe your feet. You are evil and cruel!," made the emperor very angry, but he held his peace. However, when Lady Meng threw herself from the terrace into the river, he flew into a rage.

EMPEROR: This woman is no better than any of the grass and weeds that fill all the towns and villages! Guards! Take your swords and cut up her body into little pieces, and grind her bones into powder. I want to erase every trace of this woman, this hated enemy, from the face of this earth!

NARRATOR: As the soldiers did this, each little piece of Lady Meng's body, ground to powder, turned into a little living fish. There were hundreds, thousands, possibly millions of them, all carrying the soul of Lady Meng in them, continuing to shed tears for the injustice done to them, to face authoritarian rulers with the power of love, and to speak the truth in public. Death is not the end! The power of the emperor — brutal, cruel, and inhuman as it is — is not the final power! Truth lives!

SECTION III

SPEAKING OUT OF OUR PERSONAL ENCOUNTERS

Examples of Asian Sociotheological Biographies

Thus, stories are metaphors in search of a context, waiting to be told and given new relevance.

— A. K. Ramanujan

Chapter 11

Two Encounters in My Theological Journey

ALOYSIUS PIERIS

It was a Sri Lankan Jesuit, Aloysius Pieris, who first put forward the thesis that any serious theological inquiry in Asia should grapple with its two interlocking realities — religious plurality and poverty. His readers rarely know the significant events that led to this theological discovery. Reproduced below is a moving and absorbing autobiographical piece that narrates how his theological journey changed its course after his encounters with a Buddhist monk and an underprivileged Sinhalese youth.

Aloysius Pieris is one of the most eminent of Asian theologians. His two books, *An Asian Theology of Liberation* and *Love Meets Wisdom: A Christian Experience of Buddhism,* both published by Orbis Books, are widely recognized as important sources for Asian theological themes. He runs a community-based study center near Kelaniya.

I present here *my itinerary* in the evolution of a theology and spirituality that is not only very Asian but liberating as well. It is not that I have arrived at conclusions, for the struggle still goes on within me. For that, I would like to start with two basic experiences that have determined the direction of my journey. One was a kind of insertion into the religiosity of Asia; the other, into the social problems. These two experiences could not be reconciled at first. It took time to find integration.

Hundred Years of Bitterness

The first experience was when I was chosen to do Buddhist studies. I was one of the first Catholic priests to get a doctorate in Buddhist philosophy in Sri Lanka. This was a big struggle then. It was something new. The Buddhist could not believe, much less accept, it.

This atmosphere of suspicion was wrought by the many years of estrangement between the church and the Buddhists, especially in the last century. You see, three basic issues were at stake.

One was education. Three to 4 percent of the Christian populace was controlling 90 percent of our educational institutions. And it was using education as a means of conversion. The Buddhist majority felt obligated to pass through Catholic or Christian schools to get an education and, eventually, a job. The foreign aid that flowed freely was siphoned into the schools. The schools, wittingly or not, became the powerful instruments of the church, which presented itself as a power structure.

The Buddhists resented this system and fought against it for years. As a result, the Buddhist Theological Society began running schools of its own. Unfortunately, it produced a type of school that was as bad as the Christian schools in its social structure, owing to the society's very anti-Christian, anti-Western polemical drive. Another issue was the use of the press, which was misused. The Buddhists did not have a press of their own. Not only was there a lot of literature about Christ (which need not be questioned), but also a lot of derogatory statements about Buddhism, and even about the person of the Buddha. The Buddhists felt handicapped because they did not have an instrument of retaliation. Finally, with the help of the Dutch, they managed to go to Thailand — the closest Buddhist authority from which they got help. This was fifty years after the Christians had been using the press. The Buddhist response was very polemical, even obscene. They came out with their own derogatory literature; for instance, a book that devoted one chapter to the virgin birth of Our Lady was really something to read!

Spicing this scenario were debates and public controversies. Christians challenged the Buddhists to public debate. Here, the Buddhists got rid of them because they did not have any mechanical gadgetry advantage. It was purely talk. And I must say that the Buddhists in Sri Lanka, and Buddhists on the whole, have been engaged in controversies for centuries. They practically invented the art of controversy. So the Christians were defeated by the sheer wit of Buddhist polemics. The debates became so famous that they were heard by Colonel Alcott in America. He came running to Sri Lanka. And that was how the Buddhist Theosophical Society began, with the whole Buddhist revival taking on an anti-Christian, anti-Western mien.

Thus far, it can be seen that Buddhist reaction was always a response to a Catholic or Christian initiative in a very polemical approach to interreligious encounter. The real bitterness among the Buddhists, however, was triggered by one particularly terrible misunderstanding. At that time, some Protestant missionaries were hopping from one monastery to another, speaking about Christ. The Buddhists accepted them, gave them a cup of tea, and smiled. The Protestants left greatly upset because the Buddhists just smiled without accepting Christ. The Buddhists, in turn, and as a token of goodwill, invited the Protestants to one of their ceremonies. The Protestants took this as a diabolical plot to belittle their evangelizing efforts. For them, the hour of darkness had come, and the *hour of grace* must strike. So on the day of the ceremony, despite ostentatious assurances that they were guests of honor, the missionaries distributed leaflets rather derogatory to Buddhism, with slurs on the character and person of the Buddha. Since then, no Buddhist monk could ever again bring himself to trust a Christian missionary — or a Christian, for that matter.

So you can imagine the atmosphere of suspicion into which I went to study

Buddhist philosophy. My professor was not only a Buddhist monk from the age of five; he also had a doctorate from Cambridge University. (Many monks have this double formation; they know both East and West well.) He asked me, rather distrustfully, "Father, you could go to a Christian University. Why do you want to waste your time here?" I stuck it out, though. I asked why I couldn't study Buddhism, and he said this was based on experience introspection. Somehow there was this invisible barrier between us. So it took one year and three months to get my application approved, whereas those who were less qualified in terms of academics got in rather easily.

Finally, I was given a chance to go through experience introspection while doing my doctorate. This set me on the path to becoming a monk. The meditation under personal guidance lasted one-and-a-half years. It was an important experience in my life — forgetting Christianity, to the point of denying it, to receive the fullness of the Buddhist kenosis.

The monks did not accept me at first because, even then, I did not accept them. I went to them with my index cards because I had studied in Europe. Our monks did not know English and, as far as I was concerned, those who did not know English were uneducated. What I failed to realize — because of my prejudices — was that these villagers were nurturing a tradition blessed by centuries.

Then one day, garbed in my cassock as a Catholic priest, I took a basket of fruit and flowers and, in the presence of a Buddhist leader, fell prostrate. I worshiped him and asked to be accepted as his pupil. From that day, after this act of humility, I have had no problem with Buddhist monks. And now (thank God!) they have accepted me as a scholar among them. As a Catholic priest, I have been invited to read a research paper, a new theory in Buddhist doctrine, for their monastic seminar.

This incident illustrates a point expounded in an earlier paper, "The Theology of Double Baptism." There I made a theological analysis of double baptism; that is, baptism in the "Jordan of Asian Religiosity" and baptism in the "Calvary of Asian Poverty." It was only when Jesus was humble enough to choose John the Baptist as his guru and bend down in the Jordan that his mission was proclaimed. Till then, he was not the Messiah. Messianic power was bestowed the moment he made the act of humility. Translated for our times, baptism is not to pour water on somebody and bring him or her into the church — which does not do service to anybody — but to pass through the act of humility by which the church is baptized into the Asian environment. So this conviction came to me, and it determined the one pole that is my religious experience.

Since, then, I have had another experience — harsher, more revolutionary.

A Student's Question

It was in the 1960s, when I was still working in the university that became the cradle of the 1971 revolution, that the majority of the Buddhist youth (and monks, for that matter) got disheartened by established Buddhism. Monks had landed property, a lot of wealth, and were not concerned with the problems of the country because they were well off with the government. The government supported, obeyed, and domesticated them; they, in turn, gave their sanction to the government. (This happens everywhere where there is an established religion and entrenched government. Religion and politics go together, for better or for worse.)

Most of the poor students were in economics, politics, and history, whereas the rich students were in the science faculties of the private colleges, mostly Catholic, that could afford to provide science laboratories. The big colleges produced cricketers and rugby and football players, and the private firms would employ them; the university student would arrive with great difficulty to the B.A. level — and end up a bus conductor. Obviously, despite the free education offered by Prime Minister Srimavao Bandaranaike, there was this discrepancy in the national system — one group was always in power, and religion was with that power.

Since the Buddhist youth could not turn to the church for answers to the social dimension of spirituality (a bigoted spirituality could be offered, but the church had lost its credibility), the only area open for them was Marxism. So they started on structural analysis.

Students in the villages began to say, "Our parents were duped. We shall not allow our children to be duped. We've got this much knowledge. Let's start bringing reform to this country." Whether they were right or wrong is another matter, but they took the responsibility into their hands.

I met some of the students, most of whom were undergraduates. One was a porter's son, living near a railway run. His father's job was to close the gate whenever the train passed by. It was a lowly job. This student had nothing to eat; so he used to come with a cup of tea and stay the whole day. Most of his allowances went to transportation expenses and books. In this sense, free education was just a myth; only the middle class, not the poor, could afford it. But because this student was clever, he was able to make it to the university level. He would stay in the university till 8:00 P.M. to study a bit more because there was no electricity in his house. And he would go back with a loaf of bread because it was a bit cheaper in town than in the remote area where he lived. I asked this student, given the difficulty under which he was studying, what he would do if he failed. He said, "If I fail, the train goes by my house" — which meant that suicide was a likely resource. This was the last line of frustration of the youth, and nobody realized it except those who were with them.

When I came back to my religious house, it was different. Everybody was with pipe or cigar, quite comfortable, and laughing at the prospect of Ceylonese, who were thought to be cowards, going for a revolution. And they did that until the eve of the revolution. Until bloodshed came, they could not believe it, as they were quite comfortable.

I had this ambiguous feeling of belonging to two groups, heartbroken here and there. So I asked this student to have lunch with me. Immediately his Buddhist instinct took over. "No," he said. "We never take lunch from a monk. Isn't it that you give lunch to a monk?" (See? Though he was a Marxist, as I came to know later, he still had the Buddhist instinct — just like the Italian Marxists. I know. I have been in Italy for many years, working in the slums of Naples with Marxist students. They will not believe in anything, but when they hear thunder, they immediately make the sign of the cross. This just shows their culture and the depth of religious influence.) Anyway, I told him not to mind. I gave him the social doctrines of the church. "This money with me belongs to you. I am a priest, not a monk. I am working for the transformation of the world, and I am here with this money I can share with you." He still said no.

So I told him that the money I had, according to my doctrine, was given to me for those in need. I quoted the fathers of the church, and the gospel, and stated the famous teachings of the church. (By "fathers of the church" I refer to the early Christian patriarchs who said, to wit, that if I had ten rupees, and if I don't give half of it to the one who doesn't have anything, I will be stealing five rupees from him.) Still, he was not convinced. He asked, "Is it your personal interpretation, or is it the teaching of the church?" I said it was the teaching of the church. "Then do you belong to the same church that owns all these private schools?" I said yes and no. (These are the conflicts of those in our situation.)

Finally, we were able to go for lunch. As we were taking our lunch, mostly in silence, the student turned to me and asked a very important question, which I insist should be put to all priests and nuns in Asia: *"From where do you get your money?"* I gave the wrong answer: "God gives it to me."

After this, I began to think what this student may have thought, that this must be a funny God who gives to the priest and not to him. It struck me that each time I am faced with this situation wherein I have something and somebody doesn't, and I proclaim God and my belief in God, I am preaching about an unjust God who doesn't exist. In a way, I am preaching atheism — because God is just, and nobody is just if he is not favorable to the poor. He has to be favorable to the poor, otherwise, he is not just; and if he is not just, he is not God. So each time this situation occurs, it is antitheistic, antireligious. And it has been worrying me ever since.

This child, the student, was courageous enough to invite me later for the five lessons that prepared the revolution. We fought for Christianity for four hundred years, and had 7 percent conversions in Sri Lanka, while these people, overnight, won so many. For they were in a situation of seeking liberation; we were not. They had a message; we, a doctrine. Message is quite different from doctrine. Doctrine is $(a+b)^2 = a^2 + 2ab + b^2$. You put that on the board, and everybody says yes — but it doesn't change you. Message is something you cannot prove. It is a revolutionary idea. You put it across like Mahatma Gandhi, proof or no proof — except your life witness. So this was the message they were giving. I went for two or three lessons — and than simply disappeared because I had not the courage to go on. I had my nice, comfortable home. Within a year, the revolution took place. I traced this boy and found that he had been killed in the forest. His face still comes to me regularly, asking where I get my money.

All these — my Buddhist experience of total poverty detachment, of going deep to experience, of denying everything and accepting and rediscovering God in a new dimension, and then coming back to this reality of the social dimension, of gross injustice, of religion conspiring with mammon, of building altars to mammon on the graves of the poor — have contributed to my personal synthesis. It was such that while I was teaching Buddhism and Theology of Religions in the missiological faculty of the Gregorian University in Rome, I realized, after a brief stint, that it was not the place for me. What was becoming difficult was this dissonance I was experiencing. So I told my superiors that I must have a laboratory to become a professor of Asian religions. Rome was certainly not that laboratory.

I went back to Sri Lanka in 1974 and started a little center that has developed since. The center, which is near the Buddhist University of Kelenia where I once taught, maintains a Buddhist atmosphere where youth seeking justice can meet. I continue to do Buddhist research from there, although the center is open to students of any religion. The only question we ask is whether or not the student has taken his meal — and we share whatever we have.

The initial period was one of anxiety for our center. We were thrown out of our houses; so we had to scout around for a more stable place. Finally, my order (Jesuit) bought some property at a very cheap price and allowed our Buddhist commune to build on it. Thus, we have the peculiar relationship with the order. But from that time, I have refused to accept any other donations. We worked on our garden and earned from it. I lectured; I wrote articles. And the commune earned from my earnings, too. Up until now, we are surviving on sheer earnings — and it has been nine years. Whenever I go abroad to lecture (which I do regularly), I send part of my earnings to the center. I wish I could send more but, as a scholar of Asian religions, one needs certain basic amenities like photocopying, research materials, field expenses, and the like. However, I now feel that I have answered, if only partially, the haunting question of my student friend, and that is, *I get my money through my labor.*

In essence, the aforementioned experiences — insertion into the religiosity of Asia and immersion into its social problems — have brought me to an awareness of a spirituality that is not only an orientation toward a God — an ultimate reality, a nirvana of renunciation — but also toward a cosmic involvement, manifesting the popular spirituality of the poor with whom Jesus identified himself.

Chapter 12

Mothers and Daughters, Writers and Fighters

KWOK PUI LAN

Most Asians inhabit two worlds: their indigenous cultural world, with its own distinctive stories and symbols into which they are born, and the cultural world of Western Christianity into which they are transplanted. In a personal and theological autobiography reproduced here, a Hong Kong feminist theologian recalls her personal history and the experience of inheriting two worlds — Chinese and Christian — and how it enabled her to expand her Christian identity and work out a more inclusive theology.

Kwok Pui Lan is currently on the staff of the Episcopal Divinity School, Cambridge, Massachusetts. She, along with Chung Hyun Kyung, is seen as one of the sharper voices to emerge recently on the Asian theological scene. She has written extensively on Asian theology, feminist issues, and Asian biblical hermeneutics in *Concilium, In God's Image,* and *International Review of Mission.* Her recent books include *Chinese Women and Christianity 1860–1927* (Atlanta: Scholars Press, 1992).

Source: *Inheriting Our Mothers' Gardens: Feminist Theology in Third World Perspective,* Letty M. Russell et al., eds. (Louisville: Westminster Press, 1988).

I was born in Hong Kong on the twenty-third of March, according to the Chinese lunar calendar. On this day, many Chinese in the coastal provinces of China celebrate the birthday of Mazu, the goddess who protects fisherpeople, seafarers, and maritime merchants. This is also a festive day for my family, for it is the only day in the year that my father will take a day off and go to offer thanksgiving in the temple.

I am the third child of a family of seven children. My mother gave birth to five girls before two sons came at last. Because of the patriarchal and patrilineal structure of the Chinese family, to produce a male heir used to be the most important responsibility of women in marriage. My parents had been waiting for twelve years before the sons were born, and, as can be expected, the boys were given most of the attention. From my early childhood, I questioned the legitimacy of a social system that does not treat boys and girls equally.

My mother is tall and thin but very strong. When we were young, we once moved into a new building where the water supply had not yet been adequately installed. To fetch water for the whole family, every day my mother carried two big tins full of water and slowly climbed up seven flights of stairs. This vivid image of her is lodged in my mind. Like many Chinese women of her age, she is a devout follower of folk Buddhist religion. When the moon waxes and wanes, she will offer prayers and thanksgiving sacrifices, and she also makes offerings to the ancestors. When I became a Christian in my teens, my mother did not object to my going to church. I thought that she must have found something important in her religious life.

My mother-in-law belongs to an ethnic group called the Kejia, whose women have a reputation of being powerful and independent. Contrary to the prevailing practice, the Kejia women seldom had their feet bound, since many of them had to work in the field. My mother-in-law came from a poor family and was betrothed to her husband as a child. Without learning how to read and write, she has taught herself to make all kinds of things, and her creativity often surprises me. When she lived with us in Hong Kong, she would grow many different vegetables in our backyard during the summer season. Juicy red tomatoes, fleshy white cabbages, and green Dutch beans made our garden look gorgeous. Our little daughter used to help her in watering plants and plucking weeds.

My mother-in-law does not follow any particular religious practice, but she has a profound trust in life and an unfailing spirit to struggle for survival. I have always admired people like my two mothers, who had very limited life chances yet have tried to live with dignity and integrity and to share whatever they have with others. The stories of these women have seldom been told, and their lives easily fall into oblivion. Nonetheless, it is these women who pass the wisdom of the human race from generation to generation and who provide the context of life for others. The stories of my mothers drive home to me a very precious lesson: as women living in a patriarchal cultural system, they are oppressed by men, but, never content to be treated as victims, they have struggled against the forces that seek to limit them and circumscribe their power.

My Spiritual Foremothers

When I was twelve, one of our neighbors took me to the worship service at an Anglican church. This church is one of two churches in Hong Kong built in a Chinese style, with Christian symbols and motifs embodied in Chinese architecture. I grew to like the liturgical worship, the music, and the fellowship. The vicar of the church was Deacon Huang Xianyun, who was later officially ordained as one of the two women priests in the worldwide Anglican Communion in 1971. Rev. Huang has been a strong role model for me, and her life exemplifies that women can serve the church just as men do. Rev. Huang has always preached that men and women are created equal before God, and she has encouraged women to develop their potential. Because of her influence, many women in our church volunteered to do various kinds of ministry. As a high-school girl, I used to accompany them in visiting the sick and calling on those old people who were too weak to come to church. Some of these women volunteers were widows; a few were rich; others came from poor and middle-class backgrounds. Their dedication to others in ministering to the needy helped me to see glimpses of the Divine and sustained me through many doubts and uncertainties.

Just like these women of my church, other Chinese women joined the Christian community in search of an alternative vision of society and human relationships. In the last decades of the nineteenth century, women who joined the church were poor and lower-class; the gentry and the upper-class families would not allow their wives and daughters to follow a foreign religion. To read the Bible and the catechism, these illiterate women had to be taught how to read. Bible-women were employed to translate for the missionaries and to do the home visitations. As the church became involved in social reforms, some of the Christian women participated in literacy campaigns and the antifootbinding movement and organized health-care programs and women's associations.

These activities allowed women to come together to talk about their problems and to find ways and means to tackle them. Amid all the changes in modern China, these women have tried to work for the benefit of women and contribute to society. Like other women in third-world churches, they bear witness to a faith that empowers people to break through silence and move to action. Although many of their names have been lost in history, they are my spiritual foremothers in loving memory.

Between the Two Worlds: As Chinese and as Christian

My double inheritance from my own mothers and my spiritual foremothers has raised a serious question for me: What is the connection between the lives of simple folk like my mothers and Christianity? I have long rejected the arrogance that "outside the church, there is no salvation," for it means condemning my ancestors, mothers, nieces, and nephews. In fact, in the long history of China's encounter with Christianity, the Christian population in China has scarcely exceeded one half of one percent. As a tiny minority, we live among our people in the world's most populous country, which has a long history and civilization. China not only challenges any presumptuous "universal" salvation history but also presents a world of thought, language, art, and philosophy radically different from the Christian tradition. As Chinese Christians, we have been in constant dialogue with this rich cultural heritage, long before the term "religious dialogue" was coined.

But to claim that we are both Chinese and Christian is not an easy matter; in the view of many Chinese, this claim is simply implausible. Chinese identity is defined by participation in a complicated cultural matrix of social behavior, rites, and human relationships, while Christianity is often perceived to be bound up with Western philosophy, liturgy, and cultural symbols.[1] Moreover, Christianity came to China together with the expansion of Western military aggression. We people of Hong Kong are painstakingly aware that in the first unequal treaty between China and the West, Hong Kong was ceded to the British, and at the same time missionaries were allowed to preach at China's treaty ports.

With such a heavy historical burden on our shoulders, we Chinese Christians have to vindicate ourselves to our own people: we are not the instruments of foreign aggressors, nor do we share the same religion as the oppressors. In the 1920s, religious leaders in China began the process of the indigenization of the church, so that Chinese Christians would eventually assume the tasks of self-propagation, self-support, and self-government. Some Chinese theologians at that time believed that Christianity could be the social basis for the revitalization of China. Others believed that Christianity could be a revolutionary force that would lead to social changes.

But as Chinese women, we are much more concerned about how Christianity is indigenized into the Chinese culture. The Confucian tradition has been vehemently criticized in China's recent past as advocating hierarchical social relations, strict separation between the sexes, and a backward-looking worldview. The androcentric moral teachings have been castigated as undergirding the conservative inertia of keeping China feudal and patriarchal.[2] At the same time, Christianity has been subjected to vigorous dissection and in-depth analyses to expose its dualistic tendency and patriarchal bias.[3] For some time, Chinese women have taken comfort in knowing that Jesus advocated equality of the sexes, in spite of the Jewish patriarchal custom, and that Paul's teachings on women were limited by the cultural conditions of his time.[4] But today, Jewish feminists caution us against anti-Semitic prejudices, and feminist biblical scholars argue that Paul's bias against women took place in a much wider process of patriarchalization of the early church.[5]

In a dazzling way, there is a "shaking of the foundations" on both sides, and we are confronted with a double culture shock. There is no easy path we can follow. As one Chinese poet says, "The road is long and tortuous, we have to search above and below."[6] Out of this most trying experience, we have come to face both our cultural heritage and the Christian tradition with courage and hope, that we may find new ways to do theology that will liberate us and sustain our faith.

Searching for a Liberating Faith

The crisis of meaning and identity motivates me to search passionately for my mothers' gardens. What is the source of power that they found liberating, and how were they able to maintain their integrity as women against all the forces that denied them opportunities and tried to keep them in a subordinate place? The answer to these questions is not easy to come by, since women's lives have been trivialized and their contributions often erased from our memory. For a long time, the history of Christianity was written from the missionary perspective. These books record the life and work of the missionaries but seldom relate facts about the Chinese Christians. Even when they mention mission for women, they emphasize the work "done for" Chinese women instead of telling the stories and lives of the women themselves. Chinese scholars, too, have tended to focus more on Chinese men, who could write and therefore leave us with so-called reliable historical data. We know too little about the faith and religious imagination of Chinese Christian women.

To be connected with my own roots, I have learned to value the experiences and writings of my foremothers. Many of their short testimonies, gleaned from articles in journals and small pamphlets, would not formerly have been counted as "theological data." I have also looked in alternative resources, such as songs, poems, and myths, as well as in unexpected corners, such as obituary notices. Sometimes this requires a fresh treatment of the materials: reading between the lines, attending to small details, and providing the missing links by circumstantial evidence. This meticulous work is done with a deep respect for these women, and in remembrance of their testimony to an alternative understanding of the fullness of life.

Trying to find the link to the threads of their lives, I have come to understand that they were not passive recipients of what was handed down or taught to them. They were brave enough to challenge the patriarchal tradition, both in Chinese culture as well as in Christianity. After they became Christians, some of the women refused to follow the Chinese marriage rites or to participate in the funeral ceremony, which were social enactments of patrilineal and patriarchal family ideals. In addition, some questioned the overt patriarchal bias of the Bible. A Christian woman whose name has been lost to history used a pin to cut out from her Bible Paul's injunction that wives should be submissive to their husbands. When her husband exhorted her to obey what the Bible taught, she brought out her Bible and said it did not contain such teachings. At the turn of this century, a medical doctor named Zhang Zhujun was said to be the first Chinese woman preaching in the church. Commenting on Paul's prescription that women should keep silence in the church, Dr. Zhang boldly asserted that Paul was wrong![7]

About sixty years after Chinese women started to join the church in recognizable numbers, women organized themselves in the first meeting of the Chinese National Council of Churches in 1922. Ms. Ruth Cheng addressed the Assembly and raised the issue of the ordination of women. She said:

> People in some places think that the ordination of women is out of the question and women pastors are simply impossibilities. I do not intend to advocate that the church ought to have women pastors, but I would simply like to ask the reason why women cannot have such rights. If the Western Church because of historical development and other reasons has adopted such an attitude, has the Chinese Church the same reason for doing so? If the ancient Church, with sufficient reasons, considered that women could not have such rights, are those reasons sufficient enough to be applied to the present Church?[8]

These brave acts of women demonstrated their critical discernment, as moral agents, and a radical defiance that uncompromisingly challenged those traditions that were limiting and binding for women.

To claim such a heritage for myself is a process of self-empowerment. First, it informs me that these Chinese Christian women have a history and a story that need to be recovered for the benefit of the whole church. Second, I stand in a long tradition of Chinese Christian women who, with tremendous self-respect, struggled not only for their own liberation but also for justice in church and society. Third, these women brought their experience to bear on their interpretation of Christian faith and dared to challenge the established teaching of the church. It is because of this history that I can claim to do theology from a Chinese woman's perspective.

Toward an Inclusive Theology

I have found several important insights while tending and digging in my mothers' gardens. Their religious experience and quest for liberation point to the necessity of expanding our Christian identity and developing a more inclusive theology. This involves several major shifts in our traditional theological thinking. First, it requires us to shift our attention from the Bible and tradition to people's stories. The exclusiveness of the Christian claim often stems from a narrow and mystified view of the Bible and church teaching. I admit that the Bible records many moving stories of struggle against oppression, and it continues to inspire many third-world Christians today. But I also agree with post-Christian feminists that our religious imagination cannot be based on the Bible alone, which often excludes women's experience.[9] In particular, I cannot believe that truth is revealed only in a book written almost two thousand years ago and that the Chinese have no way to participate in its inception. Let me give some concrete examples to illustrate what I mean. Coming from the southern part of China, where rice is the main food, I have often found the biblical images of bread-making and yeast-rising as alienating. I also feel a little uneasy when some Western women begin to talk about God as Bakerwoman.[10] The Chinese, who live in an agricultural setting instead of a pastoral environment, have imaged the Divine as compassionate, nonintrusive, immanent in and continuous with nature. The images and metaphors we use to talk about God are necessarily culturally conditioned, and biblical ones are no exception.

The Bible tells us stories that the Hebrew people and the Christians in the early church valued as shaping their collective memory. The Western Christian tradition represents one of the many ways to interpret this story for one's own situation. The Indians, the Burmese, the Japanese, and the Chinese all have stories that give meaning and orientation to their lives. Women in particular have a treasure chest of lullabies, songs, myths, and stories that give them a sense of who they are and where they are going. Opening this treasure chest is the first step to doing our own theology. With full confidence, we claim that our own culture and our people's aspiration are vehicles for knowing and appreciating the ultimate. This would also imply that our Christian identity must be radically expanded. Instead of fencing us from the world, it should open us to all the rich manifestations that embody the Divine.

Second, we have to move from a passive reception of the traditions to an active construction of our own theology. The missionary movement has been criticized for making third-world churches dependent on churches in Europe and America. This dependence is not just financial but, more devastatingly, theological. With an entirely different philosophical tradition, we enter into the mysterious debate of homoousia, and with no critical judgment we continue the modernist and fundamentalist debate of the missionaries, long after a partial cease-fire has been declared in the West. We try our best to study Greek and Hebrew — and Latin or German too, if we can manage — and spare little time to learn the wisdom of our own people. As half-baked theologians, we are busy solving other people's theological puzzles — and thus doing a disservice to our people and the whole church by not integrating our own culture in our theology.

All peoples must find their own way of speaking about God and generate new symbols, concepts, and models that they find congenial for expressing their religious vision. We women, who have been prevented from participating fully in this myth- and symbol-making process, must reclaim our right to do so. As a Chinese Christian woman, I have to critically reassess my double heritage, to rediscover liberating elements for building my own theology. Ironically, it is my commitment to feminism that leads me to a renewed interest and appreciation of my own cultural roots. Chinese folk religions have always been much more inclusive, and they do not exclude the female religious image and symbolism. Chinese religious sensibility has a passion for nature and longs for the integration of heaven and earth and a myriad of things. If theology is an "imaginative construction," as Gordon Kaufman says,[11] we would need constantly to combine the patterns and weave the threads in new ways to name ourselves, our world, and our God.

Third, doing our own theology requires moving away from a unified theological discourse to a plurality of voices and a genuine catholicity. The new style of theol- ogy anticipates that there will be many theologies, just as there are many different ways of cooking food. For those who are raised in a cultural tradition that con- stantly searches for the "one above many," this will imply confusion, complication, and frustration. For others, like me, who are brought up in a culture that honors many gods and goddesses, this is a true celebration of the creativity of the people.

The criterion to judge the different styles of theologizing is not codified in the Bible, and the norm of theology is not determined by whether it smells something like that of Augustine and Aquinas — or Tillich and Barth, for that matter. Instead, it lies in the praxis of the religious communities struggling for the liberation of humankind. All theologies must be judged regarding how much they contribute to the liberation and humanization of the human community. A living theology tries to bear witness to the unceasing yearning of human beings for freedom and justice; it articulates the human compassion for peace and reconciliation.

Will plurality threaten the unity and catholicity of the church? For me, unity and catholicity cannot be understood in terms of religious doctrines and beliefs but must be seen as an invitation to work together. Unity does not mean homogeneity, and catholicity does not mean sameness. Process theologian John B. Cobb, Jr., captures the meaning of unity well:

> The unity of Christianity is the unity of a historical movement. That unity does not depend on any self-identity of doctrine, vision of reality, structure of existence, or style of life. It does depend on demonstrable continuities, the appropriateness of creative changes, and the self-identification of people in relation to a particular history.[12]

The particular history that third-world people and other women's communities can identify with is that God is among the people who seek to become full human beings. Today, as we third-world women are doing our own theology, we come closer to a unity that is more inclusive and colorful and a catholicity that is more genuine and authentic. I heartily welcome this coming age of plurality in our way of doing theology, that our stories can be heard and our experiences valued in our theological imagination. To celebrate Asian women's spirit-rising, I would like to conclude by sharing a song written by my dear friend Mary Sung-ok Lee:[13]

We Are Women

We are women from Burma, China,
India, Japan, Korea, Malaysia,
Philippines, Thailand, and U.S.A.

Chorus:

Eh hey ya ho-o
Eh hey ya ho-o
Cho ku na cho wa (Oh, how good it is!)
Eh hey ya ho-o.

We are women, we are alive,
breaking our silence,
seeking solidarity.

Chorus

We are women, Yellow women,
angered by injustice,
denouncing exploitation.

Chorus

We are sisters, gathered for bonding,
mothers and daughters,
writers and fighters.

Chorus

We are women, spirit-filled women,
claiming our story,
voicing our poetry.

Chorus

Notes

1. For an insightful discussion of the two different cultural systems, refer to Jacques Gernet, *China and the Christian Impact,* trans. Janet Lloyd (Cambridge: Cambridge University Press, 1985).

2. The Confucian tradition was criticized as patriarchal in the May Fourth Movement of 1919 and was more severely condemned in the Cultural Revolution during 1966–1976. In the post-Mao era, Chinese philosophers have begun to analyze the limits and contributions of the Confucian tradition as it relates to present Chinese society.

3. See for example, Mary Daly, *Beyond God the Father* (Boston: Beacon Press, 1973), and Rosemary Radford Ruether, *Sexism and God-Talk: Toward a Feminist Theology* (Boston: Beacon Press, 1983).

4. Ding Shujing, "Funü zai jiaohui de diwei" (Women's Status in the Church), *Nu Qing Nian* 7 (2):22 (March 1928).

5. See Judith Plaskow, "Blaming Jews for Inventing Patriarchy," *Lilith* 7:12-13 (1980), and Elisabeth Schüssler Fiorenza, *In Memory of Her: A Feminist Theological Reconstruction of Christian Origins* (New York: Crossroad Publishing Co., 1983).

6. From Qu Yuan, "Li Sao" (Farewell Ode).

7. See "The History of Ms. Zhang Zhujun" in Li Youning and Zhang Yufa, eds., *Jindai Zhongguo nuguan yundong zhiliao* (Historical Materials on Modern Chinese Feminist Movement), 2 vols. (Taipei: Biographical Literature Publisher, 1975), vol. 2, p. 1380.

8. Ruth Cheng, "Women and the Church," *Chinese Recorder* 53:540 (1922).

9. Carol P. Christ, "Spiritual Quest and Women's Experience," in Carol P. Christ and Judith Plaskow, eds., *Womanspirit Rising: A Feminist Reader in Religion* (San Francisco: Harper & Row, 1979), pp. 228–245. See also her *Laughter of Aphrodite: Reflections on a Journey to the Goddess* (San Francisco: Harper & Row, 1987).

10. See the poem of Alla Bozarth-Campbell, "Bakerwoman God," in Iben Gjerding and Katherine Kinnamon, eds., *No Longer Strangers: A Resource for Women and Worship* (Geneva: World Council of Churches, 1983), p. 54.

11. Gordon D. Kaufman, *The Theological Imagination: Constructing the Concept of God* (Philadelphia: Westminster Press, 1981), pp. 263–279.

12. John B. Cobb, Jr., "Feminism and Process Thought: A Two-way Relationship," in Sheila Greeve Daveney, ed., *Feminism and Process Thought* (Lewistown, N.Y.: Edwin Mellen Press, 1981), p. 42.

13. Used by permission of Mary Sung-ok Lee.

Chapter 13

My Pilgrimage in Mission

M. M. THOMAS

Over the years, the Indian church has produced eminent lay people who have always been at the forefront in developing a suitable theology to meet indigenous needs. One of the most prominent of these lay theologians is M. M. Thomas. He became internationally known through his ecumenical activities spanning nearly four decades and locally known for his social and political involvement. Here in this article he recalls some important turning points in his spiritual-theological journey.

M. M. Thomas now lives in his hometown, Tiruvalla, in Kerala State. He has held various distinguished posts, including among others, founder and director of the Christian Institute for the Study of Religion and Society, Bangalore, and governor of the northeast Indian state of Nagaland. He has published extensively on social, cultural, and political issues. The most recent of his numerous books is *My Ecumenical Journey 1947–75,* Trivandrum: Ecumenical Publishing Centre, 1990.

Source: *International Bulletin of Missionary Research* 13 (1), 1989.

My journey has taken me through a critique of "missions" in the narrow sense to the more inclusive concept of the "mission" of the church in the modern world. Perhaps I can share this best by concentrating on some important turning points in my spiritual-theological pilgrimage.

It was through an evangelical spiritual experience as a first-year college student in Trivandrum in 1931–32 that Jesus Christ became real to me as the bearer of divine forgiveness and gave my life, awakened to adolescent urges, a principle of integration and a sense of direction. It led me to take seriously three Christian youth fellowships then active among students: (1) an informal fellowship group helping students to find new life in Christ, (2) the Youth Union, which was part of the Mar Thoma Church congregation, and (3) the interdenominational Student Christian

Movement. Through the parish Youth Union I became devoted to the church; and besides availing myself of its liturgical and sacramental resources, I joined a youth team in regular visits to a locality of low caste Hindu residences to preach Christ to them, and during the vacations I joined a student group visiting the Mar Thoma parishes to share Christ with young people. The Student Christian Movement under the leadership of K. A. Matthew, through its Bible studies and discussions on inter-church relations and current national issues, and through student surveys of slum conditions and organizing games and literacy work among the street boys, was seeking to bring students an awareness of the ecumenical and social implications of the gospel. The emphasis in my life at that period was personal devotional life and personal evangelism. I remember that for a long time Thomas à Kempis' *Imitation of Christ* was the basis of my daily self-examination; and books like Leslie Weatherhead's *Transforming Friendship,* Brother Lawrence's *Practice of the Presence of God,* and Alan H. McNeile's *Self-Training in Meditation* were resources for building my spirituality. The book *Praying Hyde* by Basil Miller impressed me so much that after my graduation in 1935, I organized the Trivandrum informal fellowship of friends into an Interceding Fellowship and made my own intercessions elaborate and systematic.

In 1935 I joined the Mar Thoma Church Ashram at Perumpavoor. There I was a part-time teacher in the school and was engaged part-time in organizing evangelistic activities of the ashram in the neighboring parishes. I remember organizing an evangelistic team to go to a rubber estate to conduct evangelistic meetings for the workers and coming away with the feeling that the gospel of salvation we preached did not have much relevance to the oppressive conditions of work and housing in which the estate workers lived. It raised many questions for me.

This was also the time when my friend M. A. Thomas had begun work as secretary of the Inter-Religious Student Fellowship. It opened for me contacts with students and nonstudent leaders of Hinduism and Islam and with their religious experiences. Debates on interfaith relations were lively in the meetings of the fellowship. The All-Kerala Conference to which Mahatma Gandhi sent a message asking that "all religions represented be treated with equal respect" and warning that if there are "mental reservations there will be no heart-fellowship" remains in memory. The "Aim and Basis" of the Inter-Religious Student Fellowship created a lot of discussion. Gandhian nonviolence also raised the social implications of religion and the meaning of the cross for politics. M. A. Thomas and I spent hours together in discussion about the truth and meaning of Christ in the interreligious setting. It was against this background that I was roused to my inquiry on Christology. It was an intellectual and spiritual struggle. Out of it came my reflections on *The Realization of the Cross* (1937) affirming the centrality of the crucified Jesus for the movement of the kingdom of God in history, which induced God's work in all religions and all urges toward love and justice. (This was published in 1972 by Christian Literature Society, Madras, as Lenten meditations.)

In 1937 I joined the Christavasram at Alleppey, where the fellowship under the leadership of Sadhu Mathai had a comprehensive vision of the gospel. They were in charge of the church's missionary work among some coastal villages; they conducted a Home for Waifs and Strays (street boys) of the town; they had interreligious dialogues. It was there that I met Svi Baliga, the Brahmin who acknowledged Christ without leaving the Hindu fold, and from whom Mathai had received *Kavi* dress initiating him into the life of a Christian *sadhu* patterned after the Hindu *samngasa*. Spontaneously Sadhuji became my guru. He put me in charge of the worship side of the ashram life; I produced a book of daily worship in Malayalam (published later), which emphasized Christian spirituality as the basis of the church's mission in the world of religions and the social life of the nation. But Sadhu Mathai felt that my spirituality was too pietistic and subjectivist and not sufficiently world-oriented. It was in search of the unity of interiority with active life that in 1938, I returned to Trivandrum, where I had my college education, to organize a home for street boys with the help of the Student Christian Movement (SCM) but under an interreligious foundation. I also took the initiative to tackle the beggar problem in the city through organized charity in cooperation with the municipal authorities. Charitable social service became the expression of my personal commitment to Christ, without emphasizing verbal witness.

It was during the period of my social service activities in Trivandrum that the political agitation for responsible government increased in the princely state of Travancore. The Student Christian Movement at its annual conference supported it and formed the Kerala Youth Christian Council of Action (YCCA) to promote Christian witness in national politics. I got deeply involved in it from the beginning as its secretary. The YCCA became a dynamic movement of thought and action among the Christian young people of Kerala, with its base in Christavasram of Sadhu Mathai (which had now moved from Alleppey to its new house in Kottayam). One of the YCCA's most challenging programs was the study courses to help young people to understand liberal secularism, Gandhism, and Marxism — ideologies influencing the Indian national movement — and to evaluate them in the light of Christian faith. R. R. Keithahn's village-oriented Gandhism, coupled with his prophetic passion and Leonard Schiff's combination of Anglo-Catholicism, Niebuhrian neoorthodoxy, and Marxism, made a tremendous contribution to our spirits and minds. The studies raised for me the role of the politics of justice in Christian social witness and the relation between faith and ideology in Christian social ethics. In pursuance of these questions, I spent a year in Bangalore reading on the theology of society and the scientific understanding of our Indian social reality.

The neoorthodoxy of Nicolas Berdyaev and Reinhold Niebuhr, along with Marxist analysis of Indian social history, gripped me. I returned to full-time work with the YCCA convinced that Marxism was a necessary ideological basis for political action for social justice in India, but that its utopianism, which elevated it to a scheme of total spiritual salvation, was a source of tyranny — and that therefore the Christian has the double task of cooperating with the communists in the politics of class struggle and intensifying the spiritual struggle against the character of communism as a scheme of salvation by works. Here class politics for justice and evangelistic witness to justification by faith became equally central to my understanding of Christian mission in India. The evangelistic witness to Christ, to be relevant, has to be within the framework of a politics of justice and not in isolation. The church as the fellowship of transcendent divine and mutual forgiveness must be present as the ultimate destiny of those involved in the necessarily tragic power-political struggles in a sinful world.

An amendment I proposed for the "Aim and Basis" of the Youth Christian

Council of Action wanted it to "accept the Catholic Christian Faith and Marxian Scientific Socialism," reacting against "both Fundamentalism that is indifferent to science and social questions and the Liberal Social Gospel which denies the fact of sin" and to offer "the Orthodox Christian Faith as in the long run the only possible basis for social and scientific realism."

It was to pursue this double task of the Christian mission that I asked for ordination in my church and for membership in the Communist party. Both rejected me, for opposite reasons. But Bishop Johanon Mar Thimotheus (later Mar Thoma metropolitan), who had participated in the YCCA activities for several years and perhaps had faith in my theological integrity, urged the church to appoint me its youth secretary. That was in 1945.

In the early 1940s Malcolm Adiseshiah of the Madras Christian College, Tambaram, began inviting me to speak at the SCM Leaders' Training Courses. For a period I was also the editor of the SCM *Student Outlook*. I also became involved in the dialogues of the Indian SCM with the British SCM and the World's Student Christian Federation (WSCF) on the Indian political situation. All this led to my being invited to Geneva as a secretary of the WSCF. From 1947 to 1950 I was full-time secretary, and from 1950 to 1953, an officer. This gave me opportunity for dialogue with the "West" within the setting of the ecumenical movement. I participated in the volume on Church and Society in preparation for the first assembly of the World Council of Churches (WCC) and had numerous conversations with J. H. Oldham, the chairman of the Church and Society Committee. I also engaged in endless discussion in the Political Commission of the WSCF, which led to the publication of the book, by J. D. McCaughey and myself, *The Christian in the World Struggle* (1951). All this made for new thinking. I had also to rethink my ideological stance in the light of India's independence and Nehru's ventures into nation-building. I began to question my thesis that political technology was a matter only of "natural necessity" and that divine justification was experienced only "after politics." This led me to a new appreciation of the ideologies of liberal democracy and Gandhian nonviolence and to a revision of my understanding of Marxism in their light. In my talk at the WSCF General Committee in 1952, I referred to this change in my approach as follows:

> There was a time when I thought that the New Age of Christ was so much beyond history that it could be experienced in politics only as Forgiveness and not as Power; that political philosophy could be only a philosophy of sinful necessities where the cross was relevant only as forgiveness to the politician and not as qualifying politics, political parties, techniques, and institutions as such.

Of course, the depth of sin in collective life made for a permanent tension between the politics of justice and redemptive love until Christ came, but "it is possible for politics itself to be redeemed of its extreme perversions and be made more or less human, if it recognizes and receives into itself the power of the gospel."

The Christian Institute for the Study of Religion and Society was founded in Bangalore in 1956 with Paul Devanandan as director and myself as associate. It was founded by the NCC of India (then the National Christian Council, now the National

Council of Churches) to help the churches understand the changing religious and social environment in which they had to discharge their mission in independent India. Devanandan was convinced that the church's faith and evangelistic mission must be set relevantly and challengingly within the context of Christian participation in nation-building and of the interfaith dialogue on the nature and destiny of human-being-in-society (anthropology) inevitable in such participation. Devanandan saw Christ at work in the struggle of Hinduism to grapple with the "new anthropology" derived from Christianity and Western culture informed by Christianity, and in the pressure this grappling exerted on the "classical theology" of Hinduism.

I had long been concerned for a secular dialogue with the political ideologies of India. Under Devanandan's influence I incorporated into my concern dialogue with Neo-Hindu religious and cultural movements. And I became interested not only in the anthropological basis of national politics but also in the exploration of an Indian theology of Christ, church, and Christian mission in this context. After the death of Devanandan in 1962, it was my effort to make the institute an instrument of this exploration. My own studies — *Acknowledged Christ of the Indian Renaissance* (1969), *Secular Ideologies of India and the Secular Meaning of Christ* (1976), and *Salvation and Humanization* (1971) — deal with the theology of mission in its several aspects. The same theological concerns within the larger world setting of secular ideological and religious pluralism were present in my participation in the life and work of the World Council of Churches over the years.

Today I spend my time in Kerala mostly doing two things: (1) keeping contact with the radical Christian social action groups in India and their theological reflections, and (2) writing my theological reflections on biblical books in the Malayalam language. For me, technical socioeconomic developmental creativity and the politics of liberation of the poor and the oppressed are the realms of modern life that most need the judgment and redemption in Jesus Christ to make them the signs of the kingdom. But my tragic sense of history prevents me from identifying any historical movement of human creativity or political liberation as totally continuous with the movement of the kingdom. The church's message is power to transform always through judgment and forgiveness in the crucified and risen Christ.

Chapter 14

My Marriage Is Not a Sacrament

ASTRID LOBO GAJIWALA

In a continent where many religious communities live alongside one another, "mixed marriages" are becoming a common feature. Such unions can either foster religious integration or prove to be a disaster. This largely depends on the nature of theological and pastoral support the couple get. In this article, Astrid, a Catholic, recounts her marriage to Kelpesh, a Hindu. With passion and feeling she describes the difficulty she had with the Catholic church in negotiating her marriage, the network of friends who supported them, the eventual marriage, the liturgy she devised, and the birth of their first child.

Astrid Lobo Gajiwala is a medical doctor practicing in Bombay, India.

Source: *In God's Image,* September, 1990.

"My marriage is not a sacrament." So says the Catholic church. The reason, I am told, is that the non-Catholic partner is an "unbeliever." So what do I say to my Hindu husband who tells me he believes that Jesus is the Son of God (Rom. 10:9), that marriage is an expression of God's love for God's creation, that the marriage ceremony is a sign of the total commitment of two persons to each other in the presence of God? Must I tell him that we are both excluded from God's strengthening and unifying grace because he doesn't have the "Catholic" label? I cannot believe this. So I focus instead on the essence of the Sacrament of Matrimony, and invite our families and friends to give us their blessings and "share in our joy as we unite ourselves in God's love."

As one who loves the church of Christ, I find this exclusion from the "sacrament" of marriage disturbing. In my search for answers to the many questions buzzing around in my head, I wrote to Samuel Rayan, S.J. His answer is one I cherish:

Saints are those who love. And love transcends all barriers of religion, race, culture, etc. It is the one human and humanizing culture. Love is the one gift in which every woman and man is rich: the one sphere in which everyone can be great and distinguished. The ability to love is the most democratic of realities. We must develop this idea and pass it on.

In the measure in which this view is correct (and I am certain it is) all human love and just relationships are sacraments of the One who is love and who loves us, humankind and their Earth. There is no reason why your marriage should not be considered a Sacrament. The Catholic Church relates the sacramentality of marriage to the Baptism of partners. But Baptism is often misunderstood as a water-ceremony. Actually Baptism is commitment, often costly commitment, to the Kingdom, its justice, its demand (Mark 10:35–45; Luke 12:49–50). All who are committed to justice and human dignity and love for brothers and sisters in need are baptized/immersed in the Christ-reality, the God-reality. And love is the heart, life and meaning of all the Sacraments.

The censure of the institutional church hung over my wedding like a cloud, casting a shadow over what should have been one of the high points of joy in my life. Getting married is an unsettling experience at the best of times, and it didn't help to have statistics quoted of "mixed" marriages that did not survive, or to be advised to get married under the Special Marriage Act so that a separation in the future would be easier. It hurt to be told by a thirteen-year-old that her Catechism teacher, a religious sister, singled out my marriage as a source of great regret to the church. I hardly expected encouragement, but I did expect openness and respect for an adult decision. Instead, as a woman who had enjoyed the affirmation of the church, I suddenly found myself feeling like an errant child — all because I chose to build a life with someone who shares my faith but not my beliefs.

I was fortunate in my interaction with my parish priest. He explored with me the problems I may face in a "mixed" marriage without making any attempt to foist his opinions on me. He dialogued with my future husband, at all times affording him respect and understanding. Other priest friends, too, warmly welcomed my Hindu beloved, responding to him not as a non-Catholic who has stolen one of the fold but as a lovable human person. It is priests such as these we will turn to when our marriage passes through dark moments, as surely it must.

For some time now, I have been reflecting on the church's attitude to marriages such as mine. The impression that lingers is one of fear — fear of losing control over one of her members, fear of losing one of the faithful, fear of losing her numerical strength. Rather than address these fears, the church chooses to sidestep them. Her reaction is one of an authoritarian parent: opposition and nonacceptance. She would rather "mixed" marriages did not exist. Unfortunately for her, not only do they exist; they are on the increase.

The church's pastoral approach to "mixed" marriages is sadly lacking. For one thing, it has no respect for the love between the partners. For another, it too is concerned about following the rules. In the process, the Catholic partner, particularly if a woman, has to face tremendous rejection. Comments like: "Couldn't you find someone in your own community?" or "Look at your family background, no wonder you are no good" or "I suppose I can say you are too old to find anyone else" make deep and lasting wounds. This is reflected in the guilt that burdens many

Catholics in "mixed" marriages — which makes me wonder, is this true witness to the liberating message of Christ? On occasion, the doors of the church are shut to these Catholics: "If you can't keep the rules, you are free to leave." In hurt and rebellion, some of them do just that. There is little scope for questioning the "rules." In time these "lost sheep" learn to build their own defense mechanisms to be able to cope with the rejection, knowing full well that even the crumbs from the Master's table are denied them (Matt. 15:21–28).

As part of my decision-making process, I sought out other Catholic women in "mixed" marriages. All their marriages had survived the ravages of differences in religion and culture. It was wonderful meeting these women, some of whom had been married for over twenty years, and hear them say how fulfilling their marriages were. Almost all the women had searched for or created their own support systems, quite independent of the church. Some had retained a close bond with the church. Others who had experienced only the pharisaical face of the church chose either to remain nominal Christians or to walk out.

My own support system is a number of deeply committed Christian women and a priest who comprise "Satya Shodak," a group concerned with restoring the human dignity of women. I experience in them the Christ I love, the Christ of the Gospels who embraces the human person. It is they who gave me shelter when I needed it, who prayed with me in my despair, who bolstered my sometimes-failing courage, who helped me build bridges, and in the end gave me the gift of a wedding ceremony my husband and I will never forget. I am fortunate, too, to know theologians who have a great love and respect for Indian religions. They have helped me understand and appreciate the Spirit that guides my husband. They have taught me to tune in to the "revealing voice" of God in other religions (*Gaudium et Spes,* 36) and have shown me by their example what it means to truly respect another human being. They remain for my Hindu husband a living witness of "Christian charity."

As I count my blessings, my thoughts go once again to the many Catholics, especially women, in "mixed" marriages. I see them as part of the marginalized within the church. Cut off from avenues of dialogue with the church, they are forever penalized with isolation because their love knew not the barriers of religion. And yet they need the church. As Christians, the church is all they have to turn to in moments of indecision regarding their spirituality and during a crisis of faith. They have constantly to balance respect for their spouse's religion with commitment to their own belief system. Given the limited, pre-Vatican II catechetical knowledge of most Catholics, how can these women ever be expected to cope on their own?

The total disregard of the church for the feelings of the Catholic partner in a "mixed" marriage is something else I cannot understand. Believing as I do that faith is the gift of the Spirit (Acts 10:44–48) and that Baptism is commitment, the Church's insistence on a law (Baptism of the children of the union) that is not even universal as a condition to a Church marriage is difficult to accept. What is more, the non-Catholic partner is expected to cooperate. Even Paul makes no such stipulation. On the contrary, he acknowledges that the children of a "mixed" marriage are "acceptable to God" (1 Cor. 7:14).

Then again, the church frowns on any kind of "non-Catholic" wedding ceremony, yet offers no alternative that would be acceptable to both partners. Is this policy meant to serve merely as a deterrent to "mixed" marriages, or does it stem from a "holier-than-thou" attitude? Adding to my confusion are the examples of John Paul II. If he could pray with heads of different religions for peace, cannot two communities, with their priests, come together to pray for God's blessings on a couple who want to pledge their lives to each other in love?

That there are problems in a "mixed" marriage is obvious to even the most casual observer. Practicing the Catholic faith in a non-Catholic environment could be difficult. I can imagine, for instance, being the odd one out in family *pujas* or during non-Christian religious festivals. I can see the inconvenience Sunday Mass may become in a household that is not bound by the obligation. Family prayer, meant to cement family relationships, could well become a source of contention. And yet none of these are insurmountable problems. They can be overcome with love, tact, creativity, and a spirit of openness to the Omnipresent Truth.

In the months since my marriage, I find that my commitment to Christ has become sharper against the backdrop of a growing appreciation of my Hindu family. I am ever conscious that they will always see me as a Christian. For most of them I will perhaps be their most visible, conscious experience of Christ. Becoming part of their family has also challenged me to discard old prejudices, to love and respect people as they are, and to search my religious practice for the Truth. For me, meeting these challenges is a process of personal growth that is very closely linked with my identity as a Christian. After all, in the final analysis, is not my Christian calling a call to embrace the human person without condition?

Facing challenges and creating acceptable alternatives have also made for a closer and more caring marital relationship. As a couple, we often find ourselves supporting each other against the efforts of those around us to change us to fit traditional patterns. In our determination to make our religions a source of unity, we have found comfort in praying together, inspiration in reflecting on our Scriptures together, and joy in sharing our discoveries of God in our lives.

But none of this is easy, and, as a practicing Catholic, I look to my church, the church of Christ, for support. I need the constant guidance of empathetic spiritual directors who are free from religious prejudices. I look forward to coming together with couples/individuals in a similar situation to mine, to be able to voice fears, share triumphs, work out frustrations, and draw strength from each other.

It is indeed a tragedy that the institutional church has chosen to close its eyes to the needs of Catholics in "mixed" marriages. For many of these Catholics, thrown into an alien culture, the strength of their relationship with their mother church in fact defines the strength of their identity as Christians. It is this relationship, too, not the external ritual, that will ultimately foster daughters and sons in Christ (Rom. 2:26–29), like Timothy of the New Testament (Acts 16:1; Phil. 2:19–23; Heb. 12:23; 1 Tim. 1:2). Unfortunately, the church in her haste to sweep their marriages under the carpet, out of sight, forgets that these "chosen" people also have a vocation. I like to believe that they are God's means of joining "a branch of the wild olive tree" to the "cultured olive tree" (Rom. 11:17) so that all who call on God (Rom. 10:10–13) may become part of the tree of salvation (1 Cor. 7:14).

My Wedding Was Not Just a "Rite"

After describing last month her experience of marrying a Hindu husband, Dr. Lobo Gajiwala gives us an account of how her wedding celebration was organized and what impact it had on her friends, Catholic and Hindu. The account will encourage others in similar circumstances to use the liturgy creatively and with sensitivity for friends of other faiths who may be our guests at the celebration.

Ironical, really. Here I was, determined to make my marriage service the heart of my wedding celebrations, and all the Catholic church had to offer me was rules: I could have the nuptial service before the Eucharistic celebration or after, or in the sacristy if my non-Catholic husband-to-be objected to the church, or I could dispense with the Eucharistic meal completely. So uncertain was the atmosphere that I began to wonder whether my invitations to priest friends would be welcome or would make them uncomfortable!

Straining under too many pressures, I had not the courage to work at a common wedding service. I chose instead to make my wedding liturgy meaningful to both my beloved and myself, as also to the "mixed" community that would be attending. I saw it as an excellent opportunity to give witness to the all-embracing love that is central to the Christian message, a love that makes no distinction between communities (Gal. 3:26–28). It was my intention, therefore, that the liturgy be as inclusive as possible, emphasizing the points of unity of the worshiping communities. Further, since my husband is a Gujarati, I had decided to have part of the service in Gujarati, as an expression of my total acceptance of him. All these nuances were strikingly brought out in the liturgy prepared by "Satya Shodak."

It is not easy planning a liturgy for a "mixed" marriage. The guest community does not share a common understanding of the marriage ritual and is, in fact, different in its very attitude to the marriage ceremony. The non-Christians present are curious. For many this is perhaps the first and only time they will enter a church or participate in a Catholic service. Some have come with reservations. Their presence is merely a sign of loyalty to the family they represent.

The Catholic party, on the other hand, comes with certain expectations. For most, the wedding ceremony is little more than a sentimental tradition. They are little concerned about the significance of the liturgy and are opposed to change. Any attempts at inculturation are, therefore, suspect. Keeping all this in mind, we aimed for a balance that would be acceptable to my family and at the same time would involve the family of my husband-to-be.

The rite of marriage began with the greeting of the wedding guests at the door of the church. This was done by representatives of the Catholic community, my women friends, who also handed out roses, in the Indian sign of welcome. The commentator introduced the service and made appropriate explanations at significant points of the ritual. For our wedding attire, my husband and I chose traditional Gujarati outfits — he, a silk *kurta* and *churidhar;* I, a red, white, and gold silk *panethar* saree. We dispensed with the usual "bridesmaid" and "bestman" and had my little nephew and niece precede us up the aisle. They too wore Indian outfits, *kurta* for him and *choli-ghagra* for her. For me, the involvement of my family was particularly important. My husband-to-be and I stood at the altar after a long and painful struggle, and the participation of my family, however restrained, was for me a very precious sign of reconciliation.

For the same reason I chose to be given away in the traditional style, by my brother. I know this made him glad, for since my father's death he has shouldered a large part of our family responsibilities. So we walked down the aisle together, to the strains of "The Wedding March." Once I was "handed over," my beloved and I moved to the main altar to light a huge brass *diya*. We especially chose the symbol of fire because of its divine significance to both communities present. As we lit the lamp, the choir (Satya Shodak) sang a *bhajan* in Gujarati, praising God. The first reading, done in English by my sister, was taken from Kahlil Gibran's *The Prophet*. It spoke of true communion in marriage, one which recognizes and encourages the uniqueness of each partner, "even as the strings of lute are alone though they quiver with the same music." The response to the reading was the well-known hymn by Rabindranath Tagore, "There are numerous strings to your lute, let me add my own among them." Like most of the hymns chosen, this was a love-song, sung to express our love for God and for each other.

At this point, we had a short homily in Gujarati by a Jesuit cousin who was the main celebrant at the thanksgiving Mass that followed. He explained the significance of the marriage vows and spoke of the wedding service as an expression of the love and joy uniting the families gathered there that evening. This was followed by the nuptials, which were blessed by my uncle and godfather. My husband and I used the traditional marriage vows and exchanged rings. In addition I was also given a blessed *mangalsutra*, which my husband placed around my neck. Our witnesses included family members from both parties. United as man and wife, we raised our hearts to God in the song: "All I ask of you is forever to remember me as loving you." This served as the entrance hymn to the Mass. Not knowing whether it was permissible to have a non-Catholic do one of the readings, we settled for my husband doing the penitential prayer, which was taken from the *Bhagavadgítá*. The first reading was done in Gujarati by a Gujarati religious sister. This served two purposes. It made the Word of God come alive to the Gujarati-speaking section of the congregation, and, hopefully, it contributed towards dispelling the myth that Christianity is for "foreigners" and the "English-speaking." The response to the reading was another Gujarati *bhajan*.

The readings themselves spoke of God's love for humanity, shown in the Son and in our love for one another (1 John 4:7–12; John 15:9–17). The Gospel was read in English and the homily preached by my parish priest and "peacemaker" in the stormy months before the wedding. He focused on the meaning of love within the bonds of marriage.

The offertory procession comprised both families, as well as common friends. For the offertory gifts, we chose typically Indian symbols (coconut, oil, *kumkum*, rice, flowers, and *ladoos*). These were decorated in traditional Gujarati style by a friend and member of Satya Shodak. The *ladoos* that were offered were distributed at the end of the Mass as *prasad*. This served to include our Hindu cocelebrators while at the same time making the point that for Catholics, the Eucharist had a deeper significance and was not to be confused with *prasad*. My husband and I took up the first *thali*, followed by his parents. My mother and brother offered the bread and wine. The prayers were offered by another close friend and member of

Satya Shodak. And finally we made of ourselves a gift to God in the beautiful hymn, "All for You, Lord." For the "sign of peace," my husband and I exchanged the *namaste* with the members of his family and mine. In retrospect, it occurred to me that this symbol of unity would have been more powerful if the two families too had come forward and greeted each other.

During Communion, the commentator said a few words on the meaning of the Eucharist for Catholics. He further mentioned that although Holy Communion was meant for Catholics only, the celebrating community was united in a very real way with God and with each other. The choir sang another of Tagore's hymns, "Lord, You Have Touched My Heart."

The Thanksgiving was a moment of the Mass that was particularly touching for me. It was a time to reach out, and a time to show appreciation, for the gift of reconciliation, for the gift of generous families, and for the gift of a community that had been truly Christian in its love, support, and service. This was done by my husband and me, each of us thanking the other's family and friends. For our concluding hymn we chose the joyful song of thanksgiving: "Sing to the Mountains."

Our reception was very simple. My husband and I met our guests over cold drinks and a couple of snacks. The toastmistress (herself a Catholic in a "mixed" marriage) wished us well on behalf of all present, and said a few encouraging words on unity in interfaith marriages. My husband and I thanked her and then proceeded to greet our well-wishers over the next hour and a half. Friends and family met and served each other, transforming what is normally just a family affair into a community celebration.

This account would not be complete without feedback from the community that was present. The "non-Catholics" loved the service, from the homily in *shudh* Gujarati to the words of the hymns. In fact, for some time after the wedding, my father-in-law would listen to the audiocassette of the hymns. The quiet, peaceful atmosphere of the church was appreciated, as was the beauty and majesty of the Holy Name Cathedral. Some of them would have liked the responses during the Mass to have also been included on the cyclostyled sheets distributed.

The response of my Catholic friends was varied. A few told me that the service had been for them a truly prayerful experience. One priest friend commented that it was "ridiculous" making a non-Catholic take a vow "in the name of the Father and of the Son and of the Holy Spirit." Another priest would have preferred a wedding service with the Word, the Offertory Procession, and the like, but without the Eucharistic prayers. The Eucharist, he believes, has meaning only for Catholics, and it is unfair to subject the others to a long service they cannot participate in completely. There is, of course, also the danger that non-Catholics will receive the Eucharist — out of curiosity, or even in the name of *prasad*. Yet another friend felt that it would have been better to have the traditional service to give the non-Christians present a taste of a Catholic-style wedding. In fact, a number of my Hindu friends had been looking forward to seeing me walk down the aisle in a flowing white gown, like in the Hindi movies!

All of these are valid suggestions. Specifically "Christian" prayers, for instance, may not always be a good idea. When recited by the non-Catholic partner, they could degenerate into empty words. On occasion, he or she may even take objection to certain phrases and sentiments expressed. On the other hand, if it is a

"Catholic" ceremony, symbols and prayers in keeping with the Christian tradition of faith are to be expected. They have a special significance to the Christian community present and offer an opportunity for religious tolerance and respect on the part of the community of differing faith. A decision in this matter, however, would to a large extent depend on the couple themselves. In our case, my husband, having had some exposure to Christian religious thought, was aware, for example, of the trinitarian concept. His pluralistic Hindu background also made it easy for him to enter into Christian words of worship.

Inclusion of the Eucharistic prayers is another point of debate. While the Canon of the Mass as we know it could be omitted, if the ceremony is acknowledged as a "Catholic" one, then I would definitely opt at least for a reading of the gospel where Christ institutes the Eucharist, followed by a Communion service. The Eucharistic meal is, after all, a high point of Christian community life. This would have to be brought out in the commentary, which would also have to emphasize the sacredness and exclusive nature of the "Body of Christ." Even curious non-Catholics would be deterred from going up for Communion if they realized that their actions would cause offense.

That a service such as this does play a part, however small, in breaking down prejudices, was evident in a little incident that took place almost a month later. A young Gujarati girl who lives next door to my husband's family got married and went to Goa for her honeymoon. On her return she gave me a medal of St. Francis Xavier. She said. "When I came for your wedding, I thought it would be the only time I would go inside a church. But I went inside the church in Goa. As I stood there I thought of you and said, I must take something back for you from here." I was quite touched.

The liturgy I have presented, though a living memorial for me, is far from perfect. It is offered mainly as a starting point for the creation of an authentic wedding service for interfaith marriages. I see such occasions as a means for concretizing the church's teaching on interreligious dialogue, for the church urges us to promote cooperation in a loving spirit with others of whatever affiliation (AG 41), and marriage involves cooperation at the deepest level. The marriage ceremony presents us with differing communities united in their goodwill and love for the couple around whom they gather. To those of us who believe that all members of the human family participate in the mystery of Christ, it is indeed a challenge to transform this social custom into a sign of a union that is "built on common love that embraces all and has its roots in God who is love" (Paul VI, Bombay, 1964).

Astrid and Kalpesh Nuptials

Introduction

We have gathered in this church to celebrate a joyful event — the nuptials of Astrid and Kalpesh — and to thank God for the love shown to them and to all of us.

In symbol and in truth we will try to make God's presence real among us today. We will pray that God, who is Love, will always be with Kalpesh and Astrid — and through their lives may become a Loving Presence to others.

The Lamp-Lighting

Astrid and Kalpesh will open today's service with the lighting of the lamp.

The light and warmth of the burning lamp is a symbol of the inspiration and love of God's presence.

•

The Choir leads us in a greeting and worship of God present among us:

> *Vandana Kariye sarajanahar* (3)
> We greet you, creator
> *Pranam thamane varamva* (3)
> Hail to you, again and again
> *Sthuthi hojo Sri Bhagavan* (3)
> Praise be to you, O God.

The Word

God is present in Fire and Light. God is also present in the Word spoken through chosen prophets. We will listen to a reading from the book *The Prophet* by Kahlil Gibran. "Marriage is a togetherness that respects and nurtures the individuality of each partner."

Then Almitra spoke again and said, And what of Marriage, master? And he answered saying: You were born together, and together you shall be for evermore. You shall be together when the white wings of death scatter your days.

Aye, you shall be together even in the silent memory of God. But let there be spaces in your togetherness. And let the winds of the heavens dance between you.

Love one another, but make not a bond of love: Let it rather be a moving sea between the shores of your souls. Fill each other's cup but drink not from one cup. Give one another of your bread but eat not from the same loaf. Sing and dance together and be joyous, but let each one of you be alone, even as the strings of a lute are alone though they quiver with the same music.

Give your hearts, but not into each other's keeping. For only the hand of life can contain your hearts. And stand together yet not too near together: For the pillars of the temple stand apart, And the oak tree and the cypress grow not in each other's shadow.

•

Our response to the reading is a hymn expressing our desire to be united in our praise and worship of God.

Refrain: There are numerous strings in your lute, let me add my own among them.

1. Then when you smite your chords, My heart will break its silence, And my heart will be one with your song.

2. Amidst your numberless stars, Let me place my own little lamp.

3. In the dance of your festival of lights, My heart will throb and My life will be one with your smile.

The Nuptial Rite

Celebrant:	My dear friends, you have come together in this church so that the Lord may seal and strengthen your love in the presence of the church's minister and this community. In this way you will be strengthened to keep mutual and lasting faith with each other and to carry out the other duties of marriage. And so, in the presence of the church, I ask you to state your intentions.
Cel:	Astrid and Kalpesh, have you come here freely and without reservation to give yourselves to each other in marriage?
Astrid and Kalpesh:	We have.
Cel:	Will you love and honor each other as man and wife for the rest of your lives?
Astrid and Kalpesh:	We will.
Cel:	Will you accept children lovingly from God and bring them up according to the law of Christ and his church?
Astrid and Kalpesh:	We will.
Cel:	Since it is your intention to enter into marriage, join your right hands, and declare your consent before God and his church.
Kalpesh:	I, Kalpesh, take you, Astrid, with joy and love to be my wife. I promise to be true to you in good times and in bad, in sickness and in health. I will love you and honor you all the days of my life.
Astrid:	I, Astrid, take you, Kalpesh, with joy and love to be my husband. I promise to be true to you in good times and in bad, in sickness and in health. I will love you and honor you all the days of my life.
Cel:	You have declared your consent before the church. May the Lord in his goodness strengthen your consent and fill you both with his blessings. What God has joined, men must not divide.
All:	Amen.

Blessing and Exchange of Rings

Cel:	Lord, bless these rings and *mangalsutra,* which I bless in your name, so that Astrid and Kalpesh who wear them may always have deep faith in each other. May they do your will and always live together in peace, goodwill, and love.
All:	Amen.

Kalpesh:	Astrid, take this ring and *mangalsutra* as a sign of my love and fidelity. In the name of the Father and of the Son and of the Holy Spirit.
Astrid:	Kalpesh, take this ring as a sign of my love and fidelity. In the name of the Father and of the Son and of the Holy Spirit.

Nuptial Blessing

Cel:	My brothers and sisters, let us ask God for God's continued blessings upon this bridegroom and his bride.
	Holy God, creator of the universe, maker of man and woman in your own likeness, source of blessing for the married life, we humbly pray to you for this bride who today is united with her husband in the bond of marriage.
	May your fullest blessing come upon her and her husband so that they may together rejoice in your gift of married love. May they be noted for their good lives, and be parents fed with virtue. Lord, may they both praise you when they are happy and turn to you in their sorrows. May they be glad that you help them in their work, and know that you are with them in their need. May they reach old age in the company of their friends, and come at last to the Kingdom of Heaven. We ask this through Christ our Lord.
All:	Amen.

The Nuptials

After a brief explanation of the whole service in Gujarathi and a short exhortation by the witnessing minister, Astrid and Kalpesh exchange the marriage vows and the priest blesses and prays for them.

•

Kalpesh and Astrid are man and wife. We join them in a joyful hymn looking forward to a happy marriage:

Refrain:	All I ask of you is forever to remember me as loving you.

1. Deep the joy of being together in one heart and for me that's just where it is.

2. As we make our way through all the joys and pain, can we sense our younger truer selves?

3. Laughter, joy and presence: the only gifts you are! Have you time? I'd like to be with you.

The Thanksgiving Mass

Cel: My sisters and brothers, we, the family and friends of Astrid and Kalpesh, have gathered together to thank God for the joy and the love that they share. The Eucharist is our act of thanksgiving, as well as an act of commitment to spread that joy and love to the world in which we live. We pause for a while now to realize how unworthy we are to be in God's presence to offer praise and worship — and we humbly ask for the grace to be less unworthy.

A Penitential Prayer

Be not offended, my Lord, if my mortal hand lacks grace to offer you oblation. Yet this hand is your gift sanctified by your touch. I will use it humbly and lift this offering of love to your feet. I will cherish my mind, for it has brought me thoughts of you, my Lord; I will cherish my heart, for it has given me vision of you, my Lord; and I will crown this life with a crown of bliss, for it has brought me to your gate.

A Divine

Response: One who is ever content and meditative, self-subjugated and possessed with firm conviction, with mind and heart dedicated to Me, one who is thus consecrated to Me is dear to Me.

Liturgy of the Word

In the first reading, which will be done in Gujarathi, we are told of another form of God's presence: God is Love, and if we love one another, God lives in us.
    Reading: 1 John 4:7–12
Our response to the reading is an expression of awareness of God present all around us:

He Bhagavan tharu nam
Sambhalatho rahu saghaletham
Gagane pavane vana upavanane
Khala Khala jharane tharu gan

O God Your name
I hear at every place
In the sky, breeze and forest
In the garden and at the "khal khal" sound of the stream I hear your
        song.

•

The Gospel passage is Jesus' command to love: Love one another, as I have loved you (John 15:9–17).

Offertory Gifts and Prayers

In the offertory procession, we offer gifts symbolizing our commitment to God's mission of love and service. And we pray that God will give us the grace to fulfil this commitment.

— Astrid and Kalpesh have committed themselves to be partners with God in the procreation and nurturing of a new family. They offer a *thali* with a coconut, *kumkum,* oil, and rice symbolizing fertility, strength, and nourishing love.

— Their parents and family members have sacrificed much in concern for the happiness of Kalpesh and Astrid. The *pedas* and flowers being offered are a symbol of the joy they wish to share with their friends.

— Bread and wine, symbols of unity and communion, are offered as a sign of our readiness to overcome barriers of religion, language, status, and to live as a community of love.
    We pray for all of us present here, that this Eucharist may be for all an inspiration to love and to work for harmony and peace.

•

The offertory hymn we sing is an expression of our gift of ourselves:

Refrain: All for you, Lord, all for you
                     Everything I give to you
                     All for you, Lord, all for you
                     Make it all your own.
                     Take my hands and feet, Lord,
                     Take them all for you
                     They are instruments, Lord, put them to your use,
                     To spread your love and give the good news,
                     All for you, my God.
                     Take my mind, my senses, feelings and desires,
                     Take my will and freedom, take my life entire,
                     I offer you myself and all I have,
                     All for you, my God.

The Sign of Peace

To show our desire of being a community of love, we greet each other and sing:

Shalom, my friend, Shalom, my friend, Shalom, Shalom.
The Peace of God be with you today, Shalom, Shalom, Shalom.
(*Repeat*)

Communion

In the sacrament of the Holy Eucharist, we Catholics believe that we receive the Body and Blood of Jesus who is our God and Savior. And so Holy Communion is meant for Catholics only.

But today's celebrating community is united with God and with each other in a very real way, and so together we thank God for being present to us and making us one:

Refrain: Lord, you have touched my heart and left me speechless.
                                     Silence is all I need to sing your praise.

1. Lord, It is you who are my cup and portion Lord,
   It is you yourself who are my prize.

2. So I will bless the Lord who gives me counsel
   And who directs my heart all through the night.

3. And so my heart is glad, my soul rejoices,
   Even my body shall in safety rest.

4. Your presence makes my life on earth a heaven.
   Your steadfast love and care for me with joy.

•

Astrid and Kalpesh are grateful to God, to their families, to their friends — and wish to express their gratitude.

•

The final prayer and blessing is our sincere wish that God, present in each one of us through this celebration — and in a special way present in Astrid and Kalpesh — may be made present to each and every one with whom we come in contact, through our lives of love and service.

•

The signing of the register is another human formality, which has its special significance. Kalpesh and Astrid have declared before God and before their family and friends that they are pledged together for life. We could take them at their word — but a written document is also useful.

As they leave the church, Astrid and Kalpesh are filled with the joy and love of God's presence — they sing and ask us to join:

Sing to the mountains, sing to the sea.
Raise your voices, lift your heart.
This is the day the Lord has made,
Let all the earth rejoice.

1. I will give thanks to you, my Lord.
   You have answered my plea.
   You have saved my soul from death.
   You are my strength and my song.

2. This is the day that the Lord has made
   Let us be glad and rejoice
   He has turned all death to life
   Sing of the glory of God.

•

Unto Us a Child Is Born (Isa. 9:6)

December 25, 1988

Christmas, I'm carrying new life. Haven't begun to show yet, Mary, another mother. Do the centuries make a difference? I wonder.

February 2, 1989

"Saw" my baby for the first time today. How fragile that little spine looks. Just seventeen weeks and already my baby is a person. Head and hands and feet curved around some imaginary pillow.

Till now it was just backaches and breathlessness, a proper diet and less traveling, no heels and a diminishing wardrobe. Suddenly I'm conscious that there's a heart pulsating inside me. We've created life!

February 13, 1989

Vertex, breach, transverse lie. That's all we seem to talk about these days. My baby seems to need a gentle shove to make it toe the line. So I sleep on one side and hug a pillow — doctor's orders. No sex please, I'm pregnant!

February 26, 1989

Four months to go and already the baby is beginning to make its presence felt. Till now I had been carrying blissfully on with home, work, and social engagements. No morning sickness or crazy cravings to disturb my routine existence. Then suddenly I can't seem to buckle my sandals anymore, my arms just aren't long enough. I have to take my blood pressure regularly, and my weight. All at once my diet has become the biggest concern of my life. A weekend out means carting a whole arsenal of pills — calcium, folic acid, etc. etc. — once a day, twice a day, thrice a day.

February 28, 1989

The first kick. Feels like a small attack of gas.

March 31, 1989

Looked in the mirror this morning. Shock. My collar bone has disappeared. The weighing scale has become an unwelcome appendage. Touched sixty at the last reckoning — fourteen kilograms overweight — yet they tell me I'm not gaining enough weight. I now have to maneuver myself in and out of trains, in between parked vehicles, around furniture. I feel like an elephant. My only consolation is that my friends tell me the extra weight suits me. Naturally, I avoid my enemies. Baby's finally in position. I can hear its heart beats with the stethoscope.

April 20, 1989

Never saw myself as aggressive, but I'm ready to fight at the slightest threat to my baby. Must be some maternal hormones. Always thought the world smiled kindly on a mother heavy with child. But roving male hands are not deterred. My blood pressure is record high.

Baby's moved again. She or he is quite persistent.

May 11, 1989

I've started waddling. And the backaches are unbearable. Turning in bed feels like I'm moving a mountain. My life is full of rules — don't bend, don't lift heavy objects, don't travel by bus or rickshaw, don't stand for too long, don't sit for too long, don't go out during the eclipse.

May 22, 1989

There's no mistaking the kicks anymore. Sharp. I feel them like waves on my abdomen. The baby's back in position. All's going to be well, it seems.

June 18, 1989

Went for a haircut. Preparing myself for the new arrival. My Chinese hairdresser says that, according to the Chinese horoscope, I'm going to get a girl. According to my scientific calculations, I'm going to get a boy. My husband's rooting for the Chinese horoscope (and secretly so am I).

June 27, 1989

My baby's had the last laugh. Transverse again, determined to present a lovely, little shoulder. It's the doctor's knife for me.

•

A couple of miracles later, I hear my husband's gleeful whisper in my ear. The Chinese horoscope was right. So much for scientific calculations. So now I am a mother.

I am still caught up in the magic of immersing myself in the act of creation. My daughter. My bones have gone into making hers. My blood has nourished her. My lifestyle has influenced her life. Yet the state doesn't consider me good enough to be a legal guardian and my family name is lost to posterity. I am allowed no sign of possession. If things are to be different for my daughter, I must work for change now.

Our creation. The months of restricted movement, the backaches, the legacy of overweight, all are balanced by the memory of her kicking inside me and the pleasure of bonding as she snuggles up to my breast. Nine months of caring have paid off. But there's still a lot more to this creation, and I'm depending on my co-creators to keep their hands in. There's no way I can manage without their caring presence.

Parent. Awesome word. There's a price to be paid for claiming my tiny share of eternity — the price of responsibility, and altered priorities, and unconditional love. I am not the free agent I once was. Motherhood is quite time-consuming. The world will have to wait a bit for my contribution. My career has to be "put on hold." My social life has to find a slot in my daughter's timetable. "Realizing my full potential" has taken on a new dimension. I worry about decent housing and a healthy environment and wholesome education. I imagine handling questions on sex and warding off precocious boyfriends. I anticipate arguments, and rebellion, and struggles for identity. They tell me it's not enough to just give life. I have to be lifegiving. Maybe what that really means is that I must make my daughter always feel lovable and loved. Isn't that a great responsibility? Will I be able to encourage her transition from child to mature adult? Will I know the right moment to let go? So many questions with answers hidden in time. Makes for a today that has new purpose. My daughter needs me to be around for a while.

For now my time is spent changing nappies, working out diet charts, and perfecting my conversational skills. Never before have I had such an avid listener. Toothless smiles and sparkling eyes, waving hands and feet, lips pursed in concentration. But the deep-throated gurgles are reserved for her father. She drifts off to sleep, head resting comfortably on his shoulder, as he sings some weird lullaby. Sound asleep, she has only to hear his voice for her eyes to flicker open in anticipation. Even now, there's no mistaking that father-daughter bond.

Makes me reflect on my bonds. New insights. I imagine my father and mother searching my face, claiming familiar features, looking out for that first sign of recognition, delighting in my smile. I feel closer to them as I begin to realize that they, too, spent sleepless nights dancing to the tune of my colic, tending that persistent fever, worrying about the money needed to give me the best. Suddenly it's easy to interpret their language of love.

Communication without words. My daughter seems to have mastered the art. A persistent cry and it's feeding time. An irritable whimper and it's bedtime. A couple of screeches and it's time to be picked up and fussed over. Dead silence and there's a "big job" coming on. Her needs are few. Life for her has not yet become complicated with frustration, anger, and hurt. Maybe I ought to learn her technique of sticking with the essentials. Her body is a delight. Holding her softness against my skin is a prayer I never tire of making. Bathing her is ritual I hate to miss. As I run my fingers over her little tummy, she squirms in anticipation and slides off my legs. She gurgles and smiles and looks into my eyes as if she understands the song I am singing. Give her half a chance and she grabs the mug with both hands and brings it to her mouth. Trying to wash her insides, I guess.

She has added new pleasure to old routines. A trip outside the house brings with it the joy of being welcomed back. As I enter the room and call her name her face lights up with a smile. I move towards her and hold out my arms. She jumps into them. The next thing I know she's climbing all over me, trying to chew my nose. I remember the hymn "Coming Home." Is this what it feels like?

Creating the right environment. According to the books, she needs attractive mobiles and colorful toys and a variety of textures to help her get the feel of this world. But she ignores all my attempts at creativity, grips my fingers, and stares at them in total fascination. The curtain blowing in the breeze catches her eye. A colored wall print takes all her attention. Everything from a leaf to a spoon is a source of wonder to her. She lives so completely in the present. No regrets about the past, no anxieties about the future. For her life is a joy, every moment to be relished. She is so eager to laugh — at me, at a passerby, at the ball in her hand, at nothing in particular. She knows well how to appreciate the gifts of life and of creation. I begin to understand better now what it means to "receive the Kingdom of God like a Child" (Mark 10:13–16).

Chapter 15

Hindu-Christian Funeral

STANLEY J. SAMARTHA

One time or other, we have all been to funeral services and sat through the solemn rituals. But the funeral that Stanley Samartha went to was different. It was an interreligious one. In this essay, Samartha narrates how the rituals associated with the ceremony transformed him and prompted him to ponder some important theological issues.

Stanley Samartha is on the staff of South Asia Theological Research Institute and the United Theological College, Bangalore, India. He was the first director of the Dialogue Program of the World Council of Churches, Geneva. His recent book, *One Christ, Many Religions: Toward a Revised Christology* was published by Orbis Books (1991).

Source: *National Christian Council Review* 108 (4), 1988.

He died on Palm Sunday morning, April 12, 1987. In a week's time he would have celebrated his eighty-sixth birthday. During the last couple of years, he was bed-ridden but could recognize his friends and sometimes talk to them. During my visits I was always impressed by his gentle face, ready smile, and soft voice. He never once complained about his illness. When I offered to pray at his bedside, he welcomed it.

He was an official in the state's department of education. He fell in love with a Christian woman and married her. He promised his father that he was not going to betray the faith of his forefathers in order to marry a Christian. The continuity of Hindu heritage through the centuries and the depth of its accumulated tradition were too precious for him to exchange for the sake of personal happiness. He kept his promise to the end. He had made his son promise him that when he died he would be cremated according to Hindu rites. The son, too, kept his promise.

It is more correct to say that he knew me than to mention that I knew him. His wife belonged to the congregation of which my father was the pastor. He and my father were great friends. He never prevented his wife and children from going to church or participating in Christian activities. With his permission my father baptized his children and, later on, confirmed them as members of the church. He also attended church services sometimes but remained a Hindu till the end of his life.

The funeral service was at four o'clock in the evening at the house of his son in Bangalore. His son told me that, remembering my father, he had asked that I be requested to say a few words about him and offer a prayer at his funeral. I gladly agreed to do so.

There was quite a large gathering at the service. He had many Hindu and Christian relatives and friends. Some of them had come from places as far away as Calcutta and Delhi, Cochin and Mangalore. They were all sitting together in the gathering. No one tried to behave like a theological porcupine or a spiritual jellyfish. They were all human beings drawn together in the common bond of grief.

In my brief speech I referred to his life as a husband, father, grandfather, and friend, mentioning that although he lived within the fellowship of a Christian family, he remained faithful to his Hindu heritage. I pointed out that even as we Christians are committed to our faith, so are our Hindu neighbors committed to theirs and that therefore we should respect one anothers' cherished beliefs and convictions.

In my prayer I made use of an Upanishadic reference to Ultimate Reality as "that from which everything is born, that by which everything that is born is sustained, and that into which everything returns at the end" (Taittiriya Upanishad III:1). Since it was Palm Sunday, I referred to the journey of Jesus, who had started the journey from the Father and was now returning to Him by way of the cross and the resurrection. I affirmed that, at the moment of death, our faith and hope as Christians are grounded in Jesus Christ, the crucified and risen Lord. The prayer was unmistakably Christian in content and character.

Christians had their service first. Jesus said, "I am the resurrection and the life; he who believes in me, though he die, yet shall he live, and whoever lives and believes in me shall never die" (John 11:25–26). Two Christian ministers were present — one in his official robe, the other in his clerical collar. The order of service of the church of South India for the occasion is beautiful and moving. The whole architectural construction with hymns, readings, and prayers has spiritual depth, theological strength, and pastoral comfort. It was a clear affirmation of Christian faith and hope in God through Jesus Christ.

Next, the Hindu friends took over. Nachiketas said to Yama (the god of death), "In the world of heaven there is no fear whatever, you are not there and no one is afraid of old age. Overcoming both hunger and thirst, and leaving sorrow behind, one rejoices in the world of heaven" (Kathopanishad 1:12). On the right side of the body, near the head, was the broken half of a coconut with a bit of camphor burning within it. On the left was a brass vessel with water from the Ganges River and leaves from *tulsi* (a plant sacred to the Hindus). An earthen pot with glowing coals was at the foot of the body.

Usually, the eldest son of the dead person officiates during a Hindu funeral ceremony (*anthyeshti*), but in this case, since his son was a Christian, the eldest son of the dead man's sister who was a Hindu took over the leadership. All this was done without the slightest bit of argument or confusion or hesitation.

The Hindu friends slowly walked around the body in a dignified procession. Usually, women do not take part in such ceremonies. But in this case, I noticed that women and children were also in the circle. Each one took some *tulsi* leaves and put a few drops of water into the mouth of the body, folded hands in the *namasthe* gesture, and touched its feet. They were quiet, solemn, and moved with a sense of rhythm. No Hindu priest was present, nor were any mantras recited.

The body was carried out both by his Hindu and Christian relatives and placed on a wooden plank, to be taken to the crematorium. And again, assisted by both his Hindu and Christian relatives, the body was placed on a green bamboo frame, on which fresh banana leaves were spread. Flowers were placed on it, sparks from the pot of fire dropped on the body, and then, at the turn of a switch, it quietly moved into the glowing door of the crematorium. The ashes were later collected and taken home.

Each rite had its distinctiveness and, perhaps in the perceptions of people, had something meaningful to say to the other. I was also struck by the differences between the two. The Christian service was formal, orderly, well-structured, and with the minister in his robe, there was not doubt that it was official. In contrast, the Hindu rite was informal, less rigid, with hardly any words uttered and no priest present. The whole group participated in the performance of the rite.

One could not but become aware of the silence that dominated the Hindu rite. No speeches were made, no mantras recited, and, with the exception of three words of a chant when the body was carried out of the house, there was no singing. The Christians, on the other hand, seemed to be very uneasy about any periods of silence. The gaps between prayers and readings were constantly being filled with the singing of English hymns to Western tunes. Except for the sign of the cross and flowers, there were no other visible symbols that could add to the meaning of Christian service. Hindus had a number of them, all taken from nature itself — flowers, coconut, *tulsi* leaves, water from the river Ganga, the bamboo framework, banana leaves and, of course, fire. *Agni* (fire) has a special place in Hindu symbolism. *Agni* is the priest of the gods and the god of priests. It is through fire that sacrifices reach God. *Agni* destroys, purifies, illumines, and is regarded as one of the five components of the cosmos.

During the whole period of about two hours, I did not notice any individuals from either group openly or discreetly seeking to separate themselves from the other. Both Christians and Hindus, without being asked, left their shoes and sandals outside before entering the room where the body was laid. It was obvious that to many Christians the Hindu rite was entirely new; it was also the first time for many Hindus to come near a Christian funeral service. Hindus and Christians will pay a visit to the house of a dead friend of either faith, but that is very different from being present during the ceremonies. Some were probably uneasy, but none showed it. Each group was eager to see what the rite of the other meant.

During the next few days, I talked to several people, both Hindu and Christian, who were present there. None expressed any difficulty or felt offended or uneasy at being present together during the ceremonies. Two Christian women told me it was a good thing that I asked people to respect their neighbors' faith. I was puzzled by the remark. Does this mean that Christians are taught not to respect their neighbors' faith? One Hindu lady, the wife of a medical doctor, told me that she was impressed with the orderliness and discipline of the Christian service and its Christian content. It was the first time that she had ever been present at such a service.

Funeral rites, Hindu or Christian, have an important contribution to make to the religious life of a community of faith.

First, based on the religious faith behind them, they are believed to influence the destiny of the person and to help in the metamorphosis of the body. When it is believed that there is only one life, more pressure and anxiety is experienced at death than when a plurality of births and deaths is believed in, offering more opportunities for the individual to realize his or her destiny. Death, however, is never regarded as the final end. It is a deliverance or transition or passage into the mystery of life, the perception of its meaning being reflected in the funeral rites.

Second, funeral rites help to comfort the bereaved. The words and symbols re-assure, strengthen, and sustain those who mourn the loss of their loved ones, thus helping to heal the wound of death.

Third, all funeral rites have a community dimension. This is one reason why so many relatives and friends make every effort to be present at a funeral. The ongoing life of the community is disturbed by the loss of one of its members. The gap left by that death has to be closed, slowly, gently, and firmly, so that the living can go on. Funeral rites thus help to revitalize the life of the community broken by death.

When the mood is one of reverence and silence, one does not feel justified in raising any questions. And yet, it may be that what strikes one deeply at the moment should be shared with others as well.

Can one body, in the utter helplessness of death, carry the weight of two religious rites? How will the destiny of the person be affected by this on the other side of death?

Can the same body be claimed by two religious groups, Hindu and Christian? Why not? Was he not related to both Hindus and Christians biologically and spiritually?

In India the distance between the temple and the church is very great, almost unbridgeable. At a time when religious fundamentalism is on the rise and the politicization of religions is on the increase, this senior friend, in his death, brought together his Hindu and Christian relatives and friends who otherwise would never have come together. Immediately after the rites, each group went away separately, perhaps never to meet again in the near future.

Is it not strange, even tragic, that life should separate religious people but that death should bring them together, even for a brief moment?

Did he live as a Christian and die as a Hindu or did he live as a Hindu and die as a Christian?

Who knows?

SECTION IV

SPEAKING FOR OURSELVES

Current Theological Concerns

On my way to the country church, I never fail to see a herd of water buffaloes grazing in the muddy field. This sight is an inspiring moment for me. Why? Because it reminds me that the people to whom I am to bring the gospel of Christ spend most of their time with these water buffaloes in the rice field. The water buffaloes tell me that I must preach to these farmers in the simplest of sentence structure and thought development. They remind me to discard all abstract ideas and to use exclusively objects that are immediately tangible. "Sticky rice," "banana," "pepper," "dog," "cat," "bicycle," "rainy season," "leaking house," "fishing," "cockfighting," "lottery," "stomachache" — these are meaningful words for them. This morning I say to myself, "I will try to bring the gospel of Christ through the medium of cockfighting!"

— Kosuke Koyama

Chapter 16

Some Perspectives on Homeland Theology in the Taiwanese Context

WANG HSIEN CHIH

At a time when there are rapid political changes in the world, when many minorities are demanding nation-states and independent rule, Taiwanese claims for self-rule continue to go unheeded. What causes anxiety is the menacing presence of China and the way outside powers use Taiwan as a political pawn. Placed in this difficult context of political uncertainty of the present and future, a Taiwanese Christian has worked out a theology which he calls "homeland theology," based on the concept of the Promised Land in Jewish history. The article that follows illustrates key features of such a theology.

Wang Hsien Chih is Professor of Theology at Taiwan Theological Seminary, Taipei, Taiwan. He has been actively engaged in evolving a homeland theology.

Source: *CTC Bulletin* 6 (2 & 3), 1986.

In the last hundred years, both the Korean and Taiwanese peoples have been dominated, suppressed, and exploited by foreign regimes, especially the Japanese military regime. Since World War II people, longing for peace and unity, have been oppressed and even killed by their own "brothers," ethnically speaking. There has been too much blood, sweat, and tears for fellow Asians in the last century! But God works through tragedy. The churches in Korea have made a wonderful witness in the history of Asian suffering.

In Taiwan we have tried to articulate the "homeland theology" with people. It is a "developing" theology. This article will deal briefly with the following three topics: (1) the emergence of the homeland issue in the theological critique of Taiwanese reality; (2) the main themes of homeland theology; and (3) some implications for theological education.

The Emergence of the Homeland Issue in the Theological Critique
of Taiwanese Reality

Historically speaking, the idea of homeland as a theological issue was first proposed by a group of theological educators in the national dialogue sponsored by the CTC (Commission on Theological Concerns) of the Christian Conference of Asia (CCA) at the Taipei YMCA, September 3–5, 1979. Taiwan, which was betrayed by her "parents" (the Manchurian Chinese) to Japan in 1895, became an "orphan" in Asia. After the defeat of Japan by the Allies in 1945, the people of Taiwan had a dream of returning home. But they have had to dream for more than thirty-seven years under martial law imposed by the new rulers from China. Worse than that, the people and the land of Taiwan continue to be treated like objects in international power games. The "orphan" wants to grow to her human dignity and to build her own home in this land, but demonic powers always destroy her humanity and exploit her land.

Under such conditions the "orphan" has had no voice at all. But the Presbyterian Church in Taiwan (PCT) has cried out for the voiceless people. When President Nixon was planning to visit mainland China in 1972, the church declared to all nations concerned:

> We, the people on Taiwan, love this island which, either by birth or chance, is our home. Some of us have roots here going back a thousand years. The majority count a residence of two or three centuries while some have come since the Second World War. We are all well aware of our different backgrounds and even conflicts, but at present we are more aware of a common certainty and shared conviction. We long to live here in peace, freedom and justice. We do not wish to be governed by Peiping.

> We note with concern that President Nixon will soon visit the Chinese Mainland. Some member countries of the United Nations are advocating the transfer of Taiwan to mainland rule, while others insist on direct negotiation between Taipei and Peiping, which means substantially the same betrayal of the people on Taiwan.

> We oppose any powerful nation disregarding the rights and wishes of fifteen million people and making unilateral decisions to their own advantage, because God has ordained and the United Nations Charter has affirmed that every people has the right to determine its own destiny (Quoted from "The Public Statement on our National Fate by the Presbyterian Church in Taiwan, December 29, 1971").

This was a solemn political and theological protest and appeal to "all nations concerned." After three and a half centuries of silence the "orphan's" brother broke the silence! Suddenly they became human beings created in the image of God. Because they proclaimed to the world that they have the God-given right to determine their own future among the nations, they became aware of their own identity as the subjects of history.

People need a home. This is a most natural thing in human history. The ancestors of the people on Taiwan, no matter whether they are Han, Hakka, Hoklo, Aborigines or some other ethnic group, came to Formosa to build a new home of peace, justice, and freedom. But this dream has always been destroyed by foreign colonial powers. Now God awakens our people by calling the PCT to declare that we have decided to build a homeland in spite of foreign or domestic domination. This idea was reaffirmed in the "Declaration on Human Rights" issued by the PCT when President Carter sent his secretary of state, Cyrus Vance, to visit the China mainland in 1977. In 1978, the United States of America cut her formal diplomatic relationship with the Republic of China. The declaration expressed the inner voice of the people on Taiwan as follows:

> Our church confesses that Jesus Christ is Lord of all mankind and believes that human rights and a homeland are gifts bestowed by God. Therefore we make this declaration set in the context of the present crisis threatening the seventeen million people of Taiwan.

Again the PCT, in its draft "Confession of Faith" in 1979, emphasized the idea of homeland in these words:

> We believe God gives man dignity, ability, responsibility and a homeland so that he may participate in God's creation and manage the world together. Therefore man shapes his social, political and economic systems, is creative in the arts and sciences, and seeks after the one true God.

The theological issue of homeland is filled with tension because the rulers on both sides of the Taiwan Strait one-sidedly claim that Taiwan is part of China and her future should be decided by the Chinese alone. The claim of the rulers distorts and diverts the authentic political history of China/Taiwan away from the people's perspective and suppresses the voice of the eighteen million people on Taiwan who have the God-ordained right to determine their own future. The rulers on both sides impose the dogma that the only future for Taiwan is "unification" and any other ideas must be condemned as heresy. Thus the PCT's claim for our self-determination has made her a suffering servant for the people and a heretic in the eyes of the rulers.

But theologically speaking, the idea of a homeland precedes or transcends the political idea of unification/separation because of its theological primacy over political expediency. For example, in the political history of Israel, the separation of the North from the South in 1 Kings 12:1–20 tells us that the unjust "yoke" and the inhuman torture, "scorpions," imposed by Solomon's son, Rehoboam, seriously violated the *chesed, mishpat,* and *shalom* of Yahweh. The political consequence of this theological violation was the disintegration not only of the kingdom but also of the peoples. Historically speaking, the political problem of unification of the North with the South had never been solved after almost three millennia of separation. But this did not stop the Israelis from dreaming of "home sweet home" and building a messianic kingdom of their own, full of *chesed, mishpat,* and *shalom.*

The Main Themes of Homeland and Theology

There are four main themes in homeland theology: people, land, power, and God. Why not people only? We all know that a people without land is just like a bird without a nest or like the "boat people" floating on an immense ocean. Conversely, a land without people is like a desert or a colonized land. And a people without participation in a political decision-making body is like a cow or a prostitute. It is because we bear the image of God that we can affirm and reaffirm our human dignity from which we are commissioned to be God's stewards to rule over the land. The power to rule in accord with the *imago Dei* brings the problems of people and land into dipolar confrontation in the history of human development.

To deal with the themes defined above, some biblical paradigms can be selected for contextual reinterpretation as follows: (a.) the Noachic Covenant (Gen. 9:8–19); (b.) the Abrahamic Covenant (Gen. 12:1–4a, and other texts); (c.) the Mosaic Covenant (Exod. 19:1–24, 18); (d.) the Davidic Covenant (2 Sam. 7:1–17); (e.) the themes of new election and new exodus in Second Isaiah, and (f.) the New Covenant in Jesus Christ. Centering around these covenants and their contexts of historical formations and transformations, the themes of homeland theology are developed as follows.

The Noachic Covenant

In this paradigm God takes the initiative to make a covenant with Noah and every living creature. This is a universal covenant with human beings and nature as a whole without "ethnocentric" and "nationalist" preoccupation. Reverence for life is the will of God for all creatures.

The Abrahamic Covenant

In this paradigm an immigration theology emerges from the call of Abraham to leave his old homeland, Ur of Babylon. Babylon as a symbol of demonic superpower, either in the form of Tiamat in Genesis or in the form of Marduk-theocratic imperialism in the Book of Revelation, is a symbol of oppression from which Abraham had to flee. He had cut his relationship with Babylonian imperialism and chauvinism. This implies that Taiwan has to struggle against "Babylon," too.

The patriarchal legend about Abraham and his tribe is an archetype for all peoples on earth. Every people needs such an archetype to identify and integrate themselves among other peoples. But it is peculiar that the people on Taiwan have no such archetype, except the aboriginal tribes, who have their own primitive versions. Therefore, it is important for the people on Taiwan to search for, or recall from, their memory a patriarchal narrative for themselves because all such previous narratives have been consistently and systematically erased by the colonial rulers in the last three centuries. When we forget history, we lose our identity. This is a cruel historical lesson that the Taiwanese have learned from their living context.

The promise of God to Abraham includes mainly three things: a land, a great nation with many descendants, and a blessing and mutual blessing between Abraham's descendants and other peoples. The universal covenant with Noah's descendants and every living creature is now narrowed down to a patriarchal covenant with Abraham's descendants that has a "nationalist" implication. The process of the nationalization of Israel always involved conflicts with other peoples who had the same God-ordained right to build their own nation. Therefore, it is important to reexamine the meaning of "blessing" and "mutual blessing" among nations in the Abrahamic covenant. Mutual blessing can be understood as a theological monopoly by Israel that always ended in mutual killing among peoples. Nationalization, mutual killing, and self-justified holy war in the name of God went hand-in-hand in the process of realizing the Abrahamic covenant in the history of Israel. Perhaps the authentic meaning of mutual blessing can be understood only when the Abrahamic archetype is radically reinterpreted in the New Testament.

In spite of the difference between the Noachic and the Abrahamic covenants, there is a common emphasis on the primacy of people over land. People are called by God to rule, to till, to build, to invent. People are the subject of civilization rather than the object. Therefore, although people cannot live without land, land belongs to the people rather than the people belonging to the land. People are subjects; they cannot be treated as objects on a certain piece of land. When China claims that historically Taiwan was part of China, this does not automatically justify the Chinese claim over the people on Taiwan. The Taiwanese have the right to manage their land. Historically, Korea was once part of China during the early Han dynasty, but this does not justify any Chinese claim over Koreans now. The Chinese could conquer the land of Korea by force, but they could not possibly conquer the people on the land by force. This theological principle of the primacy of people over land is crucially important for solving the political problem of national unification/separation.

The Mosaic Covenant

For Israelites, the Exodus event was the liberation event par excellence in the history of Israel. In Gottwald's book *The Tribes of Yahweh,* we may discern, by using sociohistorical and religious criticism, that the integration of the Mosaic revolutionary tribes under the banner of Yahweh ideology (Yahwism) was simultaneously a process of the self-unfolding of the mask of Yahweh. The name "Israel" in Hebrew literally meant "God strives" in the narrative of Jacob's struggle with the angel of Yahweh. The process of transformation from tribes into a people entailed a liberation experience and a theo-ideology. And conversely, the revelation of God can be experienced only in the process of liberation as a struggle between human beings and God. This struggle involves "participation" rather than objective investigation or reflection. Revelation experience is beyond a paper theology: it is a theo-praxis, not a theo-logos.

The Exodus event is loaded with meanings for many peoples. But there is one essential meaning: liberation means a liberation from pharaonic theocracy, the equivalent of the Chinese "Son of Heaven" theocracy. The Magna Charta for Israel was the Decalogue that forbade any theocratic articulation under Yahwism. Leaving Egypt and envisioning a "Promised Land," the Mosaic tribes had to reorganize themselves and design a new political form. It took more than "forty years" to accomplish that. One significant theme in the formation of Israel's identity emerges from the process of the integration and transformation of the Mosaic tribes. The tribes consisted of many ethnic groups who upheld Yahwism as a sacred symbol of the consolidation of the tribes into a people called Israel. This means the theopolitical ideology of Yahwism is the highest principle for the formation and identification of a people like Israel rather than the purity of ethnos, which has been the main cause of so much ethnocentric chauvinism that has stimulated so many self-justified holy wars, such as the Japanese and the Germans in World War II. Furthermore, ethnocentrism can easily be elevated to a deification of ethnic nationalism and ethnic heroes along with the "ethnologization" of their gods. The famous formula in Exodus, "I will adopt you as my own people, and I will be your God. Then you shall know that it is I, Yahweh your God, who have freed you from the Egyptians' burdens" (Exod. 6:7, *Jerusalem Bible*) may be interpreted in a broad sense, but usually in a narrow sense, as a specific "adoption" of Israel by her own "nationalistic" God Yahweh (the text is part of the document written during the Exile). It takes a prophet like Second Isaiah to break this God of narrow ethnocentric nationalism by the rearticulation of a universal God of creation and redemption.

From the desert to Canaan, the process was complicated and fraught with ambiguities. However, from a macroscopic point of view, we may discern that the so-called holy war to conquer Canaan as realization of the Abrahamic covenant could be a one-sided story based on Israel's self-concern. For the Israelites, Canaan was "a promised land of milk and honey," but for the native inhabitants of Canaan it was a "conquered land of blood and tears." The homeland of the Canaanite natives and their languages with their own history were almost lost after the establishment of the kingdom of Israel. This is always the fate of powerless people in human history. And the history and language of the powerful always triumph in a self-justified way. The sin of self-justification either in personal or communal forms distorts truth and oppresses people. The Korean and Taiwanese under Japanese colonialism experienced this truth painfully. From this contextual experience, I believe we have to ask Old Testament scholars to rewrite theology from the perspective of this truth, that is, the perspective of the powerless, the oppressed, and even the nonidentifiable peoples among nations.

The Davidic Covenant

In the process of Israel's becoming a nation after almost 450 years of settlement and enslavement in Egypt, the Exodus took place as an event of liberation from the theocracy of Pharaoh. That was a necessary step for the integration of the tribal unions into a people of Israel, an ethnopolitical integration under Yahwism, for defense against neighboring nations, and for the development of Israel as a nation. But the argument about the possibility of a new political form of kingship caused an intense debate between Samuel and the people. The transition from charismatic leadership during the period of the judges to the kingship of Saul and David maintained a long tradition of Yahweh as the sole authentic king of kings. However, the charismatic tradition was broken after David's appointment of Solomon as his successor. This dynastic-monarchical form was justified and self-ordained in the so-called Davidic Covenant (2 Samuel 7:1–17). Many Old Testament scholars consider it a controversial covenant that might be a product of the Southern tradition, which obviously was against the tradition of election of the charismatic leadership by Yahweh through the oracle of the prophets.

The tension between the Mosaic covenant and the Davidic covenant was a theo-political problem which projected the tension between Yahweh-oriented politics and king-oriented politics. The story of the split between the North and the South at the time of David's grandson Rehoboam shows that the self-ordained Southern dynasty was not well accepted by the Northern tribes, which still upheld the election tradition. The forced labor and heavy taxation systems established by Solomon tell us that the tribe of Judah imposed the "heavy yoke" and "scorpions" upon its brothers and sisters of the ten tribes in the North. This unmasked the ugliness of the self-consecrated royal power granted in the Davidic covenant. Israel was oppressed by the Egyptians, but now she started to oppress her own people because of power and greed even in the name of God.

This reminds us of the political mythology of the "Son of Heaven" in Chinese history, which guaranteed the dynastic monarchy a divine mandate of heaven. Furthermore, China has been caught in this bondage for more than five thousand years until now. (See the author's article, "The Role of Confucianism, Taoism and Folk Religions in Shaping Some Perspectives of Chinese Political Vision" in *Towards the Sovereignty of the People,* CTC-CCA, Singapore, 1983, pp. 146–52.)

The nationalism embodied in the Davidic dynasty in its "royalization" of temple, army, and economic system became virtually bankrupt after the split. The disintegration of the twelve tribes could not be stopped by a merely one-sided and self-justified claim of the South over the North. The result was mutual condemnation in the name of their gods and prolonged holy war between fellow Israelites. They had to fight against each other in an international context of rivalry between ancient superpowers. Instead of achieving national reunification, both sides fell prey to the superpowers. Here we learn the historical lesson that without justice, freedom and equality, there is no consolidation of people or possibility of reunification. Also the ugliness of power always makes use of history, such as the Deuteronomic history, which reflected mainly the perspective of the South, to cover its ugliness. Therefore, restoring the truth of history always involves confrontation with the ugliness of the powerful, who tend to suppress the powerless. Any theological educator with a faithful conscience must acknowledge this truth and pay the price of confrontation and persecution. There is no truth without the Cross! The escalation of the royal power to the level of divinity has been a natural tendency in world history and in all civilizations. The higher it is escalated, the more heavily it is judged. The fate of the South and the North was exile with the loss of both land and people.

New Election and New Exodus in Second Isaiah

The prophets had the advantage of being able to read history from a retrospective point of view. The contextual reality of being exiled to other nations became a provocative issue among the Israelites. The royal nationalism was broken while people were still dreaming of the coming of a royal messiah to rescue them from their exile. But the answer from Second Isaiah seems more provocative because he once called Cyrus the Messiah while the house of Jacob was to become a servant to bear witness to Yahweh's justice, peace, and love to all nations. This radically new role or identity of Israel among the nations entails new understanding of the meanings inherent in the Noachic, Abrahamic, Mosaic, and Davidic covenants. In Second Isaiah people are called to "remember not the former things, nor consider the things of old" (43:18). Second Isaiah mentions almost nothing about Noah (54:7), Moses, Abraham (41:8 and 51:2), or even David (just once in 55:3), while many times he says: "But you, Israel, my servant, Jacob, whom I have chosen, the offspring of Abraham, my friend, you whom I took from the ends of the earth, and called from its farthest corners, saying to you, 'You are my servant, I have chosen you and not cast you off, . . . for I am your God' " (41:8–10). The key words are: *Israel, Jacob, my servant, calling,* and *choosing.* Here we may discern that the old covenants are reinterpreted through the new election of Jacob-Israel as servant among the nations.

The theological foundation for such a new election can be understood only through a new articulation of the doctrines of creation and history. " 'I am the Lord (Yahweh), your Holy One, the Creator of Israel, your King.' Thus says the Lord, who makes a way in the sea, path in the mighty waters, who brings forth chariot and horse, army and warrior; they lie down, they cannot rise, they are extinguished, quenched like a wick" (43:15–17). "Remember these things, O Jacob, and Israel, for you are my servant; I formed you, you are my servant; O Israel, you will not be forgotten by me . . . Thus says the Lord, your Redeemer, for he formed you from the womb: 'I am the Lord, who made all things, who stretched out the heavens alone, who spread out the earth — Who was with me?' " (44:21, 24). The creator God is also the redeemer of Israel in history who shows his love for all human beings by calling Jacob-Israel to witness as a servant to all nations. Israel cannot be a messiah anymore because the messiah politics of nations such as Assyria, Babylonia, and Persia was a mere repetition of the ugly power politics that was destined to pass away. However, the servant politics that transcended the old ethnocentrism of Israel will heal the ugliness of power by vicarious suffering as it witnesses to God's creative power and redemptive love for all peoples. Even the Davidic covenant is reinterpreted in accord with the image of the suffering servant rather than of an exalted messiah (55:3–5). There will be a new Exodus for Israel to establish a new Zion, indeed, a Zion of servant politics (51:9–11).

But the people of Israel were perplexed by this new calling, which functioned in tension with the old covenants. Was Israel to be a suffering servant or a Davidic messiah? Was she to build a new Zion of servant politics or restore the old Jerusalem of power politics? Religious Judaism emerged later on. Ethnocentrism with religious patriotism replaced the prophetic image of the suffering servant until the coming of Jesus. From Second Isaiah we can learn that the reality of suffering during the Exile did not really change the ethnocentrism and the political messianism of the old Israel.

The same historical pattern has developed in Chinese history as the Han ethnocentrism and the Son of Heaven politics have enslaved Chinese peoples over several thousand years. Even the Han Chinese, who escaped from the China mainland to Taiwan after World War II, claim that there should be no idea of the Taiwanese as a people and there ought to be only one national official language in Taiwan —

Mandarin Chinese. The Taiwanese language is forbidden in the schools at every level, and the history of Taiwan can be learned only fragmentarily as an appendix to Chinese history. You can see the Han Chinese exiled in Taiwan behave like the Israelites exiled in Babylonia. They uphold political messianism and dream of the recovery of Peking (Zion) without listening to the prophetic proclamation of a new identity as the Israelites learned to understand themselves as God's suffering servant.

The New Covenant in Jesus Christ

From the time of Second Isaiah to the coming of Jesus, great empires such as those of Babylonia, Persia, Greece, and Rome rose and fell, while at the same time Judaism emerged, developed, and became the spiritual symbol of Jewish religion with a nationalistic vision. The Jews had lost their land and national identity. Although the Maccabees theoretically recovered their land for about forty years, they were actually commissioned by foreign superpowers as high priests, military governors, and ethnarchs over their fellow Jews in Palestine. What they achieved was only a relative national independence or an autonomous state under the tolerance of the superpowers — Persia, Egypt, Greece, or Rome. Most of the time they were "colonized" as Judas Maccabeus said: "The Kingdom of the Greeks was reducing Israel to slavery" (1 Macc. 8:18, *Jerusalem Bible*).

Judaism, with its ethnocentric political messianism, rejected Jesus' politics of the suffering servant which had its roots in Second Isaiah. Jesus would have loved the Minjung as Korean theologians have expounded this important perspective to us. Although Jesus did not challenge directly the colonial rulers, he did challenge the meaning of power. In his mind, the power to dominate should be radically transformed into the power to serve, with the self-offering of his own life as a paradigm (see Mark 10:4–45). This radical transformation of the meaning of power seriously threatened the power politics of self-deified messianism. This may explain why Jesus was crucified on the grounds of "sedition" or "rebellion" (John 19:19). He was considered seditious in relation to Judaism and a rebel against Caesarism. Even Paul and his coworkers were considered the "men who turned the world upside down" (Acts 11:6). This means that inherent in the paradigm of Jesus' servant politics is a high potential to "turn the world upside down," which has the potential to establish a new world order, including a new humanity and a new community in accord with the power to serve and love.

In Jesus' politics of the suffering servant, the patriarchal, ethnocentric, and nationalistic symbol of Abraham is transformed into a universal symbol of Abraham as the father of faith in the God who reveals himself in Jesus as Christ, in whom all things are created anew. The Magna Charta for Israel in the Mosaic covenant could be fulfilled only by the love of God in Christ. The Davidic political messianism had to be judged and transformed by the messianic politics of Jesus. The holy truimphalism of Israel over the natives in Canaan ought to be eradicated and replaced by a new universal brotherhood and sisterhood in Jesus Christ (Col. 3:10–11). Judaistic ethnocentrism had to be liberated by the prophetic vision of a creator-redeemer God who loves all nations and takes the form of a suffering servant to recreate all things. The Noachic cosmic vision of reverence for life embraces all of the old covenants and will be fulfilled in the symbol of the new heaven and new earth. Jesus says: "I came that they may have life, and have it abundantly" (John 10:10). Even the life of a sparrow was precious in his eyes. He loves the Minjung, encourages them, and enables them to change their life, life system, and sociopolitical system.

Jesus' followers may envision the emergence of a new heaven and a new earth. "For the first heaven and the first earth had passed away, and the sea was no more ... 'Behold, the dwelling of God is with men. He will dwell with them, and they shall be his people, and God himself will be with them' " (Rev. 21:1, 3). The old recognition formula in Exodus — "and I will take you for my people, and I will be your God; and you shall know that I am the Lord (Yahweh) your God, who has brought you out from under the burdens of the Egyptians" (6:7) — is transformed from its "patriarchal" and later "ethnocentric-nationalistic" worldview into a trans-ethnocentric and transnationalistic new world order with a new experience of God in Jesus Christ. The experience of a new world order is coexistent and coextensive with the experience of a new God in Jesus Christ who is "the compassionate God" who "disrupts" and "transposes" world history through the "communion of love" (see C. S. Song, *The Compassionate God*, Maryknoll, N.Y.: Orbis Books, 1982, pp. 255ff.).

The idea of a homeland in this new experience of God in Jesus Christ may be conceived as a process of concretion of the Kingdom of God on Taiwan. It is not an abstract speculation or theologization of a heavenly kingdom but rather a kingdom of Minjung who are struggling for the human dignity inherent in the *imago Dei*. They struggle on the land in which they have rooted their lives and hope and on which they will become a new people of God. "The compassionate God" who judges and loves all peoples and nations will break and eradicate all kinds of chauvinism, ethnocentrism, nationalism, and other self-deified "isms." The people of God on Taiwan are entrusted with this confession and enabled by it to build their own homeland with the awareness that neither capitalism nor communism can really fulfill human needs. Marx's critique of "the German Ideology" shows that without exception all kinds of *eidos* and *logos* are contaminated by some sort of "quasi-German," or ethnonationalistic, elements. Although he talks about the radical need for "human emancipation" rather than "political emancipation," his idea of achieving "universal freedom by overthrowing all existing bases of oppression," implied in his idea of "human emancipation," in reality has been distorted by nationalistic interests. The idea of "total human emancipation" in reality usually becomes human domination. There is a Russian ideology, an American ideology, a Chinese ideology, a Japanese ideology and so on. Since we acknowledge the need for the critique of these ideologies, in the homeland theology we have tried to be self-critical of such ideological enslavement. There is no theology without ideology. But self-criticism and self-transcendence of ideological enslavement may bring theologians to work together humbly for the concretion of the vision of the kingdom of Minjung in accord with the promise of the Kingdom of God.

Concluding Remarks

The idea of homeland theology has its roots in the struggle of the church and the eighteen million people on Taiwan to establish a new identity for the church and people together as the people of God on this island. The complexities of the relations among people, land, power, and God should be acknowledged in the complex context of international power groups and domestic interest groups. There is no easy way out. Homeland theology is a "theopraxis" rather than a "theologos." Consequently, theological education in the light of homeland theology must be dynamic rather than static. Being dynamic means living out the content of our faith in a living context rather than studying in the library and producing papers. The latter is static.

Under martial law what we have been doing is more significant and dangerous than what we have written. This article reveals in part what we have been doing and thinking in the last five years. For the celebration of the centenary conference in Korea, we boldly and humbly contribute these thoughts to our brothers and sisters in Christ in Korea as our little offering.

Chapter 17

Theology of Reunification

DAVID KWANG-SUN SUH

One of the most vibrant and truly indigenous theologies to emerge in Asia is the Korean *minjung* theology, *minjung* meaning "the common people." It was born in the 1970s as a theological response to, among other things, the suppression of human rights and denial of democratic process. Since then, like all theological movements, it has seen a number of changes, which include the emergence of a vigorous women's movement and the birth of a *minjung* church among the industrialized urban poor. Recently it has become conscious of the division of the country and has realized that the liberation of the *minjung* cannot be achieved by only one part of the peninsula. This essay is an early attempt to look at the whole question of reunification and reconciliation.

David Kwang-sun Suh is one of the pioneers of *minjung* theology and has written extensively about it. His latest book is *The Korean Minjung in Christ* (Hong Kong: The Christian Conference of Asia, 1991). He is on the staff of Ewha Women's University, Seoul, Korea.

Source: *Theology and Politics,* Vol. I, Yeow Choo Lak, ed. (Singapore: The Association for Theological Education in South East Asia, 1993).

Hanshik and Wandering Spirits

Hanshik is a national holiday in Korea. Officially, this day is set aside for people to plant trees over the barren hills. However, only government officials seem to engage in planting trees while the common people use this day to visit the grave sites of their ancestors. This is a day when the people pay tribute to their ancestors by offering them food and drink, planting new flowers and trees in the area surrounding the graves, and generally tending to the grass and foliage in the area. There is another memorial holiday which occurs in the first week of June. This day, unlike *Hanshik,* is in memory of soldiers and other important government figures, but the common people of Korea do not place as much significance on this day as they do on *Hanshik.*

In Chinese characters, the word *"hanshik"* refers to cold food, or eating cold food. According to Chinese folklore, rainstorms on this particular day were so harsh and strong that they would blow out the cooking fires, and thus the people had to forego cooking their food. On this day it is customary to eat cold food. My father used to tell me that the reason cold food is eaten on this day is because people have to work around the grave sites all day long with no time to cook a warm meal.

Eating cold food is no longer a problem for most of us. But millions of people are still unable to visit their ancestors' grave yards on the day of *Hanshik* because of the division of the country. There are millions of lost souls still wandering the hills, rivers, valleys, and mountains as *han*-ridden spirits, unable to rest because they lack a place to rest in peace. There are no Confucian or *mudang* priests to care for the wandering spirits who died in the Korean War between 1950 to 1953; killed in the crossfire during the run for refuge, kidnapped or fallen dead on the road to their unknown destiny; or blown up by bombs and scattered all over the countryside. For nearly forty lunar years, forty *Hanshiks* and August lunar holidays of *Chusuk,* no religion has cared for the wandering spirits of these *han*-ridden souls. No priest of *han* is forthcoming on the horizon of Korean history either to offer food and drink or to provide a final resting place to these lost souls in a free and united Korea.

Since *Hanshik* falls in our Christian Easter season, as we contemplate the death of Jesus Christ on the cross and his resurrection, we are also compelled to reflect on the death and resurrection of the lost souls who died during the process of national division which has lasted for four decades. In addition, since *Hanshik* falls in the month of April with the blossoming of azaleas and dog-berries, we think about the student martyrs of the April 19, 1960 Student Revolution as well as the other lives that ended throughout the 1970s and 1980s in order to nurture the blooming of the spring flowers of democracy and freedom. On the arbor day of *Hanshik,* as we plant trees in our small yards, we reflect on the millions of wandering souls all over the hills of Korea. And as we do, we cannot help but think about the cross they had to bear and the cross that we are all bearing — the cross of division imposed on the Korean people. On the Korean holiday of *Hanshik* during the Christian Easter season, during the cruelest month of April, we think of the death and resurrection of the divided people of Korea.

The Cross of Division

The cross of division was imposed on the Korean people by the victorious superpowers at the end of World War II. The "liberation" of Korea was the beginning of our division. It is understandable why Germany, an aggressor nation, might be cut off after World War II. On the other hand, no one seems to know why a victim of the war, like Korea, was divided up rather than Japan, the aggressor nation. Opinions regarding the division differ: some contend the division was created because of an ignorance of history; some say that the line of demarcation was drawn in order to disarm the Japanese soldiers; some claim the action was part of the American imperialistic policy of expansion; and still others assert that division reflects Soviet aggression in the Far East. What is clear, however, is that Koreans did not participate in the decision-making process; the cross of division was imposed on the Korean people by the superpowers. Moreover, the Korean people were innocent of the cross; that is, Koreans received the cross despite the fact that they were innocent of any crimes committed against the world or the superpowers. Thus, the cross of the division is a cross of *han*. (*Han* is a Korean word that describes a deeply imbedded feeling of anger, frustration, and resentment which lies in the deepest subconsciousness of the Korean psyche.)

The millions of people who lost their lives during the Korean War died unfair deaths. Russian lives were not lost defending communism in Russia, but tens of thousands of American lives were sacrificed on Korean soil in defense of freedom and democracy, and millions of Chinese lives were likewise sacrificed in defense of communism. Koreans also fought in the war under the rhetoric of defending freedom and democracy in the south, and in the north to defend communism against the threat of foreign invasion. But, in effect, the war planted the roots of division even further into the soil, partitioning off the north from the south and the south from the north. The war was not faithful to its original intention of national unification, but rather created a division among the people which was wider and deeper than when the war began in 1950.

Today, in order to keep this line of division tight and secure, nearly two million soldiers armed with the most deadly, contemporary, and sophisticated weapon systems have besieged the peninsula. In order to maintain this force, we must provide them with the comforts of expensive food, clothing, and housing. We have to purchase the most expensive weapon systems, keep the tanks oiled, repair the trucks and cranes, and keep the guns and artilleries in tiptop shape. We are forced to send our brightest and strongest sons to first-rate military academies to have them trained in the most advanced forms of technical warfare. The cross of national security and national defense has been imposed on the Korean people of both north and south. Exorbitant defense spending is the greatest barrier to the development of the north Korean economy, and one-third of the south's national budget goes annually to defense spending.

Tremendous natural and human resources are being poured into maintaining this line of division. And as if this weren't enough, the people of both north and south Korea live under the constant threat of nuclear weapons which could annihilate the peninsula. The cross of division has been forced on innocent travellers aboard airliners carrying the Korean flag. A Korean Air's flight was shot down by the Soviet Air Force in 1983, killing 269 passengers. Then again in November 1987 another Korean airliner was blown up by north Korean terrorists, which resulted in the death of 115 people. Wherever we go, we Koreans have to carry the cross of division. Under constant threats of being bombed or kidnapped, we are in fear for our lives.

Another cross of the division borne by south and north Koreans alike is the loss and separation of close family members. When tens of thousands of north Koreans left their homes to begin lives in the south, most left behind family members with only a few words of optimism expressing the hope that they might meet again in a month or two. That month or two has turned into some five hundred months. The Korean War forced families to separate and many still do not know the whereabouts of missing family members. Almost every day a missing cousin, brother, or sister reunited with family members is seen on television crying tears of joy and anguish. It is even conceivable for a missing father presumed to be dead to suddenly appear during *Hanshik* and disrupt not only the rituals of the ancestor's memorial ceremony but the normal routines of life as well. Some ten million people still separated from family members by the line of division live with this kind of uncertainty in their lives.

In order to maintain the division, north Korea has become one of the most closed totalitarian countries in the world. No letters from south Korea can enter north Korea and vice versa. No television or broadcast frequencies of the south or north can be picked up on either side of the demarcation line without serious ramifications. No papers, magazines, jokes, not even comic books, can be exchanged across this fortified line. Only gunshots, propaganda, curses, and nasty remarks are exchanged between the two sides. Any opening in this eye of the needle across the line of demarcation for dialogue or personal exchange ends up being interpreted as a "peace offensive" or results in gross verbal attacks and all-out propaganda-warfare by both sides. Nonetheless, the Korean people have not given up hope for widening that eye of the needle and continue to hope that they might perhaps be able to freely cross this line in their lifetime.

Korean democracy itself has been nailed on the cross of division for more than thirty years. A "logic of division" has been created and is now pervasive in all walks of Korean life. It is used to suppress freedom and democracy. It is the logic behind tight press control. Military dictatorships exist to make sure that national security remains protected and division is kept intact. The justifications for suppressing the labor movement are to prevent north Korean infiltration and to preserve national security. The reason to keep tabs on what ministers preach in their churches is again national security. The weight of the arguments behind maintaining national security and the anti-communist laws rests on the division. Because of this logic of division, Korean students have been prohibited from reading books on sociological analyses and the original texts of Karl Marx. The study of the liberation theologies of Latin America is prohibited except when taught for the sake of criticism. Gutiérrez's classic *A Theology of Liberation* has been banned from university bookstores.

The Korean people, nailed to the cross of division, have been robbed of freedom, justice, and basic human rights. With the red light of division, all creative and critical actions were put to a halt. With the red flag of division, frank intellectual discussions about division, democracy, human rights, justice, due process, and human dignity were all put to a stop. With the red sign of division, everyone was silenced — even faced with horrendous corruption and the cruelest violations of human rights. We have been told that as long as we are nailed to the cross of division there can be no resurrection of freedom, democracy, and human rights. We are left to die, forever nailed on the cross of division.

With clear Christian consciences, we hear the agonizing cry on the cross of division, *Eli, Eli, lama sabachthani.* This cry of *han* is a cry to God from a forsaken people. Has God forsaken the Korean people on the cross of division? When we hear the cries from our cross of division, we feel numb and powerless. We are lost; we do not know how to respond to these cries. We have no theology to help us with the pain and we have no miracles to perform to take down the suffering people from the cross of division. Nor do we possess the spirituality to endure the long years of suffering on the cross. Just as the disciples of Christ ran away from the agonizing cry on the cross, so have we been running away from the cries of the Korean people.

Resurrection and the Rice Community

On the traditional Korean holiday of *Hanshik,* which comes to us in the cruelest month of April during the Easter season, we think of death and resurrection for the dead and the living. If resurrection has only to do with the immortality of the soul, then it has nothing to do with the death of our people on the cross of division. By the same token, it has nothing to do with the death of Jesus Christ on the cross. And if resurrection is about the occurrence of a life after death and death after life, that is, history in cycle, then it is nothing more than mere vanity, for nothing under the sun will ever be new. Christian resurrection has to do with the resurrection of Jesus Christ and, we believe, it has to do with the cross of Jesus. Resurrection opposed death on the cross. In the same way, it is resistance against death on the cross of division. It is an argument against the death on the cross imposed upon us by our oppressors. Resurrection is understood as the rising up against the principalities of death on the cross of division.

A more theological understanding of the resurrection in the context of recent Korean historical developments came from a female undergraduate student. She wrote in one of her school newspapers:

> It may seem as if our history is nothing but a continuous series of sufferings on the cross without the hope of resurrection.... But Jesus who died on the cross [was] resurrected to push away the heavy tombstone to create the space for glory and salvation. Resurrection without suffering is as meaningless as death without resurrection. Likewise, the history of death and suffering of this land, this peninsula, is ready for resurrection.... As we see the deep wounds of the young Jesus, which are the suffering of the people on the streets, in the labor situation, at school and in prison, and as we see their wounds become deeper still, we are sure of the dawn of Easter with the battle cry for freedom. (Idae Hak Bok, April 4, 1988)

Our students do not give up hope in the midst of the cruelest month of April because they believe that death and suffering within the struggle for democracy are not altogether meaningless. In the middle of their death and suffering, they are able to meet with the risen Lord of the resurrection. In the cries of the people's suffering on the cross of division, we await the dawn of resurrection of the Korean people, and we possess a hope, a desperate hope for overcoming the division.

As long as we suffering people of this divided land view the cross in this historical context, we cannot help but hope for resurrection in our historical future. We cannot stop at the idea that the resurrection of Christ was his own miraculous doing. Nor can we stop at the idea that Christ's resurrection is nothing more than wishful thinking, or the memories of his disciples, or even the collective memory of the earliest Christian communities. We have to go beyond the metaphysical idea that resurrection has to do with simply the eternal life of individual souls. Resurrection is the hope of the community of the table; it is the search for people coming together at the Lord's table to eat and drink together as a community.

Jesus, the risen Lord, meets with two men on the road to Emmaus and has a conversation with them and breaks bread with them (Lk 24:13–32). The resurrected Jesus again showed himself by the Sea of Tiberias where he fed his disciples with fish laid on a charcoal fire (Jn 21:9–13). The risen Lord showed the scars of the nails on his hands to Thomas (Jn 21:24–29). And the angels told the apostles to go to the Land of Galilee, the land of suffering and oppression, to meet with the risen Lord (Mk 15:7). The resurrection is to be the memory of the disciples in the community of breaking bread together, and in touching the wounds of Jesus in the world of the suffering Galilee. As the disciples of Jesus Christ, our risen Lord, Korean Christians believe in the resurrection in the hope of bringing together scattered people to the table of the Lord in peace, in justice, and in community. We believe in the resurrection of the divided people from the cross of division, in overcoming division and obtaining resurrection through the reunification of Korea — its land and its people. We believe in the resurrection as the reclaiming of the community. In the resurrected body of Christ, we struggle for the community, the unity and commonwealth of peace with justice.

We would like to see separated families reunited not only on the television shows but in their homes, sharing rice and *kimchi* at the same table in the north and south. I would like to go back to Pyongyang myself by driving through a newly built Seoul-Pyongyang freeway. Then my family and I could visit my father's grave site, and I would offer drinks to my father by pouring Korean rice wine over the grave mound, although my Puritan father wouldn't approve of the idea of pouring rice wine over his grave.

We would like to join with north Korean Christians in an open place for worship and break bread together to celebrate the resurrected body of Christ in our common eucharist. We Koreans were overwhelmed at the news of official north Christian delegates and south Korean ecumenical leaders coming together in Switzerland to celebrate the Lord's Supper together. We experienced the resurrection of the body of Christ in that community of Christians who broke bread together in one faith even in a place so far away from home. Now we would like the chance to taste the wine we might drink together in the name of our risen Lord in the history of the divided and suffering land of Korea. We would like to celebrate our traditional holidays of *Hanshik* (arbor day) and Liberation Day (August 15) as well as *Chusuk* (the autumn festival) together at our ancestors' burial sites, sharing the best of our own food with each other, among both the living and dead. This, we believe, would truly be a celebration of the resurrection of the dead and the living alike.

Again, we believe in the resurrection in the Messianic Kingdom. As Paul says, "Then comes the end, when he delivers up the Kingdom of God the Father, after abolishing every kind of domination, authority, and power" (1 Cor 15:24). The resurrection we believe in is a socio-political one. In terms of the divided Korean people, resurrection means overcoming the state of division and achieving reunification with an eschatological vision of the Messianic Kingdom. Yes, we are theologically obsessed with the resurrection of the divided, dead nation of Korea in the eschatological Messianic Kingdom. Without this eschatological vision for the reunification of Korea, Korean Christianity would lack power in its theology and its mission within this divided and war-torn world of ours. The eschatological vision of resurrection exists in the vision of a New Earth and a New Heaven — "Now at last God has his dwelling among men. He will dwell among them and they shall be his people, and God himself will be with them. He will wipe every tear from their eyes, there shall be an end to death, and to mourning and pain; for the old order has passed away" (Rev 21:3–4).

Resurrection and Eschatological Visions of Reunification

The more we become committed to overcoming our division and realizing the reunification of Korea, the more we think and believe in the reality of the faith of resurrection. Simply and clearly, overcoming the division and realizing the reunification of Korea is the resurrection and the coming of the eschatological Kingdom of the Lord within the particular history of this land of ours.

Our eschatological vision of the resurrection is theologically connected, first, with the year of Jubilee, the favorable year of the Lord. The February 1988 general assembly of the National Council of Churches of Korea (NCCK) adopted a declaration in which the Korean Christian churches revealed their intention to carry out a movement for a Jubilee Year for Peace and Reunification in 1995. The year 1995 will be the fiftieth anniversary of liberation and at the same time the fiftieth year of the division of Korea. As in the declaration of the Jubilee by Jesus himself, Korean Christians will be empowered by the Holy Spirit to be liberated from the yoke of division to see the oppressed and the prisoners of the division return home and join their reunited families. The declaration of the Jubilee year embodies the history of salvation of the people of God. No dynasty or king has actually declared the Jubilee and seen it acted upon. But it is the promise of God in history, and with faith in this promise, the people of God have struggled, suffered on the cross and died.

We do not know whether God will allow us to celebrate the Jubilee year in 1995, or if Christians and separated families of the north and south will be able to join together to share common meals at the table of the Lord. We do not know whether the year 1995 will bring the end of hatred and conflict between brothers and sisters in the north and south. But what we do know for certain is that in our faith and conscience we cannot go beyond the fiftieth year of division and separation or remain silent about the suffering of our people on the cross of division.

However, as soon as the NCCK's declaration of the year of Jubilee was reported in the Korean press, a Christian ethicist openly criticized the declaration, stating that if the Jubilee year is actualized, it will mean the realization of socialism, and therefore the NCCK cannot escape criticism that it endorses a socialist ideology. This has been a typical way of attacking the Bible as communist literature. There is no mistake about it. The declaration of the Jubilee Year for Peace and Reunification of Korea is a movement toward the second liberation of the Korean people from the yokes of division, hatred, terrorism, murder, and the deepest sins of mutual annihilation. Therefore, internally, the movement for the Jubilee in Korea is a movement for penitence, a theologico-ethical movement which is a faith preparation for the coming of the Kingdom of God. Without a full-fledged movement of religious repentance, confessing the sins we have committed in the eyes of God —

the sins of division, distrust, mutual hatred, and mutual annihilation — we will not be able to come together with our own brothers and sisters to the table of our rice community.

Immediately following the NCCK's February 1988 declaration Christian colleagues began to criticize the movement, from mild and friendly advice and suggestions to quite open attacks, such as examples mentioned earlier. But what is basically lacking in this criticism is an articulation of their faith or the theological grounds for their opposition to the movement for the Jubilee Year of Peace and Reunification. One cannot help but question where these critics stand on the issues of reconciliation, love, justice, and repentance for their deep-seated hatred, let alone their reasons for opposing responsible Christian responses to the task of overcoming the division of Korea and realizing peace in Asia as well as the world.

Second, our eschatological vision of resurrection is connected with shalom, the peace of God which has been envisioned in the Messianic Kingdom in a New Heaven and New Earth. No present day Christian in Korea, I believe, would oppose peaceful means of overcoming Korea's division. And this concept of peace — yes, it is still only a word and concept in our time — has become a dangerous word. If "the other side" proposes peace, then it is believed as a dangerous "peace offensive." And if this side proposes peace, then it is interpreted as a "sign of weakness." And when and if Christians talk about peace, we are criticized as either religious fanatics or as being the agents of "the other side."

Despite the danger, suspicion, and disbelief, Christian efforts for peacemaking on this land are imperative, and we believe commanded by God. In practical terms, peacemaking begins with the Christian mission of raising our voices against the military build-up and intensifying tension across the line of division. Furthermore, with clear conscience, no one, neither Christian nor non-Christian of this land, could possibly advocate the use of nuclear weapons against each other. And no people of a sovereign and independent nation would welcome the perennial presence of foreign troops on their land, no matter how friendly or helpful they might be.

However, the Korean Christians' "peace proposals" in the NCCK Declaration have been criticized as "threats to peace." And we are still waiting for alternative peace proposals from our critical friends. We believe that as long as the present level of military confrontation is maintained, there can be no hope for national efforts to search for and reunite separated families, and no hope to build a road to reunification of the land. Some argue that given this present state of tension, peaceful co-existence might be an alternative. This is a fantastic illusion. First of all, present levels of military build-up preclude the possibility of peaceful co-existence, which requires mutual trust and respect. In order to maintain the present level of military balance, one side always has to out-do the other side. And the rhetoric does not promote peaceful co-existence; similarly, military deterrence always presupposes aggression from the other side.

Our critical Christian friends would ultimately not even accept the idea of peaceful co-existence, for they strongly advocate eventual unification of the peninsula. Our friends neither accept our peace proposals nor the co-existence formula. Given this, the remarks made by the Korean Association of Evangelical Theologians in response to the NCCK's proposal are interesting as well as significant. They state that 1) they agree to the proposal (of NCCK) to widen the participation of the people in policy discussions on reunification; 2) they agree to the free exchange of non-political visits across the demarcation line; and 3) they propose prayers and mission work to achieve reunification through the grace of God. These positions are asserted in spite of the fact that they oppose the NCCK's peace proposals and peaceful co-existence. They propose wide discussions on the issue of unification yet they offer only prayers.

In principle, our movement for peacemaking on the Korean peninsula and our proposals for peaceful co-existence only aim for the ultimate reunification of the people and the building of a new national community. We have no idea how to separate the issue of peace from reunification within the particular context of Korea as a people and as a nation. In Korea, division of the people and land opposes peace or peaceful co-existence. Reunification is the only road to peace, not only on the Korean peninsula but in the surrounding area as well. For nearly half a century, we have been thrashed about between the two horns of the Korean dilemma — a fragile peace or reunification. We now have the courage and the understanding to realize that "fragile peace" is no peace, and fragile peace with positive efforts for unification is, again, no peace at all. Peace on the Korean peninsula is an end in itself in the light of reunification, and reunification is also in itself an end in the light of peacemaking.

We believe that working for peace on the Korean peninsula is working for international justice and that the task of achieving unification is a task for achieving international justice. The division of Korea was a historical accident and an unfair solution. The division that was supposed to be the solution only raised more problems, to say the least. Therefore, the dialectical argument that peace must forego justice or that justice must assume an absence of peace cannot apply to the Korea case. Some latter-day Niebuhrian in Korea has made the comment that NCCK has not dealt with the justice issue in light of a balance of power. I myself had thought that this kind of argument disappeared with the American pull-out from the jungles of Vietnam. When you talk about justice from the point of peace, military strength is not necessarily being achieved. We have learned the hard way that the cost of building military strength is taking rice away from hungry children.

Maintaining international justice through military power will bring about neither peace nor justice. Justice implies forgiveness rather than retaliation; and justice is reconciliation, not mutual accusation. Justice is needed because of the sinfulness of human nature. And justice is possible because of the righteousness of the human conscience. Justice cannot be maintained through hatred and mistrust, but by trust and goodwill within the human community. Peace is opposed to justice only when the peace is unjust. The peace in Korea cannot be true peace as long as nearly two million soldiers confront each other at gunpoint across a dividing line. We must agree on a simple point regarding peace and justice in Korea, namely, that we have come to realize more and more that without peace and unification, there can be no justice, freedom, respect for human dignity, or national integrity.

Our third vision of the eschatological nature of our belief in the resurrection of a divided people on the cross of national suffering has been the subject of many questions. People ask what kind of blueprint or ideological vision we have for a united Korea. I am puzzled about the priorities of a person who asks such questions. Do we have to have some kind of a detailed blueprint about the Kingdom of God when we talk about our dreams and hopes besides what we have in the Gospel? Are we disqualified from talking about the future of a united Korea simply because we have an open and unprogrammed computer disk? The picture of our united Korea will become clearer as we begin to work step by step toward building peace on and around the Korean peninsula and implement various political, economical, cultural, scholarly, and humanitarian exchanges. And as these programs become frequent and varied, a slow but steady and certain process will be developed to achieve a political solution for unification. Then and only then will the question of a particular ideology present itself as an issue.

As we take steps to building peace and an atmosphere for wide participation by the people on the reunification issue, the question of ideology is not the most urgent problem. But when this question is raised, it is clear that the people will have to draw this ideological blueprint. For now, our blueprint is based on a dream of the Kingdom of God where space exists for the people of Korea to freely choose their own system of government as well as ideology for their own united nation. Our immediate hope is for freedom of the people in both the north and south to discuss the issues of peace and unification. This freedom will allow Koreans to live with dignity as persons and as the subjective forces within their nation and history.

Now we hear the voice of the suffering people in the divided land of Korea—

> Prepare the way for the Lord,
>   make his path straight,
> Every valley of barbed wire shall be filled with flowers,
> and every mountain and hill of nuclear mines shall be brought low,
> and the crooked will be straightened,
> and the divided line of the DMZ shall be demolished and erased from
>   the map;
> and the rough ways on the bridge of no return shall be made smooth
>   and wide for the free traffic of people;
> and all flesh shall see the salvation and liberation of God.
>
> (Lk 3:4–6, paraphrased)

Chapter 18

The Language of Human Rights:
An Ethical Esperanto?

Reflections on Universal Human Rights
from an Indian Third-World Context

FELIX WILFRED

Industrialized Western countries and international banking organizations have often used human rights as a criterion for doling out monetary aid to developing countries. Needless to say, their understanding of human rights is colored by Eurocentric values. This article offers a different concept of human rights based on an Indian understanding of the universal, which is contextually sensitive.

Felix Wilfred is Professor of Systematic Theology in St. Paul's Seminary, Tiruchiraappalli, India. His books include *Sunset in the East? Asian Challenges and Christian Involvement* (Madras: University of Madras, 1991) and *Leave the Temple: Indian Paths to Human Liberation* (Maryknoll, N.Y.: Orbis Books, 1992).

Source: *Vidyajyoti Journal of Theological Reflection* 56 (4), 1992.

A Polish oculist, Ludwik Lazar Zamenhof (1859–1917) by name, had a grand vision in his youth. Living in his native district amidst peoples of various ethnic, cultural, and linguistic extraction — Poles, Germans, Russians, and Jews — he wondered how he could help them live together in harmony and peace. The idea struck him of creating a *universal* language that belongs to none and yet will serve all people as a common medium of communication with one another. It was an attempt to reverse the story of Babel. The history and fate of this grand, stillborn linguistic child, Esperanto, need not be recounted here.

In a world that is being pulled apart by conflicting interests, values, and views, a universal ethical language on which all nations and peoples can converge is an attractive proposition. For those who are looking for a firm point in the midst of the bewildering diversity of our world and the uncertainties and doubts it brings, the ideal of human rights, like the Cartesian *ergo sum,* brings certainty and relief. But though human rights are today being promoted as a kind of world-ethic,[1] we need to dig a little deeper into their conceptual basis, assumptions, and field of praxis.

The purpose of this article is to examine the language of human rights and its claims in relation to the experiences of third-world societies, their ways of thought, histories, cultures; and their ongoing struggles for liberation. I would like to add that speaking from a third-world perspective is not simply to state one among many viewpoints. It means to look at human rights from the viewpoint of *two-thirds of humanity.* These reflections have as their immediate setting India, one of the largest third-world countries.

Different Universals

The language of human rights has, obviously, a claim to *universality.* We can identify various positions and trends concerning the universality of human rights. For some this universality means that human nature is common to all human persons; independent of nation, race, language, and culture, all human beings share in the same human nature on which certain inalienable rights are founded. The implicit assumption is that the Aristotelico-Thomistic philosophy of essences — the *philosophia perennis* — is valid for all peoples.

Others, more sensitive to cultural diversity, would see these human rights as having foundations in the various cultural traditions of peoples and in their religious universe. In this way, the universality of human rights would be vindicated. This position is open to a certain cultural relativism, namely that each culture has its own specific way of life, symbols, institutions, and the like. But then, in spite of this diversity, certain universals like human rights are considered to be valid for all.

Still for others, we should not look for human rights in its present form in the traditions of peoples. Rather what we find are homologous equivalents, that is, elements which correspond to human rights in the cultures and traditions of peoples. In this sense these rights have, nevertheless, a certain universality.

On the reverse side of this spectrum of views are those who simply reject the universal human rights tradition and deny that rights have universality. In support of it, the argument is offered, *inter alia,* that human rights are historically and culturally bound to the Western experience.

While admitting that all such positions have a point, I do not share the perspective of any one of them. I think the whole question of universality needs to be approached differently. The point at issue is not whether human rights are universal or not. The question is *what kind of universality.* And that makes a lot of difference.

It is simplistic and naive to state that human rights are not universal because they are Western in origin. Just because something has a historically and culturally conditioned origin, it does not mean that it has lost its validity. Perspectives, conceptions, ideas and values which originate among a particular people can have, in the course of time, wider and general appeal. The difference between the Western and Third World approach should not be made to consist in the origin of these rights. The fundamental difference, it seems to me, is in the *different approaches to the universal.* This makes all the difference between a Western and a third-world perspective on human rights.[2]

When faced with the fact of pluralism and diversity, the West tends to transcend the particularities by projecting a universal that would be common to all. This common or universal is viewed as being verified in the particular. The universal is applied to the particular because it is supposed to implicitly and eminently contain the particular. This kind of *common-denominator approach* can be seen in the dominant Western attitude to various issues. For example, in the face of religious pluralism, the West tends to see a common essence of all religions that would be universal, in the light of which it tries to understand each particular religion. Similarly, it sees a universal church transcending all local churches in the image of which the local churches are to be made. I think that the formulation of universal human rights is nothing but fully consistent with this Western mind-set and way of thinking in the face of plurality. It is an expression at the ethical level of this common-denominator approach to universals.

Another Western trend closely allied to the above is the process of *universalization.* It is an attempt to raise one particular to the level of universal, privileging it among other particulars. This one particular that is universalized could be an experience, event, symbol, value, and so forth.

Now, there is an intimate connection between these two trends of Western thought and approach to the universal. What is projected as universal through a common-denominator approach is not really what is common; it is often the universalization of one particular that easily becomes the essence of all others; it becomes *absolute* (free from all that is particular, concrete, or contextual) and *normative.*

The way one understands the universal is not something neutral or something that refers only to the realm of thought and ideas. The universal has a *political* connotation. Fair, comprehensive, rational, and logical as they may appear, the Western approaches to the universal tend, in fact, towards *domination.* The common-denominator conception of the universal and the process of universalization can be convenient tools in the hands of dominating powers. That is precisely what happens, unfortunately, with the system of human rights in its Western conceptual basis. More about this later on.

We can observe a different approach to the universal in most third-world societies. It offers a different conceptual framework to human rights. The universal is not viewed in terms of its comprehensiveness, absoluteness, and normativity. Nor is the universal viewed as something that overarches and transcends the particular. Rather it is a universal inextricably bound up with the context; it is a universal-in-context.

A human rights system that is bound up with the common-denominator approach to the universal will tend to overlook the specificity and peculiarity of the context where the actual struggle for humanization takes place. Third-world societies are looking for a universal that will at the same time be something contextual, something in which they can identify themselves and their experiences. As James Cone put it, "My identity with *blackness,* and what it means for millions living in a white world, controls the investigation. It is impossible for me to surrender this basic reality for a 'higher, more universal' reality. Therefore, if a higher, ultimate reality is to have meaning, it must relate to the very essence of blackness."[3]

In a unilinear cultural evolutionary perspective,[4] which is still quite pervasive, it is assumed that the "primitive" people are bound to the concrete, whereas to think in terms of the abstract and universal is a sign of higher culture and civilization. Today we realize how narrow and naïve a conception this is. In fact, microstudies in the field of anthropology offer today a wealth of materials that conclude that there is no people on earth who do not somehow relate to the universal, for without some kind of universal the ordering of society and the universe is not possible and communication cannot take place. The anthropologists are wonder-struck at the intricate and ingenious ways by which the so-called primitive people have classified and categorized thousands of plants, animals, and other objects of their experience, manifesting their capacity for the universal. Similarly, a sense of moral order and ethical conduct among all peoples is also a clear indication of their ability to think in terms of universals. However, the great difference between the Western approach to the universal and that of the third-world societies is this: the universal for the peoples of the Third World is not something outside the realm of their experience but something that is part of their experience, their life-context.

As a further illustration of the point, let me refer to the case of India. Traditional Indian thought is very much context-relative. As a well-known Japanese Indologist notes with examples, even though Indian thought is prone to abstractness, this abstractness does not transport one from the context, from the reality of experience. Linguistically, this approach to the universal is reflected in the fact that, in Sanskrit for example, the abstraction or universal that would be expressed by a singular in the Western languages is often expressed by plural forms.

> In short, Europeans generally think of the abstract notion of an abstract noun as constructed solely by means of the universal meaning which is extracted from daily experience, so that they represent it in the singular form; on the contrary, the Indians think of the abstract notion as what is included within experienced facts and so fused with them that the essential principle is often represented in plural form.[5]

Every concrete reality has its own specificity and uniqueness; it cannot be considered simply as raw material for the fabrication of a common universal. Every particular, every empirical situation should be considered on its own ground. When this is respected, there can be no generalization *sic et simpliciter.* The universal has to be many, and in relation to the context.

Such has also been a characteristic Indian approach to ethics. As A. K. Ramanujan observes,

> Universalization means putting oneself in another's place — it is the golden rule of the New Testament, Hobbes' "law of all men": Do not do unto others what you do not want done unto you. This main tradition of Judeo-Christian ethics is based on such a premise of universalization — Manu [the classical Indian lawgiver] will not understand such a premise. To be moral, for Manu, is to particularize — to ask who did what, to whom and when.... Each class (*jati*) of man has his own laws, his own proper ethic, not to be universalized.[6]

The difference in the Indian approach to the universal could also be looked at from another angle. In the common denominator approach to the universal, what is common, for example, among rivers would be the *riverness,* an abstraction which is supposed to constitute the common essence of all rivers. In the Indian approach to the universal, what is common to all rivers would be not so much riverness as the ocean. This shows how the Indian approach fuses together the universal and the concrete. In this way, the universal does not impoverish the particular by viewing it from the perspective of the minimum that it has in common with other particulars. Rather, the universal becomes truly the *fullness* and enrichment of the particular. The Indian vision of reality that sees the interrelatedness of the whole universe undergirds the conception of a particular-bound or contextual universal. The universal is not the essence distilled from out of all particulars; the particular is an integral part of the universal; even more, it is itself, in a way, the universal.

The conceptual basis of human rights rests on the Western understanding of the universal. This, in my view, is something very fundamental. The historical process by which the modern articulation of human rights came to be is only an expression of this limited understanding of the universal. This point requires some clarification.

The Birth of a Common Ground

The modern human rights system was not born alone. It has its twin brother, the modern secular nation-state system. The cluster of values and institutions represented by them was formed as a response to a critical historical situation of religious plurality. The Christian West was confronted with the serious problem of pluralism for the first time when Protestantism appeared on the religious, political, and cultural scene of Europe and the seamless garment of a homogeneous religious unity was torn asunder — with grave social and political consequences. The West did not have in its tradition stock conceptions and means to cope with this situation. As a result of the Reformation, when Western culture was divested of a homogenous *Christianitas* which had given it social unity and cohesion and was confronted with warring factions of Protestants and Catholics, it had to invent a common *third force* under which the religious differences could be sunk or subsumed. This was found to be the common *humanitas.* The nation-state was the political expression of the freshly discovered *humanum.*

In this context, the secular seems to have had a martial origin. If, for example, country *A* was at war with a neighboring country *B,* how could one be sure that the Protestant soldiers from the country *A* did not shift their loyalty to their coreligionists in country *B?* The secular came in handy as the least-common-denominator universal. By the secular, which overarched religious belonging and loyalties, the soldiers could be motivated to fight for their nation unitedly. A nationalism that transcends religious differences became an ally of the secular.

Though in its inception the human rights movement aimed at holding in check the absolute sovereignty of the rulers and the "divine right of kings," it became, in course of time, a new ethic in keeping with the ideals and values of the nation-state and the secular. The cluster of values and institutions — human rights, nation-state, secular, and so on — are based on an approach in which the universal and the common relegate the specificities and particularities — regional, religious, cultural, linguistic, ethnic — to the background. The weakness of the political institutions of the nation-state and the secular inspired by such an understanding of the universal has come to the fore today with the growing crisis of conventional political institutions in which the ethnic diversity is not seriously taken into account. This is borne out not only by the happenings in the Third World but also in Eastern Europe. The nation-state is, so to say, a *political universal* that has been privileged at the expense of the legitimate collective rights of peoples and groups for their self-determination.[7] The logic of the Western approach to the universal would justify that the diversities or pluralities apparently subsumed under the universal surrender themselves in its favor.

Now, along with the nation-state ideal, the ethics of human rights is under severe strain. It is becoming increasingly clear that the system of human rights with its basis on the Western approach to the universal is inadequate to meet the challenges and questions posed by the struggles for humanization in the Third World. The human rights tradition that once constituted a response to pluralism is not able to hold out in the situation of the plurality and diversity of today, mainly because of the limited and conditioned conceptual basis of the universal undergirding it. This system has not created room for the context, for the legitimate self-affirmation of the particular.

Social Location and Human Rights

In this context of reflection, one may raise the question whether there are not some basic things that are common to all human beings independent of the plurality of cultures, languages, and traditions. The answer cannot but be a yes. But what sort of universals? This is the crucial point.

If the process of knowledge, as the sociology of knowledge tells us, is very much conditioned and shaped not only by the physical environment in which we live but also by our social location, the class to which we belong, and the political and economic ideology we espouse, then this is true also regarding what we consider as the universal in human beings. The universal that is distilled from the history and tradition of the Western world bears the imprint of its interests and concerns. The experience of the third-world societies, on the other hand, forces us to consider certain *basic needs* as universally human — the need for food, shelter, security, interhuman relationships, self-affirmation as individuals and as a collective group, and so on. The aspirations and struggles of the third-world peoples relate to these human universals. The universals from the West, circumscribed by its economic and political interests, not only do not encounter the universally human experienced by the peoples of the Third World in the form of needs, but they even block and stifle their universals. In fact, it is in fulfilling the needs that a culture is created, a value system formed. What is happening today is that the third-world universals are conveniently passed over in silence or paid lip service. The whole world is expected to fall in line with the universals of the dominant nations and powers.

Does not perhaps the universal of human rights also fall under the same dispensation? In fact, human rights seem to be universal, as long as one does not call into question the economic and political interests of the powerful nations. The moment the people at the periphery start asserting their rights flowing from universal human needs, then human rights cease, in effect, to be the rights of all and become the commodity of privileged nations, races, or classes.

A Mixed Bag

The flaw of the human rights system is evident in the vagueness of the universal that characterizes it. The spectrum of rights to which it is open is so wide that ultimately it says little to third-world societies. Think, for example, of the clamor to have "homosexuality between consenting adults" declared as basic personal human rights. How does this compare with the plight of one million innocent Indian children who die every year of diarrhea simply because they are denied the basic human right to have clean water to drink? This is a concrete illustration of two different worlds, of almost two poles of interests and concerns, brought under one general rubric of "human rights." This kind of human rights does not respond to the vital human and survival questions with which the peoples of the Third World are concerned. It lacks teeth.

In this regard, it is good to recall here the words of Niall MacDermot, a secretary general of the International Commission of Jurists:

> One of the members of our Commission, a distinguished Professor of Law in one of the Third World countries, said to me recently, "you must always remember that human rights" — and he was referring to civil and political rights — "mean very little to a man on less than 3000 calories a day." If that is true, and in general I fear that it is, it means that human rights mean very little to two-thirds of the world's population. These rights are significant only for us, the remaining third, who consume two-thirds of the world's food resources.[8]

The question that concerns the Third World is not whether human rights are not comprehensive, meaning that they could be completed by adding new rights. This is no solution. The dominant paradigms of development, mode of governance, and economic arrangements are structurally such that they cannot effectively comprehend the rights of all, and guarantee the protection of all, even though formally the list of rights could be enlarged. In fact, in addition to the universal declaration of human rights — which was thought to reflect the liberal tradition — other social and cultural rights were added subsequently.[9] "Human rights" has become now a mixed bag in which all sorts of rights are juxtaposed.[10]

Globalization and Fragmentation

Obviously, the human rights system can and does help to reduce incidents of human rights violations. But it leaves unchallenged the structural question. It does not face the violence of structures that assaults the dignity of human persons and the rights of people. One of the reasons for this state of affairs can be traced back to its origin. As I noted earlier, the system of human rights originated as a check to state power.[11] But, the main reason lies in the two different orientations to the present situation of the world. In today's world we note two marked trends: globalization and fragmentation.[12] The advocates of human rights in the West operate from the framework of a world that is becoming — to cite an overused phrase — "a global village." The concern of the third-world societies starts instead with the unfortunate reality of a world that is fragmented socially, politically, and economically, with repercussions in the fields of culture and religion. It is in this fragmented world, full of conflicts and contradictions, that one searches painfully for greater humanization and for "fuller humanity."

In the Court of Praxis

The inadequacy of the human rights ideology to meet the concerns of the Third World and face the ethical challenges of our time becomes manifest when it is confronted with the contradictions at the level of praxis. Here the narrow conceptual foundation on which it rests becomes evident. Even more, the least-common-denominator and universalization trends that lurk under this system are triggered into action. These trends go to serve, as I noted earlier, the cause of domination and the interests of the winners in our present world. They turn the powerful of the world into a *mensura non mensurata* — a nonmeasured measure — that claims to measure and judge everybody else in the comity of nations.

Some months back, in a meeting of the foreign ministers of the European Common Market with the representatives of South East Asian countries (ASEAN), the latter were indicted for lacking in the practice of human rights. Interestingly, some years earlier these very same countries had been praised as models for the rest of the Third World. And there was no less violation of human rights at that time! Now that the economic and geopolitical interests are shifting, the discourse is changing.

One cannot but wonder whether the human rights system has not become an instrument in the hands of the self-righteous, powerful nations of the West to bully the poor nations of the Third World and continue unabated their economic and political hegemony. Human rights have become a ploy; we have come to a stage where, to put it terms of transactional analysis, the game of "I'm O.K.; you're not O.K." is played out by the Western powers vis-à-vis the third-world countries. The indictment of a third-world country for violation of human rights often means that it refuses to play the games of market economy according to the rules framed by the West.

Our suspicion about the noble sentiments voiced by the West regarding human rights has become stronger after the events relating to the Gulf War. The merchants of death continue to provide the most inhuman and lethal weapons of mass destruction to make a profit; and the high technological barbarism we witnessed during the Gulf War has exposed the shameless hypocrisy of the high-sounding human rights jargon. The very institution of the United Nations that was responsible for proclaiming the Universal Declaration of Human Rights is itself, unfortunately, being made to dance according to the tune called by the powerful nations, who never cease to mouth human rights rhetoric to achieve political and economic goals.

Some time back, the United Nations Development Program came out with an index of freedom that includes forty criteria for judging the state of freedom of the world. In the ranking of countries according to the state of freedom and practice of human rights, one cannot fail to notice Western biases and a pronounced tendency to evaluate in better light countries closer to it ideologically and politically. As Chandra Muzaffar observes, in this index a country like Israel, with a record of brutal suppression of the Palestinians, and Hong Kong, still under colonial bondage and lacking self-determination for its people, are placed high on the list.

A Race of Unequals

If one is serious about human rights, one should start by putting all nations on a footing of equality. The asymmetry and inequality in the effective role assigned to various countries in the United Nations contradicts the spirit of universality the concern for human rights is supposed to embody. Nations represent peoples. If some nations are more important, or equal than others, it means that some people are privileged and have rights others do not have. If even a body like the United Nations is instrumentalized for domination, one can well imagine the plight of the powerless poor nations of the Third World!

On the other hand, there is nothing totally new about this contradiction between profession of universal human rights and its practice. As Justice Krishna Iyer once remarked, "godly fear and earthly fraud can piously co-exist."[13] History amply bears witness to the fact that when some people were privileged as subjects of, ironically, *universal human rights,* others were oppressed and exploited. Thus slavery, colonialism, and domination over peoples of the Third World could exist side by side with the proclamation of human rights for many centuries. Even with the profession of human rights, the Jews, as a minority religious community, had to live in fear and trembling in traditional Christian nations.

I am referring to all this not only show the credibility gap — the contradiction between ideals and practice (which is there) — but also to highlight the fact that the claimed "universal" for human rights is, ironically, a *parochial* universal. It is a universal that does not encompass or meet the experiences of many nations and peoples and their rights but simply transcends them, and this "transcendence" in effect works in favor of the powerful. It is not a context-relative universal, but an absolute universal. Absolutizing and universalizing one particular has always been the logic of all dominations.

Human rights can have some ethical relevance only on the assumption that the various nations and peoples are in reality acknowledged and treated as equals. Even at the risk of sounding tautological, it must be stated that there can be equality only among equals. The deficiency of the human rights system is that it assumes all peoples as equals, which contradicts the hard facts. One forgets that what is happening in our world is "a race of unequals" in which the robust and the handicapped are placed side by side.[14] The establishment of justice and fairness in the relationships among nations is then a precondition for the human rights ethic to have an effective influence on the international scene. Otherwise, its fate is bound to be that of Esperanto.

The Process of Humanization and the Mediation of the Human through the Cultural

Looking from within, the question of capital importance for the peoples of the Third World is not so much a set of rights as the question of *humanization.* In concrete terms, it is a problem of transition from a *hierarchical* model of society to an *egalitarian* society. This is particularly true of the Indian society, which is strongly stratified and hierarchically constituted, with its caste system as the organizing principle of the social order. If not the same, similar social disparities characterize the life of many poor nations. To what extent could the system of human rights be of relevance to these "post-traditional" societies in their struggle for equality, justice, and humanization? The relevance, at least as far as the history and present experience of India shows, is very limited.

The mainspring for humanization and equality should be found in the traditions, cultures, and histories of the people, which offer rich resources. Unless one subscribes to an evolutionary view of cultures, one has to admit, on the basis of empirical facts, that every people has found its concrete way of being human. Being human is a culturally mediated reality. The culture of any people embodies its vision, values, and ideals regarding what is universally human. However, defining what is universally human is certainly not the monopoly of any one particular race, culture, or religion. Unless a people lives the law of the jungle, in which case they would not have survived, every people has found concrete ways of recognizing the duties and rights of one another in their day-to-day social life and transactions.

But do not the customs, traditions, and cultures of people contain elements which are antihuman and dehumanizing? The answer is a clear yes. Being a human product, every culture carries with it a certain ambiguity. But with equal clarity it should be stated that the solution to this ambiguity does not consist in importing a set of normative ethical standards, like human rights, from without. If being human is mediated among a people only through culture and through the process of socialization, then any change and transformation should develop from its culture and tradition.

Humanization through Social Movements

Now, if we examine closely the history of any people, with its culture and tradition, we will note that it is the movements born out of the womb of its own history that most effectively and incisively challenged the dehumanizing and antihuman ways of life. No people has remained without its rebels and prophets who have called into question the culture and the order of the society in which they lived.

In India, for example, at every epoch of its history, the inequality represented by the caste system has come under the critical scrutiny of prophetic figures who have denounced it and called for a human society. Between Gautama Buddha and Sri Narayana Guru — and Ambedkar in our century — there has been an array of prophetic figures like the medieval *bhakti* saints and the nineteenth-century Jotirao Phooley.[15] These personalities and movements are important not only for the transformation they tried to effect but also for the contributions they made to shape and widen the Indian mind in humanistic ways. "Movements emerge," as Oommen notes, "not only to correct the lags in praxis in the prevailing institutions, but to identify the gaps in theory as well."[16]

Thus, through these figures and movements, along with a deepening of what is human, there has come about also a corrective to the antihuman ideologies that legitimized the unequal and hierarchical social order. It is through them and the social movements they unleashed that the process of humanization and respect for the rights of all, especially the least in society, came to be upheld and defended — something one can hardly imagine achieved through a code of human rights.

In fact, it is the prophetic figures who symbolize the human; it is they who unleash movements of humanization. In every society prophets are the illustration of a context-related universal. Their message of humanization is a universal message invariably operative in the context of a culture, people, and history. In his or her personality the prophet combines *rootedness* and *universality*, and therefore can come out with a convincing and radical critique of society and culture — and the message goes home.

The legacy of the Western Enlightenment, with its ideal of the human, is not something new. It was tried out in India. The reform movement of the first part of the nineteenth century, with Raja Ram Mohan Roy as the pioneer, took much inspiration from the liberal and Enlightenment tradition. But it did not deliver the goods. It created some ripples in a limited circle; it could not become a nationwide or popular movement for humanization. It lacked indigenous cultural and historical roots. It is in the second part of the nineteenth century, when many streams and movements with roots in the history, culture, and tradition of the people converged, that India's vindication of the human right to self-determination gained momentum. It culminated in the liberation of India from colonial rule.

The process of humanization is far from being completed in India. One important area of struggle is the achievement of human dignity and equality for the over 150 million dalits of India. The dalits, who have all along been humiliated and kept at the bottom of society, were never considered as subjects of rights. According to the laws of Manuthe, Indian classical law-giver, they have only duties, while the upper castes are the subjects of rights.

The point I want to underline is this: in their protest and struggles against the inhumanity heaped upon them, the dalits could most naturally invoke the universal human rights. But this does not happen. The human rights tradition, if at all, has a very marginal influence. The resources for their struggle for humanization derive from a reinterpretation of their history, tradition, symbols, prophets, and social movements.

Religious Mediation of the Human and the Ethical

Another important question that concerns the third-world peoples is the interrelationship between the humanization process and the religious traditions. This is particularly relevant for India and other Asian societies, where religion is a focal point in the life of the people. Precisely because of the central place religion occupies in the life of most third-world societies, the human rights language as an "ethical Esperanto" in "no man's island" has little appeal and seems to evoke poor response.

Therefore, if the human rights question is really a human and ethical issue, then it cannot but be also a religious issue. This is all the more so today, when the liberative and humanizing potential of religious resources is being rediscovered.[17] The human should not be uprooted from the religious realm and turned into an ahistorical, neutral, abstract, and formal universal hovering over the concrete realities of human life. In fact, however, the Western human rights system arose from a distance, taking from religious loyalties and even attacking the religious sphere through the process of secularization.

If the human rights tradition is to have today any relevance to the third-world societies, it needs to somehow relate itself to the central myth or the sacral core of religion. This will not only reinforce the human but also provide the motivational force for a humanizing praxis. To put it in another way, every religious tradition has within its own belief system elements that are open to the wider horizon of the universal human. But then this universal human and the particularity of the religious myth or sacral core are so mutually interwoven that we can hardly extract one from the other. Herein lies also the source of many difficulties.

One of them is acknowledging effectively the right of religious liberty and religious pluralism. The particularity of religious belief and the collective "we" of religious loyalty is so strong that, in spite of a declared universal spirit embracing the universally human, it has been difficult, specially for the Abrahamic religious traditions, to accept "the other" particularities.[18] This is evidenced by the refusal of Christianity for centuries to admit religious pluralism as a basic human reality and the legitimacy of religious liberty. The Islamic conception makes room for other religious groups as tolerated minorities, while Judaism asserts "the right to be different." Against this background, the rise of the human rights tradition, including the right of religious liberty, was something very significant.

Concerning the Indic religious tradition, as well as religions of many other third-world societies, the human rights system could not have arisen because these religious traditions by their nature are not exclusivist. From quite early times, the Indic religious world has been characterized by pluralism as an accepted and lived value. The other, belonging in his or her religious specificity to a particular *marga* or *sampradaya*, was viewed as forming part of the one pilgrimage towards the Ultimate, even though through a different path. Pluralism as a way of life and the attitude of *sarvasamayasamabhavia*, treating all religious traditions equally, did not necessitate the intervention of a third force on the basis of a common *humanum* to create peace among religions. Instead of a religious division on the basis of *cuius regio eius religio,* India spoke of *rajadharma.* This means that amidst religious pluralism, it was the duty of the king to support all religious traditions without discrimination against anyone of them.

But then I must immediately add that the contemporary Indian society presents also a different scene. There has been a trend along religious revivalist and fundamentalist lines. This, I believe, is only a transitional phenomenon caused by several factors, examining the details of which would go beyond the scope of this discussion. To mention, however, just one important factor, there has taken place a kind of universalization of Indian religious traditions. The multiform Indian religious streams were brought under one common umbrella in the colonial period. Indic religious traditions as divergent as those that sought salvation through total renunciation and those that sought it through orgiastic ecstasy were lumped together as one religion called in "Hinduism."[19] The treating of Hinduism as a uniform and monolithic reality (which it is not and which it never has been) on the part of the fundamentalists has led to a process of *"semitization of Hinduism,"*[20] threatening the culture of millennial religious pluralism and coexistence. It is this 'semitized' Hinduism that is today locked in conflict with two Semitic religions, Islam and

Christianity. It is in this context that the system of human rights with its recognition of religious liberty can have a bearing on the present religiopolitical scene.

Checking the Excesses of State Power

Finally, one area where human rights could be of some relevance in India and other third-world societies is the state and its exercise of power. That corresponds to the earliest concerns behind the emergence of the modern human rights system. After the decolonization, many societies of the Third World adopted the nation-state system. But in their exercise of power, the state could and did go to excesses on the plea of sovereignty. Sovereignty does not, however, confer absolute power to the state over the citizens. Human rights could be helpful in holding in check the unrestrained state power that could go against the dignity and rights of its citizens. And this has to be exercised by the people themselves and their organizations.

Human rights can be considered as a brake that belongs to the nation-state machinery. One cannot have the institution of nation-state without the brake that is a part of the package. The result would be disastrous. The peoples of the Third World had their own ways of checking political power, but all these have been unfortunately destroyed.

Today in most parts of the Third World, the nation-state institution has entered into a deep crisis. Alternative modes of governance have to be found; that is the great challenge before us in the Third World. Until such alternatives are found, human rights could be a formula that could exorcise the excesses of state power and its evils. In fact, in India, the discourse about human rights began to be heard in recent times with the declaration of emergency, when a lot of human rights violations were committed by the state.[21]

Conclusion

To conclude, the human rights factor is no ethical panacea for the problems of conflict-ridden societies of the Third World. The inadequacy and limits of this universal human rights system, which in a way appears like an ethical Esperanto, are evident when confronted with other approaches to the universal. The credibility gap between theory and praxis of the human rights proclaimed by the West raises serious questions about its relevance as an ethical and normative point of reference in regulating international and intercultural relationships, all the more so as these rights are manipulated to further the political and economic ends of the powerful nations.

Human rights have, nevertheless, a limited validity for third-world societies like India that rely mainly on their own cultural, historical, and religious resources. The human rights tradition can be one more instrument in the struggles of the people towards greater humanization, and interhuman and intercollective relationships, including the religious. It is up to the people to decide in their context to what extent this particular instrument is useful in their struggle for humanization, and when and where it is to be used.

Notes

1. There is something of this tone in the presentation of Hans Küng. See his "Towards a World Ethic of World Religions," in *Concilium* 1990/2, pp. 102–19; see also Karl-Josef Kuschel, "World Religions, Human Rights and the Humanum," Ibid.

2. I would like to add that, whenever I refer to the "West" or "Western" position, I am speaking of the predominant trend in the West, being aware of the fact that there are various streams of thought and trends there. This applies also to the use of the positions or trends ascribed to the third-world societies.

3. James Cone, "The Gospel of Jesus, Black People and Black Power," reprinted in *Border Regions of Faith,* ed. Kenneth Aman (Maryknoll, N.Y.: Orbis Books, 1988), p. 152.

4. In the field of anthropology, the unilinear cultural evolutionism was represented by H. Spencer, L. H. Morgan, E. B. Tylor, and others. See Herbert Appelbaum, ed., *Perspectives in Cultural Anthropology* (Albany: State University of New York Press, 1987).

5. Hajime Nakamura, *Ways of Thinking of Eastern Peoples: India-China-Tibet-Japan,* rev. Indian Edition (Delhi: Motilal Banarsidass Publishers, 1991), p. 47; see also Raja Ram Dravid, *The Problem of Universals in Indian Philosophy* (Delhi: Motilal Banarsidass, 1972); Pratima Boes, *Between Cultures* (New Delhi: Allied Publishers, 1986).

6. A. K. Ramanujan, "Is There an Indian Way of Thinking? An Informal Essay," in McKim Marriott, ed., *India Through Hindu Categories* (New Delhi: Sae Publications, 1990), pp. 41–58. I am referring to these words, obviously, not to justify the ethic of Manu based on caste (which has come under severe indictment today with the rise of the dalit and backward caste movements and their struggle for equality) but to highlight the difference in the approach to the universal. The pattern of thinking involved here is a context-related universal.

7. See Felix Wilfred, *Sunset in the East? Asian Challenge and Christian Involvement* (Madras: University of Madras, 1991).

8. Niall MacDermot, "The Credibility Gap in Human Rights," in *The Month,* vol. 10, no. 10, 1977, p. 371.

9. Thus there is the "International Covenant on Economic, Social and Cultural Rights" and the "Covenant on Civil and Political Rights," both of which were adopted in 1966. See *Human Rights: A Compilation of International Instruments* (New York: United Nations, 1983); see also Peter Meyer, "How the International Bill of Rights was Born," in *Breakthrough,* vol. 10, no. 2–3, 1989, pp. 16–17; Patricia M. Mische, "Human Rights in the Social Dynamics of an Emerging Global Community," Ibid., pp. 10–12; "International Bill of Human Rights," *World Encyclopedia of Peace,* vol. 1 (Oxford: Pergamon Press, 1986), pp. 457–62; G. Lobo, *Human Rights in the Indian Situation* (Delhi: CBCI Commission for Justice, Peace and Development, 1991).

10. The structural inadequacies of the human rights system is not made good by adding new rights and bills relating to social, economic, and cultural realms, as has been done, for example, by the United Nations (see note 9). Nor would it suffice to prioritize the rights in such a way that the poor would be given preference, as has been proposed, for example, by David Hollenbach (*Claims in Conflict: Rethinking and Renewing the Catholic Human Rights Tradition* (New York: Paulist, 1979). What is required is a radical reconception and restructuring of human rights from the perspective of the struggling peoples of the Third World. Prioritizing the various rights could at the

most be a transitional measure. See Felix Wilfred, ed., "Human Rights on the Cross," *Jeevadhara: A Journal of Christian Interpretation,* vol. 21, no. 121, 1991.

11. The antecedents to the U.N. Declaration of the Rights of Man (December 10, 1948) were the English Bill of Rights (1688), the French Declaration of the Rights of Man and of the Citizen (1789), and the United States Bill of Rights (1791). But the origins could be traced back further in the medieval times, when the *Magna Carta* (1215) delimiting the authority of the sovereign was signed by King John of England.

12. See Felix Wilfred, *Sunset in the East?*

13. Krishna Iyer, *Human Rights and Inhuman Wrongs* (Delhi: B. R. Publishing Corporation, 1990).

14. At the microlevel this is experienced in India today, when the upper castes and classes vehemently argue in the name of equality and merit against measures meant to uplift the backward castes and classes, for centuries oppressed and discriminated against in the Indian society. The Mandal Commission, which went into the question, had to remind the upper castes and classes that in a race of unequals, the argument of equality based on merit does not bring effective justice to the lowly and the weak. See *Reservations for Backward Classes. Mandal Commission Report of the Backward Classes Commission, 1980* (Delhi: Akalank Publications, 1991).

15. S. C. Malik, ed., *Dissent, Protest and Reform in Indian Civilization* (Simla: Indian Institute of Advanced Study, 1977). See especially the contribution of the Indian historian, Romila Thapar, "Ethics, Religion and Social Protest in the First Millennium B.C. in Northern India," pp. 115–30.

16. T. K. Oommen, *Protest and Change, Studies in Social Movements* (New Delhi: Sage Publications, 1990), p. 151.

17. See the perceptive article of P. C. Joshi, "Religion, Class Conflict and Emancipation Movements: Some Reflections," *Social Action,* vol. 39, 1989, pp. 162–75; see also the "Statement of the EATWOT Consultation on Religion and Liberation," New Delhi, December 1987, in *Voices from the Third World,* vol. XI, no. 1, pp. 152–71.

18. David Hollenbach, "Human Rights in the Middle East: The Impact of Religious Diversity," *Justice, Peace and Human Rights. American Catholic Social Ethics in a Pluralistic Context* (New York: Crossroad, 1988), pp. 87–123. See also Eugene B. Borowitz, "The Torah, Written and Oral, and Human Rights: Foundations and Deficiencies," in *Concilium* 1990/2, pp. 25–33; Roger Garaudy, "Human Rights and Islam: Foundation, Tradition and Violation," Ibid., pp. 46–60.

19. Romila Thapar, "Syndicated Moksha," *Seminar* 313 (September 1985), pp. 14–22; Heinrich von Stietencron, "Hinduism: On the Proper Use of a Deceptive Term," in *Hinduism Reconsidered,* ed. Gunther D. Sontheimer and Hermann Kulke (Delhi: Manohar, 1991), pp. 11–27; Robert E. Frykenberg, "The Emergence of Modern Hinduism as a Concept and as Institution: A Reappraisal with Special Reference to South India," Ibid., pp. 29–49.

20. Rajni Kothari, interview in *Jeevadhara: A Journal of Christian Interpretation,* vol. 20, no. 115, 1990, p. 74.

21. Smithu Kothari, "The Human Rights Movement in India: A Critical Overview," *Social Action* 40, 1990, pp. 1–15.

Chapter 19

Theological Perspectives
on the Environmental Crisis

SAMUEL RAYAN

Besides the voices of feminists, the voices of environmentalists have made a deep impact on the Christian theological agenda in the last decade. The problem of ecology is probably one of the issues that cuts across both North and South and equally affects people of all faiths. This article by Samuel Rayan, who has been introduced in Section II, highlights some of the issues from an Asian angle and provides a theological undergirding based on biblical tradition, Hindu scriptural texts, and ecumenical documents.

Samuel Rayan is an Indian Jesuit and principal of the New Indian School of Ecumenical Theology in Bangalore, India.

Source: *Religion and Society* 37 (2), 1990.

    This theme of theological perspectives on the environmental crisis is related to the World Council of Churches' study on Justice, Peace, and Integrity of Creation. As we assemble here, a World Convocation on JPIC held in Seoul, Korea, is drawing to a close with a service of covenanting. They and we are united in the same concern and are held together by the same Spirit who creates and new-creates our hearts and the universe. We do well to begin with thanksgiving for, and in solidarity with, our sisters and brothers the world over who, like us, are concerned for God's earth and its future.

    I propose to proceed in four steps. The first will be a word about multiplicities and diversities in terms of the dynamic of evolution; the second step seeks to delineate the ecological crisis; the third will determine the meaning of integrity; the fourth, theological perspectives on the theme.

God's Variegated Creation

God's creation, of which we are part, is marked by endless diversity, breathtaking variety, and fascinating multiplicity — in color and shape and size and scent; in stability, flow, and movement; in structure and activity; in sensitivity and awareness; in skills and accomplishments of many kinds; in exquisitely accurate practice of highly complex chemistry and geometry; in perfect esthetics of frond and plume and song and dance. One stands in awe before the profusion of light and life, and wealth and designs, and nature's rich fantasies. One thinks of the display of beauty in the night sky with its Milky Way and myriad stars; beauty in gorgeous sunsets, in the majesty of mountains, the mystery of the sea, the splendor of the "tiger burning bright in the forests of the night"; in the delicately wrought veins of pressed rose petals; or in a drop of dew trembling at the tip of a blade of grass scintillating in the morning sun, and summing up in its tiny liquid orb, every detail of a distant grove or forest.

Following Teilhard de Chardin — scientist, poet, and theologian — we may distinguish three spheres of reality and three stages in its evolutionary history: the sphere of matter, of life, and of the mind. In each sphere and each stage there is a process of fanning out and of converging. It is the fanning out that gives rise to multiplicity and variety. An original atom or nebula explodes and evolves into this marvel of a cosmos with its galaxies, constellations, and solar systems, and its myriad elements and compounds, its variously structured and complex atoms and molecules, vibrations and radio-activity, lights and shadows, rotations and revolutions, chemisms and tactisms. One speaks of the music of the stars and of cosmic dance. Creation is symphonic.

Every earthly and historical process, on reaching a maximum of evolution, growth, and maturation, undergoes transformation and behaves in a new way or perishes. (Water, for instance, turns into steam, or a rose bush bursts in due time into glorious flower, or a baby in the womb takes the plunge into the light of day.) When the process of fanning out reaches a high point, there sets in a process of convergence: the many that the one or the few had become now seek each other to achieve a fresh fellowship, to enter into a new synthesis, to complement and enrich one another with all the wealth they have acquired and actualized, each in its distinct pilgrimage. Thus they come to recognize and live their interrelatedness and interdependence, which are always there.

Through a convergence of cosmic force and an astounding build-up of energies, life emerges. Once life comes into being, the fanning out process becomes operative, spreading life out in stupendous multiplicity of form and color, from grass to shrub to tree, to flower, fruit and seed, and scent and sweetness. Every tree, every leaf and blossom has its own style of being blossom, leaf, and tree — its own identity, "personality," and pride. At a certain level of progress and evolution in the biosphere, a new movement of convergence and synthesis takes place, giving rise to the world of animals, with the wonder and fascination of which we are familiar. This realm too advances and reaches out in its turn to new geographical areas and ever-more-complex forms till it touches the mysterious line of optimum evolution, where it undergoes transformation resulting in the phenomenon of the human. Here the earth finally becomes mind and heart, self-conscious and free.

From this point onward, the fanning out is not only chemical and biological, but cultural, specifically human. A multiplicity of lifestyles, languages, arts, stories, myths, interpretations, skills, religions, feasts, celebrations, social organizations, ways of relating to and transforming nature and of perceiving and discerning meanings are developed by women and men in various parts of the world. Nature is contemplated, respected, cultivated, used, admired, loved, probed, intimated, made a sharer in human endeavors and hopes and in human sorrows and aspirations. And sometimes it is violated and destroyed. Techniques are developed to relate to it and transform it, to actualize its latent possibilities of beauty and utility and participation in human existence. The era of techne is followed by that of technology, which introduces new patterns of relating to creation, new models bristling with problems and threats.

Ecological Crisis

It is modern technology and development ideology, as understood and practiced by a particular economic system, that have polluted the earth and led to the ecological crisis. Here we take it for granted that the crisis is familiar enough to all of us. It need not be described now in detail. A few words should suffice to refresh our memory.

Our relation to the earth and our use of the earth's resources, mediated as these are through capitalist economics, technology, and development ideology, are polluting the earth in many ways and are proving a threat to life on earth and to the planet itself. Four interrelated types of pollution are: physical, social, cultural and spiritual.

Physical pollution includes the poisoning and debilitating, followed by disease and death, of the earth, air, and water, and of living things that depend on them. Toxic chemicals used excessively as pesticides, sprays, additives, and fertilizers undermine the health and vigor of the soil and cause diseases directly through inhalation and contact and indirectly through consumption of contaminated plants and animals. Industry contributes to pollution through discharge of toxic effluent, poisonous fumes, dangerous fibers, dusts and particles (of asbestos, steel, cotton, etc.). Automobiles (the number of cars increasing from less than fifty million in 1959 to four hundred million in 1989) emit four known pollutants, besides others. Acid rain, carrying sulphur and nitrogen pollutants, degrades streams and lakes, kills forests, damages crops, affects certain birds and animals, and corrodes certain stones, metals, and glass as well as leather and paper. "Modern society has produced some 70,000 kinds of chemicals; many of these are now incorporated into the earth's global circulations. Scientists know very little about the impact of these chemicals on the natural order. What is known, however, is that these are substances with which life on earth has no prior interactions" (WCC, JPIC document no. 55, p. 14). Some of these chemicals are known to cause serious threat to life. "Others are known to be a threat to the planet's exchange of energy with the sun and outer space." (Ibid.)

It is not only lake and river water that becomes contaminated through chemicals but ground water as well, as rain and irrigation water carry poison from toxic waste sites, landfills, and chemically fertilized agricultural lands into the ground water systems. The ozone layer, which shields life on earth from excessive sun-heat and ultraviolet radiation, is being damaged and dangerously depleted by chlorofluoro-carbons, used as refrigerants, propellants, and solvents, as well as by nitrous oxide. Enormous annual increase in carbon dioxide produced by burning of fossil fuels (oil, gas, coal) and by deforestation, as well as the increase in methane and chloro-fluorocarbons, causes the greenhouse effect by restricting reradiation of energy from the earth back into space. This could add to global warming and lead to the melting of polar ice; rise in sea level; submergence of low lying land and coastal areas; change in patterns of rainfall; droughts, floods, and famines; and large scale migra-tions. Other forms of physical pollution are soil erosion, deforestation, salinization, and desertification.

There is, then, the prestigious nuclear technology and industry, which is "en-vironmentally destructive, dangerous and expensive."[1] All ionizing radiation is injurious to health, the extent of damage depending on the victim's sensitivity. A high dose of radiation to the whole body means death; lower doses could mean anything from nausea and vomiting to cancer, premature aging, genetic damage to offspring, and death of the fetus. There is risk of a large release of radioactivity over a vast expanse of land and pollution from nuclear accidents, acts of sabotage, or bombing. The horror of nuclear weapons has been burned into our consciousness from the experiences of Hiroshima and Nagasaki. As for nuclear waste, which is being accumulated in thousands of tons, no long-term solution has been developed. "Uranium extraction spells risk to health at all its stages."[2] Uranium trailing, of which there will be five hundred million of tons by the end of the year, can remain radioactive for millions of years. Other wastes could be radioactive for two hundred to three hundred years or for thousands of years. Destruction and pollution of habi-tats is accelerating everywhere. We are fast approaching a global crisis of plant and animal extinction, exhaustion of the earth's life-basing resources, and prospects of a nuclear holocaust and a charred earth.

Social pollution is an ecological problem that has to do with the habitability of our earth-home. It is manifest in the existence of massive poverty and destitu-tion, with their degrading and destructive consequences, side by side with enormous wealth and affluence indulging in vulgar ostentation and unbridled consumerism. To it correspond irresponsible and profligate practices of production and resource uti-lization. It may be seen in the imbalances and gaps that exist in the distribution of goods, jobs, and land between classes in each country and among nations on a global scale.

The "developed countries," with 26 percent of the world's population, con-sume 80 percent plus of the world's paper, metals, and commercial energy, eat fully half the world's food, and feed a quarter of the world's grain to their ani-mals. Meanwhile millions of people elsewhere are chronically undernourished, and a quarter of a million young children "die every week from frequent infection and prolonged undernutrition." Asia has many more people per square mile than Af-rica, Australia, or the Americas. A major part of the best land the world over is occupied by a minority of European peoples who took it over in the era of impe-rial conquests and still restrict immigration of non-Europeans. And yet this major global economic and ecological problem is never placed on any agenda for world reconstruction.[3]

International trade is organized to the disadvantage of the Third World. "Transnational companies operate policies in the South that are unacceptable or illegal in the North." Solutions tailored to the requirements of the First World are imposed on the Third World. IMF prescriptions are by-and-large of this sort. Other major aspects of social pollution are the colossal military spending; the growing debt crisis and the debt trap in which the poorer nations get caught; human rights violations like detention without trial and the practice of torture; the death of children to the tune of fifteen hundred every hour from hunger-related causes; the attempt of advanced countries to dump, clandestinely or for a consideration, toxic and hazardous waste, both chemical and nuclear, on Southern lands or Pacific islands where the poor live; the arrogance, aggression, and destabilization practiced by the ruling elite or rich nations, the dictatorships and government-by-assassination-and-thievery propped up by them, "contras" and mercenaries organized and paid by them to kill off popular revolutions; the maintenance of racism and caste divisions; sexist oppression and marginalization of women; the contriving of wars and famines; the mounting nuclear threat; and the increasing militarization of life, especially in the Third World. Spending money on armaments means there is less to spend on food for the people, or education, or medicine, or cleaning up of polluted water supplies. It means drive for foreign currency; cash crops for export; pushing more peasants off the land and cutting down more tropical forests. In 1985 military spending was calculated to be a million pounds a minute, while only a tiny fraction of this is available to meet actual basic needs of the vast majority of the peoples of the world. The whole social set-up seems contaminated and sick.

Cultural pollution is represented by large-scale illiteracy, which is but one of the manifestations of the neglect of the masses by the elite; by colonial and elitist devaluation of people's cultures, experiences, achievements, and wisdom; and the consequent alienation from the people, their needs and potentialities, of the colonially educated few who are now at the helm of affairs. A subtle, deep-cutting cultural and economic dependence has been built into neocolonial relationships which mark dealings between the Third World and the First. One indication of this is the uncritical borrowing of all major ideas on development and defense from old colonial sources. The economically powerful are pushing their view of things and seeking to impose their ideologies and priorities on weaker sections of society and poorer nations of the world.

Western technological culture is at the moment rampant; in the face of it, the diversity of local cultures tends to fade, is overwhelmed, and may disappear. With them might disappear much of life's poetry and some of the finest and gentlest creations of the human spirit, like old tribal ideals of life in close communion with one another and with nature. Hence Frantz Fanon's impassioned plea to us not to envy Europe's narcissism, not to follow her "motionless movement," not to imitate her in talking incessantly about humanity then murdering men and women in cold blood wherever they are found. Hence this plea to all, to go forward all the time in the company of all men and women, in a new direction, "to create the whole man, whom Europe has been incapable of bringing to triumphant birth," to bring humanity "to a different level than that which Europe has shown."[4]

Spiritual and moral pollution erupts as greed, competition, and consumerism. Its contamination becomes fatal and dehumanizing when greed, competition, and consumerism are held up and sold successfully as the highest ideals human beings can aspire to. Inherent in this disease is a shortsightedness that goes in for immediate gain and overuses scarce resources, some of which are nonrenewable and irreplaceable, unmindful of long-term effects for the earth and for future generations of humans and other living things. This scheme of things measures reality exclusively in terms of quantity and degrades everyone and everything to the level of tools — market commodities. An absence of human sensitivity, a peculiar selfishness, and voracious acquisitiveness mark the times. The many types of pollution described so far, like the dumping of toxic wastes in other people's backyards and the spending of vast resources on armaments while many mothers lack the money to buy food for their starving babies, argue for either a hardening of spiritual arteries and a loss of basic humanity or a total loss of sanity. The world of advertisements adds to this contamination by filling the air with half-truths, childish and vulgar, distorting values and priorities, and taking us for mental imbeciles.

The various types of pollution are interconnected. They cannot be dealt with separately. The Brundtland Commission Report, *Our Common Future* (1987), establishes that ecological degradation and economic deprivation are closely interlinked. Securing justice in economic life is a major step in combating ecological destruction. A JPIC (WCC) document acknowledges that "ecological degradation has everything to do with division of income and of power." It has to do with the dominant ideology and dominant economic theory, according to which (upper- and middle-class) people's material needs are unlimited, greed is extolled as need, acquisitiveness is glorified, and mounting attack on scarce resources by the already-rich is justified. It is the prevailing system of production that is anarchic and unbridled, and the underlying ideology of competitive enterprise for limitless private profit that creates the ecological threat. A crucial step to take to restore ecological balance is a critical examination of unjust social institutions like the unbalanced distribution of land and its resources and the cultural matrix in which they are rooted.

Integrity

Integrity could be understood in more ways than one. It could be the plain affirmation of a fact about God's creation; it could be the proclamation of God's purposes for the world; it could be an invitation to commit ourselves to a moral, theological, and spiritual task centering on God's earth here and now. The many nuances of the word must be held together and "integrated." We shall try to spell them out, largely following orthodox insights indicated by Gennadios Limouris in *From Sophia to Minsk Towards Seoul Seeking Justice, Peace, and Integrity of Creation* (JPIC [WCC] Resource Material no. 7.5).

Integrity could mean the dynamic process of resetting what has gone to pieces after being originally in a state of unity and wholeness. It is a way of healing and restoring to wholeness and harmony that which is sick, broken, or abused.

It could further mean complementarity of nature and history, of nature and revelation, and of their many parts and variegated phenomena. One would then be dealing with conservation, transformation, and fulfillment. Integrity here takes on an eschatological dimension.

Integrity implies and calls for "a caring attitude to nature" (to use the language of the Vancouver Assembly). Such an attitude would be an expression of the faith that "creation is from God, in God, and turns towards God," and that God bears the universe, gives it to us every day, is present to it caringly and lovingly, and is guiding it to its fulfillment beyond all disintegration and degradation, beyond all the evil we do or suffer.

Theologically integrity means "the world is stamped with goodness and freedom"; it participates in God's glory and reflects it in all its manifestations and processes. It is an epiphany of the Divine.

Integrity may be understood to mean the new creation that is the risen Christ, the Christ who makes it possible for us to become a new creation and to work for the renovation of the earth.

It can therefore be interpreted in terms of Jesus' Nazareth Manifesto, Luke 4:18; in terms, that is, of good news to the poor, sight to the blind, opening of prisons, and liberation of the oppressed; in terms of the abolition of the institutions of the powerful.

Or, finally, integrity may be expounded in terms of what Paul envisions in Romans 8:18–23 and 8:35–39. Paul's is a vision in three scenes: the frustration and the travail of human beings and of the entire cosmos; the liberation of God's children and of the earth into the freedom of God; and the security of the people and the cosmos gathered forever in the heart of God from whose love nothing, not even death, can separate us. That is the ultimate meaning and shape of integrity.

Theological Perspectives

In 1966 American historian Lynn White told the American Association for the Advancement of Science that the roots of our present ecological troubles are largely religious and Christian.[5] Others, like Lawrence Cunningham, agree that "human ecology is deeply conditioned by our beliefs." The crisis is attributed to "orthodox Christian arrogance" which holds that nature exists only to serve man. Christianity's "high anthropology," which sets the human being apart from and above all other created realities, is said, with some justification, to constitute the major historical cause of our ecological degradation. The Genesis passage about subduing and dominating the earth is often cited in support of Christianity's exploitative approach to nature.

In reply to this it is not enough to point out, as Rene Dubos does (*Wooing the Earth, 1980*), that abuse and pollution of nature are older than the Bible. Our theological anthropology needs correction; our idea of the relation between history, nature, and revelation has to be reworked. A genuine theology of nature, of the earth, and of matter must be developed. It is some of these theological perspectives on the ecological crisis that we wish to indicate here.

The Christian creed starts with a confession of God, Creator of heaven and earth, and of all that is in them, visible and invisible. After that the creed forgets everything except human beings and God's dealings with them. The first article of the creed is pregnant with a theology of matter and nature, but its promise went unfulfilled and an earth theology never came to birth. The greater promise of the Bible, too, went unheeded. The significance of the fact that the Israelite theologians placed their own national problem and Yahwistic religion in the context of creation and framed God's liberating (Exodus) intervention within God's cosmic activity was completely lost on most (Western) Christian thinkers.

Instead of creating such a theology, Christian thought and catechism became wholly anthropomorphic. Here perhaps the creed misled the way with its "for us men [humans] and for our salvation." Attention got centered exclusively on God's love for human beings. The New Testament proclamation that God loved the world (John 3:16), that God in Christ was befriending the world to himself (2 Cor. 5:19), that the whole creation is to be freed from slavery to corruption and brought into the same glorious freedom as God's human children (Rom. 8:21), and that everything in the heavens and everything on earth will be brought together under Christ as head (Eph. 1:10) has been overlooked or inadequately explored, with the result that its cosmic dreams were never given an opportunity to blossom in any theological park. The significance of the fact that the fourth Gospel founds and enshrines the story of God's salvation through Christ in the memory of creation (John 1:1–3) as well as the meaning of the fact that, both in the Old Testament and in the New, stars, skies, winds, and animals and all creatures are heralds, where a star is the first apostle of the Good News; and Psalm 19 in which the heavens and seasons of fruitfulness and good food are pointed out by Paul as evidence God gives of himself and witnesses to his presence and goodness. An anthropocentric theology insulates from our rootedness in the cosmos. It is essential that the gospel, the Bible, religion, and devotion to God and all spiritual experience be seen "in the context of creation understood as an ongoing, dynamic and ever-present reality in which we are all profoundly involved as members of one splendidly diversified and co-responsible human family."[6]

Creation is God's family born of his heart, and loved by her into existence, and nurtured daily with endless caring. Of this cosmic family of God we are (to be) *response-able* members.

The Bible posits no clear-cut and rigid distinction between nature and history. That distinction is very much an invention of Enlightenment rationalism, which felt more at home with human action based on clear and distinct ideas than with the awesome mystery of nature and life. The Bible views both natural events and historical events as signs of God's saving presence and action (see Psalm 104–107). Nature and humankind together rejoice before God and praise God together.

Genesis 1 and 2 offer the sketch of a theology of nature. Nature is something God calls into existence freely and lovingly. God is pleased with her; he admires and appreciates her; he sees she is good and lovely. She is God's beloved. Once the earth is there, she is taken into partnership with God. God said, Let there be light, and light was there. But God did not say, Let there be trees and animals. He said, rather, Let the earth bring forth (Gen. 1:11, 24), and the earth brought forth. She is God's coworker, his bride who receives his word and coparents life. Within an evolutionary frame of thought, we may contemplate God bending over the earth in creative love and throbbing expectancy as species after higher species was conceived and delivered.

The human is not only the crown of creation; the human is the endpoint of a chain of disclosures of earth's mystery. Women and men belong together with and within the secret the earth has always carried in her womb, in her limbs, in the heart of her, in all her starry and flowery and wavy dreams. The human is not a fantasy tied to the earth's branches like a paper flower from the outside. Man springs from the same depths of what is most beautiful in the depths of the earth. He is child of the earth, eagerly awaited and deeply cherished along with the rest of life. As Genesis 2 shows, the human is of the flesh of the earth and spirit-breath-kiss of God. The human is the point of convergence of the rest of life, where the earth's awareness, sensitivity, freedom and love and joy gather, come to focus and become incandescent. What the earth has been expressing in color and line and dance comes to articulation in the human. The theology humans make and the doxology they utter are in continuity with those that nature spells out.

The earth and all earthlings, including us humans, are born of God and together form God's family. There is therefore a brotherly/sisterly relationship among all creatures. What authority, then, did God give, according to Genesis 1, to human beings over the beasts of the forest, the fish in the sea, and the birds in the sky? Dominion and mastery cannot mean conquest, subjugation, tampering, or taming. All through the chapter there is not the least hint of the earth being recalcitrant, or rebellious, or uncooperative, or indifferent. She has been wholly collaborative and celebrant. Mastery and dominion must mean something other than arbitrary disposal, profligate use of grasping plunder.

Allan Boesak observes that the Hebrew word translated "to dominate" could also be rendered "to serve." It is to serve the earth that humanity is commissioned. That interpretation tallies with Genesis 2, which appoints the man to care for the earth, to till it, and keep it fruitful and beautiful, a happy home for all generations. It tallies with Jesus and God's own lordship and sovereignty over creation, which are exercised and expressed not in arbitrary, polluting, and destructive interventions but in quietly steady and faithful service. Look at the flowers, how the Father adorns them; consider the birds, how God feeds them. That is the model and the meaning of "dominion" over creation (Matt. 6:25–33).

In adopting this perspective, Jesus is strikingly consistent. You call me master and lord, says he, and you are right; but note how I have disclosed the content and meaning of lordship and masterhood by washing your feet (John 13). Dominion, authority, and power which attempts to lord it over others, be it people or nature, shall have no place among Christ's followers. Among them authority shall consist in service. Those who are aware of being first or in the crown of evolution shall be the servant of all, not the plunderer of everything. God is on our earth in Christ Jesus to serve his creation and not be served (Mark 10:35–45). The sovereignty of God is a sovereignty of love; it gives life and creates beauty. That defines for us the meaning of the dominion and mastery we as God's images and representatives are to exercise over fellow creatures. We are to love our "neighbor" as ourselves, and respect the otherness of the other. Nature plundered, stripped, broken, and left bleeding on the margin of concern is a neighbor calling for our healing, life-giving ministrations. Stop riding our high anthropology, come down from the donkey, sit at the victim's side, tend and dress her wounds with tenderness, lift her gently and nurse her back to health and beauty, and tackle the robbers who hurt her (Luke 10:25–37).

The otherness is a reality within interrelatedness. All otherness is intrinsically for-one-anotherness. God as Source, as Father/Mother, belongs with and in the family of which we humans and trees and stars and birds and seas are members. There is a unity of the human, the cosmic, the technical, and the Divine. Without nature humankind is nothing; without humankind nature is nothing; without both of these there are no tools, and without tools neither humankind nor nature is in their essential interactionary process by which we build and achieve ourselves and one another with the whole cosmic reality. As Raimundo Panikkar has said, man-machine-nature is a complex living organism, not to be vivisected or fragmented. Nature is God's providence and our product. The whole complex lives and moves and has its being in God, and God lives in the heart of every reality. God is here, in our cosmos and our history; if God is not here God is nowhere. Without humankind and nature there will be no "question" of God and no revelation of God. God is here not as the proprietor of nature and of humanity but as Source and God and Friend and Home. Therefore God needs no steward to control the creation for the benefit of the proprietor. We are not stewards but friends among friends. The Poet Kumaran Asan asks a falling flower: Are we not one, you and I? Did we not spring from the same (divine) womb? Did not the same hands that fashioned you fashion me too? Our theological vision cannot be narrower or our theological understanding shallower than those Jesus disclosed when he prayed that all might be one, that all might be in us as you are in me and I am in you (John 17:21–23; Acts 17:27–28).

It is thus our theology will be at once cosmology and Christology; our creation theology will at the same time be a soteriology, a wholistic theology and worldview, avoiding all dichotomy and fragmentation.

No created reality is pure passivity, none is wholly an object. Every creature, as a participant in the Divine, has a measure of sensitivity and enjoys a degree of autonomy, spontaneity, and freedom. A certain subjectivity is theirs. Max Horkheimer writes, "The more all nature is looked upon as mere objects in relation to human subjects, the more is the once supposedly autonomous subject emptied of any content until it finally becomes a mere name with nothing to denominate. The total transformation of each and every being into a field of means leads to the liquidation of the subject who is supposed to use them. This gives modern industrialist society its nihilist aspect" (M. Horkheimer, *The Eclipse of Reason,* 1974). All systems that treat human beings as means (imperialism, capitalism) become depersonalized. All the time we treat surrounding reality as mere objects, our own subjectivity suffers attrition; we become progressively reified. It is by dealing with creation with brotherly/sisterly regard, and learning to speak with them, to listen to them, to feel with and for them, to sense their deep and silent eloquent mystery and bear it upon our heart too, that our own subjectivity and personhood nurtures itself and ripens.

The mystery of creation, though largely missed in (Western) theology, has managed to live in the liturgy of the church, which has always celebrated grace and salvation with bread and wine, fire and water, walking and singing. The sense of mystery and of brotherly/sisterly relationship to creation flourished in the hearts of saints and singers like Benedict, Hildegard of Bingen, Francis of Assisi, Robert Bellarmine, Gerard Manley Hopkins, and all the poets of the world—and surely in the hearts of the poets of the Bible. These speak of the earth with joy and relate the earth to God, seeing it as part of God's covenant with Israel, considering the Promised Land as interior to the people's faith and fidelity. They present the universe of things as blossoming, prospering, and rejoicing, when we keep the covenant and obey the Ten Words which re-express the covenant in concrete historical terms. They experience the earth as mourning and weeping when we hurt one another or exclude God from our living and decision-making (Jer. 3:2–3; 5:23–25; 14:1–10; Lev. 26:19–20; Hos. 4:1–3). The earth suffers from the curse humans bring down on themselves, for she has always had them in view as the arrival point of her evo-lutionary pilgrimage and her final song of praise and thanks. She protests in pain when brother breaks the covenant of mercy with brother and the Cain principle be-gins to stalk her face. What are the waters of the flood but her tears shed copiously for the washing away of the filth and the cleansing of the cosmos? (See Genesis 3–4; 6–8). Throughout the Bible, from Genesis 1 and 2 to Revelation 21 and 22, the destiny of the earth and of humans are bound each to the other.

But there is more. The earth is herself partner in a covenant God makes directly with her and with all the creatures she gives birth to, bird and beast, tame and wild (Gen. 9:8–17). The rainbow, all colored and graced things, the fragrances and all pleasant and beautiful things are signs and remembrances of the lasting covenant God made with the earth. Our earth is a covenanted earth — a reality to which God has given his word and made a promise, someone God has betrothed to himself in everlasting love. Hosea recalls this truth in a poetic theology of call and response, covenant and faithfulness. God responds to the call of the earth, enabling the earth to respond in its turn (Hos. 2:16–25). That is why poems like Psalm 65 are replete with divine caring for the earth, and with deep tenderness.

There is then a mystery of the earth, a mystery of matter and of life. "Matter matters," writes Scott McCarthy in *Creation Liturgy: An Earth-Centered Theology of Worship* (1987); "it matters both to God and to people." God has not only made matter and given it to us; God has made it us, we are it. Every believer ought therefore to take the body, matter, and earth seriously as basic theological realities. Physical creation deserves from us an immense theological respect and covenanted affection and a relationship of equality such as is proposed in Saint Francis's revo-lutionary "Canticle of the Sun," in which the sun is addressed as brother, beautiful and splendid; the moon and the stars as sisters, precious and fair; the wind and air and robust fire are brothers; and water is sister, so useful and lowly, so precious, so pure. Through them all God is praised, and especially through Sister Earth, our Mother who feeds us. Many a Psalm sees the earth with its rivers, waters, and winds, its birds and beasts and snow and frost, as coworshippers of God together with us.

Richard Crashaw singing of Cana describes how "The chaste water saw her Lord and blushed" (*Lympha pudica suum vidit Dominum eteribuit*). We have here much more than a figure of speech. The line is pointing to the theological truth that cre-ation has in its depth, in its limbs — a feel for the God who made it; it senses God's presence, and thrills at God's touch. Created reality is structured like Elizabeth with the baby leaping in the womb at the approach of the Lord and his presence, how-ever hidden. The sensitivity of elements, the magnetism in things, the chemisms and tactisms of which Teilhard de Chardin speaks, the loyalty of a dog, the memory an elephant can keep, the teachability of dolphins, and the affinity between leaf and light — all seem to suggest that every creature retains in its heart the echo of the cell that brought it into being and the feel of the fingers that shaped its limbs and knit its spirit. Things remember; they remember their beginnings and their ultimate rooting;

they remember their future, beckoning them to keep evolving in a holy pilgrimage. The conclusion is that "there is no license to hack and rack the growing green"; but an invitation there is to foster fellowship with creation and to walk together hand in hand into the life and freedom of God.

To continue the mediation on the mystery of matter, it is narrated that when Christian missionaries arrived in Fiji, the islanders were surprised and puzzled at two things: one, the many layers of clothes the white Westerners wore in Fiji's hot and damp climate; and two, the religion they preached, which had little or nothing to do with the people's island, their sea, and their fish. For the Pacific people, as for Israel of old and for all aboriginal/tribal groups, the Divine is bound up with land and sea and life and life's support systems. The Divine is bound up especially with food, bread, rice. We are told that in the Pacific languages the same sound (*vanua*) stands for womb, land, and people. Without womb and land there are no people. And land and people include mountains, rivers, valleys, trees, and the earth itself (Akuila Yabaki in JPIC [WCC] document 7.1). The earth is the locus of God's presence and activity, making life possible; it is where the Divine may be encountered. All cosmic religions have this sense of the mystery of things. As Aloysius Pieris observes, they "represent the basic psychological posture that the *homo religious* (residing in each one of us) adopts subconsciously towards the mysteries of life." If we are still skeptical, Pieris would gently remind us that "after all, if the theory of evolution is really true, we were all once a mountain, the crust of the earth, the water and the fire; and that, we now carry with us as our material substratum."

It is the central message of the Bhagavadgítá, developed in chapters 9, 10, and 11 and summed up in chapter 18, that all things are held together in God, and God dwells in the heart of every reality: *Isvarah sarva bhuutaanaam harddese'rjuna tisthati.* God abides in the heart of all contingent beings. The Upanishads have similar insights: *Isavasyam idal sarvam:* this whole (universe) is pervaded (suffused) by the Lord. The very universalism of such perceptions is a pointer to its popular (tribal?) origin in the experience of the masses as against exclusivist, sectarian views of high castes and top classes. If people's stories and insights have been co-opted by dominant groups, it is imperative to reclaim them in favor of the people instead of resigning ourselves to their appropriation by encroachers and manipulators. Biblical experience concurs with people's traditions. Acts 17 is witness to the truth that in God we live and move and have our being. In a long meditation, Psalm 139 assures us that whether it be day or night we are with God, in God's hands. Paul knows that God does not live in houses made by us. The heaven is God's throne and the earth is his footstool, and earth and heaven are filled with his glory (Isa. 66:1; 6:3: Matt. 5:34–35; Acts 17:24–25). The universe is his temple, and the earth is a sacred place of glory and presence and encounter. Treat it therefore with respect and with love; take off your shoes from your feet, for the ground on which you are standing is holy ground, "and every bush is aflame with God" (Elizabeth Browning); and drive out those who profane it, turning it into a marketplace.

For biblical tradition, creation is the epiphany of the Divine, and the earth is God's self-revelation, a witness God gives concerning God-self. For whatever can be known about God (and needs to be known for our salvation) God has made known from the beginning in the world he fashioned. Only we humans have not responded to this revelation as we ought. The human conscience is also a reality of revelation, comparable to Israel's Torah, a place of light where God shows his face and meets and calls us (Rom 1:19–21; 2:14–16). The fact is that God has never left himself unwitnessed. The seasons, the rains, the fruitfulness of the earth, the food we eat, and the good cheer and health that follow are God's self-disclosure and a witness God gives unto himself. Where nature is destroyed, polluted, and plundered, where food and good cheer and health are made scarce and God's provisions for his family on this earth are so private as to become inaccessible to a great many of his children, the revelation of God is distorted, the light of his face is obstructed, and his saving purposes thwarted.

Being revelation, nature is there to be listened to and contemplated. Psalm 19 states that heavens declare the glory of God. This is a biblical example of nature contemplation. Psalm 104 is a creation poem that dwells reverently and affectionately on various features of the cosmos — light and clouds, mountains, seas and springs, birds and cattle, young lions that demand their food from God, and wine that gladdens the human heart. It was originally an Egyptian hymn written in honor of the sun-god Ra, which Israel circumcised and made their own. Psalm 29 is a similarly Israelized Canaanite (Uganda) song addressed to Baal, the lord of thunder, which contemplates nature in a thunderstorm.

The example I love best among biblical passages of nature contemplation is Matthew 6:25–33. Jesus looks at the frail flowers of the field and the birds that do not sow or reap. In them he discerns God's presence and love active like a fond Father to adorn and to nurture. God clothes the tiny, lowly, ephemeral flower with incomparable beauty and splendor. God feeds the birds with solicitude and care. Bird and flower are God's children; they are God's concern and preoccupation. They are for Jesus epiphanies of the Father, sacraments of the heart of God.

The conclusion flowing from such simple daily communion with nature is that we should make it our prime concern to seek God's reign and God's justice. The experience of the earth's beauty, of life here, is prosperity, freedom, and peace, and the meaning of nature as relation and sacrament is intrinsically bound up with the commitment to God's rule and with the practice of God's justice. God's justice consists not so much in acquitting or condemning as in providing every creature with whatever would enable it to be itself, to be active, and to blossom and come to completion. The ecological crisis is, as we have seen, part of, and an outcome of, systems of injustice and exploitation. Contemplation issuing in action for justice is a source of hope for the healing and restoration of the earth.

It is out of Jesus' habit of a contemplative approach to nature that his telling parables are born, as well as his insights into the signs of the times. John 12:24 is a tiny poem, deep and dense in meaning. In the sprouting seed Jesus discovers the entire Paschal Reality, the whole mystery of his own, and our, dying and rising. He touches with a word the commonest realities of the earth, and they open up to reveal in their depths the secrets and wonders of the Kingdom of God. The reverence and affection with which our farmers and agricultural laborers treat seed and tree and soil is pregnant with similar insights and experiences. It is perhaps to these that Tagore gives voice when he sings, "Silence, my soul, these trees are prayers" — a word compact with a whole theology of the earth. Trees are the earth's prayers, her joined and uplifted hands, a fragrant, exultant expression of the spirit of the earth.

The earth is herself a liturgical celebration with flower and incense, fruit and water, and grain and song and dance. She is a polyphonic Gloria and Halleluja.

And she is a sacrament of God: the basic sacrament symbolizing, embodying, expressing, and conveying God's love and life as well as God's loyalty and dependability. The earth shows that God is indeed the Rock the Bible names so often, on whom one may lean and build one's life with complete security. The earth gives us the experience that God is Mother and Nourisher, Bread and Rice — the basis of life. Is not the earth itself a great life-giving loaf of bread which God bakes and breaks daily for his cherished family of women and men and bird and fish and beasts, trees, worms, insects and grass of many kinds? We may encounter the Loving Mystery by breaking the bread of the earth with one another in solidarity and thanksgiving, never depriving others of earth-bread, never desecrating or polluting it, never wasting it, never privatizing it, never degrading it to the status of market commodity. Treat the earth as sacrament, symbol of interpersonal love and togetherness, its deepest meaning being life for all and a community of equality and freedom.

In giving us the earth, God gives us his own self. Every gift is a sign, a body, bearing, presenting, conveying the Giver as loving and benevolent. Think of God's earth as a sign over which God bends in unspeakable love, saying, "This is my Body, myself, this now is flesh of my flesh, bone of my bone, heart of my heart." The universe is the Body of God, God's visibility and tangibility, the way God is present to us in history: God's Body given for the life of the world. But the earth is also our body, an extension of our social existence. The human body is far more than the biological frame and mechanism inherited through evolution. Our human body is the whole complex of relationships we build with the earth through work, contemplation, and artistic production; with people through friendship, mercy, and compassion; with society through solidarity and participation in struggles against systems of death and deprivation or aggression and injustice; and with God through the options we make and the risks we take. Nature is essentially bound up with this process of building and weaving our specifically human bodily self. This self with its free and flaming creative center and its tangled earthy and cosmic interlockings can live forever as response to God's love as long as that love lasts. Within the dynamics and horizons of that love, we and nature are in the process of liberation, transformation and resurrection (Rom 8:18–39).

The body of knowledge we build up together with our science, technic, and technology also constitutes a medium of relationship with the earth, with one another, and with our final destiny. They too will be interior to our contemplation, which is not only of nature but of culture as well, and of history. Our own social, artistic, and technical creations shall be integral to our worshipful approach to God and to the work of upbuilding our resurrection body.

But is it not technology precisely that is effectively destroying and polluting the delicate harmony and balance of our earth system and creating the ecological crisis? The answer cannot be a simple yes or no. It is necessary to distinguish between technologies. There is a technical, and perhaps a technology too, that can be a servant of life for the whole earth, a servant of love and God's purposes to liberate the earth and bring it to the fullness of the freedom of God's daughters and sons. There is another technology which is lackey and the litter of avarice and "greed organized into principalities and powers" (A. Pieris's phrase) and is used to exploit people and nature in order to amass profit and power at the expanse of human beings, of their health, their life, their dignity. It is this type of technology (typified by Bhopal, Chernobyl, Three Mile Island, Minamata, Nagasaki, Bikini), born of greed and which serves greed, that has proved to be destructive, inhuman, and death-dealing, and must be challenged, stopped, and eliminated as criminal. It is the abstract rationalism that operates within "scientific" thinking as the basis of the Technology of Death that needs to be masked and fought. There is a theology of technology when this latter is for people and operates in favor of life. The other technology can yield only a demonology, for it is demons thriving on people and on the flesh of the earth.

Contemporary criticism of capitalist science and technology — of capitalist culture, politics, and economics and being hegemonies, violent and antilife — is, hopefully, preparing the way for a different system of economic theory and practice, an economics of fellowship organized as if people mattered and life was more than heaps of marketable goods. It is an economics of brotherhood/sisterhood accompanied by politics of tenderness and by science and technic undivorced from poetry, prayer, and mysticism. We hold and affirm that the mystic's and the poet's perception of reality is as valid and profound as (if not more valid and profound than) the scientist's and the technocrat's.[7]

Romans 8:18–23 is a song about the earth's final goal and glorious destiny. It is our present task and privilege to groan together with creation and share the travail in bringing forth the New Earth. For the old order of avarice and greed and privatization and selfishness and death is passing, and God is making all things new, and leading us and our earth into the depths of its own life of freedom and joy. There will be a new earth and a new heaven. This will be God's work. We are being summoned and privileged here and now to be God's coworkers in this project of liberating and renewing the Earth in the power of the Spirit. The Spirit who brooded over the beginning of creation broods over it now, and her work of renewal is in process.

Notes

1. S. Elswoth, *A Dictionary of the Environment: A Practical Guide to Today's Most Important Issues* (Grafton Books), p. 280.

2. Ibid., p. 302.

3. Tissa Balasuriya, *Planetary Theology* (London: SCM Press, 1984), pp. 21–36.

4. F. Fanon, *The Wretched of the Earth* (New York: Penguin Books, 1961), pp. 251–55.

5. Lynn White, "Historical Roots of Our Ecological Crisis," *Science,* 155, 1967, pp. 1203–7.

6. Ashish Nandy, ed., *Science, Hegemony and Violence: A Requiem for Modernity* (Bombay: Oxford University Press, 1990).

7. Sara Grant, *The Tablet,* December, 1987, p. 1353.

Chapter 20

Ethnic Conflict in Sri Lanka
and the Responsibility of the Theologian

TISSA BALASURIYA

Frequent ethnic violence has exposed militant tendencies in the various faith traditions. Among the various root causes of communalism, religion remains a key factor. Interestingly, it is not Asia's massive poverty but its multireligiosity that is threatening to undermine its social fabric and stability. The article that follows examines the ethnic violence in Sri Lanka and argues for the building up of common human communities, thus bringing together various religious and nonreligious groups to strive for a more humane and just society. It also reiterates the need to rethink our traditional theological concepts and spirituality in the face of communalism.

Tissa Balasuriya is Director of the Centre for the Study of Society and Religion, Colombo, Sri Lanka. He is actively involved in finding a peaceful solution to the current ethnic violence in Sri Lanka. His publications include *The Eucharist and Human Liberation* and *Planetary Theology*, both published by Orbis Books and essential reading for those interested in Asian theological thinking.

Source: *Responding to Communalism: The Task of Religions and Theology*, ed. S. Arokiasamy, Gujarat Sahitya Prakash, Anand: Gujarat, India, 1991.

The theologian is a religious person who reflects intellectually on spiritual experience — either as a professional scholar or a committed believer. I am reflecting here on the Sri Lankan situation and will draw more conclusions from it. Another responsibility of the theologian is to help solve these problems in order to build a just and peaceful country.

Issues and Causes

In Sri Lanka's ethnic problems, many issues are involved. Any peace group has to find out the causes of the present conflict. On the Tamil side, there are four main problems:

1. *Language*. The Tamil language is being regarded as given second place, after the Sinhala Only Act of 1956. When Sinhala was made the official language, the Tamil people felt discriminated against even though Tamil was made a national language in 1977.

2. *Education*. In this each of the ethnic groups — Sinhala, Tamil, and Muslim — can say that the others have the advantage. The Tamils had an advantage earlier, but not now.

3. *Land*. In the distribution of land among the ethnic groups, the Tamils complain that the state has been resorting to state colonization and setting Sinhala people in areas they consider "traditional Tamil homelands." The Sinhala point of view is that they have a land shortage and the Tamils have been settled in the plantation area and in the Western sea coast during the last 150 years.

4. *Employment*. The Tamils are disadvantaged after the Sinhala Act of 1956. In its 1977 election manifesto, the governing party recognized their grievances as being so serious as to bring the Sri Lanka Tamils to the point of asking for a separate state. After the ethnic conflict grew worse in August 1977, the problem of security of life itself became the main issue. The Tamil people felt that they could not trust the state and the Sinhalese-dominated army to safeguard their lives. Rajni Kothari said the same thing of some of the minorities in India in relation to the central government. The feeling of promises given to them being broken makes matters worse.

On the Sinhala side, the corresponding feeling is that they have historical disadvantages — that the colonial powers gave advantages to the minorities, that the Constitution gave safeguards to them, that the Tamils were privileged in education and employment and that the Tamils are always asking for too much. The Sinhalese feel isolated in the world in which they have a mission to preserve and propagate Buddhism in its purest form.

There is a subconscious fear among the Sinhalese of an Indian invasion. They carry an historical memory of Pandya, Chola, Chera, and Kalinga peoples coming to Sinhala as invaders. This historical memory and fear has grown larger and is likely to remain so in the future due to the Indian army's presence in Sri Lanka. (Editor: the IPKF has not been there since 1991.)

It is in this context that we have to work for justice and peace, freedom, democracy and human rights. We have to study the issues in a multidisciplinary manner. What are the myths according to which the people's perceptions are formed? What is the history of the issue and the understanding of history by the different groups?

Here the various disciplines have to come in. Psychology can help us see the stereotyping that takes place. The Sinhalese perceive the Tamils and their demands as contrary to their interests. The Tamils and Muslims have similarly distorted ways of thinking. There is also a suspicious attitude towards Tamilnadu and India based on such generalizations and long-term fears.

The issues of political parties and of power politics are also relevant to the understanding of the ethnic conflict. Different groups and persons try to retain power or come to power using the ethnic question and the communal feeling of people, such as the shift in Congress policies in the last few years to woo the majority Hindu vote. In Sri Lanka this has taken place among the main Sinhala-backed political parties, principally the governing U.N.P. and the Sri Lanka Freedom Party led by Sirimavo Bandaranaike. The power factor is important among the Tamil groups also — namely among those who are for a democratic process and the militant groups that have taken up arms. The power relation of political parties in Tamil-nadu are also relevant. The Sri Lanka issue is used by different parties in their power struggles. Even central government politics in India have a relationship to the Sri Lanka issue and to the South Asian region.

The commitment to a peaceful and just resolution of the communal issue requires an analysis of the efforts being made — the proposals and failures, and how there has been a breakdown of relationships. Those who work for justice and peace in communal relations have to go between peoples to bring about a reconciliation of persons and groups, to find a political solution.

Our task in peace groups and citizens' committees is to try to bring about just and peaceful solutions. This requires much effort because people generally have built-in prejudices. The mass media tend to pander to them and perpetuate them. The mass media here in India might have spoken of the brutalities of the Sinhala army in the last few years. Now the Indian peacekeeping force is facing similar problems and is not reacting better. But the mass media here may not quite cover these events. The mass media are concerned about profits. The governments control the radio and television.

Our Option

Our peace groups search for a rational, sensible, humane solution. We think that on the ethnic issue there can be no long-term solution by violence. On the question of class, it may be possible by a violent takeover of state power to change the class structure. It is possible to dispossess the owners of property and change class relations in a community. But people's race and ethnicity cannot be changed. The more people are attacked for their race or ethnicity, the more determined they can become in their positions. This may be true of religion also, as people do not easily change their religion. Thus conflicts of class, race, and religion cannot be solved by mere violence. If a state tries to suppress such groups, they may fight back — if not in this generation, then perhaps in the next.

Modern methods of warfare enable a small group of fifty to a hundred persons to keep an army at bay by guerrilla fighting. Such a group can make it difficult for a government to govern or hold elections. Theoretically it may be thought that a big power like India can destroy an area like Jaffna in a few hours by bombing the area. But the reality is that after about two months, the IPKF has not been able to subjugate the LTTE in the North and East of Sri Lanka.

We think that even for pragmatic reasons — in addition to the fundamental human and spiritual reasons — there must be a peaceful, negotiated, democratic, and just solution to the Sri Lanka ethnic conflict. This is our conviction, and we must build the people's will towards it. Perhaps it is only after people have suffered much that they will realize the need of such a solution.

The action for peace with justice is of this nature. We have to go round to groups, explain the lies, try to bring about consensus towards a solution. Different means such as role-playing, drama, poetry, music and song, slide shows, and recently video shows are used to build understanding. This is a work that requires much patience, listening, and perseverance.

It is necessary to organize more and more small groups that are working for peace, and these in turn must become a moral pressure for peace. The religions are an important motivation and organizational help, especially in the villages. Prayer sessions, meditations, and processions help generate the spiritual motivation and courage for action for a just peace.

The peace groups and citizens' committees take action on issues such as helping refugees, safeguarding human rights, visiting the prisoners, appealing for the lives of captives, and working politically for a compromise solution. This includes participation in negotiations between government and the militant groups as well as the other political parties. Public statements analyzing the current situation and proposing ways out are made by the citizens' committees every few months as the situation evolves. I have been involved in these activities as joint secretary, with a Buddhist monk of the Citizens' Committee for National Harmony in Colombo.

The work is not easy, however, as the peacemakers are suspected by both sides of the conflict. If I am a Sinhalese and I try to present the Sinhala point of view, the Tamils may suspect me; if I present the Tamil point of view, the Sinhalese groups may suspect me. The other day a speaker at a meeting called us "Sinhalese who are Tamil racists." We get letters from both sides attacking us. The mass media also carry such articles. Thus misunderstanding is easy, and our explanation is not accepted by some. In more recent times, as the conflict has gotten aggravated and complicated with the power struggle in the South, there are also death threats and even actual killing of moderate persons by extreme groups that do not want a peaceful solution.

It is in this process that we have to try to build a community of human beings who accept and strive for a common Sri Lankan identity. This is an eminently spiritual task of reconciling persons and groups, removing prejudices, and bringing about a political solution of power sharing through constitutional reforms. This is a task of national integration and nation building.

Religions

In this situation of ethnic conflict during the past decade, religions have had a rather ambiguous role. Four religions are present in the country: Buddhism 67 percent, Hinduism 18 percent, Islam 8 percent, Christianity 7 percent. Religions are not the lines of division in this conflict. This is particularly true of the Buddhists and the Hindus. They often worship in the same shrines. This is an important fact which is sometimes misrepresented in the foreign press, as if Buddhists were fighting Hindus.

The ethnic groups, however, have a religious affiliation in so far as the majority of the Sinhalese are Buddhists and the majority of Tamils are Hindus. Christians are in both these ethnic groups. The Muslims, too, are both Tamil and Sinhalese.

The Sri Lankan problem is mainly ethnic, and the word "communal" is not so commonly used there in relation to this conflict. The economic, social, and political factors underlie the ethnic conflict.

Religions as organizations have not yet been able to transcend their divisions, in so far as they are based on ethnicity, to work together for a just peace based on the values of religions. A religious organization was formed in 1984. It is composed of the leadership (clergy) of the four religions. It made general pleas for peace but was not able to work for consensus solutions in a permanent, practical manner. It has not been able to work together, as the conflict did escalate. In many local areas, however, the religious leaders did work together and have been the core of the citizens' committees. These have generally worked for local issues such as the relations between the armed forces, the militants, and the public; refugees; political prisoners; and so on.

The religious leaders are friendly to each other, and their places of worship are open and welcoming to all; but the religions have not emerged as agencies determined to find positive resolution of the conflict. The fundamental reason for this is that they have not taken seriously their foundational inspiration, which is one of service to humankind, motivated by the spiritual and transcendent being or value as acknowledged by them. Religions have been weakened in their spiritual fervor and have failed in our crisis — or we have failed religions on account of our selfishness.

Basic Human Groups

Whereas the major leadership of the four religions could not work together in a significant manner, we find that, in practice, individuals of common sense who give a priority to human life and practical solutions have been working together during the past decade for a harmonious and just resolution of this conflict. They belong to all religions and different ideologies, including some who may be rich, and the Marxists. The religions as religions have not come together. It is individuals who tried to find rational, just, and peaceful solutions who have been together perseveringly and publicly in this ongoing crisis. Despite ups and downs and dangers, these persons have endeavored seriously to transcend the limitations of their ethnic and religious groups, while still belonging to them.

This is an indication of Kingdom of God or what we call the "rule of righteousness." These values are not limited to any religion or to the Christian churches. In fact, sometimes what a religious group or church does is not quite in keeping with these values of right conduct. I would like to reflect with you on this situation, that the members of the peace groups and citizens' committees — or the "peace community," as they have been called — are prepared to take a common option, stand up for it, and put across their message at personal risk to themselves and their families. They are misunderstood, they have received death threats. They do not belong to one particular religion, and some have no religion.

On the other hand we see that the formal leadership of the religions are not so deeply and actively concerned with the common good of the whole country. They are often more concerned with their own ethnic or religious community, and at times they have been obstacles to the peace process. In this context we can ask, why is it that the religious groups, and more specifically Christianity as an organized religion, have not been capable of responding adequately to this crisis? It is because the life of the religious group or church is not geared to such a task. This in turn is due to their thinking and teaching; organization, patterns of worship, sacred texts and their interpretation; way of training the clergy, religious, and laity; and their activities as a religious group.

Churches

These things that make up the life of the Christian church do not give its members the helpful attitudes and education for this task of justice and peacemaking. It requires listening, study, analysis, an option for a solution that is reconciling and just. It requires risk taking, being vulnerable and subject to public criticism. The traditional church is not geared towards these. People did not become members of the church for these things. The leaders did not join the ministry, religious life, or lay organizations for these tasks.

In many ways the church is a sociological reality. People belong to it because they were born in a given family. This is true of the other religions also. Baptism was conferred on most Christians at a time when they could not make much of an option — except perhaps to cry! Most people did not choose the option to be Christian. Conversions are very few in Sri Lanka. From our experience we see that this body of persons called the church is as yet not ready for or capable of a clear option for a just peace and of working assiduously for it.

Thus if we take the worship in the churches, there is little relevance in the normal Sunday and daily worship to what has been going on in the country during the past four years. The effort to stem the daily killing does not come forth from this worship, even though there is a prayer for peace at the end of each Mass. Thus there is a certain gap between the prayer of the church and the crisis of the community. The church feasts, pilgrimages, and novenas manifest a similar inadequacy of concern. What is done in these is good itself but not related effectively to the main issue that troubles our peoples.

The churches have a concern for social services. They have always been for peace, but this is more a statement than an active performance for peace. The churches have been havens for refugees. But the churches have not yet come to the position of seriously analyzing the problems, taking different options for a political solution, and working in an area where there are risks. The other religions are also in a similar situation. This raises the serious issue of the relationship of the churches and religions to the Kingdom of God and its values.

Why has this been so? It is because the church has been organized for a different objective. The goal of the church has been to sanctify and save souls. That was our spirituality based on the prevalent theology. The experience of our ethnic conflict makes us deeply reflect on our theology, for it is not generally those who say, "Lord, Lord," and bear the banner of religion who have been enlightened, courageous, and organized to respond meaningfully to the test of this crisis.

The Task of Theology

In situations of ethnic conflict, we theologians, while helping to solve the problems, must also analyze ourselves and the churches concerning our own thinking, motivation, and action. What is there in our theological framework, in our theological culture, that helps or does not help in relating positively to ethnic problems?

The prevailing theology is still fundamentally the traditional construct that has been prevalent in the Catholic church over the past few centuries — with some modifications after Vatican II. The framework of our theology is based on an interpretation of revelation as it has been worked out from the Bible and in the tradition of the church.

Bible	— unique revelation of God — to be interpreted by the Church.
God	— Creator — of universe and of human race Fall of Adam and Eve (Eve being more blamed!) Original sin — whole of humanity incapable of salvation without a divine redeemer. We are all in sin.
Jesus Christ	— God-man Redeemer who died for our sins. The source of all grace.
Church	— set up by Jesus to carry his teaching to the whole world, communicate his grace through the sacraments. The hierarchy of the church (males) are the dispensers of the sacraments — divinely ordained teachers of the truth, administrators of the community of believers.

The church is thought of as the unique vehicle of salvation. Jesus Christ is the only one who can save human beings.

Christians are God's chosen people.

All the others are in error, falsehood.

Up to Vatican II it was held that "error had no rights."

The Christian community sanctifies itself by participating in the sacraments, specially the Eucharistic worship.

The propagation of the church is all important for human salvation.

The mission of the church is thought of primarily as the building up of the church itself, as it is the necessary means of salvation. The activities of the church are geared to this objective. Thus the schools, the social services, and the pastoral action of the church are thought of in relation to this goal.

The church was not accustomed to being active in public affairs except when its self-interest was at stake, such as concerning its schools, or concerning certain moral issues, such as birth control and abortion, which it considered were of primary importance. The leadership of the church was exercised by the hierarchy, the religious, and the leaders of the lay movements. These were generally trained to be prudent and see to their security and that of the Christian community. They were to be active and self-sacrificing for the propagation of the faith, for which no sacrifice was too great. This was the traditional self-understanding of the Christian community.

Such an orientation did not make us work with others for the building of the human community — especially where there were risks, as in the struggle for justice and in peacemaking. Nor were we accustomed and trained to be open to and work with persons of other faiths and ideologies. We regarded them as not of the fold, unbelievers, and some as pagans and atheists. We thought of ourselves as the privileged children of God, of light, and of grace. This attitude did not dispose us to be active on issues such as communal harmony and to work with others for such a goal. We served others in schools and social services quite generously, but we were not conscious that our theology could itself make us self-contented and rather complacent concerning the issues of public life.

Content of Dogma

This traditional theology is based on a dogmatic teaching that the whole of humanity is in original sin and is incapable of reaching eternal salvation without Jesus Christ and the church. This is an assumption that the church claims to know from a few sentences of the epistles of the New Testament. It is, however, something that is not knowable by human beings. It is not taught by Jesus in the gospels. It is a teaching that was developed in the church some centuries after the death of Jesus. But it places all those who are not Christians at a disadvantage. They need the church to be saved.

It was on the basis of this doctrine that the church held for many centuries that the souls of those who are not Christians are damned forever. Hence, it was argued, their bodies could also be destroyed by Christian rulers and powers unless they accepted baptism. This heritage made Christians themselves an exclusive body of chosen, privileged persons. It is on this basis that the life of the Christian community tended to be self-centered and not much concerned with issues such communal harmony.

The Christology of the church is also built on the foundation of this assumption of original sin. Only God could save humankind. Hence Jesus, in order to be Savior, has to be God. Jesus Christ is God-man. He is the source of all authority in the church. This authority is given to the apostles and their successors — the pope, the bishops, and the clergy. Since Jesus Christ is God and man, it is argued that only males can be members of the clergy.

This framework of theology is said to be from the Bible. Within this, there is a community of the church that is well organized and has an understanding of its goal, its structure of authority, and its laws. The original spiritual experience of Jesus of God as love and the commandment of God to love one another is in a sense given second place or subordinated to the ecclesiastical organization and external relationships of authority and subjects in the church. The spirituality of the church is one in which there is more emphasis on regularity, obedience, and preservation of the good name of the Christian community than on building the human community, on justice, and on peace. The training of the clergy and of religious and lay leaders is also within such a perspective. This theology has been and still is generally prevalent in most areas of the church.

How Much Have We Changed?

Such a fundamental framework of theology cannot be satisfactorily remedied in its harmful aspects by peripheral changes that do not touch its main teachings. The recent changes in relation to the other religions have been more due to external pressure than to a rethinking of theology. The rethinking in relation to the Protestant churches goes into the areas where the churches differ. But in relation to other religions, tolerance is rather a pragmatic solution due to the modern world situation especially after the Asian countries became independent. Vatican II accepts that the other religions also have spiritual values; this is an operational sort of adjustment of behavior without a deeper recasting of its dogmatic underpinnings.

We have to go deeper and question where we went wrong in the last fifteen centuries or so. This is one of the tasks of the theologian with reference to the church, namely, to find out how far and why theology itself is an obstacle to the church community being open to the others. We have to realize that we theologians are part of the problem, while we try to be part of the solution. Even where the theologians are more open, we know that the bulk of the church lives a theology and spirituality that is rather traditional and somewhat exclusivist. Recently a seminar of the Franciscan family from most of the countries in Asia was held in Manila. Participants said that in most of their areas Vatican II is still not implemented in many aspects — or not even known to the ordinary Christian people. After we had a series of lectures on theology in Sri Lanka mainly for the laity in Colombo during four months of 1987, we asked them what they would like to do next term. They wanted a series on Vatican II. Actually the church has not communicated to the base the fundamental insights of Vatican II.

Those who do forward-looking theology of an open church are small groups compared to the bulk of the church who meet as Christians at Sunday Mass. The Christian community itself is part of the problem. Our internal contribution towards overcoming communalism is the transformation of the churches themselves. Then Christians would be more active as peacemakers and workers for social justice. They would be better motivated to get out of the complacency of their day-to-day activities to participate in the difficult tasks of such a mission in our countries.

Theological Issues

Since the thinking in the church has been part of the cause of our problems, that is, of the inward-looking communalistic attitudes among Christians, we have to ask further questions. If the Bible is interpreted to be the unique Word of God, then we question the validity of the message of the other faiths and their sacred texts. This is a task the theologian must resolve if we are not to be exclusive in our claim to divine revelation.

What is the nature of redemption in Jesus Christ? Do all human beings need a relationship to Jesus in order to be saved? The other side of this problem is the view that persons of other faiths often have of the attitude of Christians towards them. They think that Christians consider them as damned or at best making only human efforts towards God.

The problems of Christology are crucial to this issue. What is the personality of Jesus? Is Jesus God-man, as proposed in the Council of Chalcedon? How is the death of Jesus to be understood as redeeming humanity? If Jesus is God, what is the value of his death, for wouldn't he have known that he would rise on the third day? On the other hand, if he did not know it, could he still be God?

How is Jesus an example for us in bearing witness to the demands of love, justice, and peace? If Jesus knew everything from the beginning, he is hardly an example that ignorant, fallible human beings can follow. Jesus would hardly be a motivating personality if he were so divine as not to share our human lot. We have to work with these issues at a deeper theological level in order to have a Jesus Christ who can be an inspiration; whose life is meaningful; whose options, risks, and sufferings can be appreciated as those of a human being who took up clear positions in a time and situation when there were problems of class exploitation, imperialism, and male domination over women. He challenged his people. Some responded and formed the Jesus-community.

What is the nature of the community of disciples Jesus gathered around him? What is the task they accepted from Jesus? How did they understand the primordial spiritual experience of Jesus of God as "Father" and of his love commandment? How did the early disciples of Jesus live? How did they cope with the problem of ethnicity and communalism in the early Church? They had to grapple with the problem of transcending the narrowness of their Jewish heritage. The first council of Jerusalem was one of opening themselves to the Spirit of God in all people.

Corresponding to such theological reflection, we have to decide on the formation of Christians today. How did Jesus form the apostles? How do we form the clergy, religious, and lay leaders today? Jesus formed his disciples in an active school of bearing witness in a hostile environment. He reflected and prayed with them. Today we have so much of theology — especially dogmas, and definitions concerning things we cannot understand — that the seminarians spend the best years of their lives within the ecclesiastical compounds. Between eighteen and twenty-six (or until age thirty in the case of Jesuits) these young men are hardly making any impact on their society. The struggle is going on outside by youth of the same age group — workers, journalists, students, insurgents, militants, and most of the armed forces. They are grappling with life issues as they see them — especially communalism. Our dedicated youth are largely cut off from them. They are secure within our seminaries and formation institutes.

The Theologian's Responsibility

Therefore we have to get back to the process of active work concerning relevant issues. Thus we can enter the heart of our problem of making justice, love, and peace the main inspirations of our society. True, there are two levels of theologizing — one by formulation, articulation in scientific terms, professional systematization; and the other by dealing with live issues as Jesus did, inspired by the Word of God as accepted by us. One's theological sensitivity is developed in the process of responding to one's own situation and its call. One primary responsibility of the theologian is to be a disciple of Jesus and to show others how to be one by a life witness. The theologian also has also to learn while in the process of living the

Christian calling in these difficult times. The theologian has to teach by accepting risk, as Jesus did. It may be as an intellectual, and not necessarily as a front ranker in some active struggles. The committed intellectual has to face risks today — in bearing constant, public witness to the oneness of all human beings in our plural, divided, and conflicting societies.

The theologian is not a mere abstract thinker or a scientific historian concerned only with the study of the past. We have to be part of the process of creating the history of our people, and this has grave obligations and risks. It is a noble vocation in which we place our spirit and mind at the service of God's rule of righteousness. The theologian has to participate in transforming action so that communities may be places in which human beings of different religions and ethnic or linguistic groups can live together and find fulfillment. This requires political, socio-economic, and psychological solutions.

In order to realize this, we have to work together with all others who are directed towards these values of a new community. In many situations this action has to be for objectives that are not in the religious field directly — promotion of human rights, social justice, care of the environment as in the Bhopal case, emergency provisions in riots. In so doing we articulate in practice the value and meaning of the new approach in theology by being God- and kingdom-centered. Jesus wants the human community built on the basis of justice, sharing, peace, truth and love. We must help change the priorities in the church. For this we must rearrange our own priorities in theologizing and pay the price for it.

The theologian has to contribute to the task of transforming the church community so that it accepts these as priorities. For this the theologians and the theological community have to transform their priorities and even the concept of what it is to do theology. It is in working for these objectives that the sacraments have meaning. The Eucharist is authentic when it is related to the sharing of food and the forgiveness of one another — both of which are essential for healthy intercommunal relations. Union with Jesus of Nazareth is intensified by such action.

Core Values

Christians can and must work with persons of all religions for these causes. We believe that all religions have a divine revelation concerning what is good, ennobling, and saving humanity. That is why religions are so universal and enduring. The core of basic teaching of the religions is very similar — almost the same thing expressed in different ways, namely, that we realize ourselves in trying to love others unselfishly. This is the core of the Jesus teaching, the love commandment. Hinduism, Buddhism, Islam, and Confucianism have a similar message.

The ideologies, in what is good in them, share a similar core of values. In Sri Lanka the older Marxist parties have been more in favor of a just and peaceful solution for the ethnic crisis than the other political parties and even the religions. They have also been campaigning more actively and been at the receiving end of bombs in their headquarters. This is a reality. In the same way groups that consider themselves rationalist and secular have been peacemakers, seeking equitable solutions. This shows us those who bear the kingdom values are not necessarily limited to the Christians or religious groups.

"Religionism"

We have therefore to articulate a theology that is genuinely open to the other, so open that we do not claim to have a monopoly on truth and goodness. We should try to cure ourselves of what I call "religionism." Just as we have casteism, classism, racism, and sexism, we can have religionism. Religionism is when one religion claims to be superior to the others, that its followers are privileged people of God. It claims a monopoly over God; it claims to have a unique, singular, universal message and teaching that is binding on all. In Christian religionism a group claims to possess Jesus and divine grace. Jesus and Buddha are universal and not limited to any religion.

Religionism is one of the causes of communal conflict, not only as a sociological phenomenon but also as a theological factor. To purify ourselves of religionism we require a great deal of humility. This is more difficult for those of us who are clergy. The higher one goes in the ecclesiastical ladder, the more difficult it becomes because one can have vested interest in the institution. A saintly person like John XXIII can be liberated of such a sense of superiority and be liberating for others.

What Is the Uniqueness of Christ?

It will then be asked, Why are we Christians? Why did we become religious or priests? We have to rethink this in depth. Jesus can be considered a universal re-deemer in so far as his teaching is the universal path to holiness and self-realization, that is, his love commandment is the way, the truth, and the life. It is also the core teaching of all the major religions of the world. Jesus is not selfish and self-centered. He is God- and human-centered. One can be a follower of Jesus and of the Buddha at the same time, as their essential teachings are the same but expressed in different forms and cultures. The examples of Jesus and of the Buddha are also meaningful and powerful motivations for me.

Our task is to build the human community with all others of goodwill. If the Buddha and Jesus were to meet today, they would not engage in a debate as to who is the greatest but rather would tend to serve each other. Holiness is of this nature — a humble service to others in truth. We have therefore a call to cure ourselves of the arrogance implicit in our exclusivist positions. It is these that have made Christianity closed to others and limiting to them.

Means and Methods

We have to evolve this rethinking of theology along with the strategies of action in our situation. We are in a world and country situation of both grave injustice and violence. The injustice is by the powerful, and the violence may be by both sides. The powerless may also have to resort to violence for getting rid of their position. Within this, how are we to be present and active as persons and groups that are for justice as well as peace? This is a dilemma, in which we can be suspected by both sides of a communal conflict. Our Fr. Michael Rodrigues was killed in a situation like that. He was for justice for the poor peasants, but nonviolent and defenseless in his means. We regard him as a martyr for social justice and peace.

We have to evaluate situations and develop active, creative means of nonviolent change if we want to avoid the violence that causes so much havoc in our communal conflicts. It is the belief of our peace groups in Sri Lanka that there is no lasting solution through violence. But while we are not for violence, we have no right to ask the others not to be violent unless we endeavor to develop methods of nonviolence that are strong and powerful enough to resolve their issues. The powers of nonviolence have not yet been adequately activated in our societies.

We are wanting in this. Our training is generally nonviolent, but not for active nonviolence in sociopolitical issues. If we have five hundred young men and women between the ages of eighteen and twenty-five for five to seven years in a school of active nonviolence, can we not do much more than the military academies or militant groups?

This is a major responsibility in the formation of clergy and religious. If the seminaries and religious families were schools of active nonviolence, soon there would be big changes in the lives of the Christian communities: and if they are open to others, the rest of society will also be greatly helped. This training can be accomplished only by some form of practical involvement in such issues even during the formative period.

There has to be a training in analyzing issues, in conflict resolution, understanding different points of view, building peace groups, and collaborating with existing groups to build mass movements for peace with justice and genuine democracy. At present the political parties are trailing the people. They are divisive in many of our countries. Even the trade unions are failing the people. We are coming to a period when there will have to be people's organizations — maybe issue-oriented ones. Rajni Kothari emphasized the role of people's organization when he visited Sri Lanka a year or two ago. The Philippines experience shows that people power can rise up on a democratic basis with freedom and consciousness. It can help rebuild our countries in a way that is nonviolent and just. This task is not over in the Philippines. The EDSA manifestations of February 1986 that drove Ferdinand and Imelda Marcos from power were the result of many years of patient work among the long-suffering people in the villages and towns.

Spirituality

Theologians can develop the spirituality of such action by articulating the people's aspirations, motivating them towards nonviolent struggles, and being alongside people in the process. We have to learn the lessons of risk taking and suffering for a cause. This is a new type of sacrifice to which we are called. It has not been part of the traditional spirituality of the Christian saints or spiritual directors. This is an area of reflection we have to work out in actual life with its new symbols — being in the demonstrations, prayer groups, different forms of public pressure.

Working together with all others, inspired by the core values of all the religions and ideologies, we can go forward together. Given our unjust and violent society, we will mentally meet the Cross in different forms. This is true not only of the local situation of Sri Lanka but also of India, South Asia, and many countries of the world. The violent are powerful, and they sell arms to both sides of our communal conflicts. They have vested interests in our countries and, they want small local wars to continue. We should not be surprised at this. Conflicts of limited intensity are propagated by the highly sophisticated arms marketing agencies of small powers and big powers. The transnational corporations also benefit from this. The powers-that-be in the world encourage small wars, such as the Iran-Iraq conflict, even while talking peace. In the international situation there are powers that will be happy if India and Pakistan arm themselves — and perhaps more so if India and China fight each other till both nations are exhausted and destabilized. This is the world of real politics in which our local communal conflicts take place. To mention this is not to be blind to our own follies but to see the network of conflicts and the spiral of violence that operate nationally and internationally. The arms dealers work on communalism to foment conflicts.

It is within such a system and situation that theologians have a grave responsibility and a necessary mission of developing the thinking and action required to save our peoples from the madness of communal conflicts which are so self-destructive. The churches as churches can work together in this effort, despite all our drawbacks, thanks to the service of the theologians in clarifying the issues. The central gospel inspiration would then be primary in our lives.

But in actual fact when we think of the relations between India and Sri Lanka, our countries and churches have not had a satisfactory communication. In Sri Lanka the government and majority community think that Tamilnadu and the Indian government helped to build up the Tamil militant groups. Here in India some think that India and Sri Lanka were not in communication with each other in this worsening situation during the past four years. There was a grave deficiency in our being disciples of Jesus in so far as we neglected these issues. We failed to be peacemakers among our ethnic and communal groups and countries. As theologians we can and must develop the analysis concerning the relations between our two countries. We can also communicate to the European and North American churches the problems of the peoples of our countries. Here our overall worldview also comes in.

The fundamental task and vocation of the theologian is to be a disciple of Jesus. The theologian has to do the intellectual analysis that is necessary, and more than that, be present where the people are in difficulty, where the poor are exploited, where life is in danger. In such a situation the theologian has to take one's cross and bear witness to the commandment of love that Jesus has taught us. Where people are divided on communal lines, we have to transcend our own narrow communal loyalties and go among the groups as peacemakers and seek a just solution for all. And if we do not want many to be killed, we urgently have to develop a powerful nonviolent movement for peace, justice, and democracy.

In Sri Lanka ten thousand have been killed in the past four years, and over one thousand persons since the Indo–Sri Lankan peace accord. If we are to avoid even worse killings in the coming years, we must be far more active than we have been. India is now involved in Sri Lanka; Indian and Sri Lankan theologians must therefore come together to seek solutions to this common issue.

We should, however, have no illusion about this task, as it calls us to get out of ourselves and change our priorities, to take up public positions and perhaps face grave risks. The final testimony of the theologian, as of any other believer or person of goodwill in such times, is the supreme price of life itself, if need be, for the service of our peoples. "The disciple is not greater than the master." "Greater love than this no one hath than to lay down one's life for others." This is the ultimate call of the Master. It is also the limit to which the theologian is called in endeavoring to be a faithful interpreter and messenger of Jesus in our society torn by communal violence. Perhaps it is the blood of martyrs that will be the source of the redemption of our countries from our present tragedy. Our resurrection cannot be without the Cross, and the Cross is not what we want but what comes our way in an effort at discipleship in these situations. The theologian as a spiritual leader has also to bear the cross and perhaps be among the front rank of those who are vulnerable. The good shepherd lays down his life for the sheep. The theologian has to break the message of Jesus to others principally by an example of authentic discipleship.

Some Conclusions from the Experiences

1. Ethnic conflict is a complex issue that has to be understood in a multi-disciplinary approach.

2. The solution has to be peaceful, just, and democratic. There is no permanent solution through violence.

3. Religions, including Christian churches, have not measured up to the exigencies of justice and peacemaking in this violent and critical situation.

4. Groups that have worked patiently and perseveringly for a nonviolent and just solution have been multireligious, multiethnic, and included persons of secular, rational, humanitarian, and Marxist inspiration. What held them together was a common search for a sensible, humane, and fair solution that tried to save human lives and respect the human dignity and rights of all in an understanding manner, trying to transcend the narrowness of each one's ethnic, religious, or ideological affiliation. They have faced grave risks together, including death threats. They have sought practical solutions in the political field and tried to build peace groups and a peace-with-justice constituency.

Some Conclusions from Theological Reflection

1. The values of these basic human groups seem to correspond to what Christian ideology calls the values of the Kingdom of God.

2. The church's failure to respond adequately is due to a moral inadequacy as well as a theological irrelevance.

3. The task of the theologian is therefore to examine where and why the prevalent theology is inadequate and recommend reorientation in thinking.

4. This has to include: rethinking on content of theology — what made us exclusive and self-centered?; a revision of priorities in theologizing — there has to be a greater relation to the reality of the situation and action towards resolving issues (this is a question of method and goal of doing theology); a revamping of the spirituality of the theologian and of the theological community. This is the challenge of the discipleship of Jesus in the context of justice and communal violence.

In a situation of communal conflict, it is the responsibility of the theologian to analyze issues in a seriously intellectual manner and be committed to building human community. Inspired by the core values of all religions and ideologies and by a seriously practical action, the theologian must face the risks involved in being a disciple of Jesus, crucified and risen.

Selected Annotated Bibliography

Section I. Speaking among Ourselves

"Asian Women Doing Theology." *Exchange* 47, 1987. Survey of materials, methodology, major themes, and the role of biblical authority.

Chung Hyun Kyung. *Struggle To Be the Sun Again: Introducing Asian Women's Theology.* Maryknoll, N.Y.: Orbis Books, 1990. An examination of the social and historical context of Asian women's theology, its concrete manifestation in Christology, Mariology, and spirituality, and its future challenges.

Dyvasinvandam, Govada. "Doing Theology with God's Purpose in India in the Context of the Dalit Struggle for a Fuller Humanity," in *Doing Theology with God's Purpose in Asia,* ATESEA Occasional Paper #10. Edited by Cho Lak. Singapore: ATESEA, 1990. A proposal for dalit liberation theology.

Endo, Tomiju. "Buraku liberation and the Church: Throw Off the Heavy Burdens and Sins which Entangle You!," *Crowned with Thorns* 6 October, 1985, p. 6. Reflections of a pastor involved in a liberation movement.

"A Glossary of Buraku Liberation Terms," in *Crowned with Thorns* 20 October, 1990, pp. 5–6. Explanation of different Buraku terms.

Gnanadason, Aruna (ed.). *Towards a Theology of Humanhood: Women's Perspectives.* Delhi: ISPCK, 1986. A collection of Indian women's theological reflections.

Irudayaraj, Xavier (ed.). *Emerging Dalit Theology.* Madurai, India: Tamilnadu Theological Seminary, 1990. A collection of essays on social and theological aspects of dalits.

Manikam, S. *Nandanar: The Dalit Martyr.* Madras: The Christian Literature Society, 1990. A historical and theological reconstruction of a Tamil dalit saint.

Manuel Raj, V. *A Santal Theology of Liberation.* Delhi: Uppal Publishing House, 1990. Liberation theology for Santals, one of the tribal communities in India.

Massey, James. *Roots: A Concise History of the Dalits.* Delhi: ISPCK, 1991. Dalits as a distinctive group of people, supported by literary, archaeological, and historical evidence.

Minz, Nirmal. "Meaning of Tribal Consciousness," *Religion and Society* 36 (2) 1989, pp. 12–23. A study of tribals in the central belt of India.

Minz, Nirmal,"Religion and Culture as Power in the Context of Tribal Aspirations in India," *Religion and Society* 33 (2) 1986, pp. 45–54.

Park Sun Ai. "Asian Women's Experience of Injustice and Reflection," in *Asian Journal of Theology* 3 (1) 1989. Cultural discrimination of women, a theological reflection based on Jesus's attitude to women, and renewal of human community and church unity from an Asian woman's perspective.

"People's Theology." *Jeevadhara: A Journal of Christian Interpretation* 22 (129) 1992. Essays on people's ways of doing theology from Christian, Islamic and feminist points of view.

Suh Jung-Soon. "The Minority Situation in Japan," in *In God's Image,* December, 1988, pp. 34–37. The nature of discrimination from the point of view of Japan's minorities.

Section II. Speaking out of Our Own Resources

Appavoo, Theophilus James. *Folklore for Change.* Madurai, India: Tamilnadu Theological Seminary, 1986. How folktales, folksongs, proverbs, puns, and riddles are used by a grassroots Tamil community for social protest and change.

Athyal, Leelama. "Despair and Hope: The Story of Yegnadatta — A Theological Reflection," *East Asia Journal of Theology* 3 (2) 1985, pp. 278–89. Use of an Indian tale for theological reflection.

Gallup, Padma. "Doing Theology — an Asian Feminist Perspective," *CTC Bulletin* 4 (3) 1983, pp. 21–27. An interpretation of Genesis 1:27–28 in the light of a popular androgynous image of Shiva as *Arthanareesvara* (half female and half male).

Lee, Peter K. H. "Re-Reading Ecclesiastes in the Light of Su Tung-p'o's Poetry," in *Ching Feng* 30 (4) 1987, pp. 214–36. Koheleth and Su Tung-p'o come from two different cultures and two different eras but by re-reading Ecclesiastes in the light of Su's poetry, the author sees new theological nuances.

Lee, Peter K. H. "Ta-T'ung and the Kingdom of God," *Ching Feng* 31 (4), 1988, pp. 225–44. Twin passages from the Confucian classic *Li yun* and two chapters of Isaiah (61 & 65) together with Luke 4:16, as a basis for Christian and Confucian dialogue and for mutual enrichment.

Lee, Peter K. H. "Two Stories of Loyalty," *Ching Feng* 32 (1) 1989, pp. 24–40. Loyalty of two women, one a Moabitess, Ruth, and the other a Chinese, Tou Ngo, and the theological implications for the multi-cultural context.

Song, C. S. *Tell Us Our Names: Story Theology from an Asian Perspective.* Maryknoll, N.Y.: Orbis Books, 1984. Selections from the Asian cultural heritage — folk tales, poems, and myths — placed imaginatively alongside biblical materials.

Section III. Speaking out of Our Personal Encounters

Amirtham, Samuel. *Stories People Make: Examples of Theological Work in Community.* Geneva: World Council of Churches, 1989.

In God's Image 11 (3) 1992. An issue which contains personal theological narratives of Asian-American women who were faced with a personal identity crisis and racism in America.

Pieris, Aloysius. "The Three Ingredients of Authentic Humanism: An Autobiographical Essay on the Religious Vows," in *Vidyajyoti Journal of Theological Reflection,* 56 (1) 1992, pp. 3–22. Starting from an analysis of the basic component of authentic humanism — the experience of beauty, humor and friendship — Pieris interprets the meaning of the religious vows.

Suh Kwang-sun, David. *The Korean Minjung in Christ.* Hong Kong: The Christian Conference of Asia, 1991. An autobiographical account of one of the initiators of Korean *minjung* theology.

Tiwari, Y. D. "From Vedic Dharma to the Christian Faith," *Religion and Society,* 10 (3) 1963, pp. 113–20. Reminiscences of a convert.

Voices from the Jungle: Burmese Youth in Transition. Tokyo: Centre for Christian Response to Asian Issues, 1989. Burmese youth who live in the Thai-Burmese border share their experiences, nightmares and dreams.

Section IV. Speaking for Ourselves

Arokiasamy, S. and Gispert-Sauch, G. (eds.). *Liberation In Asia: Theological Perspectives.* Anand, Gujarat, India: Gujarat Sahitya Prakash, 1987. Indian contributions to liberation theology.

Batumalai, S. "A Malaysian Neighbourology," in *CTC Bulletin* 9 (2 & 3) 1990, pp. 46–56. Articulation of the gospel for a Muslim context from the standpoint of the way Christ lived in solidarity with the people. A pioneering effort from Malaysia.

Chandrakanthan, A. J. V. "Emerging Trends in Asian Theology," in *East Asian Pastoral Review* 27 (314), 1990, pp. 271–80; see also *Priests & People* 5 (10) 1991, pp. 367–70. Three current responses of Asian theology — liberational, inculturational and trans-ecclesial.

Fernandez, Eleazar S. "People's Cry, Creation's Cry," in *Tugon* 12 (2) 1992, pp. 276–94. A theological and ethical reflection on ecology from the perspective of the struggling poor.

Gasper, M. Karl. "Doing Theology (in a Situation) of Struggle," in *Voices from the Third World* 14 (1) 1991, pp. 32–65. This piece is a kind of *Summa* for the Philippines theology of struggle.

Huang Po Ho. "Mission for a Promised Land: A Taiwanese Theological Perspective of Self-determination." A paper presented at Subregions Mission Consultation of the Christian Conference of Asia, Taipei, May 1992. A biblical reflection based on the migratory experience of the Israelites and the Taiwanese people.

John, T. K. (ed.) *Bread and Breath: Essays in Honor of Samuel Rayan.* Anand, Gujarat, India: Gujarat Sahitya Prakash, 1991. A collection of essays by Indian and international theologians on the future of third-world theologies, spirituality and inter-faith dialogue.

Lee, Peter K. H. "Some Critical Issues in Asian Theological Thinking," in *Ching Feng* 31 (2 & 3) 1988, pp. 124–52.

Manuel, Lawrence. "On Being Prophetic in Pakistan," in *Focus* 8 (3) 1988, pp. 167–77. Doing theology as minorities in Pakistan.

Narchison, Rosario. "Towards a Definition of Fundamentalism," in *Vidyajyoti Journal of Theological Reflection* 55 1991, pp. 255–64. Ten illustrations of how fundamentalism operates.

Noh Jong Sun. "The Effects on Korea of Un-ecological Theology," in *Liberating Life: Contemporary Approaches to Ecological Theology.* S. McFague et al., eds. Maryknoll, N.Y.: Orbis Books, 1990, pp. 125–36. Proposals for an ecological and liberating theology from a Korean *minjung* perspective.

Park Soon K. "The Unification of Korea and the Task of Feminist Theology," in *Voices from the Third World* 12 (2) 1989, pp. 104–18.

Public Statements: The General Assembly, The Presbyterian Church in Taiwan. Taipei: The Presbyterian Church in Taiwan, 1991. A compilation in chronological order of various documents issued by the Presbyterian Church on the homeland issue, human rights, etc.

Xiang Feng. "People's Theology in Taiwan," *Ching Feng,* 25 (3) 1982, pp. 148–54. Theology of powerlessness as a basis for people-centered theology in Taiwan.

Significant Asian Christian Journals in English

Asia Journal of Theology
324 Onan Road
Singapore 1542
REPUBLIC OF SINGAPORE

Arasaradi Journal of Theology
Tamilnadu Theological Seminary
Arasaradi
Madurai 625010, INDIA

Bangalore Theological Forum
United Theological College
63 Miller's Road
Bangalore 560046, INDIA

Bible Bhashyam
Sr. Thomas Apostolic
Vadavathoor P.O. No. 1
Kottayam 686010
Kerala, INDIA

The Chinese Theological Review
86 East 12th Street
Holland, MI 49423
USA

Ching Feng
Christian Study Centre
 on Chinese Religion and Culture
6/F Kiu Kin Mansion
No. 566 Nathan Road
Kowloon, HONG KONG

Christian Orient
St. Thomas Apostolic Seminary
Vadavathoor P.O. No. 1
Kottayam 686010
Kerala, INDIA

Crowned with Thorns
Baraku Liberation Centre
2–23 Miamino 5–Chome
Shijonawate City
Osaka 575, JAPAN

CTC Bulletin
Christian Conference of Asia
2 Jordan Road
Kowloon, HONG KONG

Dialogue
490/5 Havelock Road
Colombo 6, SRI LANKA

East Asian Pastoral Review
East Asian Pastoral Institute
P.O. Box 221, U P Campus
1101 Quezon City, PHILIPPINES

Focus
Pastoral Institute
G.P.O. Box 288
Multan 6000, PAKISTAN

Image: Christ and Art in Asia
Kansai Seminar House
Takenouchi-Cho
Ichijoji
Sakyo-Ku
Kyoto 606, JAPAN

In God's Image
Asian Women's Resources Centre
 for Culture and Theology
134–5 Nokbun-Dong
Eunphyong-Ku
Seoul 122–020, KOREA

Indian Missiological Review
Sacred Heart Theological College
Shillong 793008, INDIA

Indian Theological Studies
St. Peter's Pontifical Seminary
Malleswaram West P.O.
Bangalore 560055, INDIA

The Japan Christian Review
3–25 Hachiyama-Cho
Shibuya-Ku
Tokyo 150, JAPAN
(formerly *Japan Christian Quarterly*)

Jeevadhara: A Journal of
 Christian Interpretation
Theology Centre
Kottayam 686017, INDIA

Journal of Dharma
Dharmaram College
Bangalore 560029, INDIA

The Living World
Alwaye 683103
Kerala, INDIA

Masihi Sevak
United Theological College
63 Miller's Road
Bangalore 560046, INDIA

Praxis
WSCF
Kiu Kin Mansion
12/F 568 Nathan Road
Kowloon, HONG KONG

Religion and Society
Bulletin of the Christian Institute
   for the Study of Religion and Society
P.O. Box 4600
Miller's Road
Bangalore 560046, INDIA

Salaam
St. Mary
S P Mukherjee Marg
Delhi 110006, INDIA

Sevartham
Saint Albert's College
P.O. Box 5
Ranchi 834001, INDIA

*Tugon: An Ecumenical Journal of
   Discussion and Opinion*
P.O. Box 1767
Manila, PHILIPPINES

*Vidyajyoti: Journal of Theological
   Reflection*
4A Raj Niwas Marg
Delhi 110054, INDIA

Word and Worship
ATC Jyothi Book House
P.O. Box 8426
Bangalore 560084, INDIA

Index

Hong Kong, 214; dance in, 65–79; dragon-symbol and changes in modern, 98, 99, 103
Hopkins, Gerard Manley, 230
Horkheimer, Max, 230
Hsun Tze, 104, 106
Hsu Shen, 99
Huang Xianyun, 148
human rights: contrast of Western and third-world views of, 207–10, 212–16, 218; history of Western notions of, 210–11; religion and, 216–18; universal, 206–7; Western domination and, 211–12
Hyun Young-Hak, 55

Im Chul Je, 82, 83
Im Kok Chong, 22
India: approach to the universal in, 209–10; ecology and images of God in, 90–96; history of Christian theology in, 28–31; humanization through social movements in, 215–16; human rights and, 215, 216–18; theology and tribals in, 41–51
India Shuddhi Sabha, 30
International Commission of Jurists, 212
International Missionary Conferences, 29
International Monetary Fund, 225
Islam, 217, 239
Iyer, Krishna, 214

Japan: the church and the oppressed in, 23–24; history of untouchability in, 25 n. 3; oppression of Korean women by, 57; understanding of Jesus among academic theologians in, 20; understanding of Jesus among middle-class Christians in, 19. *See also* Burakumin, the
Jesus: Buddha and, 247; the Burakumin and, 15–24; of the dalits, 36–39; Indian tribals and, 48, 50–51; Korean theology and, 200–201; Taiwanese homeland theology and, 193–94
Jharkhand movement, 50
Job, 111–14
John Paul II, Pope, 164

John XXIII, Pope, 247
Josephus, 16
Jubilee year, the, 202–3
Jubilee Year for Peace and Reunification (Korea), 202–3
Judaism, 217
Justice, Peace, and Integrity of Creation (WCC convocation), 221, 223, 226

Kappen, Sebastian, 4
Kaufman, Gordon, 153
Keithahn, R. R., 158
Kim Chi Ha, 18–19, 22, 26 n. 21
Kim Tae Kon, 83
Kingdom of God: caste and, 24; in Korean theology of unification, 201–2, 205; Taiwanese homeland theology and, 194
Korea: a basis of women's theology in, 52–61; masculine images of God in the church in, 80–81; shamanism in, 81–89; theology of reunification of, 196–205
Korean Association of Evangelical Theologians, 203–4
Korean Association of Women Theologians, 60, 81
Korean War, 198
Kothari, Rajni, 237, 248
Kraemer, Hendrik, 29
Ku Chieh-kang, 105
Kudo Eiichi, 26 n. 22
Küng, Hans, 219 n. 1
kut (shaman ritual), 55, 59, 81, 86
Kwon In-Sook, 58

Lanternari, Vittorio, 17
Lao-tzu, 97–98
Lee Chi Chung, Archie, 4
liberation theology, 12; hermeneutics of Latin American, 3; in India, 30; Latin American, in Korea, 199; women and Asian male, 2
Lightfoot, J. B., 38
Li Kung, 71
Limouris, Gennadios, 226

McCarthy, Scott, 231
Macaulay, Thomas, 6
MacDermot, Niall, 212

BT 30 .A8 F76 1994

Frontiers in Asian Christian
  theology

BT 30 .A8 F76 1994

Frontiers in Asian Christian
  theology